Service Charges: Law & Practice

Sixth Edition

Service Charges: Law & Practice

Sixth Edition

Philip Freedman
CBE, QC (Hon)

Eric Shapiro BSc, FRICS, FCIArb

Brian Slater

LexisNexis | 200

Members of the LexisNexis Group worldwide

United Kingdom	RELX (UK) Limited trading as LexisNexis, 1-3 Strand, London WC2N 5JR and 9-10 St Andrew Square, Edinburgh EH2 2AF
Australia	LexisNexis Butterworths, Chatswood, New South Wales
Austria	LexisNexis Verlag ARD Orac GmbH & Co KG, Vienna
Benelux	LexisNexis Benelux, Amsterdam
Canada	LexisNexis Canada, Markham, Ontario
China	LexisNexis China, Beijing and Shanghai
France	LexisNexis SA, Paris
Germany	LexisNexis GmbH, Dusseldorf
Hong Kong	LexisNexis Hong Kong, Hong Kong
India	LexisNexis India, New Delhi
Italy	Giuffrè Editore, Milan
Japan	LexisNexis Japan, Tokyo
Malaysia	Malayan Law Journal Sdn Bhd, Kuala Lumpur
New Zealand	LexisNexis NZ Ltd, Wellington
Singapore	LexisNexis Singapore, Singapore
South Africa	LexisNexis Butterworths, Durban
USA	LexisNexis, Dayton, Ohio

Published by LexisNexis

A CIP Catalogue record for this book is available from the British Library.

ISBN 978-1-7847-3409-1

9 781784 734091

ISBN for this volume: 9781784734091

Printed and bound by Hobbs the Printers, Hampshire SO40 3WX

Visit LexisNexis at www.lexisnexis.co.uk

Preface

Service charges are almost invariably the subject of conflict between those who arrange the expenditure and those who are ultimately called upon to pay for it. Some twenty-seven years ago, the Report of the Committee of Inquiry on the Management of Privately Owned Blocks of Flats (DoE, 1985) ('the Nugee Report') revealed an almost universal holding of grievances by tenants of flats about the conduct of the management of their blocks of flats and the amount of service charges. Mutual mistrust, lack of proper consultation by landlords and managing agents, and failure to take proper account of the tenants' views seemed rife in both the residential and the commercial spheres. The position has hardly changed over the years.

In the residential sector, successive Governments have legislated to alleviate this problem, by imposing a statutory regime for residential service charges and by enabling residential flat owners to buy the freeholds of their blocks or to take over management from the landlord. The Royal Institution of Chartered Surveyors have also published a Residential Management Code (3rd edition) which has been approved by the Secretary of State and is effective from 1 June 2016.

Similar grievances are expressed by commercial tenants whose service charges can often add considerably to their businesses' occupancy costs. While bad management is all too common in many cases, problems arise simply because the parties fail to recognize each other's legitimate requirements. A guide to good practice called 'Service Charges in Commercial Properties' was published by the Royal Institution of Chartered Surveyors, on behalf of seven property industry bodies, stating that its purposes were to encourage a good working relationship and to secure co-operation between owners and occupiers through consultation and communication. That was elevated to the status of an RICS Code of Practice in 2007 and an updated and modernised new edition was issued in 2011 and in February 2014. This code has now been updated again and is due to be published at almost the same time as this new edition is being published. It is intended that its observance is to be obligatory by all Chartered Surveyors. We have made references to this new code in this book. It sets out best practice to be observed by chartered surveyors who manage property and administer service charges.

In practice a distinction can be drawn between those multi-occupied properties which are let at market rents and those which are sold on long leases (or, as in the case of some office, industrial or warehouse units, sold freehold). In the former cases, the landlord's rental income growth and capital value will usually depend upon the continuing quality of the buildings (in addition to their location and other market factors), whereas in the latter cases the ground rents (if any) are either fixed for many years or escalate on a basis usually unrelated to the state of the buildings. Landlords in the former cases have a financial stake in the maintenance and improvement of their buildings, while the interest of landlords in the latter cases may wane once all the flats or units comprised in the development have been sold, except perhaps where they hope to make a profit from the provision of services – a usually unattainable and unlawful desire, and undesirable except for a fair management fee.

Tenants, on the other hand, might be expected to have an interest in the proper maintenance of their buildings, irrespective of whether they are paying market rents under short- or medium-term leases, or ground rents under long leases. Office, light industrial and warehousing tenants require their premises and access ways to be kept in repair in order not to endanger or disrupt their processes or the flow of their goods. Office tenants expect their buildings to be maintained both for the proper functioning of their businesses or professions and to present a quality appearance to their customers or clients. Generally neither want the premises improved at their expense. Flat-owners are normally keen to have their blocks well maintained and in theory ought to be willing to pay for them to be improved to preserve or increase the asset value of their flats. However, in all cases there needs to be a balance between cost, affordability and benefit.

These factors ought to mean that there should be a good deal of common ground between the interests of landlords and tenants. However, the cost of repairing and servicing buildings is a major independent consideration for both landlords and tenants and it can impact on potential rent levels. Institutional landlords usually try to insist that lettings of commercial properties should be on clear leases, under which the tenants not only pay a full market rent, but also meet the entire costs involved in maintaining, servicing and renewing the properties. Until recently, these clear leases were the norm rather than the exception, and inclusive rents were rare save in the case of short residential lettings or very short commercial lettings. Tenants who used to be asked to pay relatively low contributions towards a limited range of services are now usually required to pay for roof renewals, the replacement of plant and equipment and other heads of expenditure which were at one time traditionally met by their landlords. The situation today is not so clear-cut since many commercial tenants are now taking shorter leases than used to be prevalent and frequently ask for capped service charges or for limitations to be placed on the costs which can be included.

Commercial tenants justifiably view their rents, service charges, general rates and water charges as a package of costs for the occupation of their premises, and take the total into account when viewing their overheads or production costs; an excessively high level of service charge can lead to a reduced level of market rent. Flat-owners have found that flats which are liable to constant high service charges are not only expensive to run but also suffer a reduction in their resale value, except in the most prestigious locations. It is, therefore, understandable that tenants of both commercial and residential properties are generally keen to minimise their service charge liabilities by opposing expenditure which they consider is unnecessary or premature and, in many cases, this may lead to a failure to take account of their own longer-term interests, as well as the interests of their landlords.

The position has been exacerbated by successive governments passing legislation, both aimed at green issues and at health and safety, which has had the effect of increasing the cost of maintaining and operating buildings. In the past, such legislation usually empowered a court to direct how the costs should be allocated between landlords and tenants if it was not dealt with by the leases, but such provisions are usually omitted from modern legislation. In many cases this creates uncertainty, particularly where the new statutory obligations were unforeseen when the leases were drafted and are not directly addressed by the lease clauses.

This book sets out to summarize the current state of the law on service charges as at June 2018 and to give guidance on management practice and on related tax and accountancy matters. Brian Slater, Chartered Tax Adviser and previously tax principal at Finers Stephens Innocent, has contributed detailed notes on VAT and on the taxation problems of service charges. Suggestions for drafting service charge clauses are also included.

The scheme of this book is to deal first with matters which are common to both residential and commercial property (**Chapter 1**) and then to deal specifically with matters which only affect residential property (**Chapter 2**), before going back to matters of a special nature, covering VAT (**Chapter 3**), sinking and reserve funds (**Chapter 4**), the special rules relating to freehold and commonhold properties (**Chapter 5**), the position relating to costs incurred in complying with statutory obligations (**Chapter 6**) and a reference to relevant codes of practice (**Chapter 7**).

Much of the case-law that we cite comes from disputes relating to residential property because that is the area most litigated, but the common law principles laid down in the cases apply generally to all types of leased property. However, the statute law on service charges mainly applies to residential property but not to commercial premises. These distinctions are drawn out in the text.

PHILIP FREEDMAN CBE, QC

Mishcon de Reya
London WC2

ERIC SHAPIRO BSc, FRICS, FCIArb

Chestertons
London EC3
1 July 2018

Contents

Table of Abbreviations

ACoP	Approved Code of Practice
ADR	Alternative dispute resolution
CCS	Commonhold community statement
CLRA 2002	Commonhold and Leasehold Reform Act 2002
CO_2	Carbon dioxide
COSHH 2002	Control of Substances Hazardous to Health Regulations 2002, SI 2002/2677
CRC Energy Efficiency Scheme	Carbon Reduction Commitment Energy Efficiency Scheme
DEC	Display energy certificate
DPA 1964	Diplomatic Privileges Act 1964
EPC	Energy performance certificate
FFT	First-tier Tribunal
GIA	Gross internal area
HA 1986	Housing Act 1986
HMRC	Her Majesty's Revenue and Customs
LRHUDA 1993	Leasehold Reform, Housing and Urban Development Act 1993
LT	Lands Tribunal
LT(C)A 1995	Landlord and Tenant (Covenants) Act 1995
LTA 1985	Landlord and Tenant Act 1985
LTA 1987	Landlord and Tenant Act 1987
LVT	Leasehold Valuation Tribunal
RICS	Royal Institution of Chartered Surveyors

RTM company	right-to-manage company
SCCR Regulations 2003	Service Charges (Consultation Requirements) (England) Regulations 2003, SI 2003/1987
SIA 1978	State Immunity Act 1978
VAT	Value added tax
VATA 1994	Value Added Tax Act 1994
VAT Regulations 1995	Value Added Tax Regulations 1995, SI 1995/2518

Table of Statutes

References are to paragraph numbers.

Table of Statutory Instruments

References are to paragraph numbers.

Table of Cases

References are to paragraph numbers.

C

D

I

J

K

L

M

N

O

P

S

T

U

V

W

Y

Z

Decisions of the European Court of Justice are listed below numerically. These decisions are also included in the preceding alphabetical list.

Chapter 1

MATTERS APPLICABLE TO COMMERCIAL AND RESIDENTIAL LEASES

For the reason given in the Preface, most of the court cases cited in this chapter are related to disputes under residential lettings but, nevertheless, the principles applied in them are (unless otherwise stated) to be taken as applying to commercial as well as residential property.

LANDLORDS, MANAGEMENT COMPANIES AND MAINTENANCE TRUSTEES

The supplier of the services

1.1 Services to a tenant may be provided by the landlord, a management company, a right to manage company or a maintenance trustee, depending upon the express or implied terms of the tenant's lease or tenancy agreement. In the case of short residential lettings and lettings of parts of commercial buildings the service obligations are usually undertaken by the landlord. Under long leases of residential flats the obligations may be imposed either on the landlord, or (quite frequently) on a management company controlled by the tenants, or occasionally on a maintenance trustee. Those maintenance obligations which are imposed by statute (eg in relation to short term residential lettings, under ss 11–16 of the Landlord and Tenant Act 1985) are almost invariably placed upon the landlord.

As to whether a particular service has to be provided as a matter of contractual obligation, as distinct from being at the landlord's discretion, see **1.13**.

The landlord

1.2 It is often advantageous to tenants if it is the landlord who is responsible for the services. In the case of larger commercial buildings the landlord will frequently be a substantial property company which, particularly where the building is let at full market rents, will be keen to preserve the value of its reversionary interest in the property. Such a landlord may be likely to ensure prompt attention to any necessary repairs to the building. However, it is unlikely to be as cost-conscious as a tenants' management company.

In the residential sector, the landlord will often be a company controlled by the tenants, as in the case of a company established to acquire the freehold of a block of flats when the freehold is bought by the tenants under the collective enfranchisement provisions of the Leasehold Reform, Housing and Urban Development Act 1993. (The alternative procedure by which such tenants can take over the management without having to buy the block, by using an 'RTM company', is discussed in **1.3**, **1.5** and **2.98**).

Management company

1.3 The management company was originally simply a device adopted by those landlords, especially in the residential sector, who wished to avoid taking on management and maintenance responsibilities. Nowadays it is even more common in that sector because the tenants will usually have a statutory right to set up a company to take over the management (see the right to manage at **1.5** and **2.95**), so it is often more convenient for landlords to establish a management company structure from the outset. The landlord incorporates a company which joins in the leases in order to covenant to carry out the service obligations, usually including all main repairs and sometimes including insurance. Normally the tenants are made members or shareholders in the company. In such cases the courts will *not* normally imply into the tenants' leases any obligation on the landlord to provide any services even if the management company defaults.

EXAMPLE

> *Hafton Properties Ltd v Camp; Camp v Silchester Court (Croydon) Management Co Ltd*[1], Official Referee: A management company joined in a 99-year lease of a flat and covenanted with the tenant that the company would provide services and manage and maintain the block. The landlord gave the tenant only a covenant for quiet enjoyment of the flat. Could the tenant claim damages from the landlord when the company failed to perform its covenants? **Held**: No.

In the residential sector, as mentioned, a management company may come into existence after the leases have been granted, in the form of a company (called an RTM company) established by tenants for the purpose of exercising the 'right to manage' – see **2.95**.

At first glance, it may seem desirable for tenants to have full control over the management and maintenance of their properties in this way, and in the case of leasehold flats a scheme involving a management company which will not be under the control of the flat-owners may be unacceptable to flat purchasers and their mortgagees, and this is increasingly expected to be the perception although this is not currently so.

However, in practice the efficiency of such companies depends on the time and enthusiasm of the tenants and problems can arise if some tenants, for their own personal reasons, wish to delay the incurring of heavy expenditure on repairs or renewals. Too often one finds blocks of flats controlled by tenants' management companies, where major repairs have been postponed indefinitely due to a majority of the tenants not wishing to fund the expenditure, or where the tenants do not want to appoint professional managing agents but lack the expertise to manage the block themselves. Severe mismanagement can lead to such companies becoming insolvent, such as where very expensive repair costs are incurred after unjustified delays and cannot be fully recovered from the tenants.

The risk of incurring costs which might not fall within the service charge, and thus might not be recovered from the tenants, has, perhaps, more serious consequences for a management company than for a commercial landlord. Since management companies normally have no assets other than the service charge monies, the inability to recover part of its expenditure could lead to the company being put into liquidation because of unpaid creditors (see *Re Cranley Mansions Ltd*[2]). This would be to the detriment of the tenants (at least, in the absence of a covenant by the landlord in the leases that he would perform the services if the company defaulted). Where this risk is perceived to arise, and the tenants will not unanimously agree to the expenditure, the directors of the company should consider making an application to the court or, in residential cases, the First-tier Tribunal (FTT), in the name of the company for a declaration that the expenditure will fall within the service charges and be recoverable from the tenants (see **1.40**).

It is possible for the articles of association of a tenants' management company to contain provisions which create an obligation on the members of the company (ie the tenants) to contribute, in that capacity, towards any costs incurred by the company which are not otherwise recoverable (see *Morshead Mansions Ltd v Mactra Properties Ltd*[3]), *di Marco v Morshead Mansions Ltd*[4]). In such cases, if the tenant transfers his lease to another person, it may be possible for the management company to refuse to register a notice of transfer of the lease while service charges payable under that lease remain unpaid (see *Mactra Properties Ltd v Morshead Mansions Ltd*[5]).

1 [1993] EGCS 101.
2 [1994] 1 WLR 1610.
3 [2006] EWCA Civ 492.
4 [2014] EWCA Civ 96.
5 [2008] EWHC 2843 (Ch).

Maintenance trustee

1.4 This is another device enabling the landlord to avoid having to undertake management and maintenance, but without passing control of such matters to the tenants. An outside company is employed to act as trustee of the maintenance fund and joins in the leases (or sometimes in a supplemental document) in order to covenant to use the fund for the provision of the specified services. If the maintenance trustee fulfils his function properly, this type of management can work well although it will usually add additional costs which may be at a level which is unacceptable.

Right to manage company

1.5 A right to manage ('RTM') company may be established by tenants to take over the management of premises containing residential flats, under the provisions of the Commonhold and Leasehold Reform Act 2002 (CLRA 2002) (see **2.98**). In such cases the RTM company assumes the role of the party providing the services under the leases, and the service charge provisions in the leases continue to apply as if the RTM company was that party (CLRA 2002, ss 96, 97).

However there is no provision in that Act for the costs of running the RTM company to be included in the service charge, so if the wording of the service charge provisions does not extend to such costs they would have to be borne separately by those tenants who are members of the company.

Terminology in this book – 'landlord'

1.6 Except where it is necessary to distinguish between landlords, management companies and maintenance trustees, the expression 'landlord' is used in this book to mean the party (whether or not actually the landlord) responsible for providing the services under the terms of the letting. Those terms may be set out in a document called a 'lease' or a 'tenancy agreement', and in this book the word 'lease' will be used to cover both.

Documents ancillary to the lease

1.7 Since arrangements between the parties to a lease may be binding on their successors even if contained in separate deeds or even 'side letters' rather than in the lease itself, all documents supplemental to the lease need to be taken into account when determining the true terms of the letting (see *System Floors Ltd v Ruralpride Ltd*[1] and, for leases granted after 1995, see the Landlord and Tenant (Covenants) Act 1995, which provides that 'landlord covenants' and 'tenant covenants' may be contained not only in the lease itself but also in any ancillary document entered into before or after the grant of the lease).

1 [1995] 1 EGLR 48, CA.

THE CONTRACTUAL BASIS OF THE SERVICE CHARGE

Basic contractual position

1.8 The lease is the contract that controls the relationship between the landlord and the tenant and, except where legislation intervenes, its provisions must normally be applied as they are expressed.

The mere fact that the tenant has the benefit of a service does not, of itself, mean that he is required to pay for that service. Generally, no tenant is obliged to pay a service charge except so far as the terms of his lease may provide for one. The precise wording of the clauses of the lease creating the landlord's obligation to provide services to his tenant and creating his entitlement to a service charge from his tenant must be considered carefully in order to ascertain the extent of the tenant's liability.

EXAMPLE

Riverlate Properties Ltd v Paul[1]: The 99-year lease of a maisonette set out the landlord's obligation to provide services in a number of separate subclauses: subclause 6(a) dealt with external and structural repairs, subclause 6(b) with insurance; subclause 6(c) with external redecoration and subclause 6(d) with payment of water rates. The tenant's covenant for contribution only mentioned the costs incurred by the landlord under subclauses 6(b) to (d). There was no reference to subclause 6(a). Was the tenant liable to contribute to the landlord's costs of carrying out external and structural repairs under clause 6(a)? **Held:** No; the provisions of lease were to be read literally the landlord had to provide those works at his own cost for the entire duration of the term of the lease.

In the case of management companies of which the tenants are members, provisions imposing service cost liabilities on tenants are occasionally contained in the articles of association of the company in addition to, or instead of, in the leases. Provisions in the articles are sometimes also used in an attempt to find an indirect route to making the tenants contribute to any shortfall arising due to the irrecoverability of an item of cost through the service charge (see **1.3**).

As to the possible inclusion of service charge arrangements in documents other than the lease itself, see **1.6**.

Lack of funds does not usually absolve a landlord from his liability to provide the services (see **1.53**). This is of particular concern in the case of a landlord company which is owned by the tenants, since such a company will often have no source of funds other than from the tenants. If that company cannot meet its expenditure from the service charges as and when costs falls due for payment, there is a risk of the company becoming insolvent. This may arise, for example, where the tenants' leases do not provide for adequate interim payments on account of service charges. Residential tenants who are considering setting up an RTE company (see **1.2**) or RTM company (see **1.3** and **1.5**) should take such issues into account and consider whether they can arrange for deficient leases to be varied in order to modernise the service charge provisions. Alternatively, in cases where a block is being purchased by agreement outside the statutory residential enfranchisement regime (and so the statutory requirements for an RTE company do not apply) the tenants might consider making provision through the articles of association for the members to contribute to any cost shortfall (see **1.3**).

Occasionally, a lease may contain a specific declaration that the intention of the service charge clause is to achieve full recoupment of all expenditure and the court would have to give weight to such a declaration when interpreting the operative provisions, but this is quite rare.

1 [1975] Ch 133, CA.

Interpreting service charge provisions

1.9 Where the wording of a service charge clause is clear, the courts will generally interpret it literally. The courts will not strain to read the clause as if every service charge is intended to ensure 100 per cent recovery of all the landlord's service costs. Even under a lease which contains a detailed service charge clause, there may be landlord's expenditure which falls outside the wording of the clause and, even though it may have been unintentional and commercially unrealistic, that cost cannot be charged to the tenant.

An early example of the application of this approach was given at **1.8** (*Riverlate Properties Ltd v Paul*) and below are further examples.

EXAMPLES

Rapid Results College v Angell[1]: The lease obliged the landlord to maintain the external walls, structure and roof of the building. The lease of the offices on the second floor required the tenant to pay 50 per cent of the cost of maintenance of the 'exterior . . . in respect of the premises being the offices on the First and Second floors'. Did the tenant have to pay towards maintenance of the roof immediately above the second floor? **Held:** No; the roof was not part of 'the exterior' of 'the first and second floor offices'. Dillon LJ said: 'It does not follow automatically . . . that the services rent must necessarily cover everything the landlords are to do . . . '

Douglas Shelf Seven Ltd v Co-Operative Wholesale Society Ltd[2], Outer House, Court of Session: The service charge clause in the lease of a unit in a shopping centre did not expressly mention the costs of security. The landlord tried to recover the cost of security by getting the managing agents to pay for the security and the landlord then contended that these costs could be included in the service charge under a provision that allowed the inclusion of the professional charges of the landlord's surveyors in connection with the management and administration of the centre. **Held:** This provision plainly covered only the surveyors' own professional charges and not sums paid by them to unskilled labour; costs cannot be recovered from a tenant through a service charge unless the wording in the lease plainly covers those costs.

Daejan Properties Ltd v Campbell[3]: The lease of a maisonette, which was termed 'the Property' and formed part of a building, required the tenant to pay as service charge 40 per cent of the costs of repairing the external walls 'of the Property'. Was this a manifest error and did the tenant have to pay 40 per cent of the costs of external repair of the whole building and not just of the costs of repairing the part abutting this flat? **Held:** No, departing from the ordinary meaning of the words was not justified (in the absence of proceedings for rectification of the lease, where the parties' true intention has to be proved) and so the landlord would have to bear the shortfall.

PR Hardman & Partners v Greenwood[4]; The costs recovery clause in an agreement to rent a mobile home pitch required the renter to pay 'general and/or water rates . . . and charges in respect of electricity water gas telephone and other services'. Did this allow the site operator to charge for administration or for any services it might itself provide? **Held:** No, the clause only required payment of charges levied by third-party utility suppliers.

A notable recent example where the literal approach to fairly clear wording worked against the tenant is the Supreme Court's decision in *Arnold v Britton*[5]. The long leases of chalets in a leisure park, granted mainly in the 1970s and 1980s, reserved service charges which the clauses initially referred to as being a proportion of the yearly estate costs but then went on to state in each case that it was to be the fixed sum of £90 per year with a provision for escalation. Some of the leases provided that the sum was to increase by 10 per cent every year, while others provided for it to increase by 10 per cent every three years. The Supreme Court appeared to accept that the lessees may not have realised that the formula would result in the service charge rising from £90 to around £2500 over 30 years. Nevertheless, the court felt (by a majority decision) that it had to interpret the clause literally and that the later provision in the clause for payment of the fixed escalating amount was, on the wording used, intended to displace the earlier reference to the proportion of the actual estate costs.

Lord Neuberger (giving the majority decision) said that when interpreting contractual provisions the court is concerned to identify the intention of the parties by reference to 'what a reasonable person having all the background knowledge which would have been available to the parties would have understood them to be using the language in the contract to mean', by focusing on the meaning of the relevant words in their documentary, factual and commercial context. That meaning has to be assessed in the light of (i) the natural and ordinary meaning of the clause, (ii) any other relevant provisions of the lease, (iii) the overall purpose of the clause and the lease, (iv) the facts and circumstances known or assumed by the parties at the time that the document was executed, and (v) commercial common sense, but (vi) disregarding subjective evidence of any party's intentions. However, he said that this was subject as follows:

- The reliance placed in some cases on commercial common sense and surrounding circumstances should not be invoked to undervalue the importance of the language of the provision which is to be construed. The exercise of interpreting a provision involves identifying what the parties meant through the eyes of a reasonable reader, and, save perhaps in a very unusual case, that meaning is most obviously to be gleaned from the language of the provision. Unlike commercial common sense and the surrounding circumstances, the parties have control over the language they use in a contract. And, again save perhaps in a very unusual case, the parties must have been specifically focusing on the issue covered by the provision when agreeing the wording of that provision.
- When considering the centrally relevant words to be interpreted, the less clear they are, the more ready the court can properly be to depart from their natural meaning. The clearer the natural meaning, the more difficult it is to justify departing from it. However, that does not justify the court embarking on an exercise of searching for, let alone constructing, drafting infelicities in order to facilitate a departure from the natural meaning. If there is a specific error in the drafting, it may often have no relevance to the issue of interpretation which the court has to resolve.
- The commercial common sense is not to be invoked retrospectively. The mere fact that a contractual arrangement, if interpreted according to its natural language, has worked out badly, or even disastrously, for one of the parties is not a reason for departing from the natural lan-

guage. Commercial common sense is only relevant to the extent of how matters would or could have been perceived by the parties, or by reasonable people in the position of the parties, as at the date that the contract was made.

- While commercial common sense is a very important factor to take into account when interpreting a contract, a court should be very slow to reject the natural meaning of a provision as correct simply because it appears to be a very imprudent term for one of the parties to have agreed, even ignoring the benefit of wisdom of hindsight. The purpose of interpretation is to identify what the parties have agreed, not what the court thinks that they should have agreed. Experience shows that it is by no means unknown for people to enter into arrangements which are ill-advised, even ignoring the benefit of wisdom of hindsight, and it is not the function of a court when interpreting an agreement to relieve a party from the consequences of his imprudence or poor advice. Accordingly, when interpreting a contract a judge should avoid re-writing it in an attempt to assist an unwise party or to penalise an astute party.
- When interpreting a contractual provision, one can only take into account facts or circumstances which existed at the time that the contract was made, and which were known or reasonably available to both parties. Given that a contract is a bilateral, or synallagmatic, arrangement involving both parties, it cannot be right, when interpreting a contractual provision, to take into account a fact or circumstance known only to one of the parties.
- Where an event subsequently occurs which was plainly not intended or contemplated by the parties, judging from the language of their contract, if it is clear what the parties would have intended, the court will give effect to that intention.

Lord Neuberger stressed that service charge clauses are not subject to any special rule of interpretation that they have to be interpreted restrictively other than in the sense that the court should not 'bring within the general words of a service charge clause anything which does not clearly belong there' (per *Rix LJ in McHale v Earl Cadogan*[6]).

A possible gloss on this approach may be where the lease provides for the services to be supplied by a management company which is controlled by the tenants. Such a company ordinarily has no assets other than the management fund and, in such cases, it will not be in a position to perform its task without full funding from the tenants. In those circumstances the courts may attempt to interpret the service charge provisions, *so far as possible*, on the basis of full recoupment of the cost of those services which the company is obliged to provide.

However, this approach will not assist the management company to recover costs which are undeniably outside a precise and unambiguous list of recoverable costs set out in the lease or in the memorandum and articles of association of the company or where a tenants' management company was not envisaged by the terms of the lease.

EXAMPLES

Embassy Court Residents' Association Ltd v Lipman[7]: The lease of a flat required the tenant to pay towards the costs of performance of the landlord's covenants (mainly for external and structural repair of the block), required the tenant to become a member of the company, and provided for the company to become the landlord by the grant to it of an overriding lease. The landlord's covenants did not mention employing managing agents, but the company, which was a company limited by guarantee of which the tenant and the other flat-owners were members, did so when the flat-owners who had been running it got fed up. Was the tenant liable to pay towards the managing agents' proper fees? **Held:** Yes; when the tenant's lease was granted the parties must have contemplated that the company should take such steps as were reasonably necessary and conducive to the performance of its administrative functions and that the flat-owners accepted an obligation to contribute, pro rata, such sums as were necessary for the discharge by the company of its necessary administrative expenditure.

Broadwater Court Management Company v Jackson-Mann[8]: A company established by the tenants of a block of flats acquired the freehold. The service charge provisions in their leases did not expressly include costs relating to annual auditing and the filing of statutory returns under the Companies Acts. Could such costs be included in the service charges? **Held:** No; this was not intended at the time when the leases were granted. (For a similar decision involving an RTM Company, see *J E Wilson v Lesley Place (RTM) Co Ltd*[9]).

Mullaney v Maybourne Grange (Croydon) Management Co Ltd[10]: The wooden window-frames in a tower block of flats gave constant trouble. The management company had them replaced by maintenance-free double glazing. Was the tenant liable to pay towards the cost of this under service charge provisions covering (a) the 'repair' of the block, or (b) the cost of providing 'additional services or amenities'? **Held:** No; installing new-type windows was neither a repair nor a service or amenity. (Note: In *Sutton (Hastoe) Housing Association v Williams*[11] the Court of Appeal did not disagree with the above decision but, nevertheless, held that in the case before them the replacement of old wooden windows with double-glazed units could be chargeable as a 'repair'; similar decisions allowing the cost of replacement windows as 'repair' have been held in *Craighead v Homes for Islington*[12] and *London Borough of Sutton v Drake*[13].)

Bratton Seymour Service Co Ltd v Oxborough[14]: The company was formed to maintain the common parts of a residential estate. The plots were sold and the conveyances imposed a covenant on each purchaser to contribute towards the costs of maintaining the drive, water supply and drainage system. Was a plot purchaser, as a member of the company, liable to contribute to the costs of the company maintaining amenity areas not mentioned in the covenant? **Held:** No; additional burdens on members cannot be added by implication into the articles of association of the company.

Where the wording used in the service charge clause is plainly unclear or ambiguous, it has often been said that the courts will generally interpret it narrowly and determine ambiguities or uncertainties in the tenant's favour, under the 'contra proferentem' rule that an ambiguous deed will be interpreted against the party who granted it (see *Gilje v Charlgrove Securities Ltd*[15], per *Mummery LJ; Earl Cadogan v 27/29 Sloane Gardens Ltd*[16], Lands Tribunal; *McHale v Earl Cadogan*[17]). However, the court should try first to extract a sensible interpretation (*Ian Morris v Blackpool Borough Council*[18]), and the courts now have guidance from the Supreme Court on the correct approach to interpreting service charge clauses in Lord Neuberger's judgment in *Arnold v Britton*[19] (summarised above).

It must also be remembered that lease provisions vary considerably and, unlike building contracts, there are no widely used standard forms of lease. Accordingly one cannot derive from the decided cases settled meanings for particular wording used in service charge clauses, but only the approach to be taken when reading such provisions.

1 (1986) 277 EG 856, CA.
2 [2007] CSOH 53.
3 [2012] EWCA Civ 5103.
4 [2017] EWCA Civ 52.
5 [2015] UKSC 36.
6 [2010] EWCA Civ 14.
7 (1984) 271 EG 545, CA.
8 (1997) EGCS 145, CA.
9 [2010] UKUT 342, LC.
10 (1986) 277 EG 1350.
11 [1988] 1 EGLR 56.
12 [2010] UKUT 47, LC.
13 [2004] LRX/69, LT.
14 [1992] EGCS 28, CA.
15 [2002] 1 EGLR 41, CA.
16 [2006] 24 EG 178.
17 [2010] EWCA Civ 14.
18 [2014] EWCA Civ 1384.
19 [2015] UKSC 36.

Sweeping-up clauses

1.10 When a lease is drafted, the landlord and his solicitor cannot be expected to foresee every conceivable item of future expenditure which should be covered by the service charge. To avoid the risk of the landlord incurring costs which might fall outside the services or works listed in the landlord's covenants or in the list of chargeable expenditure, many service charge clauses contain a 'sweeping-up' provision entitling the landlord to charge not only for the services specifically listed but also for other services which he may decide to provide.

Sweeping-up clauses are discussed in more detail at **1.14**.

Overriding leases

1.11 Sometimes, after a lease has been granted to a tenant (T), an overriding lease is granted by the landlord (L1) so as to interpose an intermediate landlord (L2) between L1 and T. An overriding lease might be of an entire building or of one or more individual flats or other parts of a building. One particular situation in which an overriding lease of an individual part might arise would be under s 19 of the Landlord and Tenant (Covenants) Act 1995 (LT(C)A 1995) (see **1.97**).

The interposition of an overriding lease can create a problem in relation to service charges which are payable to the landlord (as distinct from being payable to a third party such as a management company). Imagine that T's lease requires T to pay a service charge calculated at 10 per cent of the total service costs of the building incurred by 'the Landlord', who up to the grant of the overriding lease will be L1. This would have been drafted to reflect the fact that L1 was the landlord of the whole building and would be supplying all the services in it. As from the grant of the overriding lease, L2 becomes 'the Landlord' in place of L1, who is now L2's landlord. The overriding lease will almost certainly impose on L2 an obligation to pay to L1 the same amount of service charge as was formerly payable by T, that is 10 per cent of the service costs incurred by L1. Accordingly, L2 will expect to recover the same amount from T, who is now his tenant. However, T's lease requires him to pay only 10 per cent of the service costs incurred by 'the Landlord', who is now L2. Does this mean that T need only pay to L2 a sum equal to 10 per cent of the amount of service charge that L2 has to pay to L1, leaving L2 to meet the difference? It is hoped that this would not be the case, but finding T liable to pay 100 per cent of the service charge payable by L2 to L1 may depend on whether the text of the particular lease leaves room for the court to interpret the references to service costs incurred by 'the Landlord' as meaning those incurred by L1 rather than by L2 (see *Adelphi v Christi*[1]). (If the premises are a residential flat, L2 might be able to solve this problem by obtaining a court order varying T's lease, under s 35 of the Landlord and Tenant Act 1987 – see **2.76**.)

A related problem would arise concerning the effect of the landlord's covenants to provide the services. If T's lease imposes covenants on 'the Landlord' to maintain the structure and common parts of the entire building and to provide other services, T can now require L2 to comply with those covenants (in addition to T still having that right against L1 – see s 15(2) of the LT(C)A 1995). However, L2 will not normally be in a position to perform them himself, nor wish to do so, since his overriding lease will comprise only the part of the building which is let to T; all L2 can do in this respect is to require L1 to perform those covenants, under the terms of the overriding lease.

1 (1983) 269 EG 221.

IDENTIFYING THE CHARGEABLE COSTS

Old-fashioned contribution clauses

1.12 Older forms of lease frequently contain quite brief and restricted contribution clauses, such as:

> 'to pay a fair proportion of the cost of maintaining and repairing party walls and structures, shared pipes and wires, and other things used in common.'

In such cases there is a strong chance that many items normally included in a modern service charge clause, particularly true services (such as porterage, heating, etc) as distinct from repairs and maintenance works, may not be covered by the wording and, thus, will not be chargeable to the tenant (under the principles set out at **1.8**).

However, the scope of this type of clause may not be quite as narrow as the first impression gives.

EXAMPLES

Twyman v Charrington[1]: The tenant, in his lease of the ground floor and basement of a building, covenanted to pay a proportion of the landlord's expenditure in repairing 'mutual or party structures and other items which may belong to or be used for the demised premises in common with other premises'. Was the tenant liable to contribute towards the cost of repairs to the roof located above the second floor? **Held:** Yes; although the roof was not a party structure so far as the demised premises were concerned, it benefited every part of the building and was therefore a 'mutual' structure or, alternatively, something 'used in common'. (As to a roof being held to benefit the tenants of lower floors, also see *Princes House Ltd v Distinctive Clubs Ltd*[2] at para 57).

Daejan Properties v Bloom[3]: The lease of a commercial garage in the basement of a block of flats imposed on the tenant a covenant to contribute to the cost of 'repairing . . . all walls, fence walls, fences, drains and other conveniences . . . used in common with the owners or occupiers of adjoining or contiguous premises'. Did this include the paving, asphalt membrane and concrete slab over the garage, forming the entrance driveway of the flats? **Held:** Yes.

1 [1994] 1 EGLR 243, CA.
2 [2006] All ER (D) 117, ChD.
3 (2000) EGCS 85, CA.

Modern service charge clauses

1.13 Modern service charge clauses can be drafted in many ways but generally fall into three categories:

(1) those which directly link the service charge to the costs incurred by the landlord in performing his service covenants contained elsewhere in the lease, eg by providing that the service charge is a percentage of:

> 'the costs and expenses incurred by the Lessor in carrying out his obligations under Clause 3 of this Lease';

(2) those which list the chargeable items (usually under the title of 'Heads of Charge' or similar) quite independently of the landlord's covenants, eg by providing that the service charge is a percentage of:

> 'the costs and expenses of such works services facilities and amenities listed in Part II of this Schedule as may from time to time be provided by the Lessor';

(3) a combination of (1) and (2) extending both to the cost of performing the landlord's covenants and the cost of other, discretionary, classes of expenditure.

Type (2) and (3) provisions can be misleading as they may give the tenant the impression that the landlord is obliged to provide all the listed services, but this may not be so. The fact that the landlord is entitled to charge if he provides a particular service does not, of itself, imply that he is contractually obliged to provide that service – the provision of the service may be at his discretion.

EXAMPLES

> *Duke of Westminster v Guild*[1]: The tenant of a mews building covenanted to 'pay and contribute to the landlords a fair proportion with other lessees interested therein of the expenses of . . . repairing . . . drains . . . belonging . . . to the demised premises or . . . used jointly'. The drain serving the premises was blocked with earth. Part of the drain was situated within the demised premises (and fell within the tenant's repairing covenant) and the remainder ran beneath the landlord's private mews. The tenant constructed a new drain between the premises and the private sewer serving the mews. Could the tenant recover any of the cost from the landlord on the basis that the landlord was obliged, by implication, to repair the drain in the mews and had failed to do so? **Held**: No; such an implication was not to be inferred. The landlord had a discretion whether or not to carry out the works mentioned in the contribution covenant.
>
> *Russell v Laimond Properties Ltd*[2]: Resident porters were employed by the landlord of a block of flats for several years. The landlord covenanted 'to provide . . . the services of such maintenance staff as [he] shall consider necessary for the performance of the matters specified . . . '. The possible service charge costs were separately listed in a schedule and included the cost of porterage and of providing, maintaining and repairing a flat for staff. The landlord decided to sell the porter's flat and use outside maintenance staff. Could the flat-owners obtain an injunction to stop him? **Held**: No; a covenant by the landlord to provide a resident porter could not be inferred from the schedule of chargeable items. The covenant required a maintenance man to be available at certain times in connection with expressly mentioned matters such as the central heating system, but this did not necessarily involve him residing in the block.

Accordingly, in order to check whether a service is obligatory, the landlord's covenants must be examined.

It is of critical importance to interpret correctly the wording of the service charge clause and, if that clause refers in turn to the landlord's covenants, the wording of those covenants. If it is found that certain types of work do not fall within any of the descriptions of work set out in the detailed clauses, the sweeping-up provision (if any) will have to be considered (see **1.10** and **1.14**) in order to see whether it covers them. If it does not, the expense in question cannot be included in the service charge. Sweeping-up provisions can be found in both types of clause and the existence of a well-drawn sweeper provision will reduce the risk of the landlord incurring irrecoverable expenditure.

A number of typical items found listed in landlord's service covenants or heads of charge are discussed at **1.19–1.43**.

1 (1983) 267 EG 762, CA
2 (1984) 269 EG 947, QBD.

Costs that can be charged

1.14 The most common service charge wording is that to the effect that the tenant must pay towards the 'costs', 'expenses' or 'expenditure' of the landlord on specified works and services, usually those performed on or in respect of the building or estate containing the premises let by the lease.

The concept of 'costs' is normally wide enough to cover both direct and ancillary costs. In the case of works, the cost of carrying out works will usually include the cost of engaging surveyors to specify, arrange and supervise them. In the case of services, the cost of providing them will normally include the cost of workmen or contractors (see **1.6**). Where the service is the provision of an amenity for tenants (such as a gym or a concierge area) the cost of providing that service may include the cost of renting the necessary accommodation (see *The Gateway (Leeds) Management Ltd v Naghash and Shamsizadeh*[1]).

It may be implied that the amount of any item of cost is after crediting any contribution to that cost from a person other than the tenants who together contribute to the service charge; in *Sheffield City Council v Oliver*[2] the council as landlord of a block of flats had to give credit for government funding it received towards the cost of improvements to the building. That concept might equally apply where owners of an adjoining property have to contribute to the cost of repairing amenities that are shared with them.

It may also be implied that there is to be no double-counting of the same costs under different heads of charge (see *Phillips v Francis*[3]).

Where, as is very common, the lease defines the service charge by reference to costs incurred or paid by the landlord in relation to a particular building (such as the building containing the premises let by the lease) the landlord must be able to demonstrate that the costs relate to that building. If the lease does not expressly give the landlord the power to allocate to that building a proportion of costs incurred collectively on that and one or more other buildings, the landlord may not be entitled to include any part of those collective costs in the service charge. A recent example is in *Norwich City Council v Redford*[4], in which the Upper Tribunal held that the landlord of a residential estate could not charge the tenants a contribution towards the cost of the maintenance of communal lighting in their estate since the landlord employed the maintenance company under a single contract covering of all its properties and not just that estate, and the company charged for call-outs as well as a fixed basic charge. The landlord was unable to calculate the precise costs attributable to the tenant's building and the lease did not allow the landlord to apportion the costs on any other basis, however fair or reasonable it might be.

As for costs 'incurred' or 'expended' and the time when costs can be included in a service charge, see **1.17** and **1.75**.

1 [2015] UKUT 0333, LC.
2 [2017] EWCA Civ 225.
3 [2012] EWHC 3650 (Ch).
4 [2015] UKUT 30 LC.

Sweeping-up clauses, variation rights and the landlord's discretion

1.15 For the reasons mentioned at **1.10** and **1.13**, many service charge clauses contain provisions intended to sweep up into the service charge the cost of services or works not otherwise specifically mentioned. This may appear in the lease:

(a) in a definition of the chargeable costs, for example:

> '"Total expenditure" means the expenditure incurred by the Lessor in any accounting period in carrying out its obligations under Clause 3 of this Lease and any other costs and expenses reasonably incurred in connection with the Building';

(b) by a separate head of charge in the list of chargeable costs, for example:

> 'the cost of providing such other services and performing such other works as the landlord shall deem appropriate or desirable';

(c) by a landlord's covenant in a similar form to (b), such as:

> 'to provide such other services and perform such other acts as the landlord may deem appropriate or desirable';

(d) by a provision giving the landlord the right to vary or add to the listed services (see **1.46**).

In the example quoted in (a) above, the words in italics will catch the cost of any works or services which the landlord '*reasonably*' decides to carry out (see, for example, *Fluor Daniel Properties Ltd v Shortlands Investment Ltd*[1] and **1.50**), but which are not covered by his express obligations under clause 3 of that lease. Some sweeping-up clauses do not contain this reasonableness qualification, but give the landlord wider discretion (subject to any statutory or common law implication of reasonableness or rationality – see below and **1.49** and **2.24**). Other sweeper clauses may be drafted so as to narrow down the scope of unspecified services by confining them to matters carried out '*for the benefit of the tenants in the Building as a whole*', '*in the interests of good estate management*', or by similar limiting phrases.

The effectiveness of these clauses in sweeping up unspecified costs depends entirely on their wording taken in the context of the lease as a whole. In most cases, but not invariably, these sweeper clauses are just as narrowly construed as the main charging provisions. The use of the word 'services' in some sweeper clauses may itself have a limiting effect.

EXAMPLES

Mullaney v Maybourne Grange (Croydon) Management Co Ltd[2]: The service charge clause entitled the management company to recover the cost of 'providing and maintaining additional services or amenities'. Did this cover the costs incurred by the company in replacing wooden window frames with different maintenance-free frames? **Held:** No; since window frames were neither 'services' nor 'amenities'.

Jacob Isbicki & Co Ltd v Goulding & Bird Ltd[3]: Wall cleaning was not on the list of chargeable items in the lease, but the landlord had power at his discretion to 'add to, extend, vary or make any alteration in the rendering of the said services or any of them', and proposed to clean the external walls by sand-blasting. Could he charge for this? **Held:** No; the power quoted above gave the landlord a limited right to vary the services whilst remaining within the types of service listed, and did not give the landlord the right to embark upon a kind of service not contemplated by the main provisions. Furthermore, the proposal was not a 'service' in the normal sense.

Sun Alliance and London Assurance Co Ltd v British Railways Board[4]: The specified service costs included the cost of operating and maintaining equipment, and the sweeping-up clause covered 'the cost of providing other services'. Could the landlord include in the service charge the capital cost of installing a window-cleaner's cradle system at a cost of £70,000? **Held:** Yes; the provisions quoted were wide enough; the fact that it was capital expenditure was irrelevant (see **1.25**).

Lloyds Bank plc v Bowker Orford[5]: The service charge extended to 'any other beneficial services'. Did this include the repair of the exterior of the building and the repair and decoration of the internal common parts? **Held:** No; they were not 'services' in the sense used in the clause; the quoted words were only apt to cover matters such as lift operation, caretaking, security, cleaning and lighting the common parts and the provision of constant hot water.

Whether such clauses are likely to encompass legal and other professional costs, particularly in connection with service charge disputes, is discussed at **1.38** and **1.39**, and the inclusion of the costs of environmentally friendly measures is considered in **Chapter 6**.

Where the scope of the sweeper clause is unclear, a landlord who wishes to rely on the clause in order to be able to recover the cost of proposal expenditure should seek the tenants' agreement, failing which the landlord could apply to the court for a declaration on the point (see, for example, *Reston Ltd v Hudson*[6]). In the residential sector, the FTT has jurisdiction to decide in advance whether proposed expenditure falls within the scope of the service charge provisions of the tenant's lease and whether it meets the statutory test of reasonableness – see **2.67**). The ability to ask the court or FTT to rule in advance on the recoverability of proposed expenditure is very useful and should probably be used more frequently by landlords.

Whether sweeper clauses may at common law be subject to an implied test of reasonableness is discussed at **1.51**. Statutory reasonableness tests in the residential sector are discussed at **2.26**.

A recent legal development is to consider whether a contractual discretion has to be exercised, if not reasonably, then at least rationally and in good faith having regard to the purpose of the contract. The exercise by the landlord of a discretion given to him by the lease, such as choices about providing services, may be subject to an implied test of rationality and an implied obligation to act in good faith towards the tenant – this implication under contract law was expounded by Lord Sumption in *Hayes v Willoughby*[7] and applied by the Supreme Court to an employment contract in *Braganza v BP Shipping*[8]. It was first applied to service charges by the Court of Appeal in *Hounslow LBC v Waaler*[9] and subsequently cited by the Upper Tribunal in *COS Services Ltd v Nicholson*[10].

EXAMPLE

Hounslow LBC v Waaler[11]: The service charge clause entitled the landlord to charge for improvements carried out to the building. Did the landlord have an unfetter right under the lease to decide whether to carry out and charge for improvements comprising replacing the windows and cladding of the building? **Held:** No; the landlord had a discretion but by implication it had to exercise that discretion rationally and in good faith and consistently with its contractual purpose. (Since the case involved a residential lease, the statutory reasonableness test also applied and created a higher hurdle for the landlord to satisfy – see **2.26**).

1 [2001] EGCS 8.
2 (1986) 277 EG 1350.
3 [1989] 1 EGLR 236.
4 [1989] 2 EGLR 237.
5 (1992) 31 EG 67, ChD.
6 (1990) 2 EGLR 51, ChD.
7 [2013] UKSC 17.
8 [2015] UKSC 17.
9 [2017] EWCA Civ 45, CA.
10 [2017] UKUT 382 LC.
11 [2017] EWCA Civ 45.

A presumption against profit-making

1.16 It is likely that the courts will assume that, in the absence of clear wording to the contrary, the service charge provisions are not intended to give the landlord a profit on the provision of services but merely to provide reimbursement of cost.

EXAMPLES

Jollybird Ltd v Fairzone Ltd[1]: The lease contained an ambiguously worded heating charge clause which, on one reading, would have entitled the landlord to charge more than actual cost. Held: That interpretation must be rejected in favour of the clause being interpreted to give reimbursement only.

Earl Cadogan v 27/29 Sloane Gardens Ltd[2]: The lease contained a very clear provision allowing the landlord to include in the service charge an amount for notional rent on the caretaker's flat. The landlord's headlease did not allow the caretaker's flat to be used otherwise than as rent-free accommodation for a caretaker, so the landlord could not have obtained rent from that flat by letting it. The tenant claimed that, since the provision of the flat was at no actual or foregone cost to the landlord, the landlord could not charge anything for it. **Held:** The provision in the tenant's lease allowing the landlord to charge the notional rent was clear and unambiguous, so the landlord could charge it even though the amount was neither a cost he incurred nor an income which he had foregone.

Clear wording will prevail however unreasonable the outcome (see *Arnold v Britton*[3] at **1.9**) and where leases set out fixed percentages for tenants' service charge contributions there is no rule preventing the landlord from recovering more than 100 per cent of its total costs if the percentage contributions payable under each lease total more than 100 per cent.

The RICS Professional Statement: Service Charges in Commercial Property (see **7.1**) imposes a mandatory requirement on chartered surveyors who manage commercial property for landlords not to seek to recover from commercial tenants more than the actual costs of the provision or supply of the services, although confusingly it also states that the provisions of the leases are paramount.

1 [1990] 2 EGLR 55, CA.
2 [2006] 24 EG 178, LT.
3 [2015] UKSC 36.

Costs incurred or expended

1.17 Many service charge clauses are expressed to cover costs and expenses which the landlord 'expends' or 'incurs' or which 'become payable' by him. In some circumstances, it will be important to know whether the wording allows the charging of costs which have not yet been paid out or have not yet even fallen due, but which will become payable at a later date when work which has already been contracted between the landlord and his builders or suppliers is completed. The landlord may be keen to charge the cost to his tenants at the time or even before he contracts for the work to be done, particularly in cases where the leases will have expired by the time payment falls due or as a way of financing the work if the lease does not provide expressly for payments on account.

At first glance it may be thought that the word 'incurs' simply means that the landlord acquires the obligation to pay the cost by placing the order for the relevant works or services, but a competing interpretation is that a cost is only incurred once the conditions triggering its payment have been satisfied, such as the work or service having been carried out and the supplier having invoiced it. These points have been considered in a number of court cases.

EXAMPLES

Capital & Counties Freehold Equity Trust Ltd v BL plc[1]: The service charge covered costs which may 'be expended or incurred or become payable' in respect of the listed services. Some work was ordered by the landlord shortly before the end of the lease, to be carried out afterwards. Did costs 'incurred', in contradistinction to costs 'expended', mean costs for which a contractual commitment was entered into by the landlord even though payment might be made at a later date, so that those costs were 'incurred' before the lease expired and could be included in the service charge payable by the tenant? **Held:** No; in the context, the words 'become payable', 'expended' and 'incurred' were synonymous, and meant that payment was made or fell due during the service charge accounting period in question. The intent of the landlord's covenants and service charge provisions, read as a whole, was that the service obligations and the service charge were to be coterminous and that only services performed during the term of the lease were chargeable.

Barrington v Sloane Properties Ltd[2]: The service charge covered the 'actual cost to the Landlord' of providing the services. Building work was carried out in two phases under separate building contracts. Each contract straddled two accounting years. Could the service charge for a particular accounting year include costs relating to work carried out in that year but not yet payable under the building contract, or costs that had become payable under the building contract but were not actually paid during that year? **Held:** The date of actual payment did not matter. A liability became a 'cost' when it became contractually due for payment. Once that happened it could be included in the service charge accounts.

For a different distinction between 'cost' and 'sums expended', see *Gilje and Others v Chalgrove Securities Ltd*[3] at **1.45**.

The meaning of the word 'incurred' has been analysed by the court where it is used in a statutory provision relating to residential service charges. Section 20B of the Landlord and Tenant Act 1985 imposes a time limit by reference to when costs are 'incurred' and in *OM Property Management Ltd v Burr*[4] the Court of Appeal held that this meant when they are paid or when the landlord receives an invoice or other demand for payment from the supplier or service provider. Whether the same word has the same meaning when used in the contractual service charge provisions in a lease remains to be seen; a Chancery Division judge came to that conclusion in *Morshead Mansions Ltd v Mactra Properties Ltd*[5] and his view was followed, also in a lower court, in *Friends Life Management Services Ltd v A&A Express Building Ltd*[6], but the point has not yet come before a higher court.

It is to be noted that professional guidance and standards on accounting matters (such as FRS18 and TECH 03/11) normally require accounts to be drawn on an accruals basis, taking into account expenditure that will become payable at a later date under a legally binding commitment. That wider approach is also reflected in the RICS Service Charge Residential Management Code which has been approved by the Secretary of State – see **2.92**. Further, interpreting 'incurred' more narrowly for the purpose of s 20B of the LTA 1985, to catch only those costs that have been paid by or demanded from the landlord, may be justified on the basis that the section is quite a penal provision restricting the landlord's right to recover the costs to which it applies, and that this narrow meaning should not necessarily apply elsewhere.

For clauses allowing provision to be made for future expenditure, see **1.18**.

Landlords who are about to incur significant costs on repairs or other works should consider carefully how the timing of the works or of the due dates for payment may relate to the mechanisms in the leases for inclusion of those costs in the service charges, so that they can match the timing of receipts and payments. Where the service charge clauses do not provide for adequate interim charges or in other ways do not give the landlord sufficient flexibility, it may be necessary for the landlord to enter into contracts under which only a lump sum payment will fall due a certain time after the work is complete and with the contractor being obliged to complete the work by a particular date (even trying to make 'time of the essence'), to facilitate the collection of funds through the service charges to meet that payment. Whilst the total cost under such a contract may be higher than under a contract involving stage payments, this might be unavoidable.

1 [1987] 2 EGLR 49.
2 [2006] LRX/31/2006, LT.
3 [2001] EWCA Civ 1777.

4 [2013] EWCA Civ 479.
5 [2013] EWHC 224 (Ch).
6 [2014] EWHC 1463.

Costs incurred during the term and provision for future expenditure

1.18 In many cases the service charge provisions of a lease may be interpreted to confine the service charge to costs that the landlord incurs for works or services provided during the term of the lease.

The court in *Capital & Counties Freehold Equity Trust Ltd v B L Plc*[1] held that, in the absence of express provisions, it was to be implied that a service charge covered only those costs that were incurred during the term of the lease and could not include costs anticipated to be incurred after the end of the term.

This concept was followed by the Court of Appeal in *Brown's Operating Systems Ltd v Southwark Roman Catholic Diocesan Corporation*[2], where a tenant exercising a break clause was held to be entitled to a refund of surplus service charge payments exceeding his proportion of the expenditure incurred up to the break date.

In *Friends Life Management Services Ltd v A & A Express Building Ltd*[3], a number of related points arose. The lease expressly allowed each Financial Year's costs to include provision for costs to be incurred in a later Financial Year. The lease ended by the tenant exercising a break clause. It was held that where a provision for future expenditure had been made, a credit equal to that provision had to be brought forward in the service charge accounts and set against the actual cost of the works or services for which the provision had been made once those costs were incurred. Since the landlord conceded that the lease by implication allowed the provision only to cover expenditure to be incurred before the lease ended, it followed that any unspent balance had to be repaid to the tenant when the lease ended, whether it ended by term expiry or under a break clause. As regards calculating the tenant's final service charge liability, the accounting date for the 'Financial Year' was 31 December but the term date was 24 March and the break notice ended the term on 24 March 2010; it was held that the tenant was only liable to pay for the period to 24 March 2010 but that to calculate that liability all costs properly chargeable for the whole of the then current at Financial Year (to 31 December 2010) should be aggregated and the tenant's proportion up to 24 March 2010 was to be calculated on a day by day basis as if the costs had been incurred evenly throughout that Financial Year. Since it had been conceded by the landlord that provisions for future expenditure were limited to expenditure incurred before the lease ended, no new provision could be made in the accounts for that final Financial Year in respect of later periods and any existing provision carried forward from past Financial Years had to be credited against the final service charge liability. An accountants' certificate for accounts that wrongfully included such a further provision was held invalid.

See also **1.75** below.

1 [1987] 2 EGLR 49.
2 [2007] EWCA Civ 164.

[3] [2014] EWHC 1463 (Ch).

REPAIRS, RENEWALS, REPLACEMENTS, IMPROVEMENTS, SERVICES AND STATUTORY WORKS

Basic principles

1.19 Many service charges cover the cost of 'repair' of the exterior, main structure, common parts and shared plant machinery and service media (pipes, wires, etc) of the building. The word 'repair' commonly features in both landlord's service covenants and heads of charge (see **1.13**).

Ascertaining the scope of the word 'repair', and any other words used to describe the nature of works for which the landlord can charge, is extremely important, particularly because tenants usually resent paying for works other than straightforward maintenance or redecoration. Tenants of new buildings frequently object to being potentially liable to pay for the completion of unfinished works or the repair of inherent structural defects, whilst tenants in older buildings may object when the landlord seeks to include in the service charge the cost of refurbishing and modernising the entrance, lifts and common parts of the building or even renewing an old roof. These matters are discussed in the RICS Service Charge Residential Management Code (2nd edition) (see **2.92**).

The meaning of the word 'repair' has been considered in numerous cases and is a large complex topic; the following is only a brief summary of the position.

For the position where the landlord fails to carry out necessary repairs at the appropriate time, see **1.29**.

In some cases repairs, improvements or services are carried out under an obligation imposed by legislation. That is considered at **1.30** and **Chapter 6**.

Repair

1.20 The word 'repair' has been defined as the rectifying of damage or deterioration, that is 'the putting back into good condition of something that, having been in good condition, has fallen into bad condition' (per Lord Evershed MR in *Day v Harland and Wolff Ltd*[1]), or 'making good damage so as to leave the subject so far as possible as though it had not been damaged' (per Atkin LJ in *Anstruther-Gough-Calthorpe v McOscar*[2]). These definitions of repair have been cited with approval by the Court of Appeal in *Quick v Taff-Ely District Council*[3] and *Post Office v Aquarius Properties Ltd*[4].

Words similar to 'repair', such as 'amend', 'maintain', 'uphold', etc, will generally be interpreted as the same as 'repair': *Halliard Property Co Ltd v Nicholas Clarke Investments Ltd*[5], per French J, and *Fluor Daniel Properties Ltd v Shortlands Investment Ltd*[6] (see **1.50**).

Even if an item is plainly out of repair by virtue of having been damaged or having deteriorated compared with its previous condition, nevertheless there are limits to the remedial work falling within the scope of 'repair':

(1) the nature and standard of repair is to be determined by reference to the class and character of the property at the date on which the lease was granted, so that upgrading (unless an unavoidable result of remedying the disrepair – eg the replacement of broken Victorian sanitary fittings with currently available modern fittings) falls outside repair; thus, the 'repair' of heating and air conditioning plant means keeping it in working order so that it performs as it did when it was installed, not to the standard now expected of new plant (*Ultraworth v General Accident*[7]);

(2) the word 'repair' may not be apt to cover work which would be effectively an alteration to the whole or substantially the whole of the structure of the building, or which would produce a building of a wholly different character to that which had been let, or which would cost an amount which is out of proportion to the previous value of the building and would substantially enhance the value and life span of the building: *McDougall v Easington District Council*[8] (summarising the effect of a number of earlier authorities including the landmark decision in *Ravenseft Properties Ltd v Davstone (Holdings) Ltd*[9]).

Often the distinction between 'repair' and 'improvement' is very fine and hard to draw (see **1.26**). In some cases the issue of 'reasonableness' is invoked in determining whether proposed work is or goes beyond repair (see **1.50**).

If the landlord's duty is to 'keep' in repair, as is commonly required under modern leases, this requires him to prevent disrepair from occurring and would therefore appear to encompass preventive work where disrepair is imminent (*British Telecommunications plc v Sun Life Assurance Society plc*[10]; see **1.29**). This effectively requires a landlord to arrange regular inspections of the property to ensure that those parts for which the landlord is responsible are always in repair.

Occasionally, it is unclear whether a certain element of the building is repairable by the tenant or by the landlord. This may occur where the definition of the extent of the tenant's demise is imprecise. It may, alternatively, be unclear whether certain proposed work is within the meaning of 'repair' or other such expression used in the service charge clause, as discussed at **1.21–1.26**. In such cases, it may be prudent for the landlord to apply to the court for a declaration on the issue, as in *Reston Ltd v Hudson*[11] (see **1.21**). As to the costs of such an application, see **1.40**.

Often the service charge will be stated to cover the costs of repairing or redecorating 'when necessary'. If this is disputed, the court or tribunal can consider whether work was 'necessary' or was premature and outside the scope of the charge (see *Burge v Dome Developments Ltd*[12]).

1 [1953] 2 All ER 387.
2 [1924] 1 KB 716.
3 [1985] 3 All ER 321.
4 (1987) 54 P&CR 61.
5 (1984) 269 EG 1257.
6 [2001] EGCS 8, ChD.
7 (2000) EGCS 19, Tech & Constr Court.
8 (1989) 58 P&CR 201, CA.
9 [1979] 1 All ER 929.
10 [1995] 2 EGLR 44, CA.
11 [1990] 2 EGLR 51, ChD.

12 [2007] LON/00AU/LSC/2006/0157, LVT.

Patching or replacement

1.21 What work can reasonably be expected of a landlord where he is required to carry out repairs will depend upon the facts of each particular case (*Bradley v Chorley Borough Council*[1]).

Repair work can sometimes present a choice between patching up or replacing the damaged or deteriorated parts: *Inglis v Buttery*[2], per Lord Blackburn; *Anstruther-Gough-Calthorpe v McOscar*[3], per Scrutton LJ; *Greg v Planque*[4], per Slesser LJ. Generally, the party responsible for carrying out the repair has the choice whether to execute the long-term repair/replacement or a 'patching-up', as long as the immediate result of either course of action will be to put the dilapidated or damaged item back into proper repair.

EXAMPLES

> *Manor House Drive Ltd v Shahbazian*[5]: In the lease of a maisonette, the landlord covenanted to 'maintain repair and redecorate the main structure and roof of the building', and the tenant was liable to pay towards the costs incurred. On surveyor's advice, the landlord installed a new zinc roof. The tenant argued that the roof could have been patched up for less cost. Could the landlord recover the cost of the new roof? **Held**: Yes.
>
> *Murray v Birmingham City Council*[6]: The landlord was liable for external repairs to the tenant's house, and chose periodically to patch up the roof on a piecemeal basis whenever parts of it leaked, rather than replacing the entire roof. Had the landlord properly fulfilled his obligation? **Held**: Yes.
>
> *Reston Ltd v Hudson*[7]: The landlord, liable at the tenants' cost to 'repair' the window-frames of a block of flats, proposed to replace all the window-frames in circumstances in which a piecemeal replacement of individual timbers in many rotted frames would be impractical and more expensive. Was he entitled to do so? **Held**: Yes.

However, where an item is beyond sensible patching up, it must be replaced.

It may be implied that the landlord is under a general duty to act reasonably when deciding the type of repair work (see **1.49** and **2.24**). Certainly, where the landlord is not able to restore the premises to exactly what was there before, he must provide a repair that is reasonable (see below and *Reedbase Ltd v Fattal*[8]).

EXAMPLE

> *Stent v Monmouth District Council*[9]: The wooden front door of a council house rotted, previous wooden doors having also rotted due to the exposed location of the house. Was the council, under its obligation for external repairs, liable to replace the rotten wooden door with a new aluminium door of better design? **Held**: Yes; since that was what a reasonable landlord would do.

1 (1985) 275 EG 80, 17 HLR 305, CA.
2 (1878) 3 App Cas 552.
3 [1924] 1 KB 716.
4 [1936] 1 KB 669.

5 (1965) 195 EG 283, CA.
6 [1987] 2 EGLR 53, CA.
7 [1990] 2 EGLR 51, ChD.
8 [2018] EWCA 840, CA.
9 (1987) 54 P&CR 193, CA.

Structural and external repair

1.22 An obligation to repair, or a right to charge for the cost of repairing, the 'structure', 'exterior' or other specified part of a building must be interpreted in the context of the lease as a whole. In some cases it will be plain, even if not clearly expressed, that it is intended that the landlord's works shall include repair of all parts of the building that are not demised to the tenants. A well-drafted modern lease will make it clear whether parts of the building such as joists are the responsibility of the tenants or the landlord, but frequently one finds poorly-drafted leases which are not clear on this type of issue and in such cases it may be necessary to apply to the court to decide the matter (eg *Marlborough Park Services Ltd v Rowe*[1]).

'Structural repair', a phrase sometimes met in the context of covenants to repair the structure of a building, has been held to mean the repair of structural parts only, thus excluding repair of the finishes: *Granada Theatres Ltd v Freehold Investment (Leytonstone) Ltd*[2].

Sometimes, the service costs will cover repair of the 'main structure'. In *Samuels v Abbints Investments*[3], Ungoed-Thomas J held that a landlord's covenant to repair the 'main structure' of a block of flats required him to repair the outside bricks of the external walls (although this may have been influenced by the fact that the lease defined the plaintiff's flat as including 'the internal and external walls . . . but excluding the outside brick, steel or concrete work').

The word 'structure' has also been judicially considered in the different context of the Landlord and Tenant Act 1954. In *Romulus Trading Co Ltd v Trustees of Henry Smith's Charity*[4], it was held that the statutory expression 'work of construction' meant interference 'with the structure of the building', and it was observed that 'structure' was not necessarily confined to external and load-bearing walls, but further guidance on the meaning of the word was not given. The precise extent of 'structure' may, therefore, depend on the context.

Where the repair of structural parts necessarily entails further works, the obligation to carry out structural repair may include those further works: *Smedley v Chumley & Hawke Ltd*[5] (see **1.23**).

What if the service costs include the repair of the 'exterior' of the building? Sometimes the word 'exterior' has been given a wide meaning by the courts. In cases under the original provisions of the Housing Act 1961 (re-enacted in the Landlord and Tenant Act 1985) the 'exterior' was held to include accessways and staircases: *Brown v Liverpool Corporation*[6], but in *Kumarsamy v Edwards*[7], the Supreme Court stated that *Brown v Liverpool Corporation*[8] had been wrongly decided.

The expression 'external wall' was held in *Pembury v Lamdin*[9] to mean a wall forming part of the enclosure of the premises, not necessarily a wall exposed to the atmosphere.

Whether windows and window-frames are part of the 'exterior' or 'outside walls' of a building will depend upon the overall intent of the various clauses and the physical nature of the building. In buildings with glass curtain-walling, for example, it will often be apparent that the windows are merely sections of that curtain-walling. 'It would appear that windows in the outer wall of a building may, in certain contexts and for certain purposes, be regarded as part of the walls': Lord Evershed MR in *Holiday Fellowship Ltd v Hereford*[10]; see also *Boswell v Crucible Steel Co*[11]; *Ball v Plummer*[12].

Often the courts adopt a flexible, common-sense approach to these references to parts of the building, as in *Plough Investments Ltd v Manchester City Council*[13], where Scott J treated the phrase 'main timbers', in a landlord's repairing covenant, as referring to the steel frame of the building – there were no 'timbers' in the strict sense of wooden members.

1 [2006] EWCA Civ 436, CA.
2 [1959] Ch 952, CA.
3 (1963) 188 EG 689.
4 [1989] EGCS 165, CA.
5 (1982) 44 P&CR 50.
6 [1969] 3 All ER 1345.
7 [2016] UKSC 40.
8 [1969] 3 All ER 1345.
9 [1940] 2 All ER 434, CA.
10 [1959] 1 All ER 433.
11 [1925] 1 KB 119.
12 (1879) 23 Sol Jo 656, CA.
13 [1989] 1 EGLR 244.

Whether repair includes rectifying inherent defects

1.23 Generally speaking, the remedying of a defect found to be inherent in the construction of a building will not of itself fall within an obligation to 'repair', since the defectively constructed part will not have been previously in any better condition.

EXAMPLES

Halliard Property Co Ltd v Nicholas Clarke Investments Ltd[1]: Did the tenant's covenant to 'repair' the premises make him liable to rebuild an unsupported wall, described by the judge as a 'jerry-built structure', when it collapsed during the term of the lease? **Held:** No.

Post Office v Aquarius Properties Ltd[2]: Did the tenant's covenant to 'repair' an office building oblige the tenant to alter the construction of the basement walls so as to render the basement watertight? **Held:** No.

Quick v Taff-Ely Borough Council[3]: The windows of a council house were badly designed and were prone to cause condensation, which damaged the tenant's contents and decorations but did not damage the walls or other parts of the house itself. Did the landlord, under his covenant to 'repair' a house, have to replace them with different windows? **Held:** No.

Eyre v McCracken[4]: Water ingress, facilitated by the absence of any damp-proof course, caused damage to parts of a building. Did the necessary works of 'repair' include installing a damp-proof course? **Held:** No.

Holding & Barnes plc v Hill House Hammond Ltd[5]: The landlord covenanted to keep in repair the structure and exterior of the building. Did 'repair' include installing a damp-proof course? **Held:** No.

However, if an inherent defect in one element of a building causes damage to occur to another, previously sound, part of the building, the part so damaged will require to be rectified in a modern competent manner under the obligation to 'repair' and that may extend to remedying the underlying inherent defect if the damaged part cannot sensibly be repaired without it. This is a matter of fact and degree in each case, so it is difficult to derive precise rules which would apply in every case (compare, for example, *McCracken* and *Holding & Barnes*, above, with *Elmcroft* and *Welsh*, below).

EXAMPLES

Ravenseft Properties Ltd v Davstone (Holdings) Ltd[6]: The tenant of a building covenanted 'when where and so often as occasion shall require well and sufficiently to repair renew rebuild uphold support . . . ' the premises. The external stone cladding had not been installed with expansion joints and there were no metal ties between the stone slabs and the concrete frame. The cladding was bowing dangerously due to its expansion being greater than that of the frame. Did the tenant's covenant require him to remedy the problem in accordance with current building methods by cutting the cladding and installing ties and plastic expansion-absorbing material at a cost of about £155,000? **Held:** Yes; the fact that the building was built without expansion joints or ties did not exonerate the tenant. However, if the cost of the remedial work would have been a substantially higher proportion of the cost of rebuilding the entire building, it would have gone beyond repair.

Elmcroft Developments Ltd v Tankersley-Sawyer[7]: The landlord covenanted to 'maintain and keep the exterior of the building and the roof, the main walls, timbers and drains thereof in good and tenantable repair and condition'. Was the landlord liable to remedy deterioration caused by rising damp, the damp-proof course having been positioned below ground level? **Held:** Yes.

Smedley v Chumley & Hawke Ltd[8]: The landlord covenanted 'to keep the main walls and roof in good structural repair'. A main wall cracked because the building had been built on a partly unsupported concrete raft, one end of which had subsided. Was the landlord liable to carry out remedial work including major underpinning, since the wall could not be properly repaired otherwise? **Held:** Yes.

Welsh v Greenwich London Borough Council[9]: The landlord covenanted 'to maintain the dwelling in good condition and repair'. The property was not properly insulated and suffered from damp and condensation, which damaged the walls as well as the tenant's fittings. Was the landlord liable to provide thermal insulation? **Held:** Yes.

Where the express terms of the lease go beyond 'repair' and include obligations such as to 'rebuild', 'renew' or 'rectify inherent defects', the limitations on the scope of 'repair' will not be decisive and the additional wording must be closely examined. The covenant may, in fact, be divisible so as to provide a covenant to repair and a separate covenant to rectify inherent defects.

In *Credit Suisse v Beegas Nominees Ltd*[10], it was held that an obligation to 'keep the building in good and tenantable condition' required leaking cladding which had a design defect to be replaced by a totally new cladding system.

1 (1984) 269 EG 1257.
2 (1985) 276 EG 923, CA.
3 (1985) 276 EG 452, CA.
4 (2000) 80 P&CR 220, CA.
5 (2000) WL 877816, ChD.
6 [1979] 1 All ER 929, QBD.
7 (1984) 270 EG 140, CA.
8 (1982) 44 P&CR 50.
9 (2000) EGCS 84, CA.
10 [1994] 4 All ER 803.

Replacements and renewals

1.24 Good practice requires landlords to draw a distinction between replacing or renewing defective equipment of structures on the one hand and, on the other hand, carrying out replacements or renewals solely as improvement. The issues are discussed in various places in the RICS Professional Statement: Service Charges in Commercial Property (see **7.1**). The former type of work, unlike the latter, will often be within the scope of 'repair' and will be encompassed by many service charge clauses without special wording. Where the lease expressly includes the words 'rebuilding' or 'renewal', this is likely to widen the scope of work covered by the clause, but even a simple covenant to 'repair' will usually, by implication, include a certain amount of rebuilding and replacement of elements of the building which have deteriorated, as mentioned in **1.20**.

EXAMPLE

> *Minja Properties v Cussins*[1]: A landlord had the right to enter a building in order 'to effect repairs to the building'. Did 'repair' include replacing rusted windows with new double-glazed sealed window units? **Held:** Yes; since the windows needed replacing and renewal of parts of a building is within 'repair'.

As for plant and equipment, an obligation to 'repair' or 'maintain' such items usually carries with it an obligation to replace the plant and equipment when necessary. This will also apply where the obligation is expressed simply as a covenant to provide the particular service (eg hot water or central heating) without even mentioning the plant and equipment. The fact that the expenditure is of a capital nature, rather than revenue, is generally irrelevant. However, this implied obligation will not necessarily be taken to require or authorise the upgrading of plant and machinery which is in working order.

EXAMPLES

> *Yorkbrook Investments Ltd v Batten*[2]: The landlord covenanted to provide hot water. Was he liable to replace the boiler system when necessary, even though the lease did not expressly mention the boiler system? **Held:** Yes.

Lloyds Bank plc v Bowker Orford[3]: The service charge covered the provision of hot water and lighting of the common parts. Did this encompass not only the operation of the existing hot water and lighting systems but also the replacement of the plant and equipment when necessary and even the provision of necessary additional equipment? **Held:** Yes.

London Borough of Sutton v Drake[4]: In order to repair cladding that was in disrepair the old metal windows had to be removed. Some windows were unavoidably damaged in this process. Could the cost of repairing the cladding extend to the cost of replacing the damaged windows? **Held:** Yes.

Where the obligation is to 'repair' and it is possible (even if exceptionally expensive) to repair the item rather than replace it with something totally different, the obligation may require the expensive repair rather than the cheaper replacement.

EXAMPLE

Creska v Hammersmith London Borough Council[5]: The lease of an office building required the tenant to keep it in repair. The underfloor heating system broke down and would be very expensive to repair. Could the tenant satisfy its repairing obligation by leaving the underfloor system and installing storage heaters? **Held:** No; the existing system had to be repaired.

Also see **1.49** (as to reasonableness tests) and **4.2** (as to sinking funds, reserve funds and depreciation).

1 (1998) 30 EG 114, ChD.
2 (1985) 276 EG 545.
3 (1992) 31 EG 67, ChD.
4 [2007] LRX/69/2004, LT.
5 (1998) 37 EG 165, CA.

Capital expenditure

1.25 If a particular item of expenditure is to be chargeable to the tenants through the service charge, the wording of the service charge clause must be apt to cover the item in question; if it is, the cost is prima facie chargeable, *whether or not* the work is an improvement, a replacement or renewal, the remedying of an inherent defect, or other non-standard type of expenditure. The fact that, for some purposes, the expenditure may be considered as a capital item is normally irrelevant.

EXAMPLES

Sun Alliance and London Assurance Co Ltd v British Railways Board[1]: The specified service costs included the cost of operating and maintaining equipment, and the sweeping-up clause covered 'the cost of providing other services'. Could the landlord include in the service charge the capital cost of installing a new window-cleaner's cradle system at a cost of £70,000? **Held:** Yes.

Yorkbrook Investments Ltd v Batten[2]: The lease contained a landlord's covenant 'to provide and maintain . . . an adequate supply of heating in the hot water radiators . . . and to remedy any mechanical breakdown in the hot water and central heating systems'. Did this require the landlord to incur the capital cost of replacing antiquated and unserviceable equipment? **Held:** Yes.

Lloyds Bank plc v Bowker Orford[3]: The service charge was to cover the 'total cost' of providing the listed services, which included provision of constant hot water in the lavatories, and keeping the common parts lighted. Did this encompass capital expenditure on installing, when necessary, new hot water plant and equipment and new lighting? **Held:** Yes.

1 [1989] 2 EGLR 237.
2 (1985) 276 EG 545, CA.
3 (1992) 31 EG 67, ChD.

Improvements

1.26 Where the service costs are restricted to the cost of 'repair' or 'maintenance', the question may often arise as to the extent to which the landlord is entitled to charge for work involving improvement. This question might arise not only where the landlord wishes to carry out works which are obviously improvements (such as refurbishing common parts to a higher standard), but also where it is proposed to replace worn or damaged fittings with upgraded or environmentally friendly items (eg gas boilers for an oil-fired system, or energy-efficient light fittings for traditional lighting). As mentioned earlier, the principles of including or excluding the costs of improvements as service charge items are discussed in the RICS Codes of Practice mentioned above, particularly Part 8 of 'Service Charges in Commercial Property'.

There are four elements of the meaning of 'repair' that must be considered when approaching the technical legal question whether improvements are within the scope of 'repair'.

(1) According to the meaning of the word 'repair' (discussed at **1.20**), 'repair' only becomes necessary if the premises concerned are 'out of repair', since the word 'repair' has been defined as the rectifying of damage or deterioration. Premises are not 'out of repair' unless they have been damaged or have deteriorated from an earlier better physical condition. Thus, the treatment or replacement of the fabric of a building or its plant and machinery cannot be within the meaning of 'repair' if the item concerned is not out of repair (within the above meaning) at that time. Carrying out work to premises which have not deteriorated or been damaged is not 'repair' but improvement, and if the service charge covers only 'repair', the cost of that work would fall outside the scope of the charge. If the recoverable cost is that expended under a covenant to 'keep in repair', the cost of such work can be charged if deterioration has occurred or is clearly imminent (eg a roof at the end of its life even if not yet leaking). An example might be the replacement of old, but perfectly functioning, sanitary fittings with new fittings; since the old fittings were not out of repair, their replacement is not repair but improvement.

(2) Whilst 'repair' can include patching where to do so is reasonable practice, it is for the party liable to do the repairs to choose, in those circumstances, whether to patch or to carry out longer lasting repairs. As Mustill LJ said in *McDougall v Easington District Council*[1]: 'Often there will be a choice of methods for solving the problem . . . it must be a matter of judgment for the paying party which method to adopt.' The reference to 'the paying party' means the party responsible for carrying out the work, whether or not he can obtain reimbursement from another party. Therefore the landlord will be the paying party even if he can recover the cost of the work through a service charge. An example is *Manor House Drive Ltd v Shahbazian*[2] (summarised at **1.21**) where a landlord successfully claimed the cost of replacing the roof of a block of flats instead of patching it up. However, if the landlord unreasonably selects a more costly remedy, the tenant might have an argument against the charge, by virtue of an express or implied 'reasonableness test' (see **1.49**).

(3) The standard of work for 'repairs' is that which is necessary to bring the premises back into the condition in which, having regard to the age, character and locality of the property at the date on which the lease was granted, the premises would be reasonably fit for occupation by a reasonably minded, incoming tenant of the class who would be likely to take it and ignoring any change, during the term of the lease, in the class of persons likely to require the property. As Lord Esher MR said of a tenant's repairing covenant in *Lister v Lane and Nesham*[3], 'He has to repair that thing which he took; he is not obliged to make a new and different thing.' Carrying out work which goes beyond this standard would fall outside 'repair'; an example might be the replacement of a deteriorated linoleum floor with marble. An exception to this rule is where the work must inevitably be carried out in a way which exceeds the original standard because of current building practice (as in (4) below) or by virtue of the limited choice of materials available. A further exception is where it is reasonable to install an improved version of a particular item as the replacement for the item in disrepair – such as an aluminium, sealed door unit for a rotten wooden door (*Stent v Monmouth District Council*[4]) or double-glazed maintenance-free windows for rusted or rotten frames (*Sutton (Hastoe) Housing Association v Williams*[5]; *Minja Properties v Cussins*[6]); *Craighead v Homes for Islington*[7] and *London Borough of Sutton v Drake*[8]).

(4) If work of 'repair' is necessary because of damage or deterioration, it must normally be done in accordance with the principles of good building practice at the time the work is done and, if this involves a degree of updating, will nevertheless be considered to be within the repair. There is no notion of 'betterment' where the work can only properly be done with a degree of improvement. This rule may apply even where the work is required to remedy disrepair caused by an inherent defect although that is an area where the precise application of the law is harder to predict. In *Ravenseft Properties Ltd v Davstone (Holdings) Ltd*[9], a tenant under a covenant to 'repair' was held to be required to insert new expansion joints as an integral part of the repair of stone cladding, notwithstanding that such joints had not been incorporated in the original construction; and in *Halliard Prop-*

erty Co Ltd v Nicholas Clarke Investments Ltd[10], French J said that if the tenant was liable to reinstate a collapsed 'jerry-built' structure, the reinstatement would have had to be carried out properly and lawfully, in accordance with building regulations, codes of practice and byelaws.

If particular works fall with the scope of 'repair' under these rules, then the cost of such works can be included in the service charge if the service charge clause provides for the inclusion of the cost of 'repair' of the relevant parts of the property. Works which are outside the ambit of repair can be included in a service charge only if the service charge clause contains other provisions within which those works would fall, such as an express reference to improvements.

The difficulty of applying these rules in individual cases is illustrated by the differing conclusions of the courts in the cases summarised at **1.23**. In many cases, it will be a close judgment as to whether the rectification of a defect such as the absence of a damp-proof course or proper insulation or ventilation is required under a covenant to 'repair'.

There is, of course, no rule preventing a service charge clause from expressly requiring the tenant to pay towards improvements.

See also **1.24** in relation to the replacement of plant and machinery.

1 (1989) 58 P&CR 201.
2 (1965) 195 EG 283, CA.
3 [1893] 2 QB 212, CA.
4 (1987) 54 P&CR 193, CA.
5 [1988] 1 EGLR 56, CA.
6 (1998) 30 EG 114, ChD.
7 [2010] UKUT 47, LC.
8 [2004] LRX/69, LT.
9 [1980] QB 12.
10 (1984) 269 EG 1257.

Services and amenities

1.27 Where the lease provides that the service charge is to include the cost of providing 'services', 'amenities', or other non-works categories of expenditure, the interpretation of particular words will depend upon the context. Some leases use very general wording for these categories of cost while others go into more detail. Typically, modern leases of units in shopping centres will set out the chargeable services and amenities in detail and may for example expressly include specific items such as advertising and promotion. (For a case where the landlord agreed to be liable for a proportion of those costs, see **1.65**).

In many cases these categories of cost will be narrowly interpreted under the *contra proferentem* rule (see **1.9**) so that a right to charge for 'works' might not be construed as extending to 'services' and vice versa, depending on the context. However the courts will not normally use that rule to override a commonsense interpretation of clear provisions.

EXAMPLES

Mullaney v Maybourne Grange (Croydon) Management Co Ltd[1]: The wooden window-frames in a tower block of flats gave constant trouble. The management company had them replaced by maintenance-free double glazing. Was the tenant liable to pay towards the cost of this, under service charge provisions covering the cost of providing 'additional services or amenities'? **Held:** No; installing new-type windows was neither a service nor an amenity.

Jacob Isbicki & Co Ltd v Goulding & Bird Ltd[2]: Wall cleaning was not on the list of chargeable items in the lease but the landlord had power, at his discretion, to 'add to, extend, vary or make any alteration in the rendering of the said services or any of them', and proposed to clean the external walls by sand-blasting. Could he charge for this? **Held:** No; the proposed work was not a 'service' in the normal sense.

Lloyds Bank plc v Bowker Orford[3]: The service charge extended to 'any other beneficial services'. Did this include the repair of the exterior of the building and the repair and decoration of the internal common parts? **Held:** No, these works were not 'services' in the sense used in the clause; the quoted words were only apt to cover matters such as lift operation, caretaking, security, cleaning and lighting the common parts and the provision of constant hot water.

St Modwen Developments (Edmonton) Ltd v Tesco Stores Ltd[4]: The service charge included the cost of keeping the common parts of a shopping centre clean. Did that include the cost of arranging the collection and removal of tenants' refuse from refuse bins that the landlord provided to tenants in the service areas of the common parts? **Held:** Yes.

1 (1986) 277 EG 1350.
2 [1989] 1 EGLR 236.
3 (1992) 31 EG 67, ChD.
4 [2006] EWHC 3177 (Ch).

Utilities and energy

1.28 Some service charge clauses expressly provide that the service costs can include outgoings incurred in the provision of the services, such as energy utility costs, but even if there is no such express provision it will usually be implied that the costs of providing a service that runs on gas or electricity, such as a heating system, will include the costs of those utilities consumed in operating the system.

However, whether that extends to costs incurred under the statutory Carbon Reduction Commitment Energy Efficiency Scheme (see **6.14**) is a separate question. That question may arise where the landlord is (or is part of) an organisation required to participate in that Scheme. In that situation the landlord (or a company in the same organisation as defined in the Scheme regulations) may incur management and monitoring costs in complying with the Scheme as well as making payments required by the Scheme for the acquisition of 'allowances' permitting the organisation to purchase energy. Where the amount of such payments reflects the participators' total energy consumption and is not attributed to individual buildings, it may be that (unless the lease contains express provisions covering this point) such costs will not fall within the ambit of the service charge since normally costs which cannot be directly attributed to the building in which the tenant's premises are located will fall outside the scope of the service charge (see, eg, *Norwich City Council v Redford*[1]).

The British Property Federation has published guidance as to the choice of clauses which might be inserted into leases to deal with this issue but at present there is no consensus as to the most appropriate regime.

1 [2015] UKUT 30 LC.

Overriding limitations

1.29 Even if certain items of expenditure appear to fall within the wording of the service charge provisions of a lease, the effect of statute law or common law may be to exclude such items of expenditure from the service charge if they fail to meet certain 'reasonableness' and other tests.

This is dealt with in more detail in **1.49**, with the special rules applicable to residential lettings described in **2.24**.

Landlord's delays

1.30 If the landlord fails to carry out his repairing or redecorating obligations at the appropriate time, the effect may be to allow disrepair to worsen to a state at which costly remedial work, which otherwise would have been avoided, becomes necessary.

In some such cases, the tenants may be able to contend that these extra costs should be excluded from the service charge since they arise out of the landlord's breach of obligation, but even if this is proved it appears that the landlord can set against this the cost saving of having omitted the earlier work.

EXAMPLES

Postel Properties Ltd v Boots The Chemist[1]: The tenants argued that the need for major work to glazing was the result of lack of maintenance; moisture ingress should have been avoided by regular painting. The tenants failed to satisfy the judge, Ian Kennedy J, on the detailed facts, but in any event he said: 'The removal of the more extensive rust which time has allowed to develop does not add significantly to the overall cost . . . so far as [the landlords] may have been guilty of delay and so increase the final cost in terms of the extent of the corrosion, that is more than balanced by the saved costs of repainting in 1990 . . . '.

Continental Property Ventures Inc v White[2]: The landlord delayed carrying out repairs to a leaking pipe which exacerbated the disrepair. Were the tenants entitled to claim damages from the landlord for this breach, to compensate for the increase in repair costs? **Held:** Yes.

Princes House Ltd v Distinctive Clubs Ltd[3]: The tenant's lease capped the service charge for a limited period. The landlord delayed necessary repairs to the roof until the cap expired and by then more extensive repairs were needed. Could the tenant recover damages from the landlord equal to the amount by which the proposed charge exceeded what would have been the capped charge? **Held:** Yes.

In order for a tenant to maintain a claim against the landlord in this way, the tenant would have to be able to establish that the landlord had been obliged contractually to carry out the appropriate remedial work when it first became necessary. The scope of obligations such as to 'repair' has been discussed at **1.19–1.26**, and the question of whether the landlord is actually obliged to carry out particular works or is merely entitled to do them at his discretion has been discussed at **1.13**.

In the case of 'repair', the time when the landlord is obliged to carry out the remedial work depends upon whether the part which is out of repair is or is not included in the tenant's demise. Where it is not demised to any tenant (eg the common parts or main structure of a multi-let building, where each tenant is demised only the interior of his flat or office suite), the landlord will be expected to know the condition of the parts which he has retained and therefore he will be required to carry out repairs as soon as they become necessary. Indeed, the usual covenant to 'keep in repair' such retained parts of a building may be breached by the landlord as soon as disrepair occurs, thus effectively requiring the landlord to carry out preventive work in order to prevent disrepair from arising.

EXAMPLE

British Telecommunications plc v Sun Life Assurance Society plc[4]: A landlord covenanted to keep the external walls of a commercial building in repair. Repairs became necessary, which the landlord carried out within a reasonable time from the disrepair occurring. Was the landlord nevertheless liable to pay damages to the tenant for the period from the moment of disrepair until the repairs were completed? **Held:** Yes; since the breach of covenant to 'keep in repair' occurred immediately upon the occurrence of disrepair.

On the other hand, where the landlord's repairing obligation relates to parts which are included in a tenant's demise, the landlord's obligation to carry out repairs does not arise until the landlord has been given notice (however informally) of the state of disrepair.

EXAMPLE

O'Brien v Robinson[5]: The landlord of a house, the whole of which was let to the tenant, was under a covenant (imposed by statute) to keep the structure of the house in repair. The bedroom ceiling fell in, due to structural defect. Was the landlord liable to pay for the damage caused to the tenant's furniture and effects? **Held:** No; he was only liable to repair the ceiling. Where the disrepair is of something included in the tenant's lease, the landlord's covenant to repair requires the landlord to take action only when the landlord has information that the disrepair has occurred, and the landlord then has a reasonable opportunity to carry out the repair. The collapse of the ceiling therefore was not due to any breach of covenant by the landlord, so the landlord was not liable for the damage it caused.

However, where the landlord is required, either by the terms of the lease itself or by statute, to consult with the tenants before carrying out particular works, it will presumably be the case that the landlord's obligation to start that work will not arise until the prescribed period for consultation (or, if no period is prescribed, a reasonable period for consultation) has elapsed.

If the landlord fails to carry out necessary repairs at their due time (that time being ascertained under the above rules), he can be sued for damages for breach of covenant. The tenant's claim can extend to damages for distress and inconvenience caused to him as well as for any costs of remedying physical damage caused to his belongings.

EXAMPLE

> *Wallis v Manchester City Council*[6]: The landlord of a house, the whole of which was let to the tenant, was under a covenant (imposed by statute) to keep the structure of the house in repair. The landlord was in breach of covenant by failing to repair a collapsed wall, rotten windows, a failed damp-proof course, loose plaster, leaking rainwater pipes, etc. Could the tenant recover damages for distress and inconvenience? **Held:** Yes; the damages for distress and inconvenience should be of an amount sufficient to reflect the reduced rental value that the premises in their actual condition would have commanded compared with the rent actually payable.

A similar principle was applied in *Electricity Supply Nominees v National Magazine Co*[7], where the tenant of offices obtained damages for loss of amenity due to the landlord failing to comply with his covenant to use reasonable endeavours to maintain the lifts and air conditioning equipment, which broke down excessively often.

In *Broadwater Court Management Company v Jackson-Mann*[8], the landlord was guilty of serious delay in carrying out some necessary repairs in a block of flats and the tenant of one flat was awarded damages of £25 per month for loss of amenity.

1 (1996) 41 EG 164, QBD.
2 [2006] 16 EG 148, LT.
3 [2006] All ER (D) 117, ChD.
4 [1995] 2 EGLR 44, CA.
5 [1973] AC 912, HL.
6 [1998] 41 EG 223, CA.
7 [1998] EGCS 162, Official Referee.
8 (1997) EGCS 145, CA.

Compliance with statutory obligations

1.31 The landlord may be obliged to carry out works or provide services under obligations imposed by statutes or regulations. Traditionally such obligations have related to matters such as fire precautions, means of escape and dangerous structures, but over recent years the scope of these obligations has been widened. Costs incurred by the landlord in complying with such statutory obligations might be recovered from the tenants either where the relevant legislation includes provision for recovering costs from tenants, or where the wording of the service charges clauses or other provisions in the tenants' leases extends to these costs. Many service charge clauses, but not all, expressly cover the cost of complying with statute, and many sweeper clauses (see **1.14**) will catch these types of costs. However, there is no rule that a landlord will always be able to recover costs merely because he had to incur them by reason of being under a statutory obligation to do so.

These issues are considered further in **Chapter 6**.

INSURANCE AND DAMAGE BY INSURED RISKS

Insurance obligations

1.32 Leases of parts of buildings almost always contain a covenant by the landlord to insure the building and the landlord's plant and machinery in it.

Although old leases may only require the landlord to insure against fire, modern leases normally contain a list of other perils to be covered, including matters such as storm, flood, impact, explosion, bursting of pipes or tanks, subsidence, heave, landslip, and various other perils.

The insuring clauses may make express provision about damage caused by terrorist activity but, in the absence of such provisions, a reference to 'explosion' may be interpreted to mean an explosion due to any cause, and that might require the landlord to maintain cover for explosion caused by terrorism (*Qdime Ltd v Bath Building (Swindon) Management Co. Ltd*[1]). That is consistent with the old decision in *Enlayde Ltd v Roberts*[2] (see **1.35**).

Many leases have clauses allowing the landlord to take out insurance policies containing exclusions that are either standard in the market or are imposed in order to keep the premiums at an economic level (see **1.34**) and these often mention terrorism damage as a peril to be covered only where this can be done at a reasonable level of premium.

The landlord's insuring covenant will normally provide for the landlord either:

(a) to make good any damage caused by insurance risks; or
(b) to apply insurance monies in making good such damage.

The former provision would oblige the landlord to commence the repairs without waiting for the insurance monies to be paid to him by the insurers. As such, many landlords prefer the latter type of provision, which implies an obligation to pursue the insurance claim against the insurers with reasonable speed if it is not expressly set out in the lease.

EXAMPLE

> *Vural v Security Archives Ltd*[3]: The landlord covenanted to insure the building and to lay out insurance money, once received, in reinstating the premises, but the covenant did not expressly require him to submit or pursue a claim under the insurance. Was it implied that, if damage occurred, the landlord would make and prosecute his claim under the policy with all reasonable speed? **Held:** Yes.

This may apply even where the lease requires the tenant to insure the property but in practice the landlord insures and the tenant contributes to the premiums (*Adami v Lincoln Grange Management Company*[4]).

1 [2014] UKUT 261 LC.
2 [1917] 1 Ch 109.
3 (1990) 60 P&CR 258, ChD.

4 (1998) 17 EG 148, CA.

Insurance premiums, valuation fees and commission

1.33 Whether the cost incurred by the landlord in insuring against all of the risks that its insurance covers can be recharged to the tenants depends, as in the case of other service costs, on the wording of the lease; many leases give the landlord the right to select the insured risks at his discretion – whether this is subject to an implied limitation that he must act reasonably, and not extravagantly, and whether a landlord is obliged to 'shop around' for competitive insurance rates, is discussed at **1.49**.

Leases generally provide for the tenant to pay towards the landlord's insurance by way of 'additional rent', separately from the service charge, but occasionally the cost of insurance will, instead, be included within the scope of the service charge. The same principles should determine the ability to charge for the insurance, whichever of these formulae is adopted.

Some leases expressly allow the landlord to include, in the service charge, the cost of obtaining, usually at unspecified intervals, professional valuations for insurance purposes. Even in the absence of such a provision, it is strongly arguable that the cost of an insurance valuation can be charged where the landlord is entitled to charge the *cost* of insuring, rather than just the insurance *premiums*; the insurance valuation fee can be said to be a cost incurred in arranging the insurance (see the 'cost' argument, discussed at **1.37**).

There is some uncertainty as to whether, in the absence of express provisions in the lease on the point, a landlord or managing agent who arranges insurance through his own agency with the insurers may keep the commission paid by those insurers. The landlord's legal right to keep the commission was recognised some years ago by Leasehold Valuation Tribunals when valuing the landlord's reversion for residential enfranchisement (see *Castlebeg Investments (Jersey) Ltd v Lynch*[1]; 63 *Perham Road Ltd v Mayfield*[2]), and the RICS Professional Statement: Service Charges in Commercial Property (see **7.1**) states in paragraph 4.1.6.1 that the landlord's right to retain commission is long established.

Occasionally the concept of the landlord being entitled to retain insurance commissions is questioned, and it may be suggested that the landlord or managing agent is acting, wholly or partly, as agent for the tenant in arranging the insurance and therefore has trustee-like fiduciary duties towards the tenant which precludes the agent from making a secret profit from the transaction.

In any event it certainly seems that, unless the lease clearly states that the tenant must pay the gross premiums before any discount, the landlord or agent must give the tenants the benefit of any discount he receives from the insurers since the 'cost' of insurance will be the amount of the premiums less the discount; whether that argument can equally apply to commission paid by the insurer is unclear.

Whether tenants can challenge unreasonably high premiums is discussed at **1.49** and, in relation to residential property, at **2.33**. As to the ability of tenants to challenge the landlord's choice of insurer, see **1.51**.

1 (1989) 57 P&CR 493.
2 (1995) 2 EGLR 206.

Cost of rectifying damage by insured risks

1.34 Although few service charge clauses specifically deal with the point, it is probably to be inferred that service costs referable to remedying damage by risks covered by the landlord's insurance policies are to be first met out of the insurance monies, with only any unrecovered shortfall being charged within the service charge. Most service charge clauses are designed to afford the landlord reimbursement of actual cost and, plainly, the cost to the landlord of carrying out the work will be just the shortfall, if any, between the actual cost of the remedial work and the amount received under the insurance policy.

EXAMPLE

> *Avon Ground Rents Ltd v Cowley*[1]: The landlord was entitled to recover, under the National House Building Council's defects insurance warranty scheme, a substantial proportion of the cost of remedying certain defects in the building. Did the landlord have to credit that amount against the cost of the remedial work when calculating the service charges payable by the tenants? **Held:** Yes.

A similar approach was taken by the court in *Sheffield City Council v Oliver*[2], where a council as landlord was held liable to calculate the service charge, which included the cost of certain improvement works, only after crediting a government grant received towards the cost of those works (see **1.14**).

However, there may be an issue over meeting the shortfall, discussed at **1.35**.

1 [2018] UKUT 92, LC.
2 [2017] EWCA Civ 225.

Shortfalls in repair costs arising from excesses and exclusions

1.35 Many leases require the landlord to insure for the full rebuilding cost of the property. However, even if there is no under-insurance, a shortfall in meeting the cost of repairing insured damage might arise where the terms of the insurance policy provide, as they commonly do, for excesses or exclusions. These may be imposed in respect of risks which have materialised more frequently than originally envisaged by insurers (eg subsidence), or in relation to new perils (such as terrorist action), or threatened liabilities (such as third party liability for the effects of gradual pollution, which has commonly been excluded from policies since mid-1990).

If his insuring covenant obliges the landlord to insure for the *full reinstatement cost* (plus professional fees etc) and does not expressly allow for excesses and exclusions to be contained in the insurance policy, the landlord may arguably be in breach of his covenant if the policy does not effectively cover the full amount because of an excess or exclusion. In such a case, it might be possible for the tenants to recover the amount of the shortfall from the landlord as damages for his breach of covenant although the landlord may seek to set off the increase in premiums that would have been payable if insurers had agreed to remove the excess. It was established in *Enlayde Ltd v Roberts*[1] (summarised below) that an inability to obtain insurance cover for certain perils free of exclusions does not exonerate a landlord who gives an unqualified covenant to insure against those perils, and a similar result obtained in a mortgage case in 1940 on the same point (*Moorgate Estates Ltd v Trower*[2]).

EXAMPLE

> *Enlayde Ltd v Roberts*[3]: The landlord covenanted to insure a building against fire. It transpired that damage by enemy action, which caused a fire, was excluded from the policy. Was the landlord in breach of his insuring covenant, even though insurance without that exclusion was unavailable? **Held:** Yes.

However, it is not clear whether those decisions still stand. Since almost every insurance policy is subject to some exclusion or excess it could be argued that it should be an implied term of the lease that the insurance can be subject to normal or usual provisions of that type. This problem is particularly relevant where insurers are refusing to grant or are imposing limits on cover for certain risks, eg subsidence, acts of terrorism, etc.

1 [1917] 1 Ch 109.
2 [1940] 1 All ER 195, ChD.
3 [1917] 1 Ch 109.

MANAGING AGENTS AND OTHER PROFESSIONAL FEES AND LEGAL COSTS

Management fees

1.36 Whether management fees can be included in a service charge depends on the wording of the service charge clause. It seems that the courts will be reluctant to interpret the lease as entitling the landlord to recoup such fees, unless the wording of the service charge clause clearly provides for this. (See also **1.9**.)

A possible exception to this restrictive approach may be where, under the terms of the lease, the services are being provided by a company controlled by the tenants who cannot be expected to have the time or expertise to manage the property themselves; the company may be held, impliedly, to have power to appoint managing agents to administer its functions. However, this depends upon the individual wording used and the circumstances at the date of the lease.

(As for the landlord charging its in-house management costs or overheads, see **1.41**).

EXAMPLES

> *Embassy Court Residents' Association Ltd v Lipman*[1]: The landlord's covenants did not mention employing managing agents, but the landlord was a company limited by guarantee of which the tenant and the other flat-owners were members, and it appointed managing agents when the

flat-owners, who had been running it, got fed up. Was the tenant liable to pay towards the managing agents' proper fees? **Held:** On the facts, yes; but (per Cumming-Bruce LJ) 'If an individual [ie as distinct from a residents' company] wants to [employ managing agents] and to recover the costs from the lessee, he must include explicit provisions in his lease'.

Lloyds Bank plc v Bowker Orford[2]: The service charge schedule in the lease did not expressly provide for the service charge to include managing agents' fees, but it did contain a declaration that the tenant could not object to 'the employment of managing agents to carry out and provide on the lessors' behalf services under this Part of this Schedule'. Did this imply that managing agents' fees for general management could be included in the service charges? **Held:** No; it simply meant that the tenant could not refuse to pay for a service merely because it had been decided by the agents and not by the landlord. (However, see **1.37**.)

A clearer provision enabling managing agents' fees to be included in the service charge would be the express inclusion of managing agents' fees in any list of chargeable items in the service charge clause, or (where the service charge clause is expressed to cover the cost to the landlord of performing his covenants) the express inclusion of a landlord's covenant to employ managing agents.

Where a management fee *is* chargeable, it is likely to be interpreted (in the absence of express wording to the contrary) as meaning an appropriate fee for managing the building and administering the services, but *not* for collecting the rent on behalf of the landlord. However, this does not necessarily mean that the management fee cannot be calculated by reference to the rent, provided that it is a proper fee for administering the chargeable services and not for rent collection; nevertheless, it is unlikely to be best practice to charge this way. Indeed, the RICS Professional Statement: Service Charges in Commercial Property see (**Chapter 7**) and the RICS Code of Practice: Service Charge Residential Management Code (see **2.92**) set out best practice for setting management fees for commercial and residential property and recommend fixed fees rather than taking a percentage of service expenditure. They also distinguish between management fees (for managing and supervising services) and fees representing the cost of providing on-site staff where appropriate and the commercial Statement provides detailed guidance on staff costs in paragraph 4.1.3.4.

Where the amount of the management fee is in question, a fee comparable with that which other agents might properly charge for management, excluding rent collection, will often be a guide to what is reasonable.

EXAMPLE

Parkside Knightsbridge Ltd v Horwitz[3]: Expenditure incurred by the landlord in respect of management was chargeable. The landlord company engaged its parent company to manage the block, and by 'normal accounting processes' (ie book entries) paid the parent company a management fee based on a rough, notional allocation of its overheads. The fee was low by comparison with quotations received from four well-known firms of surveyors and managing agents. Those quotations were for the management work excluding rent collection; one firm quoted 5 per cent of the gross rents, the second 4 per cent of the gross rents, the third 15 per cent of the service costs and the fourth 14 per cent of the service costs. Could the fee be included in the service charge? **Held:** Yes; (1) it was a reasonable charge, since the quotations indicated the market cost of management; (2) it had been expended – the parent company was a separate legal entity from its subsidiary the landlord company, and the book entries counted as payment.

Some leases specify the amount of management fee that can be charged, for example as a percentage of total service costs. In one case, the lease referred to the RICS scale; this was abolished during the term of the lease, and the court held that a reasonable fee could be charged instead (*Thames Side Properties Ltd v Brixton Estate plc*[4]).

There should not be any possibility of double-counting, so where the lease allows professional fees to be charged for specifying and supervision works, the level of fees for general management should not also cover that function.

In some cases, it may be implied that professional fees are only to be included in the service charge if they are 'reasonably' or 'properly' incurred (see **1.51**).

1 (1984) 271 EG 545, CA.
2 (1992) 31 EG 67, ChD.
3 (1983) 268 EG 49, CA.
4 [1997] NPC 5, ChD.

Professional fees relating to particular chargeable items

1.37 Irrespective of whether or not general management fees are recoverable through the service charge, it may be possible for a landlord to recoup fees paid to agents or other professionals (eg building surveyors) for arranging and supervising *particular* works or services, which themselves fall within the service charge. This, however, would not entitle the landlord to recoup fees paid to the agents for *general* management of the building, unless management was mentioned as a chargeable service in its own right.

The justification for including in the service charge the professional fees for arranging particular works is that where (as is usually the case) the service charge is expressed to cover the 'cost' or 'expense' of a specified item, it can be argued that the 'cost' or 'expense' includes the cost of engaging a professional person for specifically arranging and supervising the provision of that item.

EXAMPLES

Concorde Graphics Ltd v Andromeda Investments SA[1]: Vinelott J said: 'while the costs, charges and expenses recoverable under clause 2(3) clearly do not extend to the whole fee paid to managing agents for managing the estate and collecting rents, a fee may be justifiable in so far as the managing agents are called on to arrange and supervise works and services the costs of which do fall within clause 2(3)'.

Lloyds Bank plc v Bowker Orford[2]: The service charge covered the 'total cost to the lessors . . . of providing the services'. Did this entitle the landlord to include in the service charges the managing agent's fees for organising and supervising the provision of those particular services? **Held:** Yes.

For fees to be chargeable in this way, they must relate properly to services or works which are themselves chargeable within the service charge. If the fees relate to investigation into problems which prima facie are likely to be chargeable, those fees can be charged up to the moment, if any, when the investigating professional proposes a remedy which will fall outside the chargeable categories; thereafter the fees may not be chargeable within the service charges. The lesson here is that such consultants should be instructed in stages, with their advice being considered at each stage, having regard to the scope of the service charge.

EXAMPLES

Holding & Management Ltd v Property Holding & Investment Trust plc[3]: Consulting engineers were engaged to investigate defects in the external walls of the building. The engineers prepared a report recommending a scheme of rebuilding which was so extensive that it went beyond the meaning of 'repair' and fell outside the scope of the services for which the plaintiffs, as maintenance trustees, were responsible. Nevertheless, the engineers assisted the maintenance trustees in promoting that scheme, but it was eventually withdrawn in favour of more modest remedial work. How much of the engineers' fees could be included in the service charge? **Held:** Only the fees for work done up to the time they made their report.

Plough Investments Ltd v Manchester City Council[4]: The landlord covenanted to repair and maintain the external walls and main timbers of the building, and the service charge covered the costs so incurred. Some cladding came away from a part of the steel frame which had rusted. Consulting engineers engaged by the landlord carried out a structural survey of not only that part but also the entirety of the building and proposed that all the cladding be removed and the whole frame shot-blasted and encased in concrete to stop future rusting. Since 'repair' means dealing with parts which have actually deteriorated, but not parts which are presently unaffected, this proposal was rejected by the court in favour of remedying only the parts which had deteriorated. How much of the engineers' fees could be included in the service charge? **Held:** Not the engineers' fees for reporting on the entire steel frame, but only fees in connection with work which was properly a repair, ie relating to the parts which had actually rusted. (Note: more recently it has been decided that a covenant to 'keep in repair' requires work to be done when necessary to prevent imminent disrepair occurring; see **1.20** and **1.29**.)

1 (1983) 265 EG 386, ChD.
2 (1992) 31 EG 67, ChD.
3 [1989] 1 WLR 1313, CA.
4 [1989] 1 EGLR 244, ChD.

Fees for statutory and voluntary assessments

1.38 The landlord may be under a legal obligation to arrange professional assessments of the building for, say, fire risk or the condition of asbestos, or may wish to demonstrate corporate social responsibility by voluntarily arranging an energy efficiency or environmental assessment of the building. A number of such issues are considered in **Chapter 6**.

The landlord might have difficulty in recovering the cost of a voluntary assessment through the service charge unless the sweeping-up or management provisions are sufficiently widely drawn, since, in many cases, there may not be, prior to the exercise, any indication that the fabric or services of the building are out of repair (see **1.20**), fail to comply with statutory requirements, or are otherwise in a condition requiring something to be done which would fall within the scope of the service charge. Just as many modern service charge clauses allow for periodic insurance valuations and surveys to be carried out at the tenants' expense through the service charge, an express provision entitling the landlord to carry out, and charge for, environmental and other voluntary assessments would now seem appropriate.

Legal and litigation costs

1.39 When the landlord sues a tenant for arrears of service charge and obtains judgment successfully, the landlord will usually be awarded costs, but not necessarily on a full indemnity basis (see **1.89**). Often the costs recovered from the defaulting tenant will be less than the actual legal and other costs, and in some situations (such as disputes over residential service charges) the usual position is that costs will not be awarded to the landlord even where he successfully defends his service charge calculation (see **2.67**). The question arises then whether the unrecovered costs can be recouped by the landlord under the provisions of the lease or leases, either wholly from the tenant involved in the litigation through a costs provision in the lease or from the tenants generally through the service charge.

Many leases contain tenants' covenants to pay costs in relation to notices and proceedings for breach of covenant, such as under s 146, Law of Property Act 1925. Depending on the wording and facts, such a provision may allow the landlord to demand his unrecovered litigation costs from the tenant party to the litigation even if the landlord is not awarded those costs in the proceedings.

EXAMPLE

> *Freeholders of 69 Marina, St. Leonards-on-Sea v Oram*[1]: A residential tenant complained about the amount that the landlord included in the service charge for certain repairs, so the landlord applied to the appropriate tribunal for a ruling. The tribunal assessed the amount due but, as is usual, made no order for costs. The tenant still declined to pay the service charge so the landlord served on the tenant a notice under s 146 of the Law of Property Act 1925 in respect of the failure to pay (see **1.93**). Under a standard clause in the tenant's lease, the tenant covenanted to pay all costs incurred by the landlord of and incidental to the preparation and service of a s 146 notice. The service of a notice under s 146, after the amount of service charge (if not agreed) has been determined by a tribunal, is a statutory requirement if the landlord wishes to threaten to forfeit the lease for non-payment of service charges (see **2.70**). Did the service of that notice trigger the costs clause in the lease and did that result in the landlord being entitled to be repaid all the costs he incurred in that stream of litigation? **Held:** Yes, this was a residential case where a tribunal ruling was needed before a disputed service charge would be recoverable and the ruling was

needed before the s 146 notice could be served, so the tribunal litigation was 'incidental' to the preparation of the s 146 notice for the purpose of that clause.

If the individual tenant is not liable to repay the landlord's litigation costs, the landlord may turn to the service charge provisions in the leases. However, in the absence of specific wording, a right expressed in the lease in general terms for the landlord to charge legal or other professional fees within the service charge will, generally, be construed as limited to those fees directly incurred in connection with management. This might cover the cost of taking legal advice on management or supply contracts or even in respect of enforcing, on defaulting tenants, those lease covenants which benefit the tenants generally (such as covenants not to cause nuisance or block the common parts). However, this would not, without express provision, normally cover the cost of suing particular tenants for arrears of service charges.

EXAMPLES

Sella House Ltd v Mears[2]: The service charge covered the fees of managing agents and 'other professional persons as may be necessary or desirable . . . '. Could the service charge include legal costs incurred by the landlord in seeking to recover arrears of service charges from tenants? **Held:** No.

Iperion Investments Corporation v Broadwalk House Residents Ltd[3]: The tenant of a flat embarked on unauthorised structural alterations. The landlord obtained an injunction and also, but unsuccessfully, sought forfeiture of the tenant's lease. Could the costs of the landlord's proceedings be included in the service charges under the head of the 'costs properly incurred by the landlord . . . in the proper and reasonable management' of the block? **Held:** Yes; both the injunction and forfeiture applications were incurred in 'managing' the property.

Morgan v Stainer[4]: A group of tenants sued the landlord for breaches of covenant and the case was settled, the tenants agreeing to pay certain maintenance charges and the landlord agreeing to pay the tenants' taxed legal costs which exceeded £80,000. The tenants' leases expressly required the tenants to pay towards the landlord's costs in obtaining the maintenance contributions from any tenant in the building. Could the landlord, under this clause, recover back from the tenants the costs he had paid them? **Held:** No; the costs had not been incurred for the purpose of recovering the maintenance charges but in resisting the tenants' proceedings; the agreement by the landlord to pay the costs included an implied agreement not to seek to recover them through the back door. By implication, the costs mentioned in the lease were limited to those reasonably and properly incurred, which these were not; the lease clause was not intended to apply to the type of costs involved here.

Greening v Castlenau Mansions Ltd[5]: A residential tenant unsuccessfully challenged certain service charges and the landlord sought to charge his unrecovered legal litigation costs through the service charge for the year in which the tribunal proceedings took place, by virtue of a right to charge for administration of the building including engaging lawyers and other professionals, the lease clauses being effectively the same as those in the

Sella House case (above). Were the litigation costs recoverable through the service charge? **Held:** No, the tribunal was bound to follow the decision of the Court of Appeal in Sella House.

It has been suggested that the *Sella House* decision might have been different if the landlord had been a tenants' management company with no other source of funds; see **1.9**. That might possibly be so if the original landlord that granted the lease was a residents company; in the *Greening* case the President of the Upper Tribunal did not think that the meaning of the lease could be affected by the fact that the landlord's interest was bought by a tenants' nominated company on a collective enfranchisement after the leases were granted (also see *Broadwater Court Management Company v Jackson-Mann*[6] at **1.9**).

1 [2011] EWCA Civ 1258, CA.
2 [1989] 1 EGLR 65, CA.
3 [1995] 2 EGLR 47, CA.
4 [1993] EGCS 162, ChD.
5 [2011] UKUT 326 LC.
6 (1997) EGCS 145, CA.

Costs of court applications for declarations

1.40 In some cases, particularly where the wording of the lease is unclear or the proposed works are non-routine, it may be sensible for the landlord to apply to the court for a declaration as to whether proposed works can properly be carried out and be charged within the service charge. In such a case, it may be that the costs of the court application can be included in the service charge if the service charge clause entitles the landlord to charge for the costs of management or to charge for costs which he reasonably incurred in the discharge of his obligations.

EXAMPLE

Reston Ltd v Hudson[1]: The landlord made an originating application to the court for a declaration as to whether certain proposed works could properly be carried out and be charged within the service charges under the leases, which were imprecisely drafted. Could the costs of the court application be included in the service charges under provisions in the leases permitting the charging of 'the costs of management' and 'all outgoings, costs and expenses whatsoever, which the lessor may reasonably incur in the discharge of its obligations'? **Held:** Yes. (Note: the tenants did not appear before the court and the point was decided without argument.)

1 [1990] 2 EGLR 51.

IN-HOUSE MANAGEMENT CHARGES

Charging for in-house overheads

1.41 Many substantial landlords have their own, in-house, property management departments. While some leases expressly entitle the landlord to employ staff to provide or manage the services, many do not and in the past the court was unlikely to interpret service charge clauses (in the absence of a clear provision) as entitling the landlord to include any element of cost or charge for in-house management. Traditionally, service charge clauses were interpreted as being intended to give the landlord reimbursement of sums it paid to third parties such as surveyors, contractors and suppliers, and the landlords' in-house overheads were not normally thought to be covered by general references to the cost of providing the services. However, recently the court has accepted that in-house management overheads can be treated as falling within the costs, expenses or outgoings incurred by a landlord in providing its services.

Where such costs can be included in the service charge, the question arises how much can be charged. Generally, where these costs are being included by virtue of falling within 'costs and expenses' or similar phrases, the actual salary and overhead costs must be calculated, and a round sum or percentage calculation can only be used in cases where the lease expressly allows the landlord to charge a fee for in-house management.

EXAMPLES

> *Cleve House Properties v Schildof*[1]: The landlord was a company which did not employ managing agents but carried out management in-house by its directors, and sought to charge a management fee calculated at 15 per cent of the service costs. The service charge, under the then current housing legislation, covered any 'liability incurred or amount defrayed' in respect of the services. Was the management fee chargeable? **Held:** No; the service charge was limited to sums paid out or liable to be paid out by the landlord, and this did not include overheads such as the directors' remuneration.
>
> *Wembley National Stadium Ltd v Wembley (London) Ltd*[2]: The service charge related to 'all costs fees expenses and outgoings whatsoever properly incurred by the Lessor in complying with its obligations . . . '. Did this include in-house management costs? **Held:** Yes. 'There was no reason why the wages of the employee who actually applied the tarmac to the surface of the car park should be included but the salary of he who arranged for the employee to do it and for the tarmac to be available for such application be excluded . . . the wording embraced both.'
>
> *St Modwen Developments (Edmonton) Ltd v Tesco Stores Ltd*[3]: The service charge expressly included the cost of the landlord employing staff to carry out or maintain the services. Could the landlord charge for them by charging a fee calculated at 10 per cent of the cost of the services? **Held:** No, the landlord could only charge on the basis of their wages and other actual costs and overheads, and not some arbitrary calculation however commonplace that might be.

1 (1980) CLY 1641, Deputy Judge Gray, Bloomsbury and Marylebone County Court.
2 [2007] EWHC 756 (Ch).
3 [2006] EWHC 3177 (Ch).

Landlord's group companies

1.42 Where a lease allows the landlord to charge outside managing agent's fees in the service charge, but the ability to charge in-house management costs is uncertain because the lease does not mention in-house management charges or contemplate that the landlord may employ its own staff to provide or manage the services, and the landlord would prefer to carry out the management in-house, it seems that the landlord may be able to circumvent this problem by setting up a separate, subsidiary company, appointing it as the managing agent, and paying that company a proper fee for carrying out the management. It appears that such fees can then be included in the service charge.

EXAMPLE

> *Parkside Knightsbridge Ltd v Horwitz*[1]: Expenditure incurred by the landlord in respect of management was chargeable. The landlord company engaged its parent company to manage the block and, by book entries, paid the parent company a reasonable management fee. Could the fee be included in the service charge? **Held:** Yes; the parent company was a separate legal entity from its subsidiary, the landlord company, and the book entries counted as payment.

In *Parkside*, the Court of Appeal applied the time-honoured company law rule that a subsidiary company is a separate legal entity from its holding company, so that the parent was treated as a separate agent. The application of that rule in the context of service charges is, however, perhaps surprising, since the courts have been known to 'lift the veil' or 'pierce the veil' of corporate identity in some other property cases (eg *DHN Food Distributors Ltd v London Borough of Tower Hamlets*[2]; *Hillbank Properties Ltd v Hackney London Borough Council*[3]), although the non-piercing principle has been followed by the *London Rent Assessment Committee in Eaton Square Properties v Ogilvie*[4] (see **2.41**).

1 (1983) 268 EG 49, CA.
2 [1976] 1 WLR 852.
3 (1978) 37 P&CR 218.
4 (2000) 16 EG 143.

CARETAKERS AND THEIR ACCOMMODATION

Provision of caretaker or porter

1.43 An obligation on the landlord to provide the tenants with the services of a porter or caretaker may be set out expressly in the lease, or the lease may give the landlord the discretion to provide such services if he thinks fit.

EXAMPLES

> *Hupfield v Bourne*[1]: The landlord of a block of luxury flats covenanted to 'employ such persons as shall be reasonably necessary for the due performance of [his] covenants . . . and for the proper management of the block'. He provided a resident caretaker at the time the lease was granted. Was he obliged to continue to provide a resident caretaker? **Held:** Yes; it was 'reasonably necessary' within the covenant mentioned.
>
> *Russell v Laimond Properties Ltd*[2]: Resident porters were employed by the landlord of a block of flats for several years, including when the leases were granted. The landlord covenanted 'to provide . . . the services of such

maintenance staff as [he] shall consider necessary for the performance of the matters specified . . . '. The possible service charge costs were separately listed in a schedule and included the cost of porterage and of providing, maintaining and repairing a flat for staff. Was the landlord obliged to provide a resident porter? **Held:** No; the necessary maintenance tasks could be performed by outside contractors.

(See also **1.13**.)

Where the lease contains an express covenant by the landlord to provide a resident porter, that obligation will not be fulfilled by the provision of non-resident staff, even if they perform similar specific tasks.

EXAMPLE

Posner v Scott-Lewis[3]: The landlord covenanted to provide a resident porter. The porter went to live elsewhere but remained employed by the landlord on terms that he would return daily to perform his duties. Was that sufficient compliance with the landlord's obligation? **Held:** No; the presence of a resident porter gave the tenants a feeling of enhanced security; a mandatory injunction was granted ordering the resumption of resident porterage.

1 (1974) 28 P&CR 77.
2 (1984) 269 EG 947, QBD.
3 [1987] Ch 25 see p 32.

Charging caretakers' employment costs

1.44 Even if there is no implied or express obligation on, or power for, the landlord to employ a caretaker, a right to charge the whole or part of the cost of employing one might be implied to the extent that the caretaker attends to the particular services which are expressly chargeable on the basis that the 'cost' of providing the services includes the cost of engaging someone to perform them.

EXAMPLE

Concorde Graphics Ltd v Andromeda Investments SA[1]: Vinelott J said: 'while the costs, charges and expenses recoverable under clause 2(3) clearly do not extend to the whole fee paid to managing agents for managing the estate and collecting rents, a fee may be justifiable in so far as the managing agents are called on to arrange and supervise works and services the costs of which do fall within clause 2(3). Similarly, part of the expense of providing a full-time caretaker may be attributable to work done by the caretaker in attending to matters within clause 2(3)'.

1 (1983) 265 EG 386, ChD.

Charging for staff accommodation

1.45 Many leases which require or permit the landlord to engage porters or caretakers also contain express provisions enabling the landlord to charge, within the service charge, a rent for any accommodation he might provide for the porter or caretaker (eg a caretaker's flat), in addition to the actual paid outgoings of that accommodation.

Even where the service charge clause does not expressly entitle the landlord to charge such rent, a right for the landlord to do so may be inferred if the lease contains a landlord's covenant to provide a resident or non-resident porter or caretaker and the service charge is expressed to cover all the costs and expenses of the landlord in performing his covenants. However, this is less likely to apply where the service charge clause expressly mentions certain costs relating to staff accommodation but does not mention the rental cost of providing it.

Where the landlord provides accommodation for a porter or caretaker within the property or in another building owned by the landlord, the landlord may be able to include a *notional* rent in the service charge. This is especially so where the lease allows the porter to reside away from the building; it can be reasoned that if the landlord had to arrange accommodation for the employee in a building not owned by the landlord, the landlord would have to pay rent for it and, thus, rent would be an expected cost of the service. Even where the porter is required, under the landlord's covenants, to reside in the same building, notional rent may still be treated as a 'cost', albeit in the sense of rental income forgone as opposed to money spent.

EXAMPLES

Agavil Investments Ltd v Corner[1]: The landlord covenanted to provide a resident caretaker, who was to be housed in the block or elsewhere. The service charge covered the 'costs and expenses' of providing this and other services. The caretaker lived in a flat in the block. Could the landlord include, in the service charge, a sum equal to the rent he would otherwise have obtained for that flat? **Held**: Yes.

Lloyds Bank plc v Bowker Orford[2]: The landlord covenanted to use best endeavours to provide the listed services, which included the employment and housing of a resident caretaker. The service charge covered 'the total cost to the landlord . . . of providing the services . . . and defraying the costs and expenses relating and incidental to such services'. The caretaker lived in a flat in the block. Could the landlord include, in the service charge, a sum equal to the rent he would otherwise have obtained for that flat? **Held**: Yes.

Gilje and Others v Chalgrove Securities Ltd[3]: The leases of flats in a block which included a caretaker's flat provided for the service charge to cover 'monies expended by the lessor in . . . providing the services and management and administration called for under clause 5 . . . '. The lessor's obligations under that clause included providing a resident caretaker. The list of service charge items included the cost of gas, electricity and rates of the caretaker's flat. Could the landlord include a notional rent for the flat in the service charge, either directly or by notionally paying the caretaker a higher salary to include rent? **Held**: No; so far as the clause was unclear, it was to be interpreted against the landlord. Whilst listing certain items of cost, such as gas, did not exclude all other items (contrary to Neuberger J in *Lloyds Bank v Bowker Orford*[4] – see **1.14** etc), the phrase 'monies expended' meant monies actually paid out and a reasonable prospective tenant reading the lease would not have expected the service charge to include notional rent. This was different from the position in *Agavil*[5] (above).

Earl Cadogan v 27/29 Sloane Gardens Ltd[6]: The lease contained a provision allowing the landlord to include in the service charge an amount for notional rent on the caretaker's flat. The landlord's headlease allowed the caretaker's flat to be used only for rent-free accommodation for a caretaker, so the landlord could not have obtained rent from that flat by letting it to a tenant. Did that prevent the landlord from including notional rent in the service charge? **Held:** No, since the provision allowing the charging of notional rent was clear and unambiguous.

There have been a number of residential cases where tribunals have taken the view, like the court in the *Gilje* case, that provisions allowing the landlord to charge the cost of providing a caretaker only covered the actual costs expended and not notional rent (for example, 2 Culford Gardens[7] and Oakland Court Worthing[8] and Oakland Court Worthing[9]).

Where a notional rent can be charged, according to the deputy judge in *Russell v Laimond Properties Ltd*[10] (see **1.43**), an alternative basis to market rent forgone, for assessing the 'cost' of providing such accommodation, might be a fair return for the landlord on the capital cost or value of the accommodation, but this has not been followed in the other decisions.

Where a notional rent is charged, it seems appropriate for the rent to be assessed as if the tenants were renting the flat for 'the business of providing the services to the block/estate' and thus the same basis should be used as if there was a tenancy under the Landlord and Tenant Act 1954 with rent valued in accordance with s 34 of that Act.

The cost of maintaining and decorating staff accommodation is often expressly covered by service charge provisions, but where it is not expressly mentioned the landlord might be able to include such costs by arguing that the accommodation is part of the 'common parts' of the building (see the collective enfranchisement case *Cadogan v Panagopoulos*[11]).

1 (1975) 13 October (unreported).
2 (1992) 31 EG 67, ChD.
3 [2001] EWCA Civ 1777.
4 (1992) 31 EG 67, ChD
5 (1975) 13 October (unreported).
6 [2006] 24 EG 178, LT.
7 LON/00AW/LSC/2007/0116.
8 CHI/45UH/LIS/2011/0031.
9 CHI/45UH/LIS/2011/0031.
10 (1984) 269 EG 947, QBD.
11 [2010] EWCA Civ 1259.

VARYING THE SERVICES

Basic principles

1.46 As has been seen, the lease or tenancy agreement constitutes a contract between the landlord and the tenant. Like most other contracts, it cannot be varied (subject to exceptions mentioned in **1.47** and **1.48**) otherwise than by agreement between the parties. In the absence of specific provisions in the lease allowing changes in the services, the landlord is not entitled to change or discontinue any services which the terms of the lease expressly oblige him to provide. However, landlords frequently desire to depart from the strict requirements of leases, often for perfectly valid reasons. A lease might, for example, oblige the landlord to provide hot water through an existing system; if that is an oil-fired system, a change to gas boilers would be a sensible departure.

Naturally, there is no reason why the landlord should not seek the consent of each tenant in a building to the discontinuance or substitution of a particular service. Any agreement with tenants should make it clear whether the variation is intended to endure for any substantial period (whether or not it is the full residue of the term of the lease) and should, ideally, be set out in a formal deed executed by the landlord and the tenant and expressed to bind their successors (with any mortgagee of the tenant joining to give his consent). In this way, there will be an effective variation of the lease, which will continue to apply even if the present tenant assigns the lease. However, if this is impracticable, a variation by agreement in correspondence will usually suffice in the short term, although it must be remembered that it will not bind the tenant's mortgagees nor, in some cases, an assignee.

The landlord must bear in mind, however, that if he discontinues or substitutes a service notwithstanding that one or more tenants withhold their agreement, he may be in breach of covenant towards those tenants, who could seek damages or, in appropriate cases, obtain a mandatory injunction ordering the landlord to restore the service (see *Posner v Scott-Lewis*[1] at **1.43**).

If a former tenant or guarantor has continuing liability for the tenant's obligations (see **1.96**), the amount of those liabilities cannot be increased as a result of a lease variation made on or after 1 January 1996 by the landlord and the present tenant (Landlord and Tenant (Covenants) Act 1995, s 18). Furthermore, major lease variations made without the consent of a guarantor may under common law rules have the effect of wholly releasing the guarantor from all his liabilities in respect of the lease, although minor variations will not release him (see *Metropolitan Properties Company v Bartholomew*[2]).

1 [1987] Ch 25, p 32.
2 [1995] NPC 172.

Variation clauses

1.47 Some leases contain provisions entitling the landlord to vary the services or to discontinue services which he considers obsolete, sometimes entirely at his discretion or after balloting the tenants, and in such cases a landlord who wishes to vary the services should follow the procedure laid down by the lease. However, it appears that such provisions, unless worded very carefully to give the landlord wide discretion, may be narrowly interpreted so as to limit the landlord to keep within the types of services which are specifically mentioned in the lease (see **1.14**). Where such powers are contained in non-negotiable standard clauses in leases to consumers, their effect may be restricted by consumer protection legislation, see **1.52**.

Where the landlord has the right to vary the services, it is best practice to consult the tenants and give them advance warning of any proposed changes even if the lease does not require the landlord to do so. The RICS Professional Statement: Service Charges in Commercial Property and the RICS Code of Practice: Service Charge Residential Management Code (see **2.92**) require communication with tenants and transparency about such matters.

Varying the lease

1.48 Variation by agreement is discussed at **1.46**. Where the lease of a residential flat fails to contain satisfactory provisions as to (amongst other things) services and service charges, an application might be made to the court to order the lease to be varied. This procedure is governed by Pt IV of the Landlord and Tenant Act 1987, discussed at **2.76**. It does not apply to business premises or, except as to insurance provisions, to houses.

REASONABLENESS TESTS AND CONSUMER PROTECTION

Express terms as to reasonableness

1.49 In those cases where the lease sets out a reasonableness test which qualifies the service charge, the fact that a particular type of expenditure falls within the wording of the service charge clause will not result in the sum spent on that item being chargeable to the tenant, if the tenant can successfully challenge that expenditure on the ground that it was not reasonable.

Some leases make express provision for service costs to be limited to those which the landlord 'reasonably' incurs; others simply refer to the 'reasonable cost' of providing the listed services. In some instances, there might be a difference in meaning between these. Incurring costs 'reasonably' may mean that both the decision to do the work and the actual cost of it must be reasonable, whilst 'reasonable cost' may mean merely that the amount of the cost must be reasonable for the work done but that the decision to do the work did not have to be taken reasonably.

Some leases contain an obligation on the landlord to minimise the costs so far as possible, for example:

> 'the landlord will use its reasonable endeavours to maintain the service charges reserved hereunder at the lowest figure reasonably consistent with the due performance of its obligations hereunder.'

Such provisions are sometimes found coupled with a provision excluding the tenant from objecting to the cost of individual items, such as:

> 'provided that the Tenant shall not be entitled to object to any item comprised in the service costs by reason only that the materials, works or services in question might have been obtained or performed at a lower cost.'

However, this may appear to contradict earlier references to reasonableness or a covenant to keep the charges to the minimum and will need cautious interpretation.

Some leases apply an express reasonableness test to just certain services.

EXAMPLE

> *Qdime v Bath Building (Swindon) Management Co Ltd*[1]: The insurance clauses of a lease gave the landlord the right to add cover for extra risks in addition to the list of specified insured risks 'as the landlord may in its *reasonable* discretion think fit to insure against'. The landlord had included cover for terrorism at an additional cost. Was the landlord entitled to charge that extra cost? **Held:** Yes. The reference to 'explosion' in the list of essential insured risks meant explosion from any cause and therefore arguably the landlord was required to include explosion caused by terrorism; but even if that was not the case and terrorism had been a discretionary additional risk, the landlord had not stepped outside the express test of reasonableness; that test was whether a lawful decision had been reached in all the circumstances and whether the landlord's decision fell within the range of reasonable decisions as distinct from being perverse, and the landlord had met that test.

The RICS Professional Statement: Service Charges in Commercial Property (see **7.1**) imposes a core principle on chartered surveyors who manage commercial property for landlords, to the effect that best practice recommends that both services and insurances are procured on an appropriate 'value for money' basis, that competitive quotations should be obtained for services or the costs benchmarked and that insurance policy terms should be fair and reasonable and the insurance placed with reputable insurers.

1 [2014] UKUT 261 LC.

Effect of express reasonableness tests

1.50 Express reasonableness tests use a variety of different phrases. Some leases refer to 'reasonable' costs while others (like the residential legislation) talk about costs 'reasonably incurred'. Others may refer to the landlord deciding about services 'acting reasonably'. These may not all have the same meanings.

There have been several residential case decisions on the meaning of the statutory phrase 'reasonably incurred' and these are considered at **2.26**. It is not certain whether the same interpretation would apply where that phrase is used in a commercial lease.

However, one principle followed in a number of commercial as well as residential cases is that the test requires a consideration whether the tenant, having regard to the duration of his lease and other relevant circumstances, ought fairly to contribute to the costs of the particular work or service.

EXAMPLES

> *Postel Properties Ltd v Boots The Chemist*[1]: The lease reserved as a service charge a proportion of 'the expenses and outgoings reasonably and properly incurred' by the landlord on certain works and services, including keeping

the roofs in good and substantial repair, and the landlord covenanted to carry out the work 'economically and efficiently'. The tenants disputed various costs including the cost of replacing, to an improved specification, flat roofs which were constantly leaking and had a short life expectancy. **Held:** The majority of the cost was chargeable. 'Sensible work of repair to preserve the fabric in a realistic way is entirely consistent with the duty to perform the landlord's obligations efficiently and economically.' It was 'reasonable' for the landlord to select a more durable grade of top sheeting than a basic standard and at a modest increase in cost. However, priming large areas of steel while they were accessible was a separate piece of work which was unnecessary and the cost not chargeable.

Scottish Mutual Insurance Company v Jardine[2]: The landlord carried out long-term expensive repairs to the roof of a block, ostensibly in performing its repairing obligations towards an existing tenant whose lease had only a few months left before it expired. In reality, the work was done to assist the landlord in letting a vacant part of the building. Was the short-term tenant liable to pay a full contribution towards the cost under his obligation to pay 'a fair proportion' of repair costs 'reasonably and properly incurred'? **Held:** No; these repairs had not been carried out in pursuance of the landlord's repairing covenant in his lease, under which lesser works would have been reasonable and proper having regard to the short unexpired term. A reduced contribution was payable.

Fluor Daniel Properties Ltd v Shortlands Investment Ltd[3]: The landlord of an office building covenanted to 'maintain repair amend renew . . . the air conditioning system' and to provide conditioned air at a reasonable temperature. The service charge covered the cost of performing those covenants and also had a sweeper clause covering 'the reasonable cost of carrying out other work or services of any kind whatsoever which the landlords may reasonably consider desirable for the purpose of maintaining or improving services in the Building'. The landlord also covenanted to use its best endeavours to maintain the service charge at the lowest reasonable figure, subject to no objection being made solely on the ground that a service could have been provided at lower cost. The landlord decided to replace all the air conditioning plant at the end of its normally expected lifespan, even though most of it was still working satisfactorily and rarely broke down. The tenant refused to pay towards the cost. **Held:** To replace plant which was working satisfactorily went beyond the covenant to 'maintain repair amend renew . . . ' all of which presupposed some malfunctioning which would prevent the provision of a reasonably acceptable service; for the same reason, it was also outside the scope of the covenant to provide conditioned air. As for the sweeper clause, it was not 'reasonable' to do these works since they were not reasonably required in order to maintain the service (it might have been different if the service, even if supplied to the standard applicable at the date of the lease, had ceased to conform to the reasonable current requirements of the tenants of the building). The express test of reasonableness in the sweeper clause limited the work and services to the standard such as the tenants, given the lengths of their leases, could fairly be expected to pay for – the landlord could not reasonably overlook the relatively limited interest of the paying tenants.

The question here is not whether a reasonable landlord would have decided to carry out the particular work, but rather whether the individual tenant ought reasonably to be required to pay towards its cost. In both the *Scottish Mutual* and *Fluor Daniel* cases noted above, the relative shortness of the individual tenant's lease compared with the landlord's long-term interest was a factor taken into account in deciding that the landlord's scheme of works was excessive and fell outside the recoverable service charge.

The *Fluor Daniel* decision took this approach from the Court of Appeal judgment in *Holding & Management Ltd v Property Holding & Investment Trust plc*[4] (noted at **1.51**). The issue was considered from the tenant's viewpoint even though the leases referred to costs reasonably incurred by the landlord and works which the landlord reasonably considered desirable. The reasonableness of the landlords' conduct was assessed by how far the landlords had considered the question as to what works should the particular tenants fairly be expected to pay towards.

One possible consequence of directing attention to the individual tenant's position appears to be that, even if the service charge clauses are in fact identical in all the leases in a building, particular works might fall outside the service charge under one tenant's lease but might fall within another's, simply because the leases have different unexpired terms. This would be consistent with the general rule that every lease is interpreted individually, but would undoubtedly create management problems for landlords. It remains to be seen whether the position would be different if the lease stated (as some leases do) that all the leases in the building were in the same form and that it was intended that every tenant would be liable to pay his due proportion of the service costs in order to give the landlord full recovery.

If the service charge clause does not expressly impose a reasonableness qualification, will such a qualification be implied by the courts? This question is discussed at **1.51**.

1 (1996) 41 EG 164, QB.
2 (1999) EGCS 43, QBD, Tech & Constr Ct.
3 [2001] EGCS 8, ChD.
4 [1989] 1 WLR 1313, CA.

Is there an implied test of reasonableness?

1.51 As noted at **1.15**, a landlord may by implication be constrained by a requirement to exercise any discretion he has under the lease rationally and in good faith. A stricter test would be a limitation that he must act reasonably in incurring costs that may be recovered from tenants through service charges.

Where the lease does not expressly place a limitation of reasonableness on the service charges or service expenditure, the implication was drawn by the Court of Appeal many years ago, in respect of *residential* leases, that the terms of the lease will not have been intended to give the landlord an unfettered right to be extravagant at the cost of the tenant and that it is to be implied that the landlord can only include, in the service charge, those costs which are fair and reasonable. This may be implied either in relation to the entire service charge or in respect of individual elements or heads of charge.

EXAMPLES

Finchbourne v Rodrigues[1]: The service charge was expressed to cover the costs incurred by the landlord in performing his services. The tenants challenged certain items on the grounds that the landlord had spent more than was reasonable. **Held:** There must be an implied term that the service costs claimed were to be fair and reasonable, since it cannot have been intended to give the landlord unfettered discretion to be extravagant or adopt the highest conceivable standard at the tenants' cost.

Holding & Management Ltd v Property Holding & Investment Trust plc[2]: Parts of the external walls of a block of flats needed repair. The maintenance trustees intended to carry out a major scheme of rebuilding recommended by their engineers. The tenants proposed a much less expensive scheme of repair recommended by their engineers. The leases provided for the service charge fund to be used for the 'repair' of external walls but also contained a sweeper clause that covered 'such other repairs and such improvement works and additions . . . as the Maintenance Trustee shall consider necessary to maintain the Building as a block of first class residential flats or otherwise desirable in the general interests of the tenants'. It also included 'all legal costs incurred . . . in the enforcement of the covenants . . . contained in the leases'. Could the major scheme be charged under the repair clause or the sweeper clause and could the trustees include in the service charge the legal costs of these proceedings even if they lost? **Held:** (1) The major scheme fell outside the repair clause. 'A prudent building owner bearing the costs himself might well have decided to adopt such a scheme, despite its expense. But what is in question is whether owners of 75-year leases in the building could fairly be expected to pay for such a scheme under an obligation to "repair"'. (2) The sweeper clause was not intended to overlap the 'repair' clause and did not include work to the external walls; but in any event the sweeper clause did not give the trustees a free hand to require the residents to pay for all works, whatever they might be, which the trustees might consider necessary: 'It is necessarily implicit in this paragraph that the [trustees] will act reasonably'. (3) The costs clause, read fairly, embraced only those legal costs which were *reasonably* or *properly* incurred, and the costs of pursuing an excessive scheme were not reasonably or properly incurred and so were not chargeable.

This gives rise to two questions: (1) is this reasonableness test to be implied invariably into every service charge clause; and (2) does it apply equally to business leases as to residential leases?

As to the first question, it was said in *Firstcross Ltd v Teasdale*[3] that the imposition of the reasonableness test amounted to a rule of law applicable to *every* lease reserving a variable service charge. However, the House of Lords has, in the past, rejected the creation, by the courts, of rigid rules of law for implying terms into formal documents (see *Suisse Atlantique Société d'Armement Maritime SA v NV Rotterdamsche Kohlen Centrale*[4]) and has also rejected the suggestion that the court has power to introduce terms into leases merely because they think them reasonable (see *Liverpool City Council v Irwin*[5]). The preferred view is the approach taken by the judge in *Wigglesworth v Property Holdings & Investment Trust Ltd*[6], to the effect that *Finchbourne v Rodrigues*[7] creates only a *rebuttable* presumption of a reasonableness test to be used when interpreting the wording of a lease, and that this presumption could be displaced if the implication of a reasonableness test would be inconsistent with the context. This view is supported by the decision in *Havenridge v Boston Dyers Ltd*[8], in which it was held that an express provision in a lease that the landlord could charge for 'properly' expended insurance premiums left no room for the court to infer any other qualifying words such as 'reasonably'. The sole test under that lease was whether the landlord acted 'properly', ie in the normal course of business, when arranging the insurance. This line of reasoning has been followed in another Court of Appeal decision and is now well established.

EXAMPLE

> *Berrycroft Management Co Ltd v Sinclair Gardens Investments (Kensington) Ltd*[9]: Leases of flats in a block allowed the landlord to nominate 'insurers of repute' to be used by the management company for insuring the block. The freehold changed hands and the new landlord nominated new insurers whose premiums were higher than the current insurers. Should further limitations on the landlord's choice of insurer be implied? **Held**: No; the limit on the landlord's discretion had been specified in the leases as 'insurers of repute' and no further limitation should be inferred. Provided that the new insurance was arranged in the normal course with reputable insurers, it could not be challenged. (The tenant's challenge under the legislation applicable to residential leases gave the same result – see **2.26**.)

The second question is whether the implied reasonableness test, rebuttable or not, also applies to commercial leases. In 1968, the court in *Bandar Property Holdings Ltd v JS Darwen (Successors)*[10] had held that no reasonableness test should affect the amount of insurance premium which a landlord was entitled to be reimbursed by his tenant under the terms of a commercial lease. After the decision in *Finchbourne Ltd v Rodrigues*[11], this approach was challenged in *Gleniffer Finance Corporation Ltd v Bamar Wood & Products Ltd*[12], but the point was left undecided. Furthermore, the statement in *Firstcross v Teasdale*[13], to the effect that the *Finchbourne* rule applies automatically to every variable service charge clause, did not distinguish between residential and commercial lettings, although both cases related to leases of residential flats. In the later *Berrycroft*[14] case (above), the Court of Appeal has expressed the view that the *Bandar* decision was correct and that no reasonableness test should be implied into provisions for the payment of insurance premiums.

It can be argued that in respect of commercial lettings, more than in the case of residential lettings, the tenant is normally in a good position to negotiate amendments to the offered form of lease. The Court of Appeal has refused to imply, into a commercial lease, a landlord's covenant to repair a private drain serving the demised premises, stating: 'the tenant . . . will ordinarily be well advised to demand an express covenant to this effect': *Duke of Westminster v Guild*[15]. Similar observations were made in the *Havenridge*[16] case (above). A similar cautious approach to the circumstances in which terms are to be implied into negotiated documents was taken in the leading case of *Philips Electronique Grand Public SA v British Sky Broadcasting Ltd*[17].

As mentioned at **1.49**, the RICS Professional Statement: Service Charges in Commercial Property (see **7.1**) imposes a core principle on chartered surveyors who manage commercial property for landlords, to the effect that best practice recommends that services are procured on an appropriate value for money basis and that competitive quotations are obtained or the costs benchmarked.

1 [1976] 3 All ER 581, CA.
2 [1989] 1 WLR 1313, CA.
3 (1983) 265 EG 305.
4 [1966] 2 All ER 61.
5 [1977] AC 239.
6 (1984) 270 EG 555.
7 [1976] 3 All ER 581, CA.
8 [1994] 2 EGLR 73, CA.
9 [1997] 1 EGLR 47, CA.
10 [1968] 2 All ER 305.
11 [1976] 3 All ER 581, CA.
12 (1979) 37 P&CR 208.
13 (1983) 265 EG 305.
14 [1997] 1 EGLR 47, CA.
15 (1983) 267 EG 762.
16 [1994] 2 EGLR 73, CA.
17 [1995] EMLR 472, CA.

Consumer protection legislation

1.52 The Consumer Rights Act 2015 gives rights to consumers dealing with traders. 'Consumer' means an individual acting for purposes that are wholly or mainly outside that individual's trade, business, craft or profession. It does not include, therefore, tenants who are companies or other entities or tenants who use the property for business use. 'Trader' means a person acting for purposes relating to that person's trade, business, craft or profession, whether acting personally or through another person acting in the trader's name or on the trader's behalf.

Chapter 4 of that Act applies to 'a contract to supply a service'. A lease is principally a contract to provide premises, but an important aspect in a lease of part of a building will often be the provision of services by the landlord. If the tenant under such a lease is an individual who is not using the premises for the purpose of his business and the lease can be considered to constitute a contract to supply a service, the provision of the 2015 Act most likely to apply is the provision that the contract is to be treated as including a term that the trader must perform the service with reasonable care and skill (s 49). There is also a provision that the price to be charged must be a reasonable price where the contract does not expressly fix the price or say how it is to be fixed (s 51); most leases that impose service charges expressly provide for the cost to be that incurred by the landlord, except perhaps for the landlord's in-house management charges, and it may be that s 51 would apply to such charges.

These provisions will not displace the provisions of the Landlord and Tenant Act 1985 concerning residential leases (see **2.1**) since s 53 of the 2015 Act states that it does not affect any enactment that imposes a stricter duty on the trader.

Sections 61–69 of the 2015 Act, which again only apply between traders and consumers, are largely in line with earlier legislation relating to unfair contract terms (but s 65 does not apply to contracts for the creation of an interest in land and a lease might be such a contract). Until a body of case law exists under the 2015 Act, reference to cases under the earlier similar legislation may be helpful in respect of consumer: trader situations. The Unfair Terms in Consumer Contracts Regulations 1999 applied to terms which had not been individually negotiated contained in contracts between a seller or supplier and a consumer (again being an individual, not a firm or company). Land transactions were not mentioned as being either included or excluded, but it was accepted by the courts that the 1999 Regulations were capable of applying to service charge clauses in residential leases (*R (Khatun and others) v London Borough of Newham*[1]; *Canary Riverside PTE v Schilling*[2]). The effect of the 1999 regulations, broadly, was to invalidate unfair terms, defined as terms which, contrary to the requirement of good faith, cause a significant imbalance in the parties' rights and obligations under the agreement, to the detriment of the consumer, which is similar to the provisions now in s 62(4) of the 2015 Act. In *Canary Riverside PTE v Schilling*[3] the court had to consider whether the 1999 Regulations invalidated a provision in the tenant's residential lease which allowed the landlord to include in the service costs any expenses he incurred in connection with management matters and which, as a matter of normal interpretation, could encompass costs incurred by the landlord in dealing with an application by a tenant to have a manager appointed (see **2.95**). The Lands Tribunal decided that the clause in the lease which allowed management costs to be included in the service charge was not unfair when judged under the tests set out in the 1999 regulations and was therefore not invalidated by those regulations. In *Peabody Trust v Reeve*[4], the landlord claimed that a clause in its standard form of residential tenancy agreement entitled it to effect unilateral variations in the terms of the agreement using the procedure set out in s 103 of the Housing Act 1985. The tenant argued that, even if that was the effect of the clause, it would not be binding because it fell foul of regulation 8 of the 1999 Regulations. The court decided that registered social landlords such as the Peabody Trust ceased to have rights under s 103 of the LTA 1985 after the enactment of the Housing Act 1988. However, in case that was wrong the judge also said that such a term would not be binding on a tenant by virtue of reg 8 of the 1999 Regulations because, under the grounds within reg 5(1), it would be a term that had not been individually negotiated and, contrary to good faith, would cause a significant imbalance in the rights and obligations of the parties to the detriment of the tenant. To satisfy the requirements of the 1999 Regulations, any unilateral variation of a residential tenancy agreement would at the least need to take full account of the guidelines set out by the Office of Fair Trading for tenancy agreements.

Other earlier legislation is currently preserved for circumstances other than the consumer: trader relationship now governed by the 2015 Act. The relevant earlier legislation is principally the Supply of Goods and Services Act 1982. Like s 49 of the 2015 Act, s 13 of the 1982 Act provides that, where a supplier is supplying a service in the course of a business, there is an implied term that the supplier will carry out the service with reasonable care and skill. The landlord providing services to commercial tenants will normally be doing so in the course of a business.

Furthermore, s 15 of the 1982 Act stipulates that, where the contract for the supply of a service does not specify the amount to be charged, *the charge must be reasonable*. As under the 2015 Act, it could be argued that most service charge clauses *do* specify the amount to be charged, not as a sum of money but by a formula, ie it is to be a certain proportion of the amount spend by the landlord (see dicta of *Evans LJ in Havenridge v Boston Dyers Ltd*[5]).

Under s 16 of the Supply of Goods and Services Act 1982, those implied terms can be varied by agreement between the parties. That however is subject to any limitations imposed by any other enactment.

1 [2005] EWHC 2236, QBD.
2 [2005] EW Lands LRX/65/2005.
3 [2005] EW Lands LRX/65/2005 the LT.
4 [2008] EWHC 1432 (Ch).
5 [1994] 2 EGLR 73.

FUNDING EXPENDITURE AND CHARGING INTEREST ON BORROWED FUNDS

Landlord's obligation irrespective of funding

1.53 Unless the leases state unequivocally otherwise, usually the landlord is contractually obliged to provide the services which he covenants to carry out, even if he has no funds to cover the cost.

EXAMPLES

> *Marenco v Jacramel Co Ltd*[1]: The tenant of a flat sued the landlord for breach of his covenant for external repairs. Could the landlord defend this claim on the ground that the tenants had not paid past service charges and were unwilling to give security for the cost of these further works? **Held:** No.
>
> *Francis v Cowcliffe*[2]: The tenant of a third-floor flat sought an order for specific performance of the landlord's covenant to maintain the lift. The landlord had bought a new lift but could not afford to install it. Did the landlord's lack of funds absolve him from his obligation to repair or renew the lift? **Held:** No.

If the leases do not provide for interim service charge payments, or if the interim charges are inadequate, the landlord will normally have to fund the expenditure from its own resources or by borrowings, until the service charges are ultimately collected from the tenants in accordance with the provisions of the leases.

Can the landlord withhold services from a tenant who fails to pay his service charges? Generally the answer is that he cannot. Even if the landlord's service covenant is prefaced by words such as 'subject to the tenant paying the service charge', it has been held in one case that this would not (without more explicit wording) make payment by the tenant a precondition of the landlord being obliged to continue providing the services. In *Yorkbrook Investments Ltd v Batten*[3], the landlord's covenant to provide the services began: 'Subject to the Lessee paying the Maintenance Contribution pursuant to the obligations under Clause 4 hereof . . . '. The tenant had withheld payment, alleging that the landlord was in breach of some of his obligations. The Court of Appeal held that the tenant's non-payment did not absolve the landlord of his obligation to continue to provide the services; taking the scheme of the lease as a whole and noting that the tenant could challenge individual items of service cost under the housing legislation, the court held that these words were not intended to create a condition precedent to the landlord's service covenants. However, in the more recent case of *Bluestorm Ltd v Portvale Holdings Ltd*[4], two of the three Court of Appeal judges expressed the view (obiter) that *Yorkbrook* did not establish a general rule and that in some circumstances effect might be given to clear wording which made the landlord's service obligations depend upon the tenant paying the service charge, such as where there was a direct connection between the non-payment and the non-provision of the service. The third judge in *Bluestorm* preferred to express no opinion on this subject until it came before the courts for actual decision, so the point remains uncertain.

Even if the clause was expressly worded to make payment of the service charge a precondition of the tenant's entitlement to have the benefit of the services, the withdrawal of services from a *residential* occupier might, in some cases, constitute a criminal offence under s 1(3A) of the Protection from Eviction Act 1977.

Furthermore, the tenant's liability to make payments on account will often be dependent upon the landlord complying with procedures under the service charge clause which require the landlord to make proper estimates of the annual costs.

EXAMPLE

> *Gordon v Selico Co Ltd*[5]: The maintenance trustee's covenant to provide the services began 'Subject to the payment by the Lessee of the Maintenance Contribution in accordance with the provisions of Clause 4 hereof . . . '. The lease required the maintenance trustee to make a computation of the estimated maintenance provision for the year, on which the interim demands were to be based. The maintenance trustee demanded payment of a sum not supported by any proper computation. The tenant withheld payment for various reasons, including alleging that the maintenance trustee was in breach of numerous obligations. Did this failure to pay absolve the maintenance trustee of the obligation to continue providing the services? **Held:** No; the proper computation of the annual provision under the lease was a necessary preliminary to any demand for maintenance contributions, so no proper demand had been made.

1 (1964) 191 EG 433, CA.
2 (1977) 33 P&CR 368.
3 (1985) 276 EG 545, CA.
4 [2004] EWCA Civ 289.
5 (1986) 278 EG 53, CA.

Interest on borrowed funds

1.54 As stated at **1.53**, where leases do not provide for interim payments on account of the service charge, or where they stipulate inadequately low interim payments, the landlord will normally be obliged to fund the service costs himself until such time as the service charges or excess can be demanded. Some leases expressly provide for the service charge to include interest paid by the landlord on funds borrowed to meet service expenditure, or notional interest where the landlord has paid for the services out of his own resources.

If the service charge clause is silent on this point, it was, for several years, thought to be established firmly that the courts will infer that such interest *cannot be* included in the service charge (*Boldmark Ltd v Cohen*[1]; *Frobisher (Second Investments) Ltd v Kiloran Trust Co Ltd*[2]).

However, doubt has been cast on that rule by the case of *Skilleter v Charles*[3], in which the Court of Appeal expressed the view that '. . . a term that interest should be so chargeable . . . could . . . be implied either on the basis that it is necessary to give business efficacy to the terms of the lease or, alternatively, on the basis of the officious bystander test'. The report of that case does not indicate any detailed argument on the point or any reference to the earlier cases cited above, and the decision can be argued to be confined to the particular facts, since it involved a badly drafted clause which appeared to have been intended to enable the landlord to charge his interest costs but the wording used failed to achieve that result. It is, therefore, likely that the *Boldmark* and *Frobisher* decisions remain correct indications of how this issue will be decided in other cases where the service charge clause is totally silent on the matter. The position might however be different where the landlord is a tenants' management company with no other source of funds, see **1.9**.

Where interest cannot be charged, the landlord might find it possible to arrange for the contractor engaged to carry out the works to price his work so as to include a finance cost and agree to be paid after the time when, once the work is done, service charge invoices can be sent to the tenants.

The RICS Professional Statement: Service Charges in Commercial (see **7.1**), at paragraph 4.5.11, notes that commercial leases should allow landlords to recover the reasonable and proper cost of borrowing to fund major non-cyclical or unbudgeted expenditure. The RICS residential code is silent on this point, simply noting that sometimes the landlord cannot recover through service charges interest charged on borrowings, but the same principles should logically apply. Good practice should therefore provide for the landlord to borrow on normal commercial terms in order to fund service costs where interim charges are inadequate and to include the interest and bank charges in the service charges, setting against that any interest recovered from tenants who were late in paying their contributions.

1 (1986) 277 EG 745.
2 [1980] 1 All ER 488.
3 (1992) 13 EG 113.

CONSULTATION WITH TENANTS

Good practice

1.55 Most leases lay down no procedure for tenants to be consulted before service expenditure is incurred. However, forms of lease vary so widely that it is advisable, in each case, to check whether the lease contains any specific provisions in this respect. The fact that many landlords fail to consult their tenants before incurring service costs is an unfortunate indication of the lack of thought and consideration which is prevalent in these matters.

It seems sensible (irrespective of the strict legal obligations) that landlords and their managing agents should keep their tenants informed of any changes in service arrangements which involve alterations in the practical administration of the building or in the amount of service charges, and should consult with the tenants before embarking upon any major new expenditure or substantial reorganisation of the services or administration. In addition, competitive estimates or quotations should be obtained for any items of substance to avoid allegations of extravagance (see **1.49**).

Consultation is encouraged by guidance notes and codes of practice for commercial property (see **7.1** and **7.2**). The new RICS Professional Statement: Service Charges in Commercial Property, 1st edition, lays particularly emphasis (as did the RICS's previous practice guidance on the subject) on communication and transparency between landlord and tenants. Consultation could be particularly important where voluntary (as opposed to compliance-driven) environmental initiatives are concerned. An example is the integration of environmental considerations into purchasing or tendering processes. This could arise where works are carried out or services are provided in pursuance of the landlord's obligations. Even where tenants agree, or the lease requires, that environmental considerations shall be given a place in purchasing and tendering decisions, there could be a wide range of views about how those obligations ought to be met in practice. A requirement or decision to use only environmentally benign products, or contractors with a sound environmental policy, could be interpreted in a number of ways. Environmental product information can be very difficult to interpret and claims about the 'greenness' of particular products can be misleading. Whilst industry groupings are still in the early stages of developing environmental management policies and systems, and until professional bodies and others have developed widely accepted codes of practice and guidelines, references in leases to environmental requirements are likely to be couched in broad terms. Even if a provision in a lease requires adherence to a particular guideline or code, these are unlikely to contain detailed and specific requirements. In these circumstances, landlords would be well advised to consult with their tenants on matters falling within this area.

Express consultation requirements

1.56 Where the service charge clause does lay down a consultation procedure, it might be interpreted as an absolute precondition to the tenant's liability, ie disqualifying the landlord from claiming the service charge unless he has followed the specified procedure. It is, therefore, most important for the landlord to follow strictly any consultation procedure laid down in the lease.

EXAMPLES

CIN Properties Ltd v Barclays Bank plc[1]: The clause governing contributions towards external and structural repairs required the landlord to obtain estimates or tenders in the open market and precluded him from accepting any tender or estimate or contracting for or ordering the work without the approval of the tenant, which was not to be unreasonably withheld. The landlord embarked on works in that category without observing this procedure. Did this preclude him from charging for these works? **Held:** Yes.

Northway Flats Management Co Ltd v Wimpey Pension Trustees Ltd[2]: The service charge clause contained a proviso that 'in respect of major or substantial repairs the Landlord shall, before carrying out such works submit a copy of the specification of works and estimates obtained upon such specification to the Tenant for consideration and if the Tenant shall not have raised any objection thereto within 21 days . . . the Tenant shall be deemed to have accepted the specification and estimates as reasonable . . . '. The landlord omitted to follow that procedure for major external repairs. Did this preclude him from charging for these works? **Held:** Yes.

1 [1986] 1 EGLR 59, CA.
2 (1992) 31 EG 65, CA.

Statutory rules for residential leases

1.57 The statutory provisions for compulsory consultation with tenants of residential flats are described in CHAPTER 2.

APPORTIONMENT BETWEEN TENANTS

Common methods of apportionment

1.58 The calculation of the service charge payable by any tenant must be carried out strictly in accordance with the terms of his lease. In *Kelsall v London Borough of Islington*[1] it was held that a calculation which purported to apportion costs incurred across the landlord's estate could not be used where the lease contemplated that the tenant would bear a proportion of the costs incurred in relation to the building in which his flat was located. The landlord would have to prove that a particular amount was incurred in relation to that particular building and only that amount could be used in the calculation.

The new RICS Professional Statement: Service Charges in Commercial Property (see **7.1**) states in paragraph 4.2 that managers are to provide an apportionment matrix for the building or complex to all occupiers, clearly showing the basis of calculation and the total apportionment for each schedule for each unit, so that an individual tenant should be able to clearly verify the basis and method of calculation used in arriving at his particular percentage apportionment. However, to preserve confidentiality the RICS accepts that this should exclude details of any individual concessions or other arrangements between landlords and individual tenants on the basis that these are normally borne by the landlord and will not affect other tenants, which is consistent with RICS requirements that the landlord must bear any voids and concessions (set out in core principle 24, in Part 3, paragraph 2.3 and in Appendix A to the Statement).

As for the requirement for the landlord to bear the part of the service costs as would be attributable to unlet units (voids), that requirement will in any event normally arise under a lease as a consequence of the usual provisions requiring the landlord to pay for the services and requiring the tenants to pay only their individual proportions (leaving the landlord to bear any shortfall), except in those rare cases where the drafting of the apportionment provisions allows the landlord to load the tenants of let units with contributions that would otherwise be attributable to unlet units. Some leases contain express provisions stating that the landlord must pay the service costs attributable to lettable units that are unlet or are let on leases that do not reserve full service charges, but in most cases such express provisions will be unnecessary except where the services are provided by a management company or other third party separate from the landlord and to which the landlord needs to pay the service charge for the voids.

For cases where different groups of tenants benefit from different costs, and the costs ought to be divided into different schedules, see **1.62**. The RICS Professional Statement: Service Charges in Commercial Property (see **7.1**) contains an illustration at Annex CA.

Leases vary in the method by which they define or provide for the ascertainment of each individual tenant's proportion of the relevant service costs. The most common formulae are:

(1) a fixed percentage set out in each lease;
(2) a statement in each lease that the proportion is to be determined by the ratio of rateable values of the various lettable parts of the building;
(3) a statement in each lease that the proportion is to be determined by the ratio of floor areas of the various lettable parts of the building;
(4) a statement in each lease that the proportion is to be a 'fair', 'proper', 'due' or 'reasonable' proposition, perhaps determined by the landlord's surveyor. Each of these is discussed in more detail below.

The first method (a stated, fixed percentage) is sometimes coupled with an indication of the basis on which the stated percentages have been calculated. It may also be accompanied by a provision enabling the proportions to be varied from time to time if circumstances require (see **1.63**) although this is by no means universal.

The floor space basis will not be appropriate in every case. For example, in a centrally heated building certain parts may consume more central heating than others due to higher ceilings, larger windows, or other design causes, and may justify bearing a higher proportion of the heating costs. In those cases, detailed consideration should be given to an equitable basis of apportioning any such unevenly incurred costs (see **1.61**).

The RICS Professional Statement (see **7.1**) sets out basic principles for the apportionment of service charges in paragraph 4.2, which are supplemented by examples in Appendix C.

The rateable value method cannot be imposed for new residential property since such property is no longer given a rateable value, and it is usually not appropriate for commercial property as the rateable values of different parts of a building may not correlate to their sizes or to their use of the services or amenities of the building. The RICS Professional Statement, as mentioned below, particularly advises against a rateable value apportionment.

The most modern buildings nowadays often have computerized management systems by which the usage of certain services within the lettable units (such as air conditioning, heating, hot water, etc) can be metered and recorded. Such a system can produce an apportionment for the relevant costs which matches the usage of those particular services, such as utilities. This is discussed at paragraph 4.1.6.2 of the RICS Professional Statement. To a degree this may also be possible in relation to services provided in the common parts, where swipe cards and electronic barrier systems could enable a landlord to monitor a significant proportion of the footfall generated by each lettable unit.

1 [2006] LON/00AU/LSC/2006/0399.

Proportion by reference to rateable values

1.59 The appropriateness of this method of apportionment has been commented upon at **1.58** and is discussed in paragraph 4.2.6 of the RICS Professional Statement: Service Charges in Commercial Property (see **7.1**) which generally advises against this method.

A lease which requires the apportionment to be made on this basis may provide that the tenant's proportion of the service costs is to be in the proportion which the rateable value of his demise bears to the total of the rateable values of all parts of the building *from time to time*. This may mean that the proportion must be recalculated each time the rateable value of any part of the building changes and that (unless the wording provides otherwise) the new proportion takes effect as from the date when the change in rateable value takes effect under rating law (*Moorcroft v Doxford*[1]). This can present problems when that date does not coincide with the start of the service charge accounting year, since the service charge accounts must then be split at the date of change of the rateable value, and the service charges must be separately calculated for the parts of the accounting year before and after that date. However, it may be necessary to recalculate accounts for a completed accounting period when a rateable value change is back-dated as a result of a rating appeal (*Universities Superannuation Fund v Marks & Spencer plc*[2], at first instance). In the case of residential property, rateable values ceased to be reassessed as from 1 April 1990, and so should not be incorporated into new residential leases. The use of rateable values is accordingly particularly troublesome in those mixed-use buildings which include residential as well as commercial units.

1 (1980) 254 EG 871.
2 [1991] 11 Ch 370.

Proportion by reference to floor areas

1.60 The appropriateness of this method of apportionment has been commented upon at **1.58** and is discussed in paragraph 4.2.5 of the RICS Professional Statement: Service Charges in Commercial Property (see **7.1**). Where a lease stipulates that the service costs are to be borne between the tenants in the ratio of the floor areas of their respective parts of the building *from time to time*, a recalculation will usually have to be carried out whenever any lettable part of the building is altered in a way which changes the floorspace (as in the case of the rateable value basis mentioned above). The method of measurement (net usable, gross external, etc) must be consistent throughout the building and should ideally be specified in the leases. In commercial leases it is quite common to refer to using a particular code of measurement practice. However, even such a code may need interpreting and might be the subject of disagreement (see *Kilmartin SCI (Hulton House) Ltd v Safeway Stores plc*[1]). To avoid each tenant disputing the measurement of his demise, there should be provision for one person, such as the landlord's surveyor, to determine all the relevant measurements conclusively (except, perhaps, in the case of manifest and substantial error), or for the relevant areas to be specified in the lease with any additions or variations to be decided by the landlord's surveyor or architect.

For allocating the cost of repairs or insurance of a building it is usual to use gross internal areas (GIAs) but provision should be made for adjustment in relation to differing ceiling heights.

The usage of common parts (such as staircases, service roads and areas, gardens, etc) by persons at or visiting the different lettable units may of course not match the proportions of the floor areas of those units. For example, a flat with a GIA of 75 sq m may in practice generate the same usage of common parts as a 80 sq m flat. However, any attempt to match exactly the apportionment of costs relating to the common parts to their actual usage is likely to be excessively complex and unlikely to succeed, and in most cases a degree of arbitrariness is inevitable. However it is sometimes justifiable to make an attempt to produce a more appropriate outcome.

In the case of complexes such as major shopping centres which contain units of widely varying sizes, landlords are often faced with an argument from large space users that a large unit, compared with a small unit, will not generate an amount of usage of common parts and services in direct proportion to its size – and the reverse argument is also often put forward. This would be particularly so, it is argued, in the case of large retail units in which significant areas are used for storage rather than sales. Such tenants would want a diminishing calculation to be applied either to the entire service charge or to selected items of charge. However, it is becoming less common for retail units to contain large storage areas; the ability to take daily deliveries of stock results in a greater proportion of the unit being used as sales area than was previously common. Indeed, traders in smaller units may justifiably contend that the larger units, invariably occupied by well-known multiple occupiers, attract more customers per square foot than they do themselves and that any weighting should be against the large user. If that competing argument is well founded, it may be best to abandon any fine-tuning and base the service charge apportionment on plain unadjusted floor areas. It would be risky for a landlord to grant fairly long leases with a fixed formula which might be discredited during the term of the lease at a time when the landlord has to grant new leases of other units to tenants who will not agree to the same formula; a shortfall in service charge recovery might then arise.

There is also a discussion about weighted apportionments, specifically in relation to shopping centres, in the RICS Professional Statement: Service

Charges in Commercial Property (see **7.1**) at paragraph 4.2.8. If a weighted service charge has to be adopted, one method is a points system; the relevant service costs are apportioned between the units in proportion to the service charge points allocated to them, and points are allocated to each unit according to floor areas on a reducing scale set out in the leases, for example:

- the first 1,000 sq ft of the unit: 5 points per 1,000 sq ft;
- the next 3,000 sq ft of the unit: 4 points per 1,000 sq ft;
- the next 3,000 sq ft of the unit: 3 points per 1,000 sq ft, and so on.

Another method would be to use a notional floor area arrived at by discounting the actual measured area, for example:

- the first 1,000 sq ft multiplied by 1;
- the next 3,000 sq ft multiplied by 0.8;
- the next 3,000 sq ft multiplied by 0.6, and so on.

For another example of a weighted calculation see the RICS Professional Statement: Service Charges in Commercial Property (see **7.1**) at paragraph 4.2.8. In the case of residential estates, a similar weighted points system can be adopted, but reflecting the number of persons reasonably likely to reside in each unit. Care must be taken to devise a fair system since the impact of the number of residents in a unit on the consumption of services and amenities may differ (see **1.62**). It would be possible to set out a system in which each flat was denominated as having been designed for occupation by a particular number of occupants and in which certain service costs are to be apportioned according to those numbers. For example, if the aggregate of such denominations was 105 occupants for the building a flat denominated as a three-person flat would bear 3/105 ths of the total costs of those services which are appropriate for apportioning on a per head basis (as discussed above).

Where different services are available to different groups of tenants, see the discussion at **1.62**.

1 [2006] EWHC 60 (Ch).

Fair or reasonable proportion

1.61 Where the lease provides that the service charge is to be a 'fair', or 'proper', or 'due', or 'reasonable' proportion of the total service costs, it will often state that this proportion is to be determined by the landlord's surveyor. The RICS Professional Statement: Service Charges in Commercial Property (see **7.1**) states a principle that the basis and method of apportionment should be demonstrably fair and reasonable to ensure that individual occupiers bear an appropriate proportion of the total service charge expenditure that clearly reflects the availability, benefit and use of services. Chartered surveyors have a professional duty to comply with the Professional Statement.

It is likely that, in making such a determination, the surveyor will be acting as an expert. Care must be taken to make a professionally competent and sustainable decision. Legal advice might need to be taken as to matters which should properly be taken into account, including whether such matters should be viewed at the date of the lease or having regard to subsequent events.

In one case, a judge held that in assessing a 'fair proportion' one should take into account not only the relative areas of the premises demised by each tenancy but also other factors which were relevant to fairness. This included, in that case, the short length of the unexpired term of the lease and the limited benefits which the tenant would obtain from the landlord's expenditure.

EXAMPLE

> *Scottish Mutual Insurance Company v Jardine*[1]: The lease required the tenant to pay, as a service charge, a 'fair proportion' of the costs 'reasonably and properly incurred' by the landlord in carrying out his obligations, which included repairing the exterior and structure of the building. The lease had only a few months left before it expired. The landlord carried out expensive long-term repairs to the roof of the building, instead of patching it up. The landlord's main motive in doing so was to facilitate the letting of a vacant part of the building to a new tenant. **Held**: The 'fair proportion' should not be calculated by relative floor areas, but this tenant should pay a reduced proportion reflecting the limited benefit to him due to the shortness of the unexpired term of his lease and the fact that it was not 'reasonable' for the landlord to carry out long-term repairs in order to fulfil the landlord's repairing obligations under this particular lease.

The court can review a landlord's exercise of a power in the lease to determine what is a fair or due proportion. In *Re Rowner Estates Ltd*[2], the Lands Tribunal considered a situation where a landlord reduced the service charge proportion payable by a tenant of a commercial unit in the building and increased the 'fair proportion' payable by the residential tenants. The Tribunal looked at the landlord's explanation and decided that the new percentage allocated to the residential tenants by the landlord was 'fair' and conformed to the provisions in the lease.

1 (1999) EGCS 43, QBD, Tech & Constr Ct.
2 [2007] LRX/3/2006, LT.

Unevenly shared services

1.62 In many cases, particularly in mixed-use buildings (such as blocks containing lock-up shops with separate offices or flats above), not all the tenants in the building will enjoy the benefit of the landlord's services to the same extent. For example, parts of a building may not be served by the central heating system which serves other parts, or may consume, disproportionately, more central heating energy due to higher ceilings or more windows. Certain tenants in a building may not require use of the lifts. Equally, some tenants in a building (such as those leasing lock-up shops) may have a degree of direct responsibility for the external repair of their part of the building, while tenants of other parts of the same building (eg upper-floor offices) may contribute through the service charge to the landlord's expenditure on external repairs.

The RICS Professional Statement: Service Charges in Commercial Property (see **1.12** and **7.1**), in its core principles 4 and 5, states that where different groups of tenants benefit from different costs the costs should be allocated to separate schedules and the costs within them apportioned to those tenants who benefit from them; and the basis and method of apportionment should be demonstrably fair and reasonable to ensure that individual occupiers bear an appropriate proportion of the total service costs to reflect the benefit they obtain from those services.

For these reasons, it may be desirable to divide the service charges into separate parts, with each part being individually apportioned between tenants according to usage. The RICS Professional Statement: Service Charges in Commercial Property, contains an illustration in Appendix C. However, many older leases fail to reflect those principles and require the tenant to pay a particular proportion of the total service costs incurred in relation to the building irrespective of whether the tenants benefit from the services differently.

In the case of estates involving several separate blocks, it will usually be desirable to divide service costs into different tranches so that all the tenants pay towards the maintenance of the roads and wholly communal grounds but otherwise pay only for costs relating to their own block. In the residential sector, many local authorities have traditionally spread costs across the whole of their estates, which may be convenient where tenants pay inclusive rents but will usually be inappropriate where there are tenants who pay service charges.

EXAMPLE

A two-storey building comprises a ground floor containing two lock-up shops, and an upper floor comprising four office suites of equal size. The offices are centrally heated and access is through a shared entrance hall and staircase. The shops are unheated and do not use the office entrance. All the leases impose internal repairing obligations on the tenants, with the landlord carrying out external repairs. The leases of the offices additionally require the landlord to provide central heating and to maintain the shared entrance hall and staircase. The service charge provisions of the leases should stipulate the following contributions towards the landlord's expenditure.

Demise	Contribution for central heating and shared access %	Contribution for external repairs%
Shop 1	—	25.5
Shop 2	—	25.5
Office 1	25	12.5
Office 2	25	12.5
Office 3	25	12.5
Office 4	25	12.5
	100	100.0

A more complicated example of a calculation apportioning costs in different tranches appears at example CE in Appendix C of the RICS Professional Statement: Service Charges in Commercial Property (see **7.1**).

Where the lease provides for the service charge to be calculated by applying a single percentage to the total service costs, rather than separate percentages for individual items of cost, it will be difficult for the tenant to argue that his service charge should be calculated by excluding from those total costs the cost of a particular chargeable item, merely because he does not directly benefit from it.

EXAMPLES

Broomleigh Housing Association v Hughes[1]: The lease required the tenant to pay a stated percentage of the service costs incurred by the landlord. The landlord replaced all the windows in the block apart from those of the tenant's flat, since the tenant had already replaced them, albeit without the landlord's consent. The tenant refused to pay that part of his service charge which related to the cost of installing new windows in the rest of the block. An arbitrator appointed under the Independent Housing Ombudsman Scheme found that the present landlord had permitted the tenant to retain his new windows and that the previous landlord had relieved other tenants in similar situations from contributing to such costs and held that this tenant was entitled to the same treatment. The landlord appealed to the court. **Held:** The tenant was liable to pay his specified proportion of all the service costs, as provided in his lease, even though he did not directly benefit from the new windows. The present landlord's waiver of the tenant's breach of covenant in installing his own new windows did not affect the tenant's service charge obligations, nor did the tenant have any legitimate expectation that he would be relieved from part of the contractual service charge.

Billson v Tristrem[2]: The tenant of a basement flat was liable to pay 20 per cent of the costs incurred by the landlord on various repairs, including repairs to certain common parts. Some of the common parts were used only by the tenants of the upper part of the building. The lease contained contradictory provisions as to whether the basement tenant had to pay towards costs relating to parts he did not use. **Held:** The overall intention of the lease was that the tenant would pay 20 per cent of the landlord's entire costs relating to the building, even though this included parts which did not directly benefit this tenant.

1 (1999) EGCS 134, ChD.
2 [2000] L&TR 220, CA.

Varying fixed proportions

1.63 Changes in circumstances may result in a need to change the proportions in which the total service costs are split between the tenants in a building. Some forms of lease give the landlord or his surveyor express power to vary these proportions in appropriate circumstances. If, however, the leases specify fixed proportions applicable to each flat and contain no provision for them to be varied, there are only two ways in which variation can be brought about. The first way is with the consent of each tenant whose proportion the landlord desires to alter. The problems which may arise, and the method of recording agreement on variations, are discussed at **1.46**. The second way, which is applicable if any tenant refuses to agree a variation, but only appropriate if the landlord can show that the variation is reasonable and has been brought about by lawful changes in circumstances, is to apply to the court. It appears that the court may be willing to order a variation of a lease in some circumstances, but the scope of this power is uncertain.

EXAMPLES

Pole Properties Ltd v Feinberg[1]: Alterations to the hot water system shared between two blocks of flats rendered inappropriate the proportion of the costs of running the system specified in the tenant's lease as his liability. Did the court have power to order the proportion set out in the tenant's lease to be changed to the new proper figure? **Held:** Yes.

Mylles v Hall[2]: A former caretaker's flat was sold off on a long lease. Were the tenants of the other flats in the building entitled to require a reduction of the service charge percentages specified in their leases (which added up to 100 per cent without the caretaker's flat)? **Held:** No. (Note: It appears that the court did not have the benefit of full argument on the point, and the decision may, therefore, be questioned.)

1 (1981) 259 EG 417, CA.
2 14 January 1980, unreported.

Specially requested services

1.64 Problems frequently arise where some tenants in a building require the landlord to provide services which other tenants in the same building consider unnecessary. For example, an international company occupying part of an office block may ask the landlord to provide 24-hours-a-day access, with security guards or commissionaires in attendance at all times. Other tenants in the building may be satisfied with access or security only during limited hours and may object to having to contribute towards the additional costs of night access. Whether these additional costs can be included in the total service charge payable by all the tenants depends on the wording of the service charge clauses in their leases. If it is unclear whether the additional costs are covered, it will be relevant to consider the tenants' rights under the leases. For example, if the leases give the tenants right of access over the common parts during specified hours only, it may be implied that porterage costs can only be charged so far as they relate to those specified hours of access. Whether the extra costs of late working might then be covered by a sweeping-up provision depends upon the wording of that provision. Logic suggests that the cost of services provided for the benefit of only certain tenants should be borne only by those tenants and that accords with the principles set out in the RICS Commercial Code of Practice (see **7.1**). If, therefore, some tenants ask the landlord to provide extended or additional services for their own benefit and it is not absolutely plain that the costs of these additional services will fall within the service charges payable by the tenants as a whole, the landlord should ask those tenants who are making the request to agree that they alone will pay the entire additional costs.

Landlord bearing or contributing to certain costs

1.65 Some leases provide for the landlord to bear part of the cost of providing certain services or for those costs to be excluded from the service charge. This is most common in the case of large shopping centres where the leases may provide for the landlord to meet all or part of the costs of advertising and promoting the centre, and in the case of new buildings where the costs of completing the construction and fit-out and the cost of repairs covered by construction warranties may be expressly excluded from the service charge.

The RICS Professional Statement: Service Charges in Commercial Property, at core principle 24, contains a list of items that should not normally be included in service charges, including the initial costs of the design and construction of the fabric, plant or equipment, setting up costs, etc.

As usual, the operation of such provisions depends on the precise wording and the contra proferentem rule may apply in grey areas (see **1.9**).

EXAMPLE

> *Boots UK Ltd v Trafford Centre Limited*[1]: The lease of a unit in the Trafford Centre provided that the landlord would bear 50 per cent of that part of the service costs which related to 'Promotion' which was defined as 'advertising and other forms of promotion of the Centre intended to bring additional custom to the Centre . . . '. Did the landlord have to contribute 50 per cent of the costs of providing Christmas decorations, entertainment, a Santa's Grotto and advertising on the Centre's video screens? **Held**: Generally no; most of these costs fell outside the defined meaning of 'Promotion'. The provision of decorations and entertainments for visitors in the centre was not itself any type of advertising or promotion to potential new visitors, and only that on-screen advertising which promoted the Centre as a whole might count as Promotion.

1 [2008] EWHC 3372 (Ch).

INDEXED AND FORMULAIC SERVICE CHARGES

When appropriate

1.66 Occasionally, a service charge may be of an initial specified sum of money, with increases index-linked in some way, perhaps to a published index such as the Index of Retail Prices, or linked to the cost of a particular component, such as oil or gas.

Indexing to the cost of fuel is probably most appropriate only in special cases, eg where the service charge is limited to cover hot water or heating and the specified amount of the charge is designed to include sums for maintenance or depreciation of plant, which would otherwise be difficult or cumbersome to compute on an annual cost basis.

Problems with indices and factorial formulae

1.67 The draftsman must take care to ensure that the indexation provisions are properly drawn and do not create an unintended cumulative effect that results in the increase exceeding a true reflection of the indexation. The greatest problems with published indices are that they may cease to be produced or that the basis of computation may be changed by the body which produces them. It is traditional for indexation clauses to contain provisions designed to meet these possibilities. Such provisions must be carefully examined to ensure that they achieve the intended outcome.

Mathematical formulae for increasing a fixed service charge by a pre-set multiplier can be problematic in that they may result, over a long period, in the amount becoming wildly excessive. In *Arnold v Britton*[1], it was pointed out that a provision in a 1974 lease that a £90 pa service charge would increase by 10 per cent every year, compounded, had resulted in a service charge of over £3,366 pa by 2012 – whereas RPI indexation would have given a figure of only £794 per year.

EXAMPLES

Cumshaw Ltd v Bowen[2]: The leases of flats in a house required the landlord to repair the roof and main structure of the building, and reserved a service charge of an initial specified sum, to be increased annually in proportion to the increases in the Index of Retail Prices above the figure prevailing in August 1960, namely 110.4. The clause expressly provided that if the Index of Retail Prices ceased to be published by HM Government, or was no longer available to the public, the service charge should be computed, instead, by reference to the actual cost of the services. In the mid-1970s, the government rebased the Index to a new base figure of 100, and over the years the 'basket' of commodities which made up the figure changed from that used in 1960. Could the landlord invoke the change-over clause and compute the charge by reference to actual cost, which would produce a higher service charge figure? **Held:** No; the rebasing and alteration in the basket of commodities did not mean that the Index had 'ceased', and so the change-over clause could not be invoked. Instead, the Index increase did have to be mathematically adjusted, before being used to calculate the new service charge, so as to adjust for the rebasing but not for the new basket of commodities.

Jollybird Ltd v Fairzone Ltd[3]: The charges for central heating reserved by the leases in a building were expressed to be a fair proportion of the costs incurred, with two provisos; the first imposing a minimum charge of 1.3 pence per square foot; the second being a provision that 'the sum payable may be increased proportionately at any time by the lessor if the cost of fuel for supplying such heating shall at any time exceed the cost thereof at the date of the lease'. Was this second proviso to be applied? **Held:** No; since the basic computation was to be based on the cost in any event, the second proviso was to be disregarded because it was either inappropriate or would result in the landlord making a profit on the heating charge.

The *Fairzone* case is a clear example of a badly drafted set of clauses and extreme care must be taken in the drafting of indexed service charge provisions.

Where the provisions are quite clear and largely unambiguous, the court will not interfere with the operation of those provisions merely because the tenant is surprised at the outcome and might not have agreed to accept the grant of the lease on those terms if at that time he had been aware of the future outcome (*Arnold v Britten*[4], above).

In the absence of any clear wording giving only one party the right to invoke the provision, either the landlord or the tenant can exercise a provision for a service charge to be adjusted in line with the specified index (see *IVS Enterprises Ltd v Chelsea Cloisters Management Ltd*[5]).

1 [2015] UKSC 36.
2 [1987] 1 EGLR 30, ChD.
3 [1990] 2 EGLR 55, CA.
4 [2015] UKSC 36.
5 (1994) EGCS 14, CA.

INTERIM CHARGES

Interim payments or reimbursement on demand

1.68 Some service charge clauses provide for regular payments (usually called 'interim payments') on account of the eventual charge, with the balance becoming payable when accounts of the annual costs have been prepared. Others simply provide for payment of the tenant's contribution towards the actual expenditure whenever the landlord demands payment, but without advance payments. The former category is generally found in modern leases under which substantial services are provided, whereas the latter is commonly found in older leases or those where services are minimal.

Right to interim payments

1.69 Some older leases make no provision for interim contributions, but simply provide for the tenant to pay his proportion of the landlord's actual expenditure. Depending on the precise wording, this may prevent the landlord from demanding any contributions until he has actually disbursed the expenditure. It seems that a landlord will only be entitled to demand advance payments on account of the service charge if the lease or tenancy agreement expressly makes provision for this. The point was left open in *Daitches v Bluelake Investments Ltd*[1] but it has now been held in the Lands Chamber of the Upper Tribunal in a residential case that where a lease did not make express provision for interim payments none could be demanded (*Tingdene Holiday Parks Ltd v Cox*[2]).

Where the lease fails to provide for interim payments in advance of the costs being expended, it is clearly in the landlord's interest to demand the contributions from the tenant at the earliest possible moment. In some cases the contribution clause will enable demands to be issued at any time and, in such cases, a prudent landlord or managing agent will issue a demand as soon as any significant item of expenditure has been incurred so as to recoup his costs with the minimum of delay. Whether he is entitled to charge interest for funding the expenditure may be uncertain (see **1.53**).

As to cases where interim contributions are to be based on estimated provisions, see **1.70**.

1 (1985) 275 EG 462.

2 [2011] UKUT 310, LC.

Amount of interim contribution

1.70 Where a lease provides for the payment of interim charges, the amount which the landlord or his agent is entitled to demand by way of interim charge is governed by the terms of the lease. Many modern forms of lease purport to give the landlord or his agent an unfettered discretion to dictate the amount of the interim contribution but, plainly, the preparation of proper estimates of the service costs and their circulation among the tenants is highly desirable to foster good landlord and tenant relations. Some leases expressly require the landlord to prepare and furnish the tenant with a proper estimate of the current year's anticipated expenditure, on which the interim contribution is to be based. In those cases, no interim payment will (unless the lease states otherwise) be due until that procedure has been followed.

EXAMPLE

> *Gordon v Selico Co Ltd*[1]: The lease required the maintenance trustee to make a computation of the estimated maintenance provision for the year, on which the interim demands were to be based. The maintenance trustee demanded payment of a sum not supported by any proper computation. Was that sum payable? **Held:** No; the proper computation of the annual provision under the lease was a necessary preliminary to any demand for maintenance contributions, so no proper demand had been made.

Occasionally, leases provide that the amount of the interim contributions can only be varied at specified times by the landlord or his agent giving a formal notice to the tenants and, in some cases, the increase is limited to reflecting the actual service charge of the previous accounting year. Whatever the provisions of the lease may be with regard to interim contributions, as a matter of contract the procedures laid down by such provisions must be followed closely if the tenant is to be legally obliged to pay any interim contributions.

Some very old leases provide for interim payments of only a fixed amount which are now well below the current level of service charge, resulting in the landlord having inadequate funding from the tenants until the annual service charge accounts are issued and the correspondingly high excess charges are collected. In many cases the tenants voluntarily pay a more realistic level of interim charge but that course of conduct will not entitle the landlord to sue for those higher sums unless the leases are properly varied to increase the amount of interim charge (*Fernandez v Shanterton Second Management Co Ltd*[2]).

Once an interim charge has been properly specified and demanded under the terms of the lease, it will be recoverable from the tenant, even if the preparation of the final service charge accounts of the actual expenditure is delayed, and it seems that a 'reasonable' estimate need not be based on past certified accounts.

EXAMPLE

> *Peachey Property Corporation Ltd v Henry*[3]: The lease provided for service charge accounts to be served by 6 April each year or as soon thereafter as

possible, and required the tenant to pay interim charges of 'whatever . . . the Lessor's managing agents shall certify as being a reasonable interim sum to be paid on account of the annual contribution'. The managing agents had certified a figure for interim payments in November 1959. Was that figure still binding on the tenant in 1963, the agents not having prepared any accounts in the meantime? **Held:** Yes.

1 (1986) 278 EG 53, CA.
2 (2006) LRX/153/2008, LT.
3 (1963) 188 EG 875, QBD.

Implied limits on interim contributions

1.71 So far, there has been no reported court decision indicating any common law implied term that, where the lease appears to give the landlord a discretion as to the amount he can charge on account of the service charge, such interim charges can only be demanded if they are of a reasonable amount, but a court decision to that effect might not be entirely unexpected having regard to the reasoning in *Finchbourne v Rodrigues*[1] (see **1.51**).

1 [1976] 3 All ER 581, CA.

Effect of non-payment on landlord's duties

1.72 Failure by a tenant to pay interim service charges will not normally absolve the landlord from his obligation to provide the services (see **1.53**).

Bank accounts

1.73 The RICS Professional Statement: Service Charges in Commercial Property imposes a mandatory requirement on chartered surveyors who manage commercial property for landlords to ensure that service charge monies (including reserve and sinking funds) are held in one or more discrete or virtual bank accounts separate from the landlord's or managing agent's other monies. This is plainly desirable in all cases (see **4.14**).

PREPARATION AND CERTIFICATION OF ACCOUNTS

Annual costs

1.74 As has been seen at **1.8** and **1.12**, the items which can be included in the total costs for service charge purposes are confined to those specified in the lease. Leases commonly provide for service charges to be calculated annually based on the relevant years' service costs. In such cases the landlord cannot compel the tenant to pay service charges on an ad hoc or different basis (*Leonora Investment Co v Mott Macdonald*[1]).

Similarly, under the provisions of many leases the landlord will not be entitled to demand balancing service charges (sometimes called 'excess' charges) until a valid service charge account or certificate has been issued in accordance with the terms of the lease (see **1.89**) but a delay in issuing the account or certificate will not ordinarily prevent the landlord for claiming and retaining interim charges on account (*Warrior Quay Management Company Ltd v Joachim*[2]).

Those service charge clauses which deal with the expenditure on an annual basis usually make it clear that the chargeable costs in any year are to be those costs expended or incurred during the accounting year in question. However, the wording of some service charge clauses has the effect that the cost of work contracted for by the landlord in one accounting year, but payable by him in a later accounting year, can only be included in the service charges for the period in which payment falls due (see the discussion on the meaning of 'expended' or 'incurred' at **1.16**).

Very often the lease will specify the start or end date of the accounting year but will give the landlord the right to change the dates. In the absence of any specific requirement in the lease, there may not be any need for the tenant to be notified about such a change within any particular timeframe. In *Wembley National Stadium Ltd v Wembley (London) Ltd*[3], the landlord's annual accounts for 2002 and 2003 were held to be valid even though the tenant was not notified about a change in the 2002 accounting date until the end of 2006.

Under many leases, the last accounting period falling within the term of the lease may continue to an accounting date falling after the expiry date of the lease. If the accounting period was treated under that lease as ending on the term expiry date, and other leases in the building were still continuing, the landlord would have to prepare separate service charge accounts for that particular tenant, by reference only to costs incurred up to that date, which would be very inconvenient. The preferred approach is not to treat the expiry of the lease as ending the accounting period. In some cases the lease might expressly provide that the service charge up to the expiry of the term is to be calculated by taking the full accounting years' service charge amount and apportioning it on a time basis up to the term expiry as if it had been incurred in equal daily mounts throughout the year; in the absence of an express provision to that effect, that basis of calculation may be implied (*Friends Life Management Services Ltd v A&A Express Building Ltd*[4]).

In reconciling the service charge with a particular tenant for the last accounting period in which the term expiry date of his lease falls, credit should normally be given to him for his past contributions towards any 'provision' made in a previous accounting period which has not already been applied towards the costs for which the provision was made (see *Friends Life Management Services Ltd v A&A Express Building Ltd*, above[5]).

1 [2008] EWCA Civ 857.
2 (2008) LRX/422006, LT.
3 [2007] EWHC 756 (Ch).
4 [2014] EWHC 1463 (Ch).
5 [2014] EWHC 1463 (Ch).

Apportionment of periodic costs

1.75 Some service charge clauses provide that expenditure which relates to a period which overlaps two accounting periods is to be apportioned between those periods, for example:

> 'including such reasonable part of all such expenses costs outgoings and expenditure as aforesaid which are of a periodically recurring nature (whether recurring by regular or irregular intervals) whenever disbursed incurred or made and whether prior to the commencement of the term hereof or otherwise . . . '

Such a provision would apply, for example, to annual maintenance contracts which run from a date during an accounting period; the maintenance fees payable under the contract must then be apportioned between the two accounting periods.

EXAMPLE

A lease contains a service charge clause with the above provision. The accounting period specified by the lease is from 1 January to 31 December in each year. On 1 October the landlord entered into a boiler maintenance contract for one year from that date, at a maintenance fee of £3,000 per annum. The service charge accounts for the year which includes that starting date should include the following proportion of that fee:

£3,000 x 92 days (1 Oct to 31 Dec) = £756.20

365 days

The accounts for the following accounting year would include the balance of £2,243.80, plus the duly apportioned part of the next maintenance fee, and so forth.

In *Barrington v Sloane Properties Ltd*[1], the Lands Tribunal upheld the landlord's accountant's broad method of apportioning building costs between accounting periods (by reference to the overall percentage over the whole contract and applying it pari passu to the amount certified under the contract by the year end) rather than attempting to ascertain when each item of work was done and how much it cost.

However, many managing agents take the view that this is an unnecessarily complicated approach to service charge costs and that it is simpler and equally appropriate to include the whole maintenance fee in the accounts of the year in which the fee is paid, since this is reasonable taking one year with another. They therefore prefer service charge clauses not to include any provision for apportioning periodic items across overlapping periods but to specify instead that the whole of any payment can be included in the accounts for the accounting year in which it is paid even if it relates to a service provided over a longer period. If that method of allocation is adopted without an express right to do so, it might be susceptible to challenge.

Another frequent provision is for the service costs to include provision for a reserve or sinking fund. This is discussed in detail in CHAPTER **4**.

1 [2007] LRX/31/2006.

Certificate and auditing or certification

1.76 As mentioned earlier, many modern forms of service charge clause require the landlord or his agent to prepare annual accounts of the service charge expenditure. The lease may require the accounts to be 'audited' or 'certified' by an accountant or surveyor, or simply be signed by the landlord, his agent, or his surveyor.

It is essential that the accounts should be prepared and certified strictly in accordance with the contractual provisions of the lease in order that any sums which become payable upon the issue of the accounts (such as excess service charges) will be legally recoverable from the tenants.

EXAMPLE

> *Barrington v Sloane Properties Ltd*[1]: Building works were carried out which spanned two or more service charge accounting periods specified in the lease. In relation to certain of the works, the landlord delivered a separate set of service charge accounts that did not correspond with the accounting periods mentioned in the lease. Were they valid? **Held:** No.

Also see *London Borough of Brent v Shulem B Association*[2], discussed at **2.67**.

It is usually desirable that the wording of the certificate follows the wording contained in the service charge clause referring to the certificate. Examples are given in **Appendix 1**. The RICS Professional Statement: Service Charges in Commercial Property (see **7.1**) at Appendix C4 also contains a specimen certificate.

Occasionally the category of person whom the lease requires to prepare or sign the certificate is no longer able to do so. This often arises where the lease was granted by a public body which has since sold its interest to a private sector landlord. In *St Modwen Developments (Edmonton) Ltd v Tesco Stores Ltd*[3], the lease of a unit in a shopping centre had been granted by the local council and required the annual service charge certificate to be certified by the Council's Borough Treasurer. His certificate was stated to be conclusive evidence of the matters it purports to certify. St Modwen became the landlord and their Finance Director certified the accounts, claiming to be the nearest equivalent person in the circumstances to the Borough Treasurer. The court held that the private sector landlord's finance director did not have a similar status of independence and reliability to that of a Borough Treasurer and that the mechanism in the lease for issuing service charge certificates had therefore ended. However those certification provisions in the lease were simply mechanics and the landlord was still entitled to claim service charges, but could not rely on issuing the certificates and might have to prove its calculations of the service charges if challenged.

The RICS Professional Statement: Service Charges in Commercial Property, at core principle 9, which is binding professionally on chartered surveyors who manage commercial property for landlords, states that those certifying service charge accounts should recognise that they have a duty of care to both landlords and occupiers to act with professional care, diligence, integrity and objectivity. It also provides in core principle 13 that, in addition to the manager's certificate, annual statements of service charge expenditure should be supported by an independent review of the service charge accounts in line with the ICAEW Technical Release Tech 09/14BL. The Statement gives detailed advice about reviewing and approving service charge accounts at paragraph 4.5.3.

As for auditing requirements in respect of residential service charges, see **2.54**.

1 [2007] LRX/31/2006, LT.
2 [2011] EWHC 1663 (Ch).
3 [2006] EWHC 3177 (Ch).

Time-limits

1.77 Most leases provide for the accounts or certificate to be issued 'as soon as practicable' (or similar) after the end of each accounting period. The RICS Professional Statement: Service Charges in Commercial Property (see **7.1**), in paragraph 5.12, states that this should be done within four months of the end of the accounting period in all cases of commercial lettings and the RICS Code of Practice: Service Charge Residential Management Code (see **2.92**) specifies six months for residential service charges. In any event, good practice dictates that it should be done as soon as possible following the end of the accounting period, and that budgets for the following accounting period should be prepared well before the current period ends.

Occasionally a specific time-limit is imposed by the lease itself. Time-limits laid down by a service charge clause for the preparation or service of the accounts or certificate will not normally be deemed to be 'of the essence' and, thus, delays by the landlord will not normally prevent him from eventually recovering the service charges from the tenants. It may be preferable from the landlord's viewpoint not to impose time limits for accounting when drafting service charge clauses.

EXAMPLES

West Central Investments Ltd v Borovik[1]: The lease required the landlord to have accounts prepared at the end of each accounting year and served on the tenant within two months. Accounts for 1970, 1971, 1972 and 1973 were not prepared until 1974. Was the landlord nevertheless entitled to the charges shown on them? **Held:** Yes; time was not of the essence under the two-month stipulation.

Warrior Quay Management Company Ltd v Joachim[2]: The lease required the provision of audited accounts but none had been provided for several years. Could the accounts be audited and delivered later? **Held:** Yes.

In the case of residential leases, the Landlord and Tenant Act 1987 imposes certain time-limits (see **2.48**).

1 (1977) 241 EG 609, QBD.
2 (2008) LRX/42/2006, LT.

Conclusiveness of the certificate

1.78 Leases often state that a certificate of the expenditure is binding and conclusive. In 1969, it was held that such a stipulation was invalid since it attempted to oust the jurisdiction of the court on a question of law, the question whether a particular item of expenditure fell within the service charge being a 'question of law' as it turned on the proper legal interpretation of the lease (*Re Davstone Estates Ltd's Leases*[1]). Some years later the Court of Appeal held that questions of law *can* validly be referred to the conclusive determination of an expert to whom a dispute is referred and will *not* be invalid as ousting the court's jurisdiction (*Jones v Sherwood Computer Services Ltd*[2]; followed in *Nikko Hotels (UK) Ltd v MEPC Ltd*[3]). The current position appears to be that the exact wording of the certification clause will determine whether, and to what extent, the expert's determination could be conclusive and unchallengeable, but even so it can generally only be conclusive if the expert has acted in accordance with his instructions (which by implication are to act in accordance with the terms of the lease) and there has been no fraud (*Mercury Communications Ltd v Director General of Telecommunications*[4]; *British Shipbuilders v VSEL Consortium plc*[5]; *National Grid Company Plc v M25 Group Ltd*[6]).

In *Barrington v Sloane Properties Ltd*[7], the lease stated that the service charge was to be certified by the landlord's accountant 'whose certificate in writing shall be conclusive'. The Lands Tribunal decided that certain years' service charge certificates were wrong since they included incorrect amounts. Because he had wrongly applied the provisions of the lease, the Tribunal held that the accountant had not acted in accordance with his implied instructions to follow the terms of the lease and, under the *National Grid* principle, his certificate was not conclusive (also see *Friends Life Management Services Ltd v A&A Express Building Ltd*[8]).

There have also been cases in which the courts have refused to recognise conclusive certification by anyone not wholly independent of the landlord.

EXAMPLE

> *Finchbourne v Rodrigues*[9]: The service charge was expressed to cover the costs incurred by the landlord in performing his services and the annual amount was to be ascertained and certified by the managing agents acting as experts. The 'managing agents' who issued the service charge certificate were, in reality, the same persons as the landlord. Was the certificate binding on the tenant? **Held:** No; the 'managing agents' were not independent agents as envisaged by the lease.

The safer view is, therefore, to assume that a certificate issued by anyone other than a wholly independent person cannot be conclusive. Furthermore, the possibility of the supporting invoices, etc, having to be produced to the tenant may need consideration (see **1.79**).

Where the lease does not state that a certificate is to be conclusive, the courts will not readily infer conclusive status for the certificate. If a certificate is not conclusive, either the landlord or the tenant can seek to have it reopened if there was a mistake in the calculation.

In those cases where the certificate is stated to be conclusive and the law recognises this (see earlier), the certificate will normally be binding on the landlord as well as on the tenant. If there has been a miscalculation which has resulted in under-recovery of the service costs, the landlord himself may wish to reopen the calculation. Whether he can do so will depend therefore upon the wording of the clause. Service charge clauses commonly provide that the certificate of total service costs is to be conclusive, but they do not usually provide that the statements showing the liability of individual tenants are also to be conclusive. If the miscalculation lies in those individual statements rather than in the certificate of total service costs, the landlord may be able to issue revised individual statements even if the costs certificate is conclusive, so long as the total service costs remain undisturbed.

EXAMPLE

> *Universities Superannuation Scheme v Marks & Spencer plc*[10]: The lease provided for the service costs to be certified and to be contributed between the tenants based on rateable values. After the certificate was issued and the contributions had been demanded from the tenants, the landlord realised that the apportionment had been miscalculated and had led to under-recovery of the service costs. The landlord sought to reopen the matter. **Held:** The service charge provisions had the clear purpose of reimbursing the landlord for all the service costs. The primary obligation on the tenant was to pay his proper share. The certification provisions did not state that the certificate was to be conclusive; furthermore, the certificate only covered the total costs and not the apportionments, which were in a separate statement. The landlord was entitled to reopen the apportionment and demand the balance from the tenant.

The RICS Professional Statement: Service Charges in Commercial Property (see **7.1**) notes that the law may give a tenant the right to challenge the propriety of expenditure and recommends provision for alternative dispute resolution (ADR).

The statutory provisions dealing with the certification of accounts in relation to residential flats are described in **2.54**.

As to recovery by a tenant of amounts overpaid, see **1.98**.

1 [1969] 2 Ch 378.
2 [1992] 1 WLR 277.
3 [1991] NPC 41, ChD.
4 [1996] 1 All ER 575.
5 [1997] 1 Lloyd's Rep 106.
6 [1998] EWCA Civ 1968.
7 [2007] LRX/31/2006.
8 [2014] EWHC 1463 (Ch).
9 [1976] 3 All ER 581, CA.
10 (1999) 04 EG 158, CA.

Tenant's inspection of invoices, etc

1.79 Some leases expressly give the tenant the right to inspect the service cost records, books, invoices and vouchers. Even if the lease does not give the tenant an express right of inspection, it is normally considered good management practice for the landlord or his agents to allow inspection in order to foster a good landlord and tenant relationship and to avoid distrust. This is specifically required in the case of commercial lettings by the RICS Professional Statement: Service Charges in Commercial Property (see **7.1**). It is only by 'transparent' management that the paying party can be convinced that the sums claimed are properly payable. Transparency is a core principle of the RICS Professional Statement: Service Charges in Commercial Property (see **7.1**).

In addition, in many cases the landlord would be obliged to produce these items on disclosure in the course of any legal proceedings for recovery of the service charge. An exception may be where the lease provides that the certified accounts will be conclusive as to the amount spent on individual items of cost – see **1.78**.

DETERMINATION OF DISPUTES

Express provisions in the lease

1.80 Some leases make express provision as to the means of determining disputes about the service charge. They may, for example, provide for the dispute to be referred to arbitration. The RICS Professional Statement: Service Charges in Commercial Property (see **7.1**) contains recommendations for alternative dispute resolution procedures in commercial lettings in paragraph 4.6.3.

For reasons explained in **Chapter 2**, it is no longer appropriate for residential leases to provide procedures for dispute resolution in relation to service charges since such provisions will be overridden by the jurisdiction of the Leasehold Valuation Tribunal under the Landlord and Tenant Act 1985 as amended.

If a commercial lease provides that a dispute over service charges is to be decided by the landlord's surveyor, the court will normally infer this to mean an *independent* surveyor who is not connected with the landlord or his managing agents, since the inference is drawn that the surveyor must be in a position to consider the dispute in a quasi-arbitral capacity and must, therefore, be sufficiently independent of the parties connected with the dispute.

EXAMPLE

> *Concorde Graphics Ltd v Andromeda Investments SA*[1]: The service charge clause provided that any 'difference' as to the service charge was to be settled by 'the landlord's surveyor', whose decision was to be final and binding. The tenant disputed the service charge. A firm of agents were both the managing agents and the landlord's surveyors. Was their certificate of the service charge final and binding? **Held**: No; the managing agents clearly cannot perform the duty of deciding the difference which has arisen – as managing agents they, on behalf of the landlord, had made the claim that the tenant disputed; the landlord must appoint other surveyors to determine the dispute.
>
> (See also *Finchbourne v Rodrigues*[2] at **1.78**.)

1 (1983) 265 EG 386, ChD.
2 [1976] 3 All ER 581, CA.

Where the lease is silent

1.81 If the terms of the lease do not specify any means of determining a dispute in relation to the service charge, there are three alternative procedures which might be adopted:

(1) the landlord and the tenant might agree in writing to refer the matter to the determination of a third party acting as either an expert or an arbitrator; or
(2) one party or the other might apply to the court for a declaration on the true interpretation of the lease or on the correctness of the service charge certificate and calculation; or
(3) the landlord might sue the tenant for payment of the service charge, with the tenant defending the action on the ground that the amount claimed is wrong.

In some cases, particularly where the wording of the lease is unclear or the proposed works are non-routine, it may be sensible for the landlord to apply to the court for a declaration as to whether proposed works can properly be carried out and be charged within the service charge. In such a case it may be that the costs of the court application can be included in the service charge if the service charge clause entitles the landlord to charge for the costs of management or to charge for costs which he reasonably incur in the discharge of his obligations (*Reston Ltd v Hudson*[1]).

Prior to embarking on these formal procedures, the parties should try to resolve their dispute by mediation if they both agree. This is likely to be the most cost-effective method of dispute resolution.

Where the landlord successfully sues a tenant for disputed service charges, the landlord can expect to be awarded his costs, but (at least if the dispute appears to be made in good faith) normally on the standard basis (under which less than the full costs are recovered) and not on an indemnity basis (see *Church Commissioners for England v Metroland Ltd*[2], where the tenant unsuccessfully argued against the landlord's interpretation of the lease and also unsuccessfully sought rectification of the lease).

The procedure for determining disputes under the statutory provisions applicable to residential flats is set out in **2.66**.

1 [1990] 2 EGLR 51.
2 [1996] EGCS 44, ChD.

ASSIGNMENT OF LEASE

Investigation prior to assignment of lease

1.82 Before a prospective assignee agrees to take an assignment of a lease under which a service charge is payable, he (or his solicitor or surveyor) should make enquiries on the following matters with the present tenant and, if possible, the landlord or managing agent:

(a) the level of service charges over the preceding three years, including the current estimated level;

(b) any likely increase in that level over the next few years;
(c) any major renewals, repairs or improvements likely to cause a severe increase in the service charge at a future time;
(d) the extent to which such future costs are covered by sinking or reserve funds;
(e) whether all service charges have been paid, in full, for past completed accounting years;
(f) whether there are or have been disputes concerning the service charges;
(g) whether there is likely to be a shortfall between the amounts paid on account and the final amounts due for the current or preceding accounting period.

Where such a shortfall will become payable on a date after the lease has been acquired, the new tenant will be liable to pay it (see **1.83** and **1.84**) and in such cases he should enter into a contractual arrangement with the assignor by which the assignor accepts liability for his due proportion of the shortfall, and in some cases it may be appropriate for his solicitors to make a retention from the sale proceeds of the lease as security.

Even truthful replies to the enquiries and investigations mentioned above will be no substitute for a proper survey of the building or estate, and enquiries of other existing tenants. It is surprising how many purchasers fail to investigate seriously or take professional advice as to what might be a substantial financial liability.

Effect of assignment of lease

1.83 Some, but not all, leases are registered at the Land Registry. Originally, only leases granted for terms of 21 years or more had to be registered. As a result of the Land Registration Act 2002, that period was reduced and applies both to the grant of new leases for terms of seven years or more and to assignments of leases having seven years or more unexpired.

If a lease is not registered at the Land Registry and does not need to be registered under the provisions mentioned above, it becomes vested in the assignee immediately on the completion of a deed of assignment. Consequently, once the landlord or managing agent becomes aware of an assignment having taken place, all notices under the lease and all demands for sums thereafter becoming due should be addressed to the assignee.

However, in the case of a lease which is already registered, or is required to be registered, at the Land Registry, the lease does not vest in the assignee until the assignment deed (in this case, called a 'transfer') has been registered at the Land Registry. During the gap between the completion of the transfer deed and its registration, the lease remains vested in the assigning tenant although the assignee owns it beneficially (or 'in equity' as the law puts it). Accordingly, during that period, notices and demands from the landlord should be served on both the assigning tenant and the assignee. Where the landlord serves a notice to forfeit under s 146 of the Law of Property Act 1925 in that situation, the assignee will be entitled to the usual rights to seek relief from forfeiture (*Brown & Root Technology Ltd v Sun Alliance & London Assurance Co Ltd*[1]; *High Street Investments v Bellshore Property Investments*[2]).

Once the assignment or transfer takes effect under the above rules, the assignee becomes liable, at common law and (in respect of leases which are not 'new tenancies' – mentioned below) by the Law of Property Act 1925, from that date onwards to pay the rents reserved by the lease and to perform all those covenants in the lease which 'touch and concern the land'. These covenants are usually taken to include all obligations relating to the state of the property, including covenants to pay service charges. However, it is generally considered that this is confined to covenants between the tenant and the actual landlord, so that a third party (such as a separate management company) cannot hold an assignee liable on covenants made by the tenant with the third party unless the assignee delivers to the third party a deed in which he covenants to observe those covenanted obligations (or, where a licence to assign is needed, includes such a direct covenant in the licence deed).

The Landlord and Tenant (Covenants) Act 1995 ('LT(C)A 1995') introduced new, rather clearer, provisions on this subject in respect of 'new tenancies'. These are leases granted on or after 1 January 1996, but excluding those granted pursuant to legally binding agreements for lease, options, pre-emption agreements or court orders made before that date (LT(C)A 1995, s 1(3), (6), (7)). When a 'new tenancy' is assigned, s 3 of the LT(C)A 1995 provides that the assignee becomes liable, as from the assignment, to comply with all the tenant's subsisting obligations other than any of a purely personal nature. This covers obligations not only towards the landlord but also to a third party such as a separate management company (LT(C)A 1995, s 12).

An assignment or transfer of a lease is valid to vest the lease in the assignee, even if the lease stipulates that the landlord's consent was required for an assignment and that consent was not obtained.

EXAMPLE

> *Old Grovebury Manor Farm Ltd v Seymour Plant Sales*[3]: The original tenant assigned his lease in breach of his covenant not to assign it without the landlord's consent. The landlord served a forfeiture notice under s 146 of the Law of Property Act 1925 on the original tenant. Was it a valid notice? Held: No; the unauthorised assignment was effective to vest the lease in the assignee, who was now the tenant, so the notice should have been served on the assignee.

If the assignment took place without the consent of the landlord where required by the lease, the landlord may wish to consider seeking forfeiture of the lease, in which event nothing should be done which is consistent with the lease still continuing (eg registering the notice of assignment, or demanding or accepting rent or service charges).

The provisions of the Law of Property Act 1925, s 196 apply to notices 'required to be served' by any instrument affecting property, unless the instrument evinces a contrary intention and s 196 will, therefore, normally apply to any notice which a lease requires the landlord to serve on the tenant. Furthermore, the provisions probably also apply to notices which the lease merely empowers, but does not 'require', the landlord to serve (in *Holwell Securities Ltd v Hughes*[4], it was held that a notice exercising an option fell within s 196, which is plainly a notice which the grantee need not serve if he does not want to, but is required to serve if he wants to exercise the option).

Where s 196 applies, notices can be addressed to the tenant merely as 'the Lessee' of the premises concerned, without his name (see s 196(2)), and this is useful where the landlord is uncertain of the assignee's correct name.

1 [1997] 18 EG 123, CA.
2 [1996] 35 EG 87, CA.
3 (1979) 252 EG 1103, CA.
4 [1974] 1 All ER 161, CA.

Is assignee liable for arrears of service charge?

1.84 In the absence of any specific provision in the lease (or in any licence for assignment or deed of covenant) is an assignee of the lease liable for unpaid service charges which became due and payable before the date of the assignment to him?

If the service charge is reserved as rent (usually as an additional rent to the basic rent for the premises) the answer (where the lease which was assigned is not a 'new tenancy', see **1.83**) is that the assignee is not liable for sums payable in respect of a period falling prior to the date of assignment, because rent is to be treated as accruing from day to day under the provisions of the Apportionment Act 1870 (*Parry v Robinson Wylie Ltd*[1], in which an assignee was held not to be liable for a backlog of increased rent following a review where the review date preceded the assignment).

Where, instead of reserving the service charge as rent, there is simply a tenant's covenant to pay the service charge, the answer is similar: the assignee is not liable for sums which became payable on a date prior to the assignment. This is because under the common law an assignee is liable only for his own breaches of covenant and will not be liable for a predecessor's breaches unless they are 'continuing' breaches of covenant (such as a failure to repair the premises). Thus, the assignee will be free from liability for his predecessor's 'once-and-for-all' breaches, and it seems that failure to pay a sum of money (rent or service charge) on the date it becomes due is a 'once-and-for-all' breach (*London and County (A & D) Ltd v Wilfred Sportsman Ltd*[2]; *Re National Jazz Centre Ltd*[3]). The person who was the tenant when the sum fell due remains liable to the landlord to pay it and can be sued for payment, but the assignee cannot be sued unless he gave the landlord a direct covenant to pay future *and past* rents and service charges, which is unusual.

This, seemingly, does not preclude the landlord from seeking to forfeit the lease for non-payment of service charge, even after the defaulting tenant has assigned the lease. A threat of forfeiture might encourage the assignee to pay the arrears.

Where the assigned lease is a 'new tenancy' (see **1.83**), the Landlord and Tenant (Covenants) Act 1995 provides that the assignee is not liable for defaults occurring before the assignment to him (LT(C)A 1995, s 23(1)).

A distinction must be drawn between the date on which service charges become due for payment and the period to which they relate. The above rules concern service charge payments which fell due when the lease was still vested in the previous tenant and had not yet been assigned to the assignee. Where a lease provides for a service charge shortfall (sometimes called an excess service charge) to be paid following the issue of a certificate or account, the above rules apply to such a payment by reference to the date when it is payable, whether or not it relates to an earlier period. Thus in cases where the lease is assigned after the end of an accounting period but before the issue of the certificate or account, the landlord can hold the assignee liable to pay the shortfall shown on the certificate or account, since that amount will fall due for payment on a date when the lease has already been assigned to the assignee. The ability of the assignee to recover all or part of that shortfall from the assignor will depend upon any contractual arrangements made between them (see **1.82**).

It must also be noted that the right to forfeit a lease on the grounds of a once-and-for-all breach (as distinct from a continuing breach) can be lost or 'waived' by the landlord or his agent, after becoming aware of the breach, doing any act which indicates that the landlord is treating the lease as still subsisting (such as giving a licence to assign, registering a notice of assignment from the assignee, or demanding further rent or service charges). Thus, if the landlord wishes to bring forfeiture proceedings against the assignee, perhaps to pressurise him into paying the arrears, no act of waiver should be carried out before the claim of forfeiture is issued and served.

Where the lease requires the landlord's consent to be obtained for assignments, the landlord should consider withholding consent if there are substantial arrears of rent or service charges. However, the question of the reasonableness of withholding consent is a complicated topic outside the scope of this book (particularly with regard to the risk of the landlord being liable in damages under the Landlord and Tenant Act 1988 for delaying or refusing consent without good reason). Where consent for assignment is not required, the landlord might refuse to register notices of assignment until arrears are paid off. Whatever the legality of this device, it is often successful in practice.

1 (1987) 54 P&CR 187.
2 [1970] 2 All ER 600, CA.
3 [1988] 38 EG 142.

CHANGES OF LANDLORD

Landlord's obligations

1.85 On a transfer of the landlord's interest in a property, the new landlord becomes liable to perform all those landlord's covenants in leases granted before 1 January 1996 which 'run with the land' (Law of Property Act 1925, s 142). This will normally include the covenant to provide the landlord's services. Similarly, in respect of the landlord's obligations under 'new tenancies' (see **1.83**), all those obligations become binding on the new landlord as from the transfer to him of the landlord's interest, except any landlord's obligations of a purely personal nature (LT(C)A 1995, s 3).

The previous landlord is not by implication released from his covenants in the lease, and if he is the original landlord named in the lease he may have continuing liability. In that case, so long as he remains liable on the landlord's covenants to provide the services, he continues to have the benefit of the tenant's covenant to pay the service charges (see LT(C)A 1995, s 6(2) and *Wembley National Stadium Ltd v Wembley (London) Ltd*[1]).

Where the change of landlord results from the landlord granting an overriding lease, particular issues can arise in relation to service charges (see **1.11**).

1 [2007] EWHC 756 (Ch).

Benefit of tenant's obligations

1.86 The new landlord also becomes entitled to enforce the tenants' obligations under the leases. In relation to tenancies which are not 'new tenancies' under the LT(C)A 1995, this includes the right to sue tenants for arrears of rent or service charges which fell due before he became their landlord (*London and County (A & D) Ltd v Wilfred Sportsman Ltd*[1]) (see **1.84**). In relation to tenancies which are 'new tenancies' under the LT(C)A 1995, the new landlord's rights against the tenant are confined to matters arising (or, in the case of continuing breaches, continuing) after he has acquired the reversion to the lease, unless rights in relation to prior defaults are assigned to him by the old landlord (LT(C)A 1995, s 23(1), (2)), although this would not prevent the new landlord from forfeiting the lease on the ground of past arrears of service charge (LT(C)A 1995, s 23(3)).

A new landlord should, therefore, ensure that he (and any new managing agent he may appoint) takes over all records, contracts and other papers relating to the management of the building and the service charge functions, and takes control of any unexpended service charge funds, including reserve or sinking funds. Where the new landlord will be dealing with the collection of service charges which include costs expended before he became the landlord, he should ensure that the contract under which he is buying the building entitles him to call upon the old landlord to comply with all relevant terms of the leases and all statutory requirements. These may include the supply of summaries of the costs, the provision of proper annual accounts and certificates, and the right of tenants to inspect invoices and other records.

As mentioned at **1.85**, the previous landlord may still have the benefit of the tenant's covenant to pay the service charges if he remains liable under the landlord's covenants in the lease (see LT(C)A 1995, s 6(2) and *Wembley National Stadium Ltd v Wembley (London) Ltd*[2]). The new landlord may want to provide in his purchase contract that after completion of the sale the old landlord will not enforce the tenant's covenants in the leases without the new landlord's consent.

1 [1970] 2 All ER 600, CA.
2 [2007] EWHC 756 (Ch).

Notice to tenants of change of landlord

1.87 When there is a change of landlord, each tenant should be notified in writing immediately. This is compulsory in the case of residential property (Landlord and Tenant Act 1985, s 3) and is desirable for every type of property to avoid tenants continuing to pay rent or service charges to the old landlord, which they are entitled to do until they receive the notice (Law of Property Act 1925, s 151).

Handover on change of landlord

1.88 The RICS Professional Statement: Service Charges in Commercial Property contains, in paragraph 4.5.8, detailed provisions to be observed by chartered surveyors when there is a change of landlord, concerning the handover of the service charge management and funds. It recommends that these are reflected by solicitors when drafting contracts for the sale of the landlord's interest in the building.

RECOVERY OF ARREARS AND OTHER REMEDIES

Preconditions for claiming arrears

1.89 The service charge will fall contractually due only once all procedures laid down by the lease for fixing and demanding the service charge have been followed, including the observance of any procedure laid down for determining any dispute, should there be one.

EXAMPLES

Concorde Graphics Ltd v Andromeda Investments SA[1]: The service charge clause provided that any difference as to the service charge was to be settled by the landlord's surveyor, whose decision was to be final and binding. The landlord obtained payment of a disputed service charge demand by threatening distress. Was this lawful? **Held:** No; the dispute procedure laid down in the lease had to be observed before any enforcement could take place.

Canary Riverside PTE v Schilling[2]: The lease required the landlord to give the tenant written notice of any revised estimate of the annual service costs where it exceeded the previously notified estimate. The landlord incurred some significant unanticipated expenses but failed to give the tenant a revised estimate and simply demanded increased service charge payments. **Held:** The landlord had failed to comply with the procedure required to make such additional service charge payable, so the landlord was not entitled to recover the increased amount in the year in question.

Warrior Quay Management Company Ltd v Joachim[3]: The lease required the provision of audited accounts and provided that the tenant would then be liable to pay any balancing charge. No audited accounts had been provided. Could the tenants be sued for balancing charges? **Held:** No, not until audited accounts had been delivered.

Accordingly, no action should be brought for recovery of alleged arrears of service charge unless all accounts and certificates specified in the lease have been properly prepared and delivered to the tenant and, if the lease specifies that a dispute must be settled by a particular procedure (eg by an independent surveyor) and there is a dispute on the matter, the specified procedure must be followed.

As for arrears of service charge which became payable on a date prior to a change of tenant upon an assignment of the lease, see **1.82**.

As for arrears due when the tenant or occupier is a foreign state or foreign diplomat, see **1.99**.

1 (1983) 265 EG 386, ChD.
2 [2005] EW Lands LRX/65/2005.
3 (2008) LRX/42/2006, LT.

Set-off of damages for breaches of landlord's covenants

1.90 Where the landlord has been in breach of covenant and the tenant claims damages, the tenant can (subject to one proviso) set off that claim against the sums payable to the landlord under the lease, even if the damages claim is unliquidated (ie the monetary amount is not ascertained) at the time the sums fall payable (*British Anzani (Felixstowe) Ltd v International Marine Management (UK) Ltd*[1]; *Melville v Grapelodge Developments Ltd*[2]; *Lee-Parker v Izzet*[3]). Therefore, in proceedings by the landlord for recovery of service charges, the tenant may be entitled to claim set-off for any damages to which he may be entitled due to breach of covenant by the landlord. An example might be where the tenant claims that the service costs have been increased due to the landlord's failure to carry out necessary repairs at the appropriate time (see **1.29**).

However, the court has a discretion whether or not to allow such 'equitable' set-off, and may not allow the tenant to exercise the right if the tenant's conduct would make it unfair to do so (*Bluestorm Ltd v Portvale Holdings Ltd*[4]).

The tenant generally does not have a right of set-off where the lease expressly prohibits any set-off from the service charge. It was previously questioned whether a provision excluding set-off is effective to prevent set-off being claimed in the course of legal proceedings, since set-off is governed by the rules of the court. However, there has since been a line of cases in which the validity of a prohibition on set-off has been accepted (see *Hong Kong & Shanghai Banking Corp v Kloeckner & Co AG*[5]; *Stewart Gill Ltd v Horatio Myer & Co Ltd*[6]; *Coca-Cola Financial Corporation v Finsat International Ltd*[7]). The prohibition in the lease must expressly refer to 'set-off'; a requirement to pay without 'any deduction' is not to be construed as prohibiting set-off (*Connaught Restaurants Ltd v Indoor Leisure Ltd*[8]; *Edlington Properties Ltd v J H Fenner & Co Ltd*[9]).

Statute law may, in some cases, invalidate a prohibition against set-off. Where a party to an agreement contracts as a consumer on the other's written standard terms of business, consumer protection legislation may operate, see **1.52**.

1 [1979] 2 All ER 1063.
2 (1979) 254 EG 1193.
3 [1971] 1 WLR 1688.
4 [2004] EWCA Civ 289.
5 [1990] 2 QB 514.
6 [1992] 2 All ER 257.
7 [1996] 3 WLR 849.

8 [1993] 2 EGLR 108, CA

9 [2006] EWCA Civ 403.

Claiming interest for late payment

1.91 Leases often make express provision for the tenant to pay interest on rent and (sometimes) on other sums which are not paid within a certain time after their due date. In the event of non-payment of service charges by the tenant, the lease should be checked to see whether the tenant is contractually obliged to pay interest and, if so, for what period and at what rate.

If the lease does not expressly provide for interest to be paid on arrears, there will be no contractual obligation on the tenant to pay interest. However, if the landlord commences court proceedings against the tenant for recovery of the arrears, interest can be included in those proceedings by virtue of s 35A of the Senior Courts Act 1981 in relation to High Court proceedings and by virtue of s 69 of the County Courts Act 1984 in relation to actions in the county court. Although interest under s 35A is at the discretion of the court, it is a discretion which must be exercised judicially (*Allied London Investments Ltd v Hambro Life Assurance*[1]).

1 (1985) 274 EG 148.

Recovery as if rent

1.92 If the service charges are reserved in the lease by way of additional rent, or if the lease provides that arrears of service charge are recoverable as if they were rent, the type of proceedings which can be brought for recovery of arrears include those designed for the recovery of arrears of rent (see *Escalus Properties Ltd v Robinson and Others*[1]).

That previously meant that the ancient remedy of distress was available, although that remedy was abolished with effect from 6 April 2014 by the Tribunals, Court and Enforcement Act 2007, s 71.

Such a provision in the lease is equally capable of being invoked by the tenant as the landlord; thus in the *Escalus* case it resulted in the tenant's mortgagees being entitled to automatic relief from forfeiture (which is applicable to arrears of rent) on tendering the arrears of service charge.

Where the tenant is bankrupt, insolvent, in liquidation or in administration, the various statutory regimes which apply in those circumstances may restrict the rights of landlords to enforce their usual remedies for non-payment of service charges and for other breaches by the tenant of the provisions of the lease. More detail on that subject is outside the scope of this book.

No sum can be recovered unless it is due and payable under the terms of the lease.

EXAMPLE

D'Jan v Bond Street Estates plc[2]: Although the lease provided for regular, quarterly advance payments of the estimated service charge, recoverable as if rent, the landlord had a practice of demanding, at the end of each quarter, a payment in arrear based on his actual expenditure. The tenant stopped a cheque which he had given the landlord under this procedure, since he was dissatisfied with the work done. Could the landlord claim the amount involved (and use the then-available remedy of distraint)? **Held:** No; in the absence of any specific agreement substituting the adopted procedure in place of the procedure laid down in the lease, the landlord cannot claim sums other than when they are payable under the terms of the lease.

1 [1995] 4 All ER 852, CA.
2 [1993] EGCS 43, CA.

Forfeiture

1.93 If the landlord wishes to seek forfeiture on the ground of non-payment of service charges, he must first serve on the tenant a notice, under s 146 of the Law of Property Act 1925, specifying the default and requiring the tenant to pay within a reasonable time. The reasonable time (which need not be specified in the notice) need not be very long; 14 days will probably suffice. However, if the service charge is reserved as additional rent, there will be no need to serve as 146 notice, since forfeiture for non-payment of rent is excluded from s 146 (s 146(11)).

If no notice under s 146 is required, or if the requisite notice has been served and payment has not been received within a reasonable time from service of the notice, the landlord will be entitled to proceed to seek forfeiture of the lease.

Since non-payment of a sum when it falls due is a once-and-for-all breach of covenant (see **1.84**), the right to forfeit must be preserved by avoiding acts of waiver.

If the tenant seeks relief from forfeiture under s 146, the landlord may be able to persuade the court to impose serious terms designed to ensure that the arrears of service charge are paid speedily; in some cases, even more onerous terms may be imposed (see *Khar v Delbounty*[1]).

Where the tenant is bankrupt, insolvent, in liquidation or in administration, the various statutory regimes which apply in those circumstances may restrict the rights of landlords to enforce their usual remedies for non-payment of service charges and for other breaches by the tenant of the provisions of the lease. More detail on that subject is outside the scope of this book.

As to the special rules relating to the forfeiture of residential leases, see **2.71**.

1 [1996] NPC 163, CA.

Withholding of services

1.94 The question whether a landlord can withhold services from a tenant who has failed to pay his service charges is considered at **1.53**.

Costs of the proceedings

1.95 If the landlord obtains judgment against the tenant for arrears of service charge, he will normally be awarded his costs of the proceedings. The basis of awarded costs is at the discretion of the court but, usually, costs are awarded on the 'standard' basis of 'a reasonable amount in respect of all costs reasonably incurred', with any doubts being resolved in the payer's favour, and the costs being 'taxed' by the court, if they have not been agreed between the parties.

However, costs can be awarded on an 'indemnity' basis where it appears to the court to be appropriate and, on that basis, all costs are allowed, except insofar as they are of an unreasonable amount or have been unreasonably incurred, with any doubt being resolved in favour of the receiving party. Where the lease expressly provides for costs to be recovered on a full indemnity basis the court will give weight to this, although it is not conclusive, and it does not avoid the power of the court to assess costs (*Bank of Baroda v Panessar*[1]; *Gomba Holdings (UK) Ltd v Minories Finance Ltd (No 2)*[2]; *Church Commissioners for England v Ibrahim*[3]).

The wording of the lease as to indemnity costs must be clear and unambiguous on this. In *Primeridge Ltd v Jean Muir Ltd*[4], a clause entitling the landlord to 'all proper costs' when recovering arrears was held not to mean a full indemnity for costs, contrasting with the entitlement to 'all costs, charges and expenses which you may incur' in the *Baroda* case, which was interpreted as a full indemnity. The phrase 'indemnity basis' is not essential to achieve this; the expression 'all expenses incurred by the lessor' may have the same effect (see *Fairview Investments Ltd v Sharma*[5]).

1 [1986] 3 All ER 751.
2 [1993] Ch 171, CA.
3 [1997] 03 EG 136, CA.
4 [1992] 1 EGLR 273.
5 (1999) 14 October (unreported), CA.

Liability of previous lessees

1.96 A lease is a contract between the landlord and the tenant. One result of this is that, in respect of leases other than 'new tenancies' (see **1.83**), the original tenant (and any guarantor for him) remains bound by the obligations under the lease, including the obligation to pay service charges, throughout the entire term of the lease, notwithstanding that he may have assigned the lease. Consequently, the original tenant (and any guarantors) can usually be sued for service charges payable under the lease arising at any time during the contractual term of the lease. In such cases a notice claiming arrears from that original tenant or guarantor must be given in a prescribed form and within a strict time limit from the due date (see **1.97**).

Where the lease has changed hands a number of times, it may also be possible to sue the intervening assignees if they gave the landlord direct covenants that they would pay the rents and service charges throughout the residue of the term of the lease (see *Royton Industries Ltd v Lawrence*[1]). Such direct covenants may be contained in a licence for assignment (where the landlord's licence for assigning is required) or in a separate deed of covenant. Again, in such cases a notice claiming arrears from such persons must be given in a prescribed form and within a strict time limit (see **1.97**).

However, in respect of leases which are 'new tenancies' under the Landlord and Tenant (Covenants) Act 1995 (see **1.83**), a previous tenant will not have continuing liability for defaults occurring after he lawfully assigned the lease (LT(C)A 1995, s 5) and the same applies to a guarantor for that tenant (LT(C)A 1995, s 24), but they remain liable for defaults occurring prior to the assignment (LT(C)A 1995, s 24(1)). Further, the assignee might be required to give the landlord an authorised guarantee agreement under the LT(C)A 1995, s 16, in cases where the landlord's consent for the assignment is required. Under an authorised guarantee agreement, the assignor agrees to be a guarantor for the assignee's liabilities under the lease, up to the time of the next lawful assignment.

In respect of business premises which an assignee, under the provisions of Pt II of the Landlord and Tenant Act 1954, continues to occupy beyond the expiry of the term of the lease, original and intervening tenants who are liable under the above rules will not normally be liable for service charges in respect of a period after the term expiry date, since the Act operates by continuing the 'tenancy' between the then tenant and the then landlord, rather than by extending the contractual term. However, they might be liable if the lease expressly provides for this, eg where the 'term' is defined in the lease as including any period of statutory continuation.

EXAMPLES

Thames Manufacturing Co v Perrotts (Nichol & Peyton) Ltd and Others[2]: Perrotts were the original tenants under a 1972 lease, and the second, third and fourth defendants were the sureties for them. The lease was assigned, with the landlord's consent, in January 1980 to the fifth defendant, who lost the protection of the Landlord and Tenant Act 1954 but failed to vacate when the lease expired in June 1980 and failed to remedy dilapidations. Were Perrotts and their sureties liable to the landlord for damages for disrepair? **Held:** Yes; as original tenant and sureties their liability continued, even in respect of a period in which, having assigned the lease, they were not in a position to perform the repairs.

City of London Corporation v Fell[3]: In 1979 the original tenant assigned his lease to a company. The company held over, under Part II of the Landlord and Tenant Act 1954 after the expiry of the lease in 1986, but then went into liquidation and did not pay rent for that period. The lease did not refer to a holding-over period in the definition of the term. Was the original tenant liable? **Held:** No.

Herbert Duncan Ltd v Cluttons[4]: The original tenant assigned his lease to an assignee. The lease included a covenant for payment of rent throughout the term, which was defined as including any period of continuation under the Landlord and Tenant Act 1954. The assignee held over, under the Landlord and Tenant Act 1954, after the expiry of the lease in 1990. The landlord obtained a consent order for interim rent for that period, but the assignee did not pay it. Was the original tenant liable? **Held:** Yes (but only for rent at the level last payable contractually under the lease, and not for the additional amount bringing it to the level of the interim rent, since that extra amount was payable by reason of the Act rather than by reason of the lease).

1 [1994] 1 EGLR 110.
2 (1984) 271 EG 284, ChD.
3 [1993] 2 EGLR 131, HL.
4 [1993] 1 EGLR 93, CA.

Notice of claim for arrears

1.97 If the landlord wishes to claim payment of service charges from a former tenant or former guarantor who has continuing liability (see **1.96**), he must serve on that person a notice in a prescribed form (Form 1) within 6 months of the sum in question first becoming due under the lease (Landlord and Tenant (Covenants) Act 1995, s 17). Service of the notice is a precondition for liability. If the notice is not served within the six-month period, the former tenant or guarantor will not be liable for that particular payment. A specimen of the prescribed form appears in **Appendix 1**.

The operation of s 17 of the LT(C)A 1995 was considered in *Scottish & Newcastle plc v Raguz*[1] which concerned recovery from a former tenant of a backlog of increased rent following a late rent review. The court held that, under s 17, where the sum due is a payment on account of a final amount which is not yet ascertained, as in the case of payments on account of an unascertained increased rent, a notice in Form 1, including the prescribed statement (in paragraph 4 of Form 1) that the amount due may subsequently be increased, must be served on the former tenant (or guarantor) in relation to each interim payment within six months of the interim payment becoming due, and a further notice (in Form 2) claiming any balance must be served on him, claiming payment of the balance, within three months of the ascertainment of the final amount. The court held that the balance could not be recovered from the former tenant (using a Form 2 claim) unless a Form 1 notice had been served on him in respect of the interim payment, even if the interim payment has been made by the current tenant. These principles, if correct, will probably apply equally to interim service charges and balancing charges. It is understood that the *Raguz* case is to be appealed, arguing for an alternative interpretation of s 17 of the LT(C)A 1995, and a more realistic procedure may emerge from the outcome of that appeal.

If a former tenant or guarantor pays arrears in response to a statutory notice, he may be entitled to require the landlord to grant him an overriding lease under s 19 of the LT(C)A 1995.

1 [2006] EWHC 821, ChD.

RECOVERY OF OVERPAYMENTS

1.98 It used to be that where an overpayment was made due to a mistake by the paying party as to the correct amount legally due from him, he could not recover the overpaid amount for the payee (see, eg, the *Concorde Graphics* *case* (1983) 265 EG 386) at **1.89**) because of an ancient rule that payments made under a mistake of law were not recoverable.

However, the House of Lords decided in 1998 that this rule was no longer good law (*Kleinwort Benson v Lincoln City Council*[1]). This change in the law has enabled tenants to reclaim excess rent that they paid to the landlord by mistake (eg *Nurdin & Peacock plc v DB Ramsden & Co (No 2)*[2]) and the same will presumably apply to the recovery of an overpayment of service charge if it is found that a lesser sum should have been paid. Exactly what limitation rules will apply to claims relating to payments made several years earlier has yet to be determined.

1 [1998] 4 All ER 513, HL.
2 (1999) 09 EG 175.

DIPLOMATIC AND STATE IMMUNITY

State immunity

1.99 A tenant which is a foreign state will enjoy certain immunity from legal proceedings in the UK courts, under the State Immunity Act 1978 (SIA 1978), although the immunity can be waived (see **1.100**). The immunity is subject to a number of exceptions set out in the SIA 1978 which (amongst other things) allow proceedings to be brought against the relevant state relating to its interest, possession or use of immoveable property in the UK or relating to its obligations arising out of such interest, possession or use (s 6(1)). However, this exception does not allow a UK court to issue injunctions, orders for specific performance or orders for recovery of possession against a foreign state in relation to land or other property, unless the state has expressly agreed to submit to those remedies (s 13(2)). Accordingly, these provisions normally allow a landlord to enforce covenants in leases only by claiming damages for breach.

An alternative basis under which a landlord could seek exception from the tenant's state immunity might be under s 3 of the SIA 1978, which allows proceedings to be brought against a foreign state for breaches of contract where the broken obligation was to be performed wholly or partly in the UK. Since a lease is a form of contract, s 3 appears (like s 6) to allow landlords to bring actions for breach of covenant under a lease, although the courts have indicated, without deciding the point, that it may be more appropriate to use the exception under s 6(1) mentioned above in such cases (per May LJ in Intpro Properties *(UK) Ltd v Sauvel*[1]).

The exceptions to immunity in ss 3 and 6 of the SIA 1978do not allow a landlord to seek possession of premises if they are being used for the purpose of a diplomatic mission (SIA 1978, s 16(1)(b); *Intpro Properties (UK) Ltd v Sauvel* (above)[2]; Diplomatic Privileges Act 1964, Sch 1, Art 22; *Westminster City Council v Government of the Islamic Republic of Iran*[3]). As for the special protection enjoyed by such premises, see **1.102**.

1 [1983] 2 All ER 495, CA.
2 [1983] 2 All ER 495, CA.
3 [1986] 3 All ER 284, ChD.

Waiver of state immunity

1.100 State immunity from court proceedings will not apply if the state has agreed in writing to submit to the jurisdiction of the UK courts (SIA 1978, s 2(1)). However, simply agreeing to submit to that jurisdiction is not sufficient to allow a UK court to issue injunctions, orders for specific performance or orders for recovery of possession against the foreign state in relation to land or other property, unless the state has expressly agreed to submit to those remedies (SIA 1978, s 13(2)).

Diplomats

1.101 A tenant who is a foreign diplomatic officer will enjoy personal immunity from civil proceedings in the UK courts under Art 31 of Sch 1 to the Diplomatic Privileges Act 1964 (DPA 1964). This immunity is also given to members of his family forming part of his household, unless they are UK citizens (Art 37). Again there are exceptions to immunity set out in that Act, but the exceptions are more limited than in the case of state immunity. The relevant exceptions will allow a landlord to bring 'a real action relating to private immoveable property' (but not property held for use as a diplomatic mission for the foreign state – see below) and 'an action relating to a professional or commercial activity exercised by the diplomatic agent in the . . . [UK] . . . outside his official functions'. These would presumably allow a landlord, for example, to bring proceedings against a foreign diplomat in respect of a lease of premises which the diplomat used for the purpose of a business outside the scope of his diplomatic functions.

As for immunity in relation to leases of residential premises occupied by diplomats, see **2.93**.

Premises used as a mission

1.102 Where the premises, whoever is the tenant, are used as a professional mission for the purposes of the foreign state, further special rules apply. The premises are inviolable; officers of the UK government must not enter them; the UK government is under a duty to take all appropriate steps to protect the premises against any intrusion; and the premises are immune from search, requisition, attachment or execution (DPA 1964, Sch 1, Art 22; *Westminster City Council v Government of the Islamic Republic of Iran*[1]). This prevents the landlord from entering the premises or seeking forfeiture of the lease.

1 [1986] 3 All ER 284, ChD.

Waiver of diplomatic immunity

1.103 As in the case of state immunity, both a diplomat's personal immunity and the immunity of a mission can be waived. The waiver must be by the foreign state (DPA 1964, Sch 1, Art 32, para 1) or by the head of the mission (DPA 1964, s 2(3)). Merely submitting to the jurisdiction of the English courts is not sufficient to allow the execution of a judgment obtained under that jurisdiction; unless execution is also expressly mentioned in the waiver, there will be immunity from execution of a judgment even if the court has jurisdiction to issue the judgment itself (DPA 1964, Sch 1, Art 34, para 4).

Chapter 2

SPECIAL RULES FOR RESIDENTIAL LETTINGS

OVERVIEW AND APPLICATION OF THE LANDLORD AND TENANT ACT 1985

Overview

2.1 The Landlord and Tenant Act 1985 (as amended by certain subsequent Acts) sets out a statutory code for service charges and related matters in respect of residential dwellings. Its most important features are:

(a) service costs can only be recovered if they are reasonably incurred;
(b) only works or services performed to a reasonable standard can be charged;
(c) prior consultation is required in respect of certain costs; and
(d) tenants must be given written warnings in respect of any costs which will be included in a demand which will be served on them more than 18 months after the costs are incurred.

The legislation operates by adding a layer of conditions and requirements to those which are contained in the lease. Accordingly, when assessing the liability to service charges of the tenant of a residential property, one starts by determining the contractual scope of the service charge (see **Chapter 1**) and then one applies the statutory provisions. In general terms, the statutory code applies (subject to the exemptions set out in **2.3**) to cost-related, variable service charges levied by a landlord or management company in respect of residential dwellings. It does not apply to fixed (static or index-linked) service charges or to premises occupied wholly or mainly for business purposes.

The main changes to the original provisions of the LTA 1985 were affected by the Housing Act 1996 and the Commonhold and Leasehold Reform Act 2002. Extracts from the legislation appear in **Appendix 2**. Where dates of coming into force are given these generally apply to property in England. Different dates usually apply in Wales because that requires an order of the National Assembly for Wales.

In addition to this legislation, which specifically relates to service charges, the provisions of certain general consumer protection legislation may apply, as discussed at **1.52**.

2.1 *Special Rules for Residential Lettings*

In relation to statutory control over service charges payable under residential estate management schemes, see **5.12** et seq.

The tribunal that mainly deals with disputes under LTA 1985 was originally the Leasehold Valuation Tribunal ('LVT') but, following a re-organisation of the courts and tribunals service as at 1 April 2011, it is now known as the First-tier Tribunal ('FTT'). In this book the LVT is mentioned in relation to the period before the change and FTT in relation to the current period.

Scope

2.2 Subject to the exemptions mentioned at **2.3**, s 18 of the Landlord and Tenant Act 1985 ('LTA 1985') provides that the statutory code will apply to:

(1) a *service charge*;
(2) of which all or part will *vary according to the relevant costs*;
(3) which is *payable* as part of, or in addition to, rent *by the tenant*;
(4) of a *dwelling*.

These elements are considered in turn below:

(1) *Service charge* means payment for 'services, repairs, maintenance, improvements or insurance or the landlord's costs of management' (LTA 1985, s 18(1)). The fact that the definition of 'service charge' refers only to 'services, repairs, maintenance, improvements or insurance or . . . management' does not have the effect of limiting service charges to these matters; if the cost of anything else is covered by the service charge clause in the lease, that cost can be included in the service charge without the constraints of the LTA 1985 being applied to that particular cost (*Sutton (Hastoe) Housing Association v Williams*[1]; In the Matter of Bedfordshire Pilgrims Housing Association (2000) 23 March (unreported), Lands Tribunal).
It has been suggested by the Lands Tribunal that service charge items such as notional rent for caretakers' flats, not being actual costs incurred by the landlord, fall outside the scope of s 18 for this reason (*Earl Cadogan v 27/29 Sloane Gardens Ltd*[2], Lands Tribunal).
Rent actually paid for premises used for the provision of services may be caught, such as where a management company pays rent to the landlord of the building for parts let to the management company such as reception suites and fitness rooms (*Warwickshire Hamlets Ltd v Gedden*[3], *The Gateway (Leeds) Management Ltd v Naghash*[4]).
The inclusion of the cost of 'improvements' as an element of the service charges caught by the LTA 1985 was added by Sch 9 to the Commonhold and Leasehold Reform Act 2002, with effect from 30 September 2003. Prior to that, the cost of improvements was not subject to these statutory controls (see the *Sutton (Hastoe)* case, above).
(2) *Vary according to the relevant costs* does not only encompass a service charge which is directly proportionate to the costs involved. It is wide enough to cover a service charge of a fixed initial amount which increases mathematically in proportion to the cost of just one element (*Fountain Hoteliers Ltd v Legge-Bourke*[5]) or a case where one year's service charge reflects the previous years' service costs shortfall

(*Re Southern Housing Group Ltd*[6]). On the other hand, this regime does not apply to inclusive rents which a landlord can vary under Housing Act 1988 sections 13 or 14 where the variation is not directly linked to the cost of services (*Home Group Ltd v Lewis*[7]).

The *relevant costs* referred to here are the 'costs or estimated costs incurred or to be incurred by or on behalf of the landlord or a superior landlord in connection with the matters for which the service charge is payable' and includes overheads (LTA 1985, s 18(2) and (3)). For this purpose landlord means 'any person who has the right to enforce payment of a service charge' (LTA 1985 s 30) and can include a third party to the lease such as a management company (*Paddington Basin Developments Ltd and others v West End Quay Estate Management Ltd and another*[8]).

(3) *Payable by the tenant* means payable by a person in his capacity as a tenant. These provisions do not apply to sums payable by a person who is a tenant but has to pay them in a different capacity, such as where the tenant is also a shareholder or member of the landlord company and has to pay a service cost shortfall under the provisions of the memorandum or articles of association of the company, even if it relates to service costs that the company cannot recover under the service charge (*Morshead Mansions Ltd v di Marco*[9]).

Tenant includes a statutory tenant (within the Rent Act 1977 or the Rent (Agriculture) Act 1976); but where the rent is registered under Pt IV of the Rent Act 1977, these provisions apply only if a variable service charge is registered under s 71(4) of the 1977 Act (LTA 1985, s 27).

Where the dwelling or part of it is sublet, 'tenant' includes the subtenant (LTA 1985, s 30). It is not stated here that '"tenant" means the subtenant' but merely 'includes' the subtenant and it leaves the possibility that both the tenant and the subtenant can be tenants having the protection of the Act. Accordingly the tenant can claim protection against service charges demanded from him by the freeholder, and the subtenant can claim the protection of the Act when the tenant seeks to recover that service charge from the subtenant (see **2.4**).

(4) *Dwelling* means a building or part of a building occupied or intended to be occupied as a separate dwelling, together with any yard, garden, outhouses and appurtenances belonging to it or usually enjoyed with it (LTA 1985, s 38). Premises of a residential type which are let wholly or mainly for business purposes, such as flats let for use as medical surgeries, are not 'dwellings' for this purpose (*Buckley v Bowerbeck Properties Ltd*[10]).

There are conflicting case decisions as to whether a 'dwelling' has to be a permanent home or could include a holiday home (*King v Udlaw*[11]; *Phillips v Francis*[12]).

In *Caddick v Whitsand Bay Holiday Park Ltd*[13], it was held that a movable 'lodge' on a plot in a holiday park held on a long lease was not a building, since it could be taken apart and put back together elsewhere without any process of demolition or even any process that could fairly be described as re-erection. It was not attached to the plot in any way that made it a fixture and was therefore not a 'dwelling' for the purpose of LTA 1985.

Student accommodation can be a 'dwelling' but a pod or bedroom which has the use of shared living areas is not a 'separate dwelling' and is outside the scope of LTA 1985 (*JLK Ltd v Ezekwe*[14]).

Since the singular includes the plural in legislation, LTA 1985 applies not only to individual leases of single dwellings but also to leases which demise more than just a single dwelling. It covers cases where the lease demises, say, a flat and a car-parking space or garage to be used with it, or even two or more flats (see *Heron Maple House Ltd v Central Estates Ltd*[15] and *Oakfern Properties Ltd v Ruddy*[16] and see **2.4**).

A separate set of statutory controls was introduced by the Commonhold and Leasehold Reform Act 2002 in relation to 'administration charges' and amended by the Housing Act 2016, s 131. This applies to various charges made by landlords which fall outside the scope of 'service charges', for example charges made by landlords for supplying tenants with documents for inspection and copying facilities in relation to service charge expenditure, interest charged on late payments, and certain litigation costs, and the rules are described at **2.114**.

1 [1988] 1 EGLR 56, CA.
2 [2006] 24 EG 178.
3 [2010] UKUT 75, LC.
4 [2015] UKUT 0333, LC.
5 30 November 1981, unreported.
6 [2010] UKUT 237, LT.
7 (2007) LRX/176/2006, LT.
8 [2010] EWHC 83 (Ch).
9 [2008] EWCA Civ 1731.
10 (2009) 1 EG 78, LVT.
11 [2008] 20 RG 138, LT.
12 [2010] 24 EG 118, QB.
13 [2015] UKUT 63, LC.
14 [2017] UKUT 277, LC.
15 [2002] 13 EG 102.
16 [2006] EWCA Civ 1389.

Particular landlords

2.3 Section 26 of the LTA 1985 exempts from the statutory code tenancies granted by:

(a) a local authority;
(b) a new town corporation; or
(c) the Development Board for Rural Wales,

unless they are 'long tenancies'. A long tenancy granted by such a specified body will be subject to the provisions of LTA 1985, ss 18–24 but not s 25 which relates to offences.

The following are defined by s 26(2) as 'long tenancies' for this purpose:

(a) a tenancy for a fixed term exceeding 21 years, whether or not terminable earlier by tenant's notice or by forfeiture;

(b) a tenancy which is perpetually renewable (and, therefore, is deemed by s 145 and the Fifteenth Schedule to the Law of Property Act 1922 to be for a term of 2,000 years) unless it is a subtenancy granted out of a superior tenancy which is not a long tenancy; and
(c) a tenancy granted under the 'right to buy' provisions of Pt V of the Housing Act 1985.

A tenancy granted by one of the bodies mentioned, which is terminable by notice after the death of the tenant, will not be treated as a long tenancy (and will, therefore, be outside the statutory code) unless granted by a grant-registered housing association at a discounted premium in accordance with a proper shared-ownership lease scheme (LTA 1985, s 26(3)).

Where a right to manage (RTM) company takes over the management of the property (see **2.95**), most of the statutory provisions of the LTA 1985, and other related legislation, will continue to apply (see **2.109**).

The application of this regime to the Crown, as landlord, is set out (so far as brought into force by commencement orders) by the Commonhold and Leasehold Reform Act 2002, s 172 and Sch 14 and by the Landlord and Tenant Act 1987 (LTA 1987), s 56. In broad terms, most of the provisions of the statutory regime which are in force at the publication date of this book apply to the Crown apart from those relating to the appointment of managers, the right to manage and the holding of service charge funds on trust; in individual cases reference should be made to the detailed statutory provisions if the Crown has an interest in the relevant property.

Headlease and mixed use lettings

2.4 Because s 18 can apply to leases which demise multiple flats and can apply to subtenants as well as tenants (see **2.2**), the regime imposed by LTA 1985 can apply where all or part of a building is comprised in a headlease out of which individual flats have been sublet, and even if another part of the building is used for non-residential purposes – for example, buildings with flats on the upper floors and shops or offices on the lower floors.

EXAMPLES

Heron Maple House Ltd v Central Estates Ltd[1], Central London County Court: A mixed commercial and residential block was managed by the freeholder. The residential section, which included a substantial number of flats, was let on a headlease. The headlessee sublet the whole of that section to a subtenant who subunderlet the individual flats. All the leases reserved service charges which included sums expended by the freeholder on major repairs. The freeholder incurred large expenditure which, if the LTA 1985 applied, fell within the requirements of the Act for consulting with tenants and obtaining competitive quotations (see **2.7**). However, the freeholder had not consulted the headlessee and the headlessee had not consulted his subtenant. Could the freeholder and/or the headlesseerecover those costs? **Held:** No; LTA 1985 applied to the service charges payable both under the headlease and under the sub-leases, so in the absence of complying with the compulsory consultation requirements the freeholder could not recover the expenditure from the headlessee who could not (even if he paid it voluntarily) recover it from the subtenant.

Oakfern Properties Ltd v Ruddy[2]: A mixed use building contained an upper residential part which was let to a headlessee who sublet the individual flats and recharged the subtenants of the flats with the service charge levied by the freeholder. Could the individual subtenants require the LVT to review the service charges claimed by the freeholder from the headlessee? **Held:** Yes.

In the *Oakfern* case the court noted that there were 'anomalies' in applying LTA 1985 to these circumstances. Although the judgment refers to the consultation regime (see **2.7**), the court did not attempt to explain exactly how that regime would apply in these circumstances and that is probably one of the 'anomalies' that the court had in mind. That has now been addressed in *Foundling Court and O'Donnell Court v Camden London Borough Council*[3] (see **2.7**).

1 [2002] 13 EG 102.
2 [2006] EWCA Civ 1389, CA.
3 [2016] UKUT 366, LC.

Utilities, energy supplies and district heating and cooling services

2.5 The question arises whether charges for utilities such as water, gas, electricity, drainage, heating, cooling and electronic communication services fall within the definition of service charges under LTA 1985 where the tenant's lease, or a collateral document, places an obligation on the tenant to pay such charges. Traditionally telephone, gas, electricity and water services have for many years been supplied by utility companies, and about 20 years ago sewerage functions were taken over by water companies from local councils. Whilst many leases contain a tenant's covenant to pay for telephone, gas, electricity, water and drainage services enjoyed by the tenant, it has not generally been suggested that the existence of such a provision brings those charges within the LTA 1985.

Recently, technological advances for improving energy efficiency have led to many new flats in blocks and some new houses on estates being served by heating (and sometimes cooling) from communal systems, the operation of which in many cases is outsourced by the landlord to supply companies. These new systems normally operate by feeding hot water (or, for cooling, chilled water) to an interface unit which heats (or cools) the water in the heating or cooling system within each flat. Often the energy consumed by the flat's system is measured by metering the flow and change in temperature of the communal system's water running through the interface unit.

Where the landlord includes such a communal heating system in a new building and enters into a contract with a supply company to operate the system and/or (if the landlord's communal system itself does not include boilers or chillers) to provide it with heated or chilled water, frequently the landlord will have drawn the leases to include a covenant by the tenant to enter into a contract directly with the supply company for obtaining the heating and/or cooling supply and for paying the costs. There may be a provision that the landlord will provide the service if the supply company ceases to do so.

As noted at **2.2**, the definition of 'service charge' in s 18(1) relates to charges that vary according to the 'relevant costs' which are defined as the 'costs or estimated costs incurred or to be incurred *by or on behalf of the landlord or a superior landlord* in connection with the matters for which the service charge is payable' (LTA 1985, s 18(2) and (3)). For this purpose landlord means 'any person who has the right to enforce payment of a service charge' (LTA 1985 s 30) and can include a third party to the lease such as a management company (*Paddington Basin Developments Ltd and others v West End Quay Estate Management Ltd and another*[1]).

It may possibly be argued that the supply company is a 'person who has the right to enforce payment of a service charge' because the lease requires the tenant to enter into the contract with the supply company and so that contract is collateral to the lease. If that argument were to be accepted, the charges for heating and cooling might fall within the scope of LTA 1985. Indeed, it may be thought anomalous that the protection of LTA 1985 would apply if the heating or cooling were supplied by the landlord but not where the landlord outsources them.

1 [2010] EWHC 83 (Ch).

Tenant's proportion

2.6 The focus of s 18 (and of the reasonableness test in s 19 – see **2.26**) on the 'relevant costs', being the costs that are reflected in the service charge, as distinct from the amount of the contribution towards them that is payable by any particular tenant, meant that, until the LVT's jurisdiction was enlarged in 2002, any issue about the percentage of the relevant costs that was payable by the tenant appeared to be outside the scope of LTA 1985. However, the enlarging of the LVT's (now the FTT's) jurisdiction to include, under s 27A, how much the particular tenant has to pay by way of service charge (see **2.67**) has created a tension with the scope of ss 18 and 19.

Where the lease specifies mathematically the proportion (as a percentage or fraction) of the service costs that is payable by the tenant of that lease, the FTT can determine under s 9 how much of the underlying costs have been reasonably incurred (see **2.9**) and can check under s 27A that the tenant's contribution has been duly calculated by applying the specified proportion, but has no jurisdiction to change that proportion (see *Canary Riverside v Schilling*[1]; *Re Rowner Estates*[2]; *Warrior Quay Management Company Ltd v Joachim and others*[3]).

Any variation of the proportion can only be considered by the on an application under LTA 1987 to order a variation of the lease, but even in such cases it has been held that the FTT's power of variation under s 35(4) of that Act only applies where the tenants' contributions add up to either more than 100 per cent of the cost or less than 100 per cent of the cost and that the FTT does not have jurisdiction to vary the proportion payable by each tenant, however unfair the allocation, if they add up to 100 per cent (*Morgan v Fletcher*[4] and see **2.76**).

Similarly the FTT cannot change the payment regime set out in the lease (*Southend-on-Sea Borough Council v Skiggs*[5]).

On the other hand, the FTT does have power under s 27A to review any decision of the landlord or his surveyor as to the tenant's proportion where the lease provides for it to be a 'fair proportion' or some similar expression or gives the landlord or his surveyor the right to decide the tenant's proportion (see *Re Rowner Estates*[6] (above). The question will not be whether the proportion arrived at is reasonable within the reasonableness test of s 19, since that test only applies to the underlying costs, but will be whether the proportion was in accordance with the terms of the lease, which may require a 'fair' or 'due' proportion or may simply require (perhaps by implication) that the landlord or his surveyor acts properly and in good faith and does not produce a manifestly wrong result. If the terms of the lease are not crystal clear as to the assessment, for example by referring to floor areas without reference to a specific code of measurement, the FTT may be able to make an appropriate determination under s 27A (see *Zenabell Ltd v Dedeoglu*[7]).

1 (2005) LRX/65/2005, LT.
2 (2007) LRX/3/2006, LT.
3 (2008) LRX/42/2006, LT.
4 [2009] UKUT 186, LRX/81/2008, LC.
5 [2006] 21 EG 132.
6 (2007) LRX/3/2006, LT.
7 (2006) LON/OOA)/LIS/2005/011500.

CONSULTATION WITH TENANTS AND OBTAINING ESTIMATES

Terms of the lease

2.7 Most leases do not lay down any procedure for tenants to be consulted before service expenditure is incurred. However, forms of lease vary so widely that it is advisable, in each case, to check whether the lease contains any specific provisions in this respect (see **1.55**).

Just as in the case of other types of letting, consultation prior to major expenditure is desirable in any event to foster the landlord and tenant relationship and smooth the way for the ultimate recovery of the costs through the service charge. Furthermore, in the case of flats sold on long leases, the ground landlord has little financial interest in the running of the block and is, in reality (although perhaps not in law), merely acting as agent for the tenants in administering the services. He should, therefore, act in their best interests and take account of their views, since it is their interests which are affected by his decision. In some cases this may be best done by convening a meeting of the tenants in a local hall at a time when the majority of them can attend.

Scope of the statutory consultation procedure

2.8 The current rules were introduced by regulations made under the Commonhold and Leasehold Reform Act 2002 as from 31 October 2003. Certain transitional provisions under the Commonhold and Leasehold Reform Act 2002 (Commencement No 2 and Savings) (England) Order 2003[1] preserve the earlier rules in some situations where works began, or were consulted upon, before that date.

The current provisions affecting properties in England are principally contained in the Service Charges (Consultation Requirements) (England) Regulations 2003[2] (SCCR Regulations 2003) and by the Public Contracts Regulations 2006. There are separate but similar regulations affecting properties in Wales.

The Regulations cover both works exceeding specified cost thresholds ('qualifying works') and long-term contracts (for works or services) running for over 12 months at costs exceeding specified thresholds ('qualifying long term agreements'). The details of the cost thresholds levels and consultation procedures are contained in regulations and can be changed from time to time by the Secretary of State.

'Qualifying long-term agreements' are currently, in general terms, any contracts under which 'relevant costs' (ie costs which will be reflected in service charges to which LTA 1985 applies) will be payable, which will run for over 12 months and where the contribution payable by any tenant would exceed £100 in any accounting period. This can include a long term agreement entered into by a landlord or management company with a third party who agrees to manage the provision of some or all of the services whose cost is recoverable through the service charges.

EXAMPLE

> *Paddington Basin Developments Ltd and others v West End Quay Estate Management Ltd*[3]: An estate management company that was a party to over 400 leases of residential flats entered, without consulting the tenants, into an agreement by deed engaging a company set up by the developer to manage the estate for a minimum period of 25 years and to carry out the services that the estate management company was to provide under the residential leases. Was that deed a long term agreement within the ambit of the consultation requirements so that each flat owner's contributions to the costs arising under it were capped at £100 per year? **Held:** Yes.

However, the following are excluded:

(a) employment contracts;
(b) a management agreement between a local housing authority and a tenant management organisation under the Housing Act 1985, s 27AB(8), or a body established under the Local Government Act 2000, s 2;
(c) contracts between companies in the same group;
(d) contracts for not more than five years entered into entered into at a time when there are no tenants of the building or the premises;
(e) contracts existing before 31 October 2003 even if running for more than 12 months after that date;

(f) contracts entered into under the Public Works or Public Supply regulations (as were then in force) which were advertised pursuant to those regulations before 31 October 2003.

Under exemption (d), a developer of a new block of flats can put in place contracts running for not more than five years before there are any tenants. Does that stop once a sale contract is entered into for the grant of a lease of any flat in the block, or only once the sale is completed by grant of the lease? The guidance note at the end of the Regulations refers to 'buildings or other premises which are untenanted when the agreement is entered into' which seems to indicate the latter, but the guidance is not legally binding.

In *Corvan (Properties) Ltd v Abdel-Mahmoud*[4] the Upper Tribunal held that a management agreement which was expressed to be for a period of only 12 months was a 'qualifying agreement' since it contained a provision that it would continue after that period until ended by three months' notice, and on the wording it would in fact run for at least 15 months.

Many building contracts contain provisions requiring the contractor to return to the property and make good defects that become apparent up to a year after the main work has been completed. It may be that such contracts are to be treated as being for a period of over 12 months, even where the main work is to be completed in less than 12 months.

'Qualifying Works' are any works to which any tenant will have to contribute more than £250. Under the previous regulations, each package of works was treated separately. At first instance it was held that, since the current regulations focus on the cost when defining Qualifying Works, it must mean the cost of ALL works that are to be charged through the service charge for any one accounting period: *Phillips v Francis*[5]. That unfortunate decision has now been overturned by the Court of Appeal, holding that the £250 threshold applies to each 'set of works', irrespective of whether it is being charged in one accounting year or spread, and that this must be applied on a common-sense basis in each situation: *Phillips v Francis*[6].

Since the consultation requirements apply to service costs to which 'any' tenant would have to pay an amount over the relevant financial threshold, all tenants who would have to contribute to those costs must be consulted even if only some of them (or even just one of them) would have to pay a contribution exceeding the threshold and the rest would pay contributions below the threshold.

In most situations there have to be two separate consultation periods of at least 30 days each, one following the landlord giving tenants an initial notice of his intentions and the other following him notifying them of his firm proposals based on estimates received from potential contractors, and those estimates are not to be obtained before the initial consultation period has expired. The procedure before contracts can be entered into will therefore usually be quite lengthy.

As to how the regime might apply where a freeholder levies service charges on a headlessee who recharges them to subtenants of individual flats (see **2.4**), the first issue would be how the cost thresholds mentioned above are to be applied. The application of the regulations in those circumstances is unclear. On one possible interpretation, considered but not decided at the Lands Tribunal in

Oakfern Properties Ltd v Ruddy[7], if a headlease comprises, say, 26 flats and the superior landlord intends to incur service costs of £260 attributable to all the flats, that would exceed the threshold of £250 per tenant if one treated the headlessee as the tenant, and would trigger consultation even though the cost per flat is only £10, which at first sight appears anomalous. The second issue is whether the superior landlord must directly consult both the headlessee and the subtenants, as discussed at **2.4** and at **2.16**. Plainly the regulations were not drafted with these issues in mind.

1 SI 2003/1986.
2 SI 2003/1987, as amended by SI 2004/2665.
3 [2101] EWHC 833 (Ch).
4 [2017] UKUT 228, LC.
5 [2012] EWHC 3650 (Ch).
6 [2014] EWCA Civ 1395.
7 (2005) LRX/93/2005.

The consultation requirements

2.9 There are five different sets of consultation requirements set out in the Schedules to the SCCR Regulations 2003:

(1) Schedule 1 – for entering into a qualifying long term agreement (not governed by the Public Contracts Regulations).
(2) Schedule 2 – for entering into a qualifying long term agreement governed by the Public Contracts Regulations.
(3) Schedule 3 – for carrying out qualifying works either:
  (a) under a qualifying long term agreement; or
  (b) under an agreement made by the landlord before 31 October 2003 where any of the work is carried out after 31 December 2003; or
  (c) under a contract within the Public Works or Public Supply regulations (as were then in force) which was advertised before 31 October 2003 where any of the work is carried out after 31 October 2003.
(4) Schedule 4, Pt I – for carrying out other qualifying works which have to be publicly advertised under the Public Contracts Regulations.
(5) Schedule 4, Pt 2 – for carrying out all other qualifying works.

These sets of requirements are summarised below. It is likely that, in relation to private sector landlords, the first and last of these will most commonly apply.

Under some of the requirements mentioned below, estimates are to be obtained from persons 'wholly unconnected with the landlord'. The meaning of this is elaborated by para 12(6) of Sch 1, which imposes an assumption that various categories of people (and any company they control or manage) are connected with the landlord (including those persons who control or manage a company landlord), including 'close relatives' who are defined in reg 2. The very comprehensive definition of this phrase includes people such as spouses, cohabitees (of opposite or same sex if living as a couple), parents, children, siblings, in-laws, etc. The rules also catch the position where the proposed contractor is a partnership of whom the landlord, or a 'close relative' of the landlord, is a partner.

Consultation for entering into a qualifying long term agreement (not public contracts)

2.10 Schedule 1 to the SCCR Regulations 2003 sets out these requirements in great detail. In outline, a written initial notice of intention must be given to each tenant and any recognised tenants' association, setting out the intention to enter into the agreement; describing the goods or services it will cover (or indicating reasonably where and when details can be inspected); giving reasons for wanting to enter into the agreement; if works are involved, giving reasons why they are necessary; inviting written observations within 30 days (specifying the end date and the address for sending them); and inviting written nominations within 30 days (specifying the end date and the address for sending them) of contractors from whom estimates should be sought. Paragraph 5(10) of Sch 1 requires further information to be given where the long term agreement is for the appointment of a managing agent.

The landlord must then 'have regard' (see **2.17**) to any observations received during the specified period, and only then must the landlord seek estimates from contractors. Apart from contractors of the landlord's choosing, the regulations require the landlord to seek estimates from contractors suggested by the tenants. If a recognised tenants' association responds and nominates just one contractor, the landlord must try to obtain an estimate from that contractor. If only one tenant responds and he nominates just one contractor, the landlord must try to obtain an estimate from that contractor. If a number of tenants respond and each makes a single nomination but of different contractors, the landlord must try to obtain an estimate from the contractor with the highest number of nominations (or from those contractors who tie for top position); if there are no contractors with a clear majority, the landlord must choose at least one of the nominated contractors from whom to seek an estimate. If any tenant nominates more than one contractor, the landlord must choose at least one contractor suggested by a tenant from whom to seek an estimate. If a recognised tenants' association nominates more than one contractor, the landlord must choose at least one of them (not being anyone already chosen by the landlord from persons nominated by tenants) from whom to seek an estimate.

Having followed that process and obtained estimates, the landlord must prepare at least two alternative proposals for entry into the proposed long term agreement. At least one proposal must be with a contractor who is 'wholly unconnected with the landlord' (see **2.9**), and any connection of the landlord with any proposed contractor must be stated. If the landlord has received an estimate from a contractor who was nominated by or on behalf of the tenants, at least one of the landlord's proposals must be based on it. If reasonably possible, the landlord must also state his estimate of each tenant's contribution to the costs to be incurred under each proposal; failing that he must if reasonably possible state his estimate of the total contribution applicable to the building in which each tenant's flat is situated; and failing that he must if reasonably possible state the current unit cost or hourly rate for the relevant supply or works. Any proposal which is or includes the appointment of a managing agent must also state whether or not the proposed agent is a member of a professional body or trade association (naming it) and whether or not he subscribes to any relevant code of practice or voluntary accreditation scheme relating to managing agents. Each proposal must state its intended duration and any intended provisions for varying the costs to be incurred under it. If the landlord received observations from tenants in response to his initial notice, the proposals must summarise the observations and the landlord's response to them. Written notice must be given to each tenant and to any recognised tenants' association, either accompanied by a copy of these proposals or reasonably specifying where and when they can be inspected, and inviting written observations on them to be given within 30 days (specifying the end date and the address for sending them).

Next, the landlord must 'have regard' (see **2.17**) to any observations received from a tenant or recognised tenants' association during that specified period, before entering into the long term agreement. If the landlord enters into the agreement with someone who was neither nominated by a tenant or a recognised tenants' association, nor gave the lowest estimate, the landlord must, within 21 days of entering into the agreement, give written notice to each tenant and any recognised tenants' association, setting out his reasons for making that agreement (or reasonably specifying where and when a statement of reasons can be inspected) and summarising any observations he received in respect of his proposals and giving his responses (or reasonably specifying where and when a summary and response can be inspected).

Any inspection facilities provided under the above must include copying facilities or the landlord must provide copies of the items inspected. The landlord cannot make any charge for these.

Consultation for entering into a qualifying long term agreement within the public contracts regime

2.11 Schedule 2 to the SCCR Regulations 2003 sets out these requirements in detail. They largely follow the same procedure as in Sch 1 (see **2.10**) but with certain differences due to the fact that tenders will be invited by the publication of public advertisements under the relevant public sector regulations. The initial notice must state that nominations of persons from whom estimates should be sought are not being invited from the tenants because public notice of the proposed works or services is to be given. Following the initial consultation and the public advertising, the landlord must prepare a single proposal rather than alternative proposals. The remaining rules, including those as to facilities and copying, are in general the same as above.

Consultation for qualifying works to be carried out under a qualifying long-term agreement (or under an agreement made or publicly advertised before 31 October 2003)

2.12 Schedule 3 to the SCCR Regulations 2003 sets out these requirements in detail. In outline, a written initial notice of intention must be given to each tenant and any recognised tenants' association, describing the works (or indicating reasonably where and when details can be inspected); giving reasons why they are necessary; giving the landlord's estimate of the likely total cost;

and inviting written observations within 30 days (specifying the end date and the address for sending them) as to the works or the estimated cost.

The landlord must then 'have regard' to any such observations received during the specified period, and must respond in writing to them within 21 days of receipt. Because the works are to be carried out under an existing agreement, many of the features under the other consultation requirements do not arise. The rules as to facilities and copying are the same as above.

Consultation for qualifying works which have to be publicly advertised under the Public Contracts Regulations

2.13 Schedule 4, Pt 1 to the SCCR Regulations 2003 sets out these requirements in detail. In outline, a written notice of intention must be given to each tenant and any recognised tenants' association, describing the works (or indicating reasonably where and when details can be inspected); giving reasons why they are necessary; stating that nominations of persons from whom estimates should be sought are not being invited because public notice of the proposed works is to be given; and inviting written observations within 30 days (specifying the end date and the address for sending them) as to the works. Then the landlord must 'have regard' to any observations received during the specified period.

Following that process and the public tendering procedure, the landlord must prepare a written statement proposing a contract for the works, detailing the proposed contracting parties; stating any connection of the landlord with any proposed contracting party (see **2.9**); if reasonably possible, stating the landlord's estimate of each tenant's contribution to the costs to be incurred under the proposal (or, failing that, if reasonably possible stating his estimate of the total contribution applicable to the building in which each tenant's flat is situated; and failing that if reasonably possible stating the current unit cost or hourly rate for the relevant supply or works, failing which the landlord must give reasons why these sums cannot be specified yet and state when he expects to be able to do so); and if the landlord received observations in response to his initial notice, he must summarise the observations and state his responses to them. The landlord must give a written notice to each tenant and any recognised tenants' association, either accompanied by a copy of this statement or reasonably specifying where and when it can be inspected, and inviting written observations within 30 days (specifying the end date and the address for sending them).

Again, the landlord must 'have regard' to any observations received from a tenant or recognised tenants' association during the specified period, and within 21 days of receipt the landlord must respond in writing to any such observations.

The rules as to facilities, copying and connection with the landlord are the same as set out above.

Consultation on all other qualifying works – of general application

2.14 Schedule 4, Pt 2 to the SCCR Regulations 2003 sets out these requirements in detail. In outline, a written notice of intention must be given to each tenant and any recognised tenants' association, describing the works (or indicating reasonably where and when details can be inspected); giving reasons why they are necessary; inviting written observations within 30 days (specifying the end date and the address for sending them) as to the works; and inviting written nominations within 30 days (specifying the end date and the address for sending them) of contractors from whom estimates should be sought.

The landlord must then 'have regard' to any observations received during the specified period. After that the landlord must seek estimates from contractors, including not only any of the landlord's choosing but also those nominated by tenants, as follows. If a recognised tenants' association responds and nominates just one contractor, the landlord must try to obtain an estimate from that contractor. If only one tenant responds and he nominates just one contractor, the landlord must try to obtain an estimate from that contractor. If a number of tenants respond and each makes a single nomination but of different contractors, the landlord must try to obtain an estimate from the contractor with the highest number of nominations (or from those contractors who tie for top position); if there are no contractors with a clear majority, the landlord must choose at least one of the nominated contractors from whom to seek an estimate. If any tenant nominates more than one contractor, the landlord must seek an estimate from at least one contractor suggested by a tenant. If a recognised tenants' association nominates more than one contractor, the landlord must seek an estimate from at least one of them (not being anyone the landlord has already chosen from tenants' nominations).

Following that process, the landlord must prepare a written statement giving details of the estimated costs under at least two estimates. At least one of the estimates must be from someone wholly unconnected with the landlord (see **2.9**). These estimates must include any obtained from nominated contractors. If the landlord received observations in response to his initial notice, he must summarise the observations and state his responses to them. The landlord must give copies of the statement to each tenant and any recognised tenants' association, and reasonably specify where and when all the estimates obtained by the landlord can be inspected (not just those detailed in the statement) and inviting written observations on the estimates within 30 days (specifying the end date and the address for sending them). The landlord must then 'have regard' to any observations received from a tenant or recognised tenants' association during the specified period.

If the landlord contracts for the works with someone who neither was nominated by a tenant nor by any recognised tenants' association, nor gave the lowest estimate, the landlord must, within 21 days of contracting, give written notice to each tenant and any recognised tenants' association setting out his reasons for making that agreement (or reasonably specifying where and when a statement of reasons can be inspected); and summarising and giving his responses to any observations received in response to his last notice (or reasonably specifying where and when a summary and response can be inspected).

Where the landlord's proposals for the intended works change during the process, for example where tenants make alternative suggestions in response to the initial consultation or potential contractors propose alternative materials or methods in response to the invitations to provide estimates, or where there are changes proposed during the carrying out of the works, the landlord must consider whether the change is so material that any phase of the consultation process must be repeated. This will depend on the facts of each case and relevant considerations will include whether the proposals remained substantially the same, whether there would be a large or small change in the costs, whether the change affects only a relatively small part of the works where inviting new tenders might be unrealistic, and what best property management might be in the circumstances, and regard should be had to the fact that the tenants will still be protected by the reasonableness test in LTA 1985, s 19 (*Reedbase Ltd v Fattal*[1]).

1 [2018] EWCA Civ 840.

Works taking over a year

2.15 In the case of work ordered by private sector landlords, as has been seen, the basic position is that if any tenant will have to contribute over £250 to the cost of work, consultation must take place in accordance with Sch 4, Pt 2 and no consultation is needed where the costs are below that threshold.

However, the position will be different if the landlord is entering into a new contract for that work and that contract will run for over a year. That might be the case if the contract covered a lengthy piece of work or several jobs to be run in sequence, or possibly if it merely included a defect remedy period taking the period of performance of the contract to over a year. In such cases one must ascertain if it is over the threshold for consultation under the 'long term agreement' category (ie if the contribution from any tenant will be over £100 in any accounting year) in which case the consultation required is under Sch 1 instead of under Sch 4, Pt 2.

The reason for this is that the reg 7(4) states that the provisions of Sch 4, Pt 2 do not apply where Sch 1 applies. In such a case the landlord has to explain the need for the works only if the contribution would be over £250 in relation to those works (see Sch 1, para 1(2)(c)).

Where an existing long term agreement is running and the work is to be ordered under it, and the sum which any tenant would have to contribute to that work exceeds £250, consultation for ordering that work will be required under Sch 3.

Time Limits

2.16 The requirement to give tenants 30 days to respond under the regulations is expressed as requiring the landlord to specify a response to be given within '30 days beginning with the date of the notice'. This must mean the date when the notice is delivered to the tenant or, if that is not certain, the date when law treats the notice as being delivered (*Trafford Housing Trust Ltd v Rubinstein and others*[1]).

Unfortunately neither the regulations nor the 1985 Act contain any provisions regarding delivery of notices nor do they expressly incorporate any of the statutory provisions as to deemed service of notices (such as in s 196 of the

Law of Property Act) so the judge in the *Trafford* case wanted to apply s 7 of the Interpretation Act 1978 under which a notice required or authorised by an Act, if sent with a letter by pre-paid post, is deemed to be served at the time when the letter would be delivered in the ordinary course of post. However, the landlord had used a commercial delivery service which did not publish its expected delivery periods so the court had no evidence of that period. The FTT had been willing to assume that the letters had been delivered on the second working day after they were posted and the judge found no reason to disagree. This leaves the position rather unclear and landlords would be well advised either to have the notices hand delivered or send them by post with letters and specify a final date for responses which is more than just 30 days after the date when they propose to post them.

1 [2013] UKUT 0581, LC.

'Having regard' to the tenants' views

2.17 In *Hounslow London Borough Council v Waaler*[1], the Court of Appeal said that the landlord, in deciding the nature and extent of any intended work of service, must give more weight to the tenant's views in deciding whether to incur costs under a discretionary provision in the lease than where the landlord is obliged to do the work or provide the service. That case also applied to landlord's decisions about service charges the concept that a contractual discretion must be exercised rationally and in good faith (see **1.15**).

1 [2017] EWCA Civ 45.

Headleases

2.18 As mentioned at **2.4**, the question arises how to comply with the consultation procedure where there is a headlessee between the landlord who intends to do qualifying works or enter into a qualifying contract and the individual subtenants of flats who will have to contribute to the costs through the service charges that they pay to the headlessee.

The timetable under the procedure does not allow sufficient time for the superior landlord to consult the headlessee and then for the headlessee to consult the subtenants. Accordingly it has been held in *Lessees of Foundling Court and O'Donnell Court v Camden London Borough Council*[1] that the correct method of complying is for the superior landlord to consult the headlessee and the subtenants at the same time.

In cases where the superior landlord may not know the identity of every sub-tenant who may be liable to contribute towards the costs, the Upper Tribunal suggested that consultation notices might be addressed to 'the leaseholder' and sent to each flat. However it pointed out that the 1985 Act and the SCCR Regulations 2003 do not have any express provisions regarding deemed service of these notices so the position is unclear (see **2.16**).

1 [2016] UKUT 366, LC.

Effect of non-compliance

2.19 If consultation in accordance with the regulations is required but is not carried out, then (subject to the FTT's right to dispense with the requirements, mentioned at **2.20**) the landlord is barred from recovering from the tenants any contributions towards sums payable under the relevant long term agreement or qualifying works above the amount of the relevant financial threshold mentioned at **2.8** (LTA 1985, s 20(1), (6) and (7)). Accordingly, under the current regulations no tenant could be required, in such cases, to pay more than £100 per year towards costs arising under a qualifying long term contract or more than £250 towards the cost of qualifying works.

For an example of a ruling that a breach of the consultation requirements may result in the costs recoverable from the tenants being capped in this way, see *Paddington Basin Developments Ltd and others v West Quay Estate Management Company Ltd* (at **2.8**).

Dispensing with the requirements

2.20 In some cases a landlord cannot comply with a particular aspect of the regime for a practical reason outside his control. For example if only one potential contractor out of a number responds to an invitation to tender the landlord will be unable to put forward more than one proposal for proceeding.

In other cases the nature of the landlord's operations may lead to difficulties, so for example it may be difficult for local authorities or large housing associations to comply fully with the consultation process where they employ contractors under contracts spanning several buildings or estates and cannot tell individual tenants which costs are relevant to their particular buildings. Adopting a broad brush approach may not comply with the Regulations – it is necessary for the landlord to provide information as to the costs that would be incurred on the particular building to whose service costs that particular group of tenants is liable to contribute through their service charges (see for example *Islington London Borough v Abdel-Malik*[1]).

Similarly, where a local authority provides heat and light to its tenants and charges them the cost, it would not comply with the Regulations if the local authority conducted negotiations for the bulk purchase of energy as a joint exercise with other similar bodies through a club or group structure without following the consultation regime, even if this was intended to maximise their bargaining power and produce the lowest possible energy costs for the tenants.

As mentioned earlier, the question also arises how to comply with the consultation procedure where a headlease exists between the landlord who intends to do qualifying works or enter into a qualifying contract and the individual subtenants of flats who will have to contribute to the costs through the service charges that they pay to the headlessee. The timetable under the procedure does not allow for the superior landlord to consult the headlessee and for the headlessee then to have sufficient time to consult the subtenants, so it is likely that the correct method of complying is for the superior landlord to consult the headlessee and the subtenants at the same time. This is not spelled out in the SCCR Regulations 2003 but as stated at **2.18** this approach has recently been followed by the Upper Tribunal, Lands Chamber, in Lessees of

Foundling Court and O'Donnell Court v Camden LBC[2]. In cases where the superior landlord may not know the identity of every sub-tenant who may be liable to contribute towards the costs, the Upper Tribunal suggested that consultation notices might be addressed to 'the leaseholder' and sent to each flat, but pointed out that the 1985 Act and the SCCR Regulations 2003 do not have any express provisions regarding deemed service of these notices so the position was unclear.

A solution in such cases of difficulty may be to seek dispensation from the FTT to allow one or more elements of the consultation process to be omitted or varied and this should preferably be done in advance if practicable. The FTT has power under LTA 1985, s 20ZA to order the dispensing with all or part of the consultation requirements where the FTT is satisfied that it is reasonable to do so and it has the power to impose conditions when granting dispensation: *Daejan Investments Ltd v Benson*[3].

Dispensing with all or part of the consultation process is quite common in the public sector. For example, where councils enter into collective bargaining with utility supply companies for bulk or long term supply contracts for gas, water or electricity, this will benefit tenants by keeping costs down but it is not practical to consult all the council 's tenants in accordance with the above regime. In such cases the FTT may order the council to dispense with most of the consultation process[4].

In the case of emergency works, the FTT can retrospectively waive the consultation requirement but the landlord or his agent should ensure that the steps taken without following the proper procedure should be confined to those which are necessary to deal with the emergency, and that the proper consultation procedure should be followed closely in respect of less urgent elements of the work (see, for example, the London Borough of Islington's application in respect of Caroline Martyn House[5]).

Before the decision of the Supreme Court in *Daejan Investments Ltd v Benson* there had been two competing views as to the giving of dispensation. One view was that the FTT should not grant it where the landlord has flouted the procedure since that may encourage landlords to ignore the regulations. The competing view was that the most important test was whether tenants have been prejudiced by any failure to follow the consultation process, and the landlord should not be penalised for minor breaches that do not adversely affect the tenants. It was also said that, although the financial consequences of granting or refusing dispensation are irrelevant, a more lenient approach may be taken where the landlord is a leaseholder-controlled company where they are spending their own money (*Eltham Properties Ltd v Kenny*[6]; *Daejan Investments Ltd v Benson*[7]). However, the majority view of the Supreme Court in *Daejan Investments Ltd v Benson* was that the focus should be on whether the landlord is seeking to charge higher costs than would have applied if the consultation process was followed, and his failure to follow the process is less relevant (although Lord Neuberger observed that a serious failure to follow the process may often financially prejudice the tenant, eg where the landlord fails to seek competitive tenders). The Supreme Court also held that the FTT could impose a condition limiting the chargeable costs when giving dispensation – in that case the landlord had to bear a discount of nearly 20 per cent off the cost of the works.

No dispensation was given in the *Trafford* case mentioned at **2.16** where the landlord specified a latest response date that gave tenants less than 30 days to respond from the date when they were expected to receive their consultation notices.

It must be remembered that whether the consultation procedure has been followed or dispensation obtained, the tenants can still challenge the costs under the reasonableness test in LTA 1985, s 19 (*Reedbase Ltd v Fattal*[8]).

1 [2007] LRX/90/2006, LT.
2 [2016] UKUT 366, LC.
3 [2013] UKSC 14, Supreme Court.
4 *Southwark London Borough Council* [2006] LON/00BE/LDC/0083 LVT; *Corporation of London* [2005] LON/00AA /LDC/2005/0022 LVT.
5 (2011) LON/OOAU/LDC/2010/0095.
6 [2007] LRX/161/2006, LT.
7 [2011] EWCA Civ 38.
8 [2018] EWCA Civ 840.

Recognition of tenants' associations

2.21 Recognition of tenants' associations for the purpose of the service charge provisions of the LTA 1985 is governed by s 29 of that Act. The rules are:

(1) the association must comprise 'qualifying tenants' with or without other tenants. 'Qualifying tenants' is defined in s 29(4) as tenants who may be required by the terms of their leases to contribute by service charges to the same service costs;
(2) the association must either be:
   (a) recognised by the landlord, who must give written notice to the secretary of the association that he recognises it for these purposes, or
   (b) recognised by a certificate of a member of the local Rent Assessment Committee panel;
(3) a landlord's notice can be withdrawn by six months' written notice and a certificate can be cancelled;
(4) the Secretary of State has power to make regulations in connection with Rent Assessment Committee Panel applications and certificates.

Thus, if the landlord refuses to recognise a tenants' association, the association can apply to the panel for a recognition certificate. An appeal from the panel's decision may be made to the High Court. An early example was *R v London Rent Assessment Panel, ex parte Trustees of Henry Smith's Charity Estate*[1], in which the High Court upheld a landlord's objection to the recognition of a tenants' association representing tenants in five blocks of flats, on the ground that each block should have its own association so as to represent one service charge regime.

The Department for Communities and Local Government and HM Courts and Tribunal Service have published guidance that an association should be recognised if it has membership representing at least 60 per cent of the number of tenants contributing to the service charge, but that is guidance and not a regulation.

In *Rosslyn Mansions Tenants' Association v Winstonworth Ltd*[2], the Upper Tribunal held first that it had jurisdiction to hear an appeal by the tenants' association from the First-tier Tribunal's decision and then held that the First-tier Tribunal had given incorrect reasons for rejecting the association's application for recognition. There was evidence of poor management, neglect of the common parts and lack of transparency in the management and control of the building, and the members of the association were together liable for over 65 per cent by value of the service costs. However, the block contained 13 flats of which eight were demised on long leases and only four tenants out of that eight were members of the association; the other four long lease tenants did not want to join the association and opposed its recognition (indeed, one of them actually controlled the freeholder company) and the participating tenants represented by number only 57 per cent of the number of tenants liable to pay service charges, which was below the 60 per cent figure mentioned in guidance published by the DCLG and by the HM Courts & Tribunal Service. The First-tier Tribunal based its decision on that point and on the basis that the association had not allowed the tenants holding short term rentals of the other flats to join the association. Quashing the decision of the First-tier Tribunal, the Upper Tribunal said that the tribunal had a wide discretion under s 29; there was no presumption in favour of, or against, recognising an association; the numerical proportion of service charge contributing tenants who join the association is a relevant factor but is not decisive (and the government guidance on that point is not binding); and that the financial proportion of the service costs borne by the members of the association is relevant. It referred the case back to the First-tier Tribunal for reconsideration on that basis.

1 [1988] 1 EGLR 34.
2 [2015] UKUT 0011, LC.

Surveyors appointed by tenants' associations

2.22 A recognised tenants' association has power to appoint a surveyor for the purposes set out in Housing Act 1996 (HA 1996), s 84, namely, to advise on any matters relating to, or which may give rise to, service charges payable to a landlord by one or more members of that association. By s 84(2) of HA 1996, only a surveyor who is qualified to carry out a management audit can be appointed (see **2.85**).

The appointment is effected by the association giving written notice to the landlord setting out the name and address of the surveyor, the duration of his appointment and the matters in respect of which he is appointed. The appointment will cease for the purposes of s 84 if the association so notifies the landlord in writing or if the association ceases to exist.

The detailed powers of the surveyor are set out in Sch 4 to the HA 1996. This allows the surveyor to appoint assistants and gives the surveyor the right to require the landlord or any other relevant person to afford him reasonable facilities for inspecting those documents of which he reasonably requires sight for the purposes of his functions, and to afford him reasonable facilities for taking copies of or extracts from those documents. The 'other relevant person' will be anyone who is responsible for applying the proceeds of the service charge or is under an obligation to the tenant in respect of any of the works or services covered by the service charge. The surveyor is to give notice to the landlord or other person of the facilities that he requires, and the facilities are to be provided within one week or as soon as reasonably practical. A reasonable charge may be made by the landlord or other person for providing copying facilities. No direct charge can be made for allowing inspection of documents, but if the terms of the lease allow the service charge to include management costs which are defined widely enough to include the cost of providing any of these facilities to the surveyor, the landlord is entitled to include them in the costs on which the service charge is based.

The surveyor also has the right, under Sch 4, to inspect any common parts of the relevant building, or any other premises affected by the management functions reflected in the service charge. On being requested to do so, the landlord must afford the surveyor reasonable access to those premises for inspection. Again, the landlord cannot make a direct charge for giving this access, but this does not prevent him from including any costs of doing so as part of his management costs within the service charge, if the service charge clause permits.

The county court has jurisdiction to deal with disputes arising out of these provisions. The Schedule also contains provisions dealing with the situation where the landlord, after receiving a notice or request from the surveyor, disposes of his interest in the property. In addition, it deals with a situation where a superior landlord holds, or has control of, service charge documents.

Tenants' associations obtaining information from landlord

2.23 When regulations are made under s 29A of the LTA 1985, which was added to that Act in July 2016, qualifying tenants who establish a tenants' association and wish to seek its formal recognition will be entitled to ask landlords for contact details for other qualifying tenants. Under the proposals, landlords will need to ask all such other qualifying tenants for their consent to pass their contact details onto a tenants' association when an association's secretary is seeking formal recognition under s 29 of the Act.

The Government has carried out a consultation for this purpose but no regulations had been published by the publication date of this book.

It is expected that the process of obtaining consent from the other qualifying tenants and the uses to which the details are put will need to comply with the Data Protection Act 1998 and the General Data Protection Regulation (EU) 2016/679.

REASONABLENESS TESTS

Overriding of contractual terms

2.24 As mentioned in **1.49**, the fact that a particular type of expenditure falls within the wording of the service charge clause may not necessarily result in the sum spent on that expenditure being recoverable from the tenant. Even careful adoption of the statutory consultation procedure described above does not guarantee that the cost will be chargeable. The reason for this is that there are two further ways in which the tenant can challenge individual items of expenditure in the courts. The first is under the common law and the second is under statute.

Common law rule

2.25 This has been considered (at **1.49**) in respect of the assumption drawn by the courts that the terms of a residential lease will not have been intended to give the landlord an unfettered right to be extravagant at the cost of the tenant. Consequently, variable service charge clauses in residential leases may be subject to an implied term that expenditure can only be included if it was incurred reasonably.

Statutory tests of reasonableness

2.26 Where s 18 of the LTA 1985 applies (see **2.2**) the provisions of s 19 of the Act provide two statutory limitations (in addition to any common law implied test of reasonableness) on the costs which can be included in the service charge ('relevant costs'):

(1) costs can be taken into account only to the extent that they are reasonably incurred; and
(2) costs incurred on the provision of services or the carrying out of works are only to be taken into account if the services or works are of a reasonable standard.

Test (1) is that the costs have been 'reasonably incurred', not that they are 'reasonable' in amount (see *Forcelux Ltd v Sweetman and Parker*[1]; *Veena SA v Cheong*[2]). This does not mean that the amount is irrelevant but that it is not the whole issue and to answer the question whether the cost was 'reasonably incurred' one must apply two tests:

(a) was the landlord's decision-making process appropriate and properly effected in accordance with the terms of the lease and reasonable under the provisions of LTA 1985 and proper practice (as indicated for example by an approved Code of Practice – see *Longmint Ltd v Eggleton*[3] see **2.92**); and
(b) was the amount incurred, to which the tenants are require to contribute, reasonable as distinct from being out of line with the market norm (per PR Francis in the *Forcelux* case).

The *Forcelux* decision has been cited with approval by the Court of Appeal in *Hounslow LBC v Waaler*[4].

In *Garside and Anson v RFYC Ltd* and *B R Maunder Taylor*[5], the Upper Tribunal gave a wide meaning to 'reasonably incurred' and took the view that this could include the timing of works in cases where it might be reasonable to spread the carrying out of the works and the incurring of any substantial costs over more than one accounting year, in order to ease the financial burden on the contributing tenants.

The meaning of 'to the extent that' in s 18 is that, if unnecessarily extensive work is carried out, the costs of such part of the work as is reasonably necessary can be included in the service charge, but the costs of the remainder cannot.

In respect of Test (2), where services or works are carried out to a less than reasonable standard, the court will allow the landlord to make a fair charge for the work done, on a quantum meruit basis (*Yorkbrook Investment Ltd v Batten*[6]).

The application of the reasonableness test to various elements of service charges is considered at **2.27–2.29**.

In relation to interim charges on account of service charges, see **2.49**.

1 (2001) LRX/14/2000, LT.
2 (2003) LRX/45/2000, LT.
3 (2009) LON/OOAJ/LSC/2009, LT.
4 [2017] EWCA Civ 45.
5 [2011] UKUT 367, LC.
6 (1985) 276 EG 545, CA.

Reasonableness in respect of repairs

2.27 When tests of reasonableness are applied to repair costs, the length of the tenants' leases may be relevant (see **1.49**). Certainly under the statutory tests (see **2.26**) the reasonable decision that the landlord is required to make can take into account value for money for the tenant over the term of the lease, where spending rather more now will save more money in the longer term (*Wandsworth Council v Griffin*[1]).

In *Garside and Anson v RFYC Ltd* and *B R Maunder Taylor*[2], the Upper Tribunal (as mentioned earlier) gave a wide meaning to 'reasonably incurred' and took the view that this could include the timing of works in cases where it might be reasonable to spread the carrying out of the works and the incurring of any substantial costs over more than one accounting year, in order to ease the financial burden on the contributing tenants.

If the scope of necessary work has been increased due to the landlord having delayed the repairs, this does not mean that the greater amount of work is not 'reasonably incurred' but the tenant might have a separate claim in damages against the landlord for breach of covenant (see **1.28** and *Continental Property Ventures Inc v White*[3]).

If the landlord incurs costs on work which he could have procured without cost under a warranty claim or guarantee, he will not have 'reasonably incurred' that work (*Continental Property Ventures Inc v White*[4]), and insurance proceeds in respect of the repair of insured damage should be credited against the costs (*Avon Ground Rents Ltd v Cowley*[5]).

EXAMPLE

> *Wandsworth London Borough Council v Griffin*[6]: The landlord of a block of flats replaced leaking flat roofs with pitched roofs and replaced the defective metal-framed windows with uPVC double-glazed units. The tenant argued that the landlord should have simply replaced the roof

coverings and overhauled the window-frames. **Held:** These costs were 'reasonably incurred' since they were better value for money over the terms of the leases, taking into account both initial and future costs, even though the initial cost alone was higher. Further, the landlord was entitled to take account of the work needed to the whole of its estate, which had been built as a single estate and was still being managed as such.

1 [2000] 26 EG 147, LT.
2 [2011] UKUT 367, LC.
3 [2006] 16 EG 148, LT.
4 [2006] 16 EG 148, LT.
5 [2018] UKUT 92, LC.
6 [2000] 26 EG 147, LT.

Reasonableness in respect of insurance costs

2.28 In relation to insurance premiums, it used to be said these will meet the statutory reasonableness test if they are incurred at arm's length in the market in the normal course of management even if they are not the lowest premiums available (*Berrycroft Management Co v Sinclair Gardens Investments*[1]). However, in *Forcelux Ltd v Sweetman and Parker*[2] (see **2.26**) the tribunal considered the landlord's detailed process in selecting the insurance (not simply whether it was at arm's length in the market) as well as considering the level of premium.

The *Berrycroft* approach was followed in *Avon Estates (London) Ltd v Sinclair Gardens Investments (Kensington) Ltd*[3], where the Tribunal said that under the reasonableness test the landlord must either prove that the rate of premium is representative of the market rate (the second limb under *Forcelux*) or that the landlord met the *Berrycroft* test of whether the insurance was obtained in the market and at arm's length. However, in *COS Services Ltd v Nicholson*[4], the Upper Tribunal reviewed these earlier decisions and in view of the *Waaler* decision in the Court of Appeal (see **1.15** and **2.17**) it decided to follow the *Forcelux* case and consider both the landlord's decision-making process and the financial outcome. Accordingly the Upper Tribunal required to see both that the process of selecting the insurer and policy was reasonable and that the outcome was that the premiums were not excessive. The landlord failed to meet the second limb of the test since the tenants demonstrated that similar cover could be obtained from other insurers for considerably lower premiums, in some cases one quarter of the premiums that the landlord had paid.

The FTT has ruled in several other cases that high levels of premium had not been 'reasonably incurred' and that the service charge could include only a substantially lower sum for insurance. However, the FTT may expect the tenant to demonstrate that the premiums he has challenged are unreasonably high: in *Westleigh Properties Ltd v Primeregal Ltd*[5] the LVT rejected the tenant's challenge to the level of premiums because the tenant had made no attempt to obtain alternative quotations and the landlord said that their insurance brokers had obtained other quotations.

In *Qdime v Bath Building (Swindon) Management Co Ltd*[6], the Upper Tribunal held that a landlord who included, at additional cost, cover for terrorism had not stepped outside his right under the lease to include additional risks 'as the landlord may in its reasonable discretion think fit to insure against' and that the test was whether a lawful decision had been reached in all the circumstances falling within the range of reasonable decisions as distinct from being perverse. Furthermore, the desirability of a landlord considering whether to include cover for terrorism damage was set out in the RICS Service Charge Residential Management Code and that counted in the landlord's favour.

In *Williams v Southwark Borough Council*[7], it was held that the landlord was not required to give the tenants credit for commission it had obtained from the insurer.

EXAMPLES

> *Forcelux Ltd v Sweetman and Parker*[8]: The landlord had insured several blocks under a single policy. Its brokers had obtained quotations from only a limited number of nationally known insurers, but there were benefits that flowed through to the tenants from having such a policy (such as reduced administrative costs, cover for alternative accommodation, and reduced subsidence excesses). Were the premiums reasonably incurred? **Held**: Yes. The landlord had met the first requirement that the landlord's decision-making process was reasonable and had met the second requirement that the resulting cost was not out of line with the market.
>
> *COS Services Ltd v Nicholson*[9]: The tenants demonstrated that similar insurance cover could be obtained from other insurers for considerably lower premiums, in some cases one quarter of the premiums that the landlord had paid. Were the premiums reasonably incurred? Held: No. The second limb of the reasonableness test under the Forcelux principles was not met since the cost was out of line with the market.

Some older forms of lease require each tenant to insure his own flat and in such cases the landlord does not normally have the right to insure the whole building, which can lead to anomalies if some of the leases do provide for the landlord to insure (see, for example, *Loy v Marchwalk Ltd*[10]).

1 [1996] EGCS 143, CA.
2 (2001) LRX/14/2000.
3 [2013] UKUT 264, LC.
4 [2017] UKUT 382, LC.
5 (2006) LON/OOAN/LSC/2005/0326.
6 [2014] UKUT 261, LC.
7 (2001) 33 HLR 22.
8 (2001) LRX/14/2000.
9 [2017] UKUT 382, LC.
10 (2004) LN/OOAU/LSC/2004/0078, LVT.

Reasonableness in respect of amenity costs

2.29 Service charges often extend to the cost incurred on reception areas, fitness rooms, concierge or caretaking services or other amenties. Costs incurred in providing such services are subject to the statutory reasonableness test (see **2.26**).

Even in relation to payments such as rent paid by a management company for accommodation used in the supply of services (eg concierge accommodation or a residents' gym) the reasonableness test will apply and the FTT can limit what is recoverable through the service charge to what rent is reasonable even if the management company has to lease the accommodation at a higher rent from the landlord (*The Gateway (Leeds) Management Ltd v Naghash*[1]).

EXAMPLE

> *Gilje and Others v Charlgrove Securities Ltd*[2], Judge Rich QC: The lease imposed an obligation on the landlord to provide a resident housekeeper, but the county court determined that, on the true interpretation of the lease, the landlord was not entitled to include in the service charge a notional rent for the housekeeper's flat. The landlord sought to overcome this by agreeing an increased salary for the housekeeper but paying her an amount after deducting the weekly rental value of the flat. Could the whole of that salary be included in the service charge? **Held:** No; since such an excessive salary would not be 'reasonably incurred'.

1 [2015] UKUT 0333, LC.
2 [2000] 44 EG 148, LT.

Reasonableness in respect of management fees

2.30 In respect of service charges caught by s 18 of the LTA 1985 (see **2.1**), s 18(1) expressly applies the statutory rules under that Act to 'the landlord's costs of management'. Hence, the reasonableness tests under s 19 (see **2.26**) will apply to management charges. The FTT is not bound by any formula in the lease for fixing the amount of management fees, and where the management function has been carried out to a poor standard, the FTT may set a low level of fee (see the discussion at **2.26**).

Many residential tenants will be able to seek a 'management audit' to assess whether the service charge functions are being discharged in an efficient and effective manner (see **2.85**).

If the service charge clause expressly permits the landlord to charge for in-house management, such a charge will normally be caught by s 18 and will be subject to the reasonableness tests mentioned, since s 18(3)(a) defines 'costs' as including overheads.

Management fees may be treated as 'reasonably incurred' if they amount to a 'reasonable charge', the reasonableness of which can be evidenced by a comparison with fees charged by other managing agents: *Parkside Knightsbridge Ltd v Horwitz*[1] (see **1.42**). Recent decisions by FTTs on the level of management fees have varied. Some have been fixed at between 12 per cent and 15 per cent of the total service costs, whilst others have been fixed at a rate per flat, eg £200 per flat (see also **1.36**). In the *Primeregal* case (see **2.28**) the FTT observed that tenants in smaller blocks may incur proportionately greater management costs than those in larger blocks because the cost cannot be spread over a larger number of flats.

In the *Loy* case (see **2.28**) a management fee of only £15 per flat was allowed since the amount of management performed was negligible. Where the managing agent has failed to comply with the Management Code for Residential Premises (see **2.92**) that can be take into account when determining a reasonable management fee (*Longmint Ltd v Eggleton*[2]).

While there is no perfect method of charging management fees, probably the level of fees ought to relate so far as possible to the time and effort involved. There are certain fairly predictable elements of the management function, principally relating to maintaining accounts, demanding and receiving payments, and producing demands and certificates of the service charges. There are other more variable but nevertheless generally routine functions, such as supervising staff and contractors dealing with day-to-day matters such as cleaning, gardening and maintenance. Finally there are less predictable functions such as those relating to major works, including compliance with the highly regulated consultation and tendering process (see **2.7**). Fixed fees may well be appropriate for the first two categories of function. It is probably fair that fees for the third category should reflect the time, professionalism and responsibility involved and often a convenient measure will be the cost of the work, with the fees being calculated as a percentage of that cost. However, that itself may involve a number of issues such as whether the calculation is based on the gross cost or the cost net of VAT (in most cases the VAT will not be recoverable by the landlord as input tax and must be charged on to the tenants). At the end of the day, the FTT may need to be satisfied that the overall management fees are 'reasonable'.

Where the management function has been carried out to a poor standard, the FTT may set a lower level of fee (*Margolin v Tackle*[3]), eg as a percentage of costs (*Longmint Ltd v Marcus*[4]). The FTT is not bound by any formula in the lease for fixing the amount of management fees.

Where the service charge clause allows the landlord to include professional fees that do not fall within 'management' and do not relate directly to the provision of 'services, repairs, maintenance, improvements or insurance' (see **2.2**), such as service charge litigation costs (see **1.39**), these costs may not fall within the ambit of the reasonableness tests under s 19, but they may fall within the statutory provisions relating to 'administration charges' – see **2.114**.

The selection of managing agents is itself covered separately by s 30B of the LTA 1985 (see **2.74**) and where applicable by the consultation requirements relating to long term agreements (see **2.7**).

The procedure for a tenant to challenge the service charge under s 19 of the LTA 1985 is set out at **2.67**. The charging of unreasonable service charges is also a ground on which tenants may apply to the court to appoint a manager to run the building in place of the landlord (LTA 1987, s 24, as amended by HA 1996, s 85).

1 (1983) 268 EG 49, CA.
2 (2009) LON/OOAJ/LSC/2009, LT.
3 [2005] Lands Tribunal.
4 [2004] 3 EGLR 171, LT.

GRANT AIDED WORKS

Application of these rules

2.31 The rules in s 20A of the LTA 1985 relating to grant aided works apply to service charges covered by s 18 of that Act (see **2.1**).

Credit for grants

2.32 By s 20A of the LTA 1985, where otherwise chargeable costs are incurred for which a grant has been or is to be paid under Pt XV of the Housing Act 1985 or Pt VIII of the Local Government and Housing Act 1989, the amount of the grant is to be deducted from the costs so as to reduce the service charge by that amount.

This also applies to the outstanding balance relating to external works determined for the landlord under s 130(3) and (4) of the Local Government and Housing Act 1989 where the landlord participates as an assisted participant in a group repair scheme under Pt VIII of that Act.

While other categories of government grants towards the cost of works to residential blocks are not expressly mentioned in s 20A, case law supports the view that they too must be credited against the service costs (see **1.34** and *Sheffield City Council v Oliver*[1]).

1 [2017] EWCA Civ 225.

COSTS OF PROCEEDINGS RELATING TO SERVICE CHARGES

Costs of proceedings

2.33 The common law position concerning the inclusion in management fees of legal and other costs relating to court and tribunal proceedings between the landlord and a tenant has been discussed at **1.39** and **1.40**. The wording of a service charge clause may be wide enough to extend to expenses of management including dealing with service charge disputes or tribunal or court procedures relating to management matters and even the recovery of service charges from the tenants generally, which might include the cost of suing them for payment.

Where the service charge clause allows the landlord to include professional fees that do not fall within 'management' and do not relate directly to the provision of 'services, repairs, maintenance, improvements or insurance' (see **2.2**), such as service charge litigation costs (see **1.39**), these costs may not fall within the ambit of the reasonableness tests under s 19, (see **2.26**) but they may fall within the statutory provisions relating to 'administration charges' – see **2.114**.

Costs relating to FTT proceedings in relation to service charge disputes are governed by regulations and by s 175 of and Sch 12 to the Commonhold and Leasehold Reform Act 2002 and generally even a successful landlord cannot usually recover his costs directly from the other party to the proceedings (see **2.67** and **Appendix 2**).

In the case of the service charge coming within s 18 of the LTA 1985 (see **2.2**), s 20C of the LTA 1985 allows a tenant to make an application to the FTT for an order that all or any of the costs incurred or to be incurred by the landlord in connection with proceedings under the LTA 1985 are to be excluded from the service charge payable by that tenant or by any other person or persons specified in the application (eg the other tenants contributing to the same service charge). The application under s 20C is to be made to the court or tribunal in which the proceedings are taking place. If the proceedings have been concluded, the application may be made afterwards. The court or tribunal may make such order as it considers just and equitable in the circumstances but it has been said that this power should be used by the FTT sparingly since it cuts down the landlord's express contractual rights under the leases (*Sherbani v Doren Ltd*[1]). However, it has also been said that where costs of the proceedings are awarded against the landlord (eg by a court or by the Upper Tribunal on an appeal from the FTT) an order under s 20C should also be made (see *Iperion Investments Corporation v Broadwalk House Residents Ltd*[2]; *Veena SA v Cheong*[3]).

At first glance it might appear that the provisions of para 10(4) of Sch 12 to the Commonhold and Leasehold Reform Act 2002 (CLRA 2002) completely prohibit landlords from recovering costs relating to FTT proceedings, either directly from the other parties to the proceedings or indirectly through service charges, but in view of the provisions of s 20C (which was not expressly repealed or amended by the CLRA 2002) that interpretation has been held by both the Central London County Court and the Lands Tribunal to be an incorrect reading of Sch 12 (*Staghold Ltd v Takeda*[4], Central London County Court; *Canary Riverside PTE v Schilling*[5]). Whether this view will be upheld by the superior courts remains to be seen.

An appeal from the FTT's decision under s 20C can be made to the Upper Tribunal (Lands Chamber), which was formerly the Lands Tribunal, with the leave of the FTT or, if the FTT refuses leave, with the leave of the Upper Tribunal (LTA 1985, s 31A(6)). The Tribunal has expressed the view that such an appeal in relation to costs orders should not be a rehearing, but should be handled as a true appeal in which the FTT's discretion, if properly exercised, should not ordinarily be interfered with (*Barrington Court Developments Ltd v Barrington Court Residents Association*[6]). In such cases the onus is on the appellant to show that the FTT's decision about costs was wrong (*Fernandez v Shanterton Second Management Company Ltd*[7]).

As to the costs of such proceedings and appeals, see also **2.67**.

EXAMPLES

> *Iperion Investments Corporation v Broadwalk House Residents Ltd*[8]: The landlord of a block of flats invalidly purported to forfeit the lease of a tenant who had embarked on unauthorised alterations. The tenant obtained a court order against the landlord to regain possession of the flat and the landlord obtained an injunction to stop the alterations. The landlord was ordered to pay half the tenant's costs of the proceedings. The service charge provisions of the tenant's lease allowed the landlord to include the costs he incurred in those proceedings. Was the judge right to make an order under s 20C that this tenant's service charge was not to include any costs relating to the proceedings? **Held:** Yes; the obvious circumstance which Parliament

must be taken to have had in mind in enacting s 20C is a case where a tenant has been successful in litigation against the landlord and yet the costs of the proceedings are within the service charge that would otherwise be recoverable from the tenant.

Tenants of Langford Court v Doren Ltd[9]: The LVT appointed a manager under the LTA 1987 on the application of the tenants, but refused to make a s 20C order excluding from the service charges the costs incurred by the landlord in opposing that application, because over half of the various grounds put forward by the tenants in support of their application were unfounded and the tenants' aggressive and unco-operative attitude towards the landlord's manager had contributed to the problems. Was the LVT justified in exercising its discretion under s 20C in that way? Held: Yes; the Lands Tribunal would not interfere with the LVT's exercise of its discretion under s 20C in these circumstances.

1 (2001) LRX/37/2000.
2 [1995] 2 EGLR 47, CA.
3 (2003) LRX/45/2000, LT.
4 [2005] PLSCS 16.
5 [2005] EW Lands LRX/65/2005.
6 [2001] 29 EG 128, LT.
7 (2007) LRX/153/2006, LT.
8 [1995] 2 EGLR 47, CA.
9 (2001) 5 March (unreported), LT.

IRRECOVERABLE COSTS UNDER SHORT LETTINGS

Tenancies for under seven years (ss 11–13 of the LTA 1985)

2.34 A short tenancy of a dwelling may be affected by the provisions of ss 11–12 of the LTA 1985 (formerly ss 32–33 of the Housing Act 1961) or ss 8–10 of the LTA 1985 (formerly ss 6–7 of the Housing Act 1957). Where these provisions apply, they impose repairing obligations on the landlord *and* prohibit or restrict the recovery of the costs from the tenant.

The type of tenancy to which ss 11–12 of the LTA 1985 apply is defined in s 13 of the Act to cover:

(1) any tenancy of a dwelling;
(2) granted on or after 24 October 1961;
(3) for a term of *less* than seven years (or granted for a term exceeding seven years but with a landlord's option to terminate it within the first seven years) without a tenant's option for renewal which, if exercised, would result in a total term of seven years or more.

The length of the term under (3) above is measured from the date from which the lease or agreement expresses the term to run, or the date when the tenancy was actually granted, whichever is later. For example, if a lease granting a term of seven years from 25 March 2002 was not actually granted until 27 March 2002, the term will be treated under the LTA 1985 as being less than seven years (ie from 27 March 2002 to 25 March 2009, a term of seven years, less two days) and would be caught by s 13.

However, these provisions do not apply to:

(1) tenancies which are comprised in an agricultural holding (LTA 1985, s 14(3));
(2) leases granted after 3 October 1980 to the Crown, a government department, a local authority, a registered housing association or certain other bodies (LTA 1985, s 14(4) and (5));
(3) business tenancies to which Pt II of the Landlord and Tenant Act 1954 applies (LTA 1985, s 32(2));
(4) short tenancies granted on a renewal where the previous tenancy fell outside the s 11 rules (LTA 1985, s 14(3)).

Landlord's obligations under s 11 of the LTA 1985

2.35 Tenancies caught by s 13 of the LTA 1985 are subject to the provisions of s 11(1) of the Act, which make the landlord liable, *at his own cost*, to:

(a) keep in repair the structure and exterior of the dwelling, including the drains, gutters and external pipes;
(b) keep in repair and proper working order the installations in the dwelling for the supply of water, gas, electricity and sanitation; and
(c) keep in repair and proper working order the installations in the dwelling for space heating and hot water.

Since the landlord is liable to carry out such repairs *at his own cost*, he cannot include those costs in any service charges levied on the tenant (LTA 1985, s 11(5)).

The extent of these obligations is discussed below.

Parts of a building to which the landlord's statutory obligations apply

2.36 The reference in s 11(1)(a) of the LTA 1985 to 'structure and exterior', in relation to a dwelling (such as a flat) which forms only part of a building, means the structure and exterior of all those parts of the building in which the landlord has 'an estate or interest', and not just the structure and exterior of the demised premises (s 11(1A)(a)). The 'structure' has been held to include the plaster on the walls and ceilings (*Grand v Gill*[1]).

It was previously held by the courts that the essential means of access to a dwelling should be treated as part of the 'exterior' of that dwelling, although amenity areas, such as a rear yard, might not (see *Douglas-Scott v Scorgie*[2]; *Brown v Liverpool Corporation*[3] and *Hopwood v Rugeley Urban District Council*[4]). However, in the recent case of *Kumarasamy v Edwards*[5], the Supreme Court held that *Brown v Liverpool Corporation* had been wrongly decided and that an outside paved area giving access to the building was plainly not part of the building and so fell outside the scope of s 11.

In respect of the installations referred to in s 11(1)(b) and (c), such as central heating boilers and systems which serve the demised premises but are located elsewhere in the building, the test is whether they form part of any building in which the landlord has 'an estate or interest' or alternatively are owned by the landlord or in its control (s 11(1A)(b)).

In all these provisions, the 'landlord' means the immediate landlord of the short letting (s 16(c)), so where the long leaseholder of a flat has sublet it on a short letting to which s 11 applies, his duties under s 11 to his subtenant apply both to the flat and to any parts of the building (and any service installations in those parts) in which he has 'an estate or interest', but not areas outside the building. In *Niazi Services v van der Loo*[6], Jacob J in the High Court said that these duties did not include the repair of the common parts over which the long leaseholder merely had rights of use, but in the recent case of *Kumarasamy v Edwards*[7], the Supreme Court held that this was wrong since such a right of use is an easement and as a matter of law it is an 'interest' in that part of the building. This would also apply to those structures of the building giving support and shelter to the flat where, under the express or implied terms of his lease, the long leaseholder has rights of shelter and support from those structures. Accordingly the long leaseholder of a flat which he sublets on a short letting may have responsibility to his sub-tenant under s 11 for the repair of the structures enclosing, supporting and sheltering his flat and the communal service installations in the building that serve the flat. That responsibility would however be subject to certain limitations.

Those limitations are first that the provisions of s 11(1A) do not require the landlord to carry out any works or repairs unless the disrepair or lack of working order affects the tenant's enjoyment of the demised premises or any common parts which he is entitled to use under his tenancy (s 11(1B)). Secondly, it is implied that a landlord who is not himself entitled to be present in the parts of the building that he has let which are in disrepair cannot have liability to carry out repairs under s 11 until he has been given notice of the disrepair (*Kumarasamy v Edwards*, following *O'Brien v Robinson*[8] and similar cases). Thirdly, where the disrepair is in a part of the building over which the landlord's rights do not include the right for him to carry out the repairs himself, he has a defence against a claim by his tenant under s 11 if he can prove that he has used all reasonable endeavours to obtain, but has been unable to obtain, the right to carry out the repairs (s 11(3A)). That might apply where there is disrepair in the common parts or communal service installations in a block and the landlord is the long leaseholder of only the flat, has no right under his lease to carry out repairs in those other parts of the building and has approached the superior landlord but has been refused the right to carry out such repairs. However, in *Kumarasamy v Edwards* it was said that the landlord would be expected to pass on to the superior landlord any notification the landlord received of such disrepair.

1 [2011] EWCA Civ 554.
2 [1984] 1 All ER 1086.
3 [1969] 3 All ER 1345.
4 [1975] 1 WLR 373.
5 [2016] UKSC 40.
6 [2004] EWCA Civ 52.
7 [2016] UKUT SC 40.
8 [1973] AC 912, HL.

Extent of the landlord's obligations under s 11 of the LTA 1985

2.37 The obligations imposed by s 11 on the landlord do not require him:

(a) to carry out any works or repairs which would be covered by the tenant's duty to use the premises in a tenant-like manner;
(b) to rebuild or reinstate the premises after damage or destruction by fire or by tempest, flood or other inevitable accident; or
(c) to repair or maintain anything which the tenant is entitled to remove from the dwelling (s 11(2)).

In determining the standard of repair required of the landlord, regard shall be had to the age, character and prospective life of the dwelling and its locality (s 11(3)).

Furthermore, the obligation to keep the relevant parts of the building in 'repair' is itself a limited obligation, by reason of the restricted meaning given by the courts to the word 'repair' (see **1.20**). In *McDougall v Easington District Council*[1], the Court of Appeal held that, by using the word 'repair', s 11 did not require the landlord to remedy major defects in the original construction and design of the dwellings which would have involved major structural alterations changing the character of the buildings. For the same reason, s 11 does not require the landlord to install new items which were not previously provided. Hence, it has been held that a landlord is not liable to install a damp-proof course where none had existed previously, nor to lag previously unlagged water pipes against frost, nor to replace window-frames whose design made them prone to condensation (even though this resulted in dampness which damaged internal decorations) (*Wainwright v Leeds City Council*[2]; *Wycombe Health Authority v Barnett*[3]; *Quick v Taff-Ely Borough Council*[4]; *Eyre v McCracken*[5]).

On the other hand, if internal redecoration is required as a consequence of repairs which the landlord is liable to carry out under s 11, the landlord is responsible for the necessary consequential redecoration and, if the landlord delays carrying out that redecoration, the tenant may be entitled to damages for the inconvenience of having to live in the premises in their poor decorative condition (*McGreal v Wake*[6]; *Bradley v Chorley Borough Council*[7]).

The obligations to keep installations in proper working order have been the subject of some recent cases.

EXAMPLES

Sykes v Harry[8]: A gas fire in a flat let on a shorthold tenancy was defective. The landlord did not enter into a service contract for its maintenance, had not inspected the flat and was unaware of the defect. Carbon monoxide poisoning made the tenant ill. Held: The landlord is liable in damages under the Defective Premises Act 1972, s 4 for personal injury caused by his failure to comply with his obligation to maintain installations under LTA 1985, s 11, even if he does not have actual notice of the defect, where he has not taken reasonable care.

O'Connor v Old Etonian Housing Association Ltd[9]: The landlord of a block of flats replaced old large water pipes with small bore pipes. Initially there was no problem, but later the mains water pressure decreased and the tenant's top floor flat, held on a short tenancy, ceased to get a proper supply, which would not have happened with the old larger pipes. The landlord could have installed a pump to rectify this, but did not. Six years later the water authority built a new pumping station which increased the mains pressure and solved the problem. Was the landlord liable in the meantime for breach of the covenant implied by LTA 1985, s 11(1)(b) to 'keep in . . . proper working order' the water pipes? **Held:** No; the small bore pipes were still in proper working order; when installed they had been properly designed and constructed and had worked effectively; at the time of installation a substantial long-term drop in water pressure could not have been reasonably anticipated.

1 (1989) 58 P&CR 201.
2 (1984) 270 EG 1289.
3 (1982) 264 EG 619.
4 [1986] QB 809.
5 (2000) 80 P&CR 220, CA.
6 (1984) 269 EG 1254.
7 (1985) 275 EG 801.
8 (2001) 17 EG 221, CA.
9 [2002] EWCA Civ 150 (unreported), CA.

Lettings of houses at low rents (ss 8–10 of the LTA 1985)

2.38 The LTA 1985 re-enacts some very old statutory rules concerning houses let at low rents. Sections 8–10 apply to a contract for the letting of a house if the rent does not exceed the amount set out in Table 1 below. At the publication date of this book there was a bill in Parliament to update these provisions.

Section 8(6) provides that 'house' includes part of a house, but it is not clear whether it includes a flat in a purpose-built block.

Date of making contract	*Rent limit*
Before 31 July 1923	In London: £40 Elsewhere: £26 or £16 (See Note (1))
On or after 31 July 1923 but before 6 July 1957	In London: £40 Elsewhere: £26
On or after 6 July 1957	In London: £80 Elsewhere: £52

Notes

(1) The applicable figure for contracts made before 31 July 1923, is £26 in the case of premises situated in a borough or urban district which, at the date of the contract, had, according to the last published census, a population of 50,000 or more. In the case of a house situated elsewhere, the figure is £16.

(2) The references to 'London' are, in relation to contracts made before 1 April 1965, to the administrative county of London and, in relation to contracts made on or after that date, to Greater London exclusive of the outer London boroughs.

The provisions of ss 8–10 of the LTA do not apply to a letting for three years or more if it contains an obligation on the tenant to put the premises into a condition reasonably fit for human habitation. For this purpose, a tenancy containing an option for either party to terminate the letting before the expiry of three years counts as a tenancy for less than three years. While, in some instances, a tenant's covenant to 'keep' premises in repair will be construed so as to include an obligation on the tenant to put the premises into repair at the outset of the letting (*Proudfoot v Hart*[1]), this appears to apply only where the premises are in disrepair at the commencement of the letting.

Since a lease is, in law, a 'contract', it would seem possible that, under the above rules, ss 8–10 of the LTA 1985 might apply to a long lease of a house granted at a premium and reserving a nominal ground rent if the tenant's repairing covenant is simply to 'keep' (and not 'put') the house in good repair. However, if the expression 'rent' is apt to include all sums payable to the landlord by the tenant under the terms of the tenancy, including a service charge, the effect would be, in many cases, to take the letting outside the rent limits set out in Table 1 (above).

1 (1890) 25 QB 42.

Effect of ss 8–10 of the LTA 1985

2.39 Tenancies to which ss 8–10 of the LTA 1985 apply carry an implied condition on the landlord's part that the house is fit for human habitation at the outset of the letting, and an implied obligation on the part of the landlord to keep it fit for human habitation during the letting. The cost of any works required to comply with these provisions cannot be charged to the tenant.

The criteria for fitness for human habitation are set out in s 10 of the LTA 1985. These are repair, stability, freedom from damp, internal arrangement, natural lighting, ventilation, water supply, drainage and sanitation conveniences, cooking and food preparation facilities and waste water disposal facilities. A house is to be regarded as unfit if (but only if) it is so defective in any one or more of these matters so that it is not reasonably suitable for occupation in that condition.

SERVICE CHARGE LIMITS UNDER RENT ACT PROTECTED TENANCIES AND RIGHT TO BUY LEASES

Rent Act protected tenancies

Introduction

2.40 Some short and periodic (eg quarterly) residential lettings constitute protected tenancies under the Rent Act 1977, as amended. The details of Rent Act protection, apart from those relating to service charges, are outside the scope of this book.

Until a rent is registered under the Rent Acts there is no limit on the amount of rent chargeable under a protected tenancy. However, once, and for so long as, a rent is registered the registration serves to specify the maximum which can be charged to the tenant by way of rent *and* service charge. The rent may either be registered as a fixed sum inclusive of a notional service charge, or with a separate variable service charge.

Registered rents with variable service charges

2.41 If the tenant's lease or tenancy agreement contains provisions for a variable service charge, and the rent officer or rent assessment committee considers that the terms of those provisions for variability of the charge are reasonable, the rent may be registered as a basic rent with an additional, separate, variable service charge (Rent Act 1977, s 71(4)). It must be remembered that service charges under a letting granted for a term of under seven years (including a periodic letting) cannot include the cost of works covered by ss 11–12 of the LTA 1985 (see **2.34**).

This power under s 71(4) is restricted to incorporating, in the rent registration, the *identical formula* for the variable service charge as that contained in the contractual tenancy. The rent cannot be registered with a different version of that formula. Accordingly, if, as is quite common, the contractual tenancy reserves, by way of service charge, a proportion of the amount by which the service expenditure may increase above the expenditure in a specified base year, the variable service charge can only be incorporated in the rent registration using exactly the same formula *including the same base year* (*Wigglesworth v Property Holding & Investment Trust Ltd*[1]; *Betts v Vivamat Properties Ltd*[2]).

In *Firstcross Ltd v Teasdale*[3] the court considered that when determining the reasonableness of the contractual variability provisions contained in the lease or tenancy agreement, the court was bound to take into account the implied limitation of reasonableness laid down in *Finchbourne v Rodrigues*[4] (see **1.51**). However, in *Wigglesworth v Property Holding & Investment Trust Ltd*[5] (above) the court took a different view and considered that s 71 required the contractual provisions of the lease or tenancy agreement to be considered on their own, to see whether they passed the test of reasonableness under that section.

In a case where the landlord was a co-operative which was owned by the tenants and incorporated under the Industrial and Friendly Societies Act 1965, it was held reasonable to have a clause which provided for the service charge to be a sum fixed each year by the annual general meeting of the co-operative, the rules of which (together with statutory provisions) provided for annual meetings, audited accounts, and other proper arrangements (*Re Heathview Tenants' Co-operative Ltd*[6]).

A rent registration is not to include a service charge where the services are provided by a company which is separate from a landlord (even if it is in the same group) and where the tenant pays for the services separately from the rent and the landlord is not personally liable to provide or procure the provision of the services (*Eaton Square Properties v Ogilvie*[7], London Rent Assessment Committee).

1 (1984) 270 EG 555.
2 (1984) 270 EG 849.
3 (1983) 265 EG 305.

4 [1976] 3 All ER 581, CA.
5 (1984) 270 EG 555.
6 (1981) 258 EG 644.
7 (2000) 16 EG 143.

Registered rents inclusive of service charges

2.42 If the contractual tenancy does not include a variable service charge clause (or if it does, but the Rent Officer or Rent Assessment Committee considers that the variability provisions of the clause are not reasonable), an inclusive rent will be registered incorporating a fixed service charge element. Under s 67 of the Rent Act 1977, as amended by s 59 of the Housing Act 1980, the landlord must, when applying for registration of a fair rent, submit details and calculations of the service costs referable to the particular dwelling. Once again, these cannot include the cost of works falling within ss 11–12 of the LTA 1985 where applicable (see **2.34**).

The Rent Officer is not bound by a mathematical calculation of the service costs in cases where this might result in an unrealistic figure. For example, in the case of a centrally heated flat in a block in which most other flats had been disconnected from the heating system, the actual mathematical cost of supplying the heating to that flat might be excessively high and will then be substituted by a typical, reasonable, heating charge (*R v London Rent Assessment Panel, ex parte Cliftvylle Properties Ltd*[1]).

The landlord is entitled to include in his calculation of the service element, an allowance for depreciation of the service equipment (boilers, lifts, tanks, etc) and an element in respect of profit to the landlord on the provision of services (*Regis Property Co Ltd v Dudley*[2]; *Metropolitan Properties Co (FGC) Ltd v Lannon*[3]; *Metropolitan Properties Co (FGC) Ltd v Good*[4]; *Metropolitan Properties Co Ltd v Noble*[5]; *Perseus Property Co Ltd v Burberry*[6]). This 'profit' is intended to go towards the landlord's costs of financing the provision of the services and providing the capital money for the purchase of the service equipment.

If a rent is registered with a fixed charge element based on estimates and, subsequently, it is found that the actual service costs are less than the estimates, the tenant nevertheless, cannot have the rent registration varied or set aside (*Legal and General Assurance Society v Keane*[7]). But where there is an appeal from the Rent Officer's determination to the Rent Assessment Committee, the landlord is entitled to place, before the committee, updated details of service costs which were not available at the time of the rent officer's consideration of the matter (*Daejan Properties Ltd v Chambers*[8]).

1 (1983) 266 EG 44.
2 [1959] AC 370.
3 [1968] 1 All ER 354.
4 (1981) 260 EG 67.
5 [1968] 2 All ER 313.
6 (1984) 273 EG 405.
7 (1979) 38 P&CR 399.
8 (1986) 277 EG 308.

Statutory tenancies on expiry of long leases

2.43 Part I of the Landlord and Tenant Act 1954 contains provisions for certain residential tenants to become assured tenants under the Housing Act 1980 (as amended), on the expiry of a long lease at a low rent. The detailed rules are outside the scope of this book.

Where the long lease reserved a service charge, any service charges payable in respect of a period prior to the commencement of the statutory tenancy will be recoverable from the tenant, even after that date, since the proviso to s 10(1) of the Landlord and Tenant Act 1954 excludes, from the extinguishment of past liabilities, sums payable in respect of parts of the building other than the demised premises (*Blatherwick (Services) Ltd v King*[1]).

1 [1991] 2 EGLR 39, CA.

Right to buy leases

Introduction

2.44 The grant of long, shared-ownership leases under the right to buy legislation is governed by ss 143 et seq of the Housing Act 1985, the details of which go beyond the scope of this book. However, the Sixth Schedule to the Housing Act 1985 contains provisions restricting the service charges which can be imposed under such leases.

Service charge provisions

2.45 The Sixth Schedule to the Housing Act 1985 sets out limitations upon service charges under shared ownership leases granted in pursuance of the right to buy, and these are summarised (in outline only) below.

(1) Where the premises comprise a flat, the tenant can be required to pay a 'reasonable part' of the costs of discharging or insuring against the obligations imposed by the covenants implied by para 14(2) of the Sixth Schedule (which covers the repair of the structure and the exterior of the building, the making good of defects in the structure, the repair of common parts, the maintenance at a reasonable level of the services to which the tenant is entitled, and the repair of installations connected with those services) (para 16A(1)(a) of the Sixth Schedule).
The lease can, however, require the payment of a service charge contribution of a fixed sum with increases being index-linked; the provisions of para 16B only apply to service charges which vary according to the amount of costs incurred (*Coventry City Council v Cole*[1]).

(2) The tenant can, in the case of a house or a flat, be required to pay a 'reasonable part' of the costs of insuring against the obligation implied by para 14(3) (which covers rebuilding or reinstating the building in the event of damage by fire, tempest, flood or other normally insured peril) (para 16A(1)(b) of the Sixth Schedule).

(3) However, the amount recoverable from the tenant of a flat in respect of the cost of repairs (including making good structural defects) during the 'initial period' of the lease (generally the first five accounting years – see para 16B(4)) is restricted by reference to the amount of estimated cost notified to the tenant by the landlord's notice under s 125 of the Housing Act 1985 plus an inflation allowance (para 16B(1) to (3) of the Sixth Schedule). The rate of inflation allowance is prescribed from time to time by regulations and currently, in relation to England, set out in the Housing (Right to Buy) (Service Charges) (Amendment) (England) Order 2007[2].

(4) The lease of a flat can require the tenant to pay towards improvements to be carried out to the flat, the building or other land, if notified in the s 125 notice, and during the 'initial period' (generally the first five years of the term – see para 16C(4)) the amount recoverable in this respect is limited by reference to the estimate contained in the s 125 notice, plus an inflation allowance (para 16C(1) to (3) of the Sixth Schedule).

1 [1994] 1 WLR 398, CA.
2 SI 2007/384.

NOTICES, SERVICE CHARGE DEMANDS AND TIME-LIMITS

Need for notice of landlord's address for service

2.46 Section 48 of the LTA 1987 provides that no rent or service charge will be due from any tenant of premises which are or include a dwelling (except those within Pt II of the Landlord and Tenant Act 1954 – relating to business premises) unless the landlord has served on the tenant a written notice giving the tenant an address in England or Wales at which notices (including notices in proceedings) can be served on the landlord by the tenant.

In *Dallhold Estates (UK) Pty Ltd v Lindsay Trading Properties Inc*[1], the Court of Appeal held that this meant that the rent was not due until the s 48 notice was served, at which time any rent which would otherwise have been in arrears became due immediately.

The section does not make it clear exactly when a notice needs to be served, but it seems appropriate that every residential tenant should be served with a s 48 notice well before any rent or service charge falls due or is to be demanded, and that each assignee should be given one as soon as the landlord or his agent learns of the assignment.

A specimen notice is given in **Appendix 1**. Formality of wording is not required (*Rogan v Woodfield*[2]) and strictly there is no need to state expressly that the address is being given 'for service' (*Drew-Morgan v Hamid-Zadeh*[3]). However, the statutory provisions for service charge demands require particular wording to be used (see **2.47**).

1 [1994] EGLR 99, CA.
2 [1994] EGCS 145, CA.
3 (1999) EGCS 72, CA.

Forms of service charge demand

2.47 In addition to the above requirement, ss 46 and 47 of the LTA 1987 impose requirements for rent and service charge demands addressed to those tenants. The requirements are that every demand must set out:

(1) the name and address of the landlord; and
(2) if that address is not in England or Wales, an address in England or Wales at which notices (including notices in proceedings) may be served on the landlord by the tenant.

Unless a receiver or manager is administering the service charge under a court order, no service charge will be payable on a demand which omits the above information until that information is supplied in writing (s 47(2) of the LTA 1987).

Furthermore, s 21B of the LTA 1985, inserted by the Commonhold and Leasehold Reform Act 2002, requires any demand for service charges within the regime of LTA 1985 to be accompanied by a summary of the tenant's rights and obligations concerning service charges, using the wording prescribed in regulations. The tenant's obligation to pay is suspended until this requirement is satisfied. The current required wording is set out in the Service Charges (Summary of Rights and Obligations and Transitional Provision) (England) Regulations 2007 and the Service Charges (Summary of Rights and Obligations and Transitional Provision) (Wales) Regulations 2007. That wording, including its heading, must be on a sheet of paper that accompanies each service charge demand, including demands for interim charges as well as demands for final balances; and sending the summary sheet separately from the demand does not satisfy the requirement (*Tingdene Holiday Parks Ltd v Cox*[1]).

1 [2011] UKUT 310, LT.

Time-limits for demanding payment

2.48 There is an extremely important time-limit imposed by s 20B of the LTA 1985. Where the Act applies, a service charge demand cannot include costs, even if the costs are within the scope of s 18 (see **2.1**), which are incurred more than 18 months before the demand for payment is served on the tenant, unless a written notice was given to the tenant during the 18 months beginning with the date when the costs were incurred, warning him that the costs were incurred and that he would, subsequently, be required to contribute to them through the service charge.

The 18 months period runs from the date when the costs were 'incurred'. Where the costs relate to work carried out under a building contract, it may be necessary to analyse the terms of the contract to identify what event triggers the cost being 'incurred' (per Morgan J in *London Borough of Brent v Shulem B Association Ltd*[1]) and that might not be an easy exercise.

In *O M Property Management Ltd v Burr*[2], the Upper Tribunal held that under the LTA 1985 a 'cost' was not a liability – a liability becomes a 'cost' only when it is made concrete by being paid or possibly by being set down in an invoice or in a certificate under a building contract. Thus the 18 months under s 20B ran from the date when the liability is properly invoiced to the landlord, and not the date when the service was ordered, obtained or used. However that was an unusual case in which gas charges were invoiced by the wrong supply company and were repaid; when the correct supply company invoiced them and the landlord paid the invoices, the tenants claimed that it was too late to recover the cost from them due of s 20B. That plainly had little merit and not surprisingly the landlord won, but the decision does leave a rather unusual result.

A further twist arose in *Westmark (Lettings) Ltd v Peddle*[3], where liability for costs incurred by a superior landlord was being passed down a chain of leaseholders. The FTT held that s 20B was triggered for all the tiers of tenant when the cost was incurred by the superior landlord who commissioned the relevant work. Depending on the number of successive underlettings, any other interpretation could result in the occupation tenant having to pay for the work several years after it had been billed by the contractor. However the Upper Tribunal overturned that decision and applied s 20B to each leaseholder sequentially so that each leaseholder has 18 months either to invoice or notify his immediate tenant once he receives a demand for payment from his own immediate landlord. The judge took the view that the risk of an intermediate leaseholder being unable to pass the liability down to his tenant was more serious than the issue that tenants at the bottom of the chain might be paying for work long after it was carried out.

The 'demand' for payment referred to in s 20B is a demand which both complies with the relevant provisions of the lease relating to demands for payment of service charges and can properly be called a 'demand' for the purpose of s 20B. For the latter purpose (and normally also for the former) it must require payment of a specified sum (*London Borough of Brent v Shulem B Association Ltd*[4], above).

In the absence of such a demand being made within the relevant 18 months period, the costs will only be recoverable if during that period a notice was given complying with s 20B, and for this purpose it is essential that the notice specifies the amount of the costs incurred, otherwise they will be irrecoverable (*Westminster City Council v Hammond*[5]; *London Borough of Brent v Shulem B Association Ltd*[6], above). In the *Shulem B* case, Morgan J said that the requirement under s 20B was that the written notice to be given within the 18 months period must state the amount of costs that have been incurred and that the tenant may be required to contribute towards that amount, but it need not state the amount of the tenant's contribution. Where the amount is not yet ascertained, he said that an estimate must be given and the landlord may err on the high side, but simply stating that costs have been incurred does not suffice.

However, the limit under s 20B does not apply where the tenant's contribution to the costs is fully covered by interim charges which have been collected on account and there is simply a delay in producing the final service charge accounts, since no further demand for the payment is involved and s 20B only applies to late demands. This was first held in *Gilje v Charlegrove Securities*[7]) and although the judge's reasoning in the *Gilje* case was criticised by some robust FTT decisions to the contrary effect, it was followed and cited with approval in both the Lands Tribunal and the County Court (see *Islington London Borough Council v Abdel-Malek*[8], *Brennan v St Paul's Court Ltd*[9] and *Paddington Walk Management Ltd v Governors of the Peabody Trust*[10], HH Judge Hazel Williamson QC), and by the Upper Tribunal (Lands Chamber) in *Holding & Management (Solitaire) Ltd v Sherwin*[11]. It has now been approved by the Court of Appeal in *Skelton v DBS Homes (Kings Hill) Ltd*[12].

Accordingly, it seems that where interim charges relating to the relevant costs have been demanded before the expiry of the 18 month period, the sums so collected are unaffected by s 20B and only any balancing charge will be subject to the s 20B limitation and that charge will not be recoverable if it was demanded outside the 18 months period without a sufficient notice having been given during that period as to the amount on which the balancing charge may be based (*Holding & Management (Solitaire) Ltd v Sherwin*[13]).

Where, under the terms of the tenant's lease, the demand cannot be made until a service charge certificate or account has been prepared, compliance with the above procedure will be important if the preparation of the certificate or account may be delayed.

At one time it was expected that a further, extremely important, time-limit would be introduced by the proposed new s 21(2), to be inserted by the Commonhold and Leasehold Reform Act 2002 with effect from a date that was yet to be fixed. This, if it is brought into force, would impose a deadline for the service of accounts and certificates (see **2.55**) and will allow tenants to withhold payments in cases of default (see **2.68**). However there is doubt as to whether this will be brought into force.

As for the time-limits for making demands of former tenants and their guarantors, see **1.97**.

1 [2011] EWHC 1663 (Ch).
2 [2012] UKUT 2, LC.
3 [2017] UKUT 449, LC.
4 [2011] EWHC 1663 (Ch).
5 [1995] LAG Bulletin, December, p 19, Central London County Court.
6 [2011] EWHC 1663 (Ch).
7 [2003] EWHC 1284 (Ch).
8 [2008] L&TR 2, LT.
9 [2010] UKUT 403, LC.
10 [2010] L&TR 6, Central London County Court.
11 [2010] UKUT 412, LC.
12 [2017] EWCA Civ 1139.
13 [2011] UKUT 412, LC.

INTERIM CHARGES

Common law position

2.49 The contractual position in respect of the entitlement to charge interim charges has been discussed at **1.68**. So far, there has been no reported case indicating any common law implied term that *interim* charges must be reasonable, but a court decision to that effect might not be entirely unexpected, having regard to the reasoning in *Finchbourne v Rodrigues*[1] (see **1.51**).

1 [1976] 3 All ER 581, CA.

Statutory limits on advance payments

2.50 Where s 18 of the LTA 1985 applies (see **2.1**), s 19(2) of that Act provides that, in respect of any service charge which is payable before the costs are incurred:

(1) no greater amount shall be so payable than is reasonable; and
(2) after the relevant costs have been incurred, any necessary adjustments shall be made by repayment, reduction in subsequent charges, or otherwise.

This permits both interim charges and reserve fund contributions (see *FCH Housing and Care v Burns*[1]), so long as the amounts demanded do not exceed a reasonable sum. The provisions of s 19(2) do not specify how soon 'after' the costs are incurred the adjustment must be made. The court might well imply that the adjustment must be within a reasonable time of the actual expenditure and, where the lease provides for annual accounting and certification, it is anticipated that the court would accept that procedure as complying with this requirement, assuming that the preparation and certification of the accounts were to be carried out within a reasonable time after the expiry of the accounting year.

In relation to interim charges, in *Knapper v Francis*[2] it was held that the landlord could meet the reasonableness test in respect of payments on account, commonly known as interim service charges, by reference to the expectation of expenditure at the date of demand even if it transpired later that some of the expenditure was not actually incurred during the relevant accounting period and the landlord intended to retain it for later expenditure.

Where any of the costs to be reflected in interim charges may be wholly or partly funded from insurance monies, that should be taken into account to reduce the interim charges (*Avon Ground Rents Ltd v Cowley*[3]).

EXAMPLE

> *Avon Ground Rents Ltd v Cowley*[4]: The landlord had to replace a failed waterproof membrane. The cost was largely to be covered by the NHBC new build defects insurance scheme. The leases allowed the landlord to require the tenants to make interim payments on account. Could the landlord base its interim charges on the full expected cost of the works ignoring the near-certainty of receiving the insurance monies? **Held:** No. The lease contained provisions for interim payments and the tribunal was not concerned with the question whether those provisions were reasonable but was concerned whether the amount demanded was reasonable under section 19(2) of the LTA 1985. Contributions equal to the full cost of the remedial work were not reasonable where insurance monies of a near-equivalent amount were anticipated and there was no reason to think that they would be withheld or delayed.

Note also the time-limit provisions of s 20B of the LTA 1985 where a final demand may not be available to be served within 18 months of the costs being incurred (see **2.48**).

The procedure for the tenant to challenge the amounts demanded by the landlord is set out at **2.67**.

In *Knapper v Francis*[5] (above) it was also held that s19(2) does not give the FTT jurisdiction to order the landlord to repay to the tenant a surplus by which interim charges exceed the final service charge, saying that 'the true purpose of the second limb of section 19(2) is unclear'. Service charge clauses generally have an express provision dealing with the crediting or repayment of surpluses.

1 [2007] LRX/9/2006, LT.
2 [2017] UKUT 3, LC, the Upper Tribunal (Lands Chamber).
3 [2018] UKUT 92, LC.
4 [2018] UKUT 92, LC.
5 [2017] UKUT 3, LC, the Upper Tribunal (Lands Chamber).

Inadequate interim charge provisions

2.51 If the lease fails to provide for sufficient interim charges, an application to the court to vary the lease should be considered (see **2.76**).

Trust of interim payments

2.52 Interim payments, until expended, are generally to be held on trust as described at **2.62**, although some landlords are exempt from that rule.

Designated accounts

2.53 The amendments made by the Commonhold and Leasehold Reform Act 2002 include a new s 42A to the LTA 1987, not yet in force.

This provides that interim payments (and other sums such as sinking funds) which are held on trust under the LTA 1987, s 42 (see **2.62**) must be held by the payee in a 'designated account' at a 'relevant financial institution'. The Secretary of State may make regulations identifying 'relevant financial institutions' and describing the type of account that can be used for this purpose. The institution must be notified in writing that the account is designated to receive the payments in question (ie sums collected by way of service charge from all those tenants who are contributing to the same service costs) and no other payments.

The contributing tenants will have the right to be given reasonable facilities to inspect, or to be given copies of, documents evidencing compliance with these requirements (eg bank statements). This right can also be exercised by the secretary of a recognised tenants' association (see **2.21**). They can exercise this right by giving written notice to the landlord or the rent collector and the inspection facilities or copies must be provided to them within 21 days. A reasonable charge can be made for supplying copies. No charge can be made for being given inspection facilities, but any costs incurred by the payee in providing those facilities can be treated as part of his costs of management, so such costs could be included in the service charges if management costs are chargeable under the terms of the relevant leases.

Tenants may withhold further service charge payments if they have reasonable grounds for believing that the payee is not complying with the duty to pay the sums into a designated account with a relevant financial institution. Any provisions of the tenant's lease which would apply to the non-payment (eg landlord's right of forfeiture) or late payment (eg landlord's right to charge interest) of the amount withheld are suspended in relation to that amount during the period in which the tenant is allowed to withhold payment.

Failure to comply with the requirements of s 42A without reasonable excuse is the committal of an offence (LTA 1987, s 42B). Where the payee is a company or other corporate body, the offence will be committed personally by any director, manager, secretary or similar officer of the body who has consented to or connived in the offence. This also applies to members of the body who manage its affairs. Proceedings under these provisions can be brought by a local housing authority (within s 1 of the Housing Act 1985).

The Secretary of State may make regulations which exclude certain categories of landlords from these requirements (LTA 1987, s 42A(9A)).

PREPARATION AND CERTIFICATION OF ACCOUNTS

Requirements of the lease

2.54 Requirements of the lease are discussed at **1.74**. Where statutes impose requirements in respect of the preparation and certification of accounts (see below), those will normally be *in addition* to, rather than replacing, the contractual requirements of the lease.

If the lease provides that the accounts or certificates produced in accordance with the terms of the lease are conclusive as to the amount payable by the tenant, that may or may not be the end of the matter in non-residential cases (see the discussion at **1.78**) but it is likely that any such provision is overridden in respect of cases falling within LTA 1985 by the power given to the FTT by s 27A(6) of that Act (see **2.66**).

Provision of statements of account

2.55 Where s 18 of the LTA 1985 applies (see **2.1**), the landlord must supply, to each tenant who is liable to pay a service charge, a written statement of account for every accounting period (s 21). Until the amendment to s 21 made in 2002 comes into force, this duty only arises upon the tenant (or the secretary of a recognised tenants' association) making a request for the accounts.

Section 21(5) provides that the summary must:

(1) set out the costs in a way which shows how they are, or will be, reflected in the demands for service charges,

(2) state whether any of the costs relate to works which are grant-aided (see **2.31** above),

(3) summarise any costs in respect of which no demand for payment was received by the landlord during the twelve-month period to which the relevant service charge account relates,

(4) summarise any costs in respect of which a demand for payment was received during that period but payment was not made during the period,

(5) summarise any costs where a demand for payment was received and payment was made during that period,

(6) specify the total amount received by the landlord down to the end of the twelve-month period on account of service charges and still standing to the credit of the tenants at the end of that period.

If the landlord fails to comply with such a request, that is a criminal offence rendering the landlord liable to be fined (see **2.68**), but it does not give the tenant a civil remedy to sue for delivery of the summary (*di Marco v Morshead Mansions Ltd*[1]).

A new requirement for the landlord, without request, to issue regular statements, complying with different requirements, was included in the Commonhold and Leasehold Reform Act 2002, s 152 but has not been brought into force. It would have been accompanied by provisions to the effect that the landlord's failure to comply with these requirements entitled the tenant to withhold payments of service charges (see **2.68**).

1 [2014] EWCA Civ 96.

Certification of statements of accounts

2.56 The accountant's certificate under the amended s 21 (if bought into force) will have to state:

(a) that in his opinion the statement of account deals fairly with the matters with which it is required to deal under s 21 of the LTA 1985; and

(b) that the costs stated in the summary are sufficiently supported by accounts, receipts and other documents which have been produced to him.

Regulations may impose further requirements for these certificates (see **2.55**).

Apparently, the accountant is *not* required to consider whether the costs were incurred in accordance with the reasonableness and consultation requirements of ss 19 and 20 of the LTA 1985.

The qualifications of the accountant must fall within s 28 of the LTA 1985. He must eligible for appointment as a 'statutory auditor' under Pt 42 of the Companies Act 2006. Accordingly, he must be a member of a 'recognised supervisory body' such as the Institute of Chartered Accountants in England and Wales, the Institute of Chartered Accountants of Scotland, the Association of Certified Accountants, the Institute of Chartered Accountants in Ireland, or any other body established in the UK and recognised under Sch 10 of the Companies Act 2006. Alternatively, he can be a person authorised by the

Secretary of State under s 1221 of the Companies Act 2006 as being a person with similar qualifications obtained outside the UK. However, a body corporate (except a Scottish firm), an officer or employee of the landlord or of a company in the same group as the landlord, or a person who is a partner or employee of any such officer or employee, cannot act as accountant for these purposes. Special rules apply where the landlord is one of certain specified public bodies listed in the LTA 1985, s 28(6).

Advance warning of late demands

2.57 As mentioned and considered more fully at **2.48**, the LTA 1985 precludes a demand from including relevant costs incurred more than 18 months prior to the service of the demand on the tenant, unless a warning notice under s 20B was given to the tenant within that period of 18 months.

Tenants' inspection of invoices

2.58 Some leases give the tenant the right to inspect the service charge records, books, invoices and vouchers. In addition to any such contractual rights, where s 18 of the LTA 1985 applies, a tenant who is entitled to receive a statement of account pursuant to s 21 has the right under s 22 of the LTA 1985 to be given reasonable facilities to inspect and copy (or take down extracts from) the accounts, receipts and other documents relevant to the matter to be dealt with in the statement of account (see **2.55**).

The inspection and copying facilities must be made available within 28 days of the tenant making a written request. The tenant must make his request within 12 months of the end of the relevant accounting period, except where the landlord issues the statement of account (exactly or substantially conforming to the requirements of s 21) more than 6 months after the end of the accounting period, in which event the tenant's time to request inspection of the vouchers and other supporting documents is extended to the date 6 months after the statement is actually issued to him. The request can be served on the landlord or the person who collects rent on his behalf (or on his agent specified in the rent book or similar document). Where there is a recognised tenants' association, a tenant may authorise the secretary of the association to carry out the inspection on his behalf.

The inspection facilities must be made available, free of charge, to the person inspecting, although this does not preclude the costs so incurred by the landlord being charged in the service charges as management costs if the service charge clause in the lease permits. The landlord is, however, entitled to make a reasonable charge for providing copying facilities.

These provisions have been amended by Sch 10 to the Commonhold and Leasehold Reform Act 2002 to ensure that they apply to service charge payments provided by just one tenant just as they apply to contributions from two or more tenants.

Service of tenants' requests under s 22 of the LTA 1985

2.59 By virtue of s 22(5) of the LTA 1985 (as existing and also as to be amended by the Commonhold and Leasehold Reform Act 2002), the tenant's written request for inspection of accounts, receipts and other supporting documents may be served either on the landlord, or on the person who collects rent on behalf of the landlord, or on any other agent of the landlord named as such in the rent book or similar document.

Service charges levied by superior landlords

2.60 Where the landlord's own interest in the property is leasehold, the service costs incurred by the landlord may have been paid (wholly or partly) to the superior landlord. In such circumstances, if the landlord needs information from the superior landlord in order to prepare the statement of account and obtain the accountant's certificate under s 21, he can require that information from the superior landlord, who must comply within a reasonable time (s 23(1)). Similarly, if the landlord receives a request under s 22 from his tenant, he can, in turn, make a similar request to his own landlord, who is obliged to comply with the request within a reasonable time (s 23(2)). If there is a chain of leases, s 23 enables the request to be repeated as far up the chain as necessary. It will be appreciated that the provisions of s 23 are necessary because the immediate landlord may not have the benefit of the LTA 1985 *vis-à-vis* his own landlord.

Under the new s 23A, where the landlord or superior landlord parts with his interest in the premises while obligations under ss 21–23 remain outstanding, the obligations will be enforceable against his successor so far as he becomes able to fulfil them.

Offences of non-compliance

2.61 If any person (other than bodies excluded by s 26(1) – see **2.3** above) without reasonable excuse fails to perform any duty under s 21–23, that person can, under LTA 1985 s 25, be found guilty of an offence and liable on summary conviction to a fine not exceeding level 4 on the standard scale under the Criminal Justice Act 1982 s 37.

If the offence is committed by a company with the consent or connivance of, or due to the neglect of, a director, manager, secretary or similar officer of the company or any person purporting to act in that capacity, he as well as the company will be guilty of the offence.

TRUST OF SERVICE CHARGE FUNDS

Service charges to which the statutory provisions apply

2.62 This is governed by s 42(1) of the LTA 1987, and covers payments in respect of service charges to which s 18 of the LTA 1985 applies (see **2.1**) but does not apply to payments by tenants of 'exempt landlords' (see **2.63**). By virtue of amendments made by the Commonhold and Leasehold Reform Act 2002, Sch 10, these provisions now apply even where there is only one contributing tenant.

Funds to be held on trust

2.63 Any sums paid by the contributing tenants by way of service charges, and any investments representing those sums, must (together with any accruing income) be held by the landlord (or other person to whom the service charges are paid) either as a single trust fund or in two or more separate trust funds, on trust to defray costs incurred (by himself or any other person) in connection with the matters for which the service charges were payable, and any balance being on trust for the persons who are the contributing tenants for the time being (LTA 1987, s 42(2) and (3)). However, this does not apply to contributions made by tenants of 'exempt landlords' as defined in the LTA 1987, s 58(1), which are principally local councils, development corporations, housing action trusts, charitable housing trusts, registered housing associations and unregistered fully mutual housing associations.

As to the requirements for designated accounts for funds held on trust, see **2.53**.

Investment of funds

2.64 Section 42(5) of the LTA 1987 gives power to the Secretary of State to make Orders as to how these trust funds must be invested.

The Service Charge Contributions (Authorised Investments) Order 1988[1], which came into force on 1 April 1989, provides that any sums standing to the credit of any trust fund under s 42 of the LTA 1987 may be:

(a) deposited at interest with the Bank of England; or
(b) deposited in the UK at interest with a person carrying on, in the UK, a deposit-taking business (within the meaning of the Banking Act 1987); or
(c) deposited at interest with, or invested in shares in, a building society (within the meaning of the Building Societies Act 1986).

Paragraph (b) would encompass authorised banks and licensed deposit-takers.

1 SI 1988/1284.

Ultimate entitlement to the funds

2.65 On the termination of the lease of a contributing tenant, the tenant cannot withdraw his share of the fund, but:

(a) if at that time there are other contributing tenants whose leases are continuing, the whole fund will continue to be held on trust, for those remaining contributing tenants, to meet the relevant costs (LTA 1987, s 42(6));

(b) once all contributing tenants' leases have terminated, any remaining trust fund is to be dissolved as at the termination date of the last lease, and any assets in the fund will belong to the landlord (LTA 1987, s 42(7)).

However, by s 42(8) the above is subject to any provisions in the tenant's lease which may provide otherwise.

DISPUTES OVER SERVICE CHARGES

Tenancies to which the rules apply

2.66 The rules set out below apply to service charges to which s 18 of the LTA 1985 applies (see **2.2**).

Determination of disputes

2.67 Under LTA 1985, s 27A the First-tier Tribunal (FTT) has jurisdiction to determine the matters listed below. The current rules giving powers to tribunals were introduced by the amendments to LTA 1985 made by the Commonhold and Leasehold Reform Act 2002.

The tribunals are also 'courts' for the purposes of the Senior Courts Act 1981 and accordingly they can exercise the jurisdiction given to courts by that Act, including powers to make orders under s 42 of that Act against vexatious litigants (*Attorney General v Singer*[1].)

The FTT can interpret and apply not only the statutory tests of reasonableness (see **2.26**) and other statutory limitations (see **2.33–2.54**) but also the terms of the lease (see CHAPTER **1** and **2.8**).

However, if the interpretation of the terms of the lease presents difficult issues of law, the Lands Tribunal has cautioned that the FTT is encouraged to leave those aspects to the court (*Longmint Ltd v Marcus*[2]).

The jurisdiction of the FTT under s 27A(1) gives the FTT power to decide whether a service charge is payable and the FTT can be asked to decide:

(1) who has to pay;
(2) who is to receive the payment;
(3) how much is payable;
(4) when it has to be paid; and
(5) how it is to be paid.

This is a two stage process – first the FTT must decide if a cost is recoverable under the terms of the lease and, if it is, then it must decide if it was reasonably incurred within the meaning in the 1985 Act (*Carey-Morgan v de Walden*[3]).

The FTT can also be asked under s 27A(2) to decide in advance:

(1) whether a service charge would be payable for the cost of specific proposed services, repairs, maintenance, improvements, insurance or management; and if so:
(2) who would have to pay;

(3) who would be entitled to receive the payment;
(4) how much would be payable;
(5) when it would be payable; and
(6) how it would be payable.

A typical example of the FTT using this jurisdiction to interpret the terms of the lease is *R (on the application of Sinclair Gardens Investments Ltd) v Lands Tribunal*[4], in which the Court of Appeal upheld the FTT's decision on whether certain works amounted to 'repair' within the service charge clause of the lease.

The provisions of s 27A allowing the FTT to interpret the provisions of the lease do not give the FTT the right to override those provisions, so that (for example) when interpreting the provisions of the lease as to when payments are to be made, the FTT has no power to give tenants more time to pay (*Southend-on-Sea Borough Council v Skiggs*[5], Lands Tribunal). The FTT's powers under s 27A to determine the proportion of the relevant costs that a tenant is liable to pay is considered separately at **2.4**.

Section 27A refers to amounts which may be payable by way of 'service charge'. The view has been taken that this is intended to give the FTT a wide jurisdiction (see *Continental Property Ventures v White*[6]; *Ruddy v Oakfern Properties Ltd*[7]; *Craighead v Homes for Islington Ltd*[8]). On that basis the reference here to 'a service charge' may not be limited by the definition of that phrase in s 18 (which is limited to amounts payable 'for services, repairs, maintenance, improvements or insurance or . . . management . . . the whole or part of which varies or may vary according to the relevant costs', see **2.2**), but may extend to every cost that the lease includes in the contractual service charge.

However it has been held that s 27A does not give the FTT jurisdiction to review the exercise of a public body landlord's discretion to reduce service charges under its statutory powers (see *Craighead v Homes for Islington Ltd*[9] and **2.94**) since that is a matter of public law.

The FTT's jurisdiction is declaratory and it has no power to order a landlord to repay to the tenant an overpayment of service charge even if the effect of the FTT's decision is that an overpayment was made (*R v London Leasehold Valuation Tribunal, ex parte Daejan Properties Ltd*[10]; *Warrior Quay Management Company Ltd v Joachim*[11]). The tenant would have to apply to the court to order it to be repaid.

No application can be made to the FTT under s 27A in respect of anything which:

(a) the tenant has agreed or admitted (but merely paying an amount demanded is not itself an admission or agreement of liability);
(b) has been, or is to be, referred to arbitration under an agreement to arbitrate that the parties in dispute have entered into after the dispute has arisen (arbitration clauses in the lease no longer prevent the FTT deciding the dispute);
(c) has been decided by a court; or
(d) has been decided by an arbitral tribunal under an agreement to arbitrate entered into after the dispute arose.

The provision that payment of the amount demanded is not an admission or agreement of liability, coupled with other textual changes, may in certain circumstances avoid the dangers for tenants of making payments without reserving their position to object to the charges (see *Daejan Properties Ltd v London Leasehold Valuation Tribunal*[12]). However, in *Cain v Islington London Borough Council*[13], the Lower Chamber upheld the FTT's decision that the tenant had by his conduct 'agreed or admitted' the service charges within paragraph (a) above, where the service charges had been paid without protest between 2001 and 2007 and the tenant did not query them until 2014.

Section 27A(6) provides that an agreement by the tenant of a dwelling (other than an agreement to arbitrate made after the particular dispute has arisen) is void in so far as it purports to provide for a determination in a particular manner or on particular evidence of any question which may be the subject of an application under s 27A(1) or (2). In *Barrington v Sloane Properties Ltd*[14], it was said that this overrode the provisions of the lease which stated that the service charge certificates were conclusive, enabling the tribunal to determine what was payable, and this interpretation certainly appears to be necessary to allow the FTT's jurisdiction to have real effect, although the point was left open by Morgan J in *London Borough of Brent v Shulem B Association*[15]. The procedure for applications to the FTT to determine service charge disputes is governed by Sch 12 of the Commonhold and Leasehold Reform Act 2002 and regulations made under it. An appeal may be made from an FTT determination to the Upper Tribunal (Lands Chamber), formerly the Lands Tribunal, but only with the leave of the FTT or the Upper Tribunal, under s 175 of the CLRA 2002. The Upper Tribunal has expressed the view that an appeal relating to a ruling under s 20C about the recovery of the cost of the proceedings (see **2.33**) should not be a rehearing but should be handled as a true appeal in which the FTT's discretion, if properly exercised, should not ordinarily be interfered with (*Barrington Court Developments Ltd v Barrington Court Residents Association*[16]). In relation to appeals on other matters, such as on the interpretation of the lease or the application of the reasonableness tests, a rehearing is usual (*Veena SA v Cheong*[17]).

It is possible that the 'tenant' who may apply to the FTT can include a former tenant who is liable to pay the service charge where the present tenant has defaulted (see *Re Sarum Properties Ltd's Application*[18]).

1 [2012] Div Ct (unreported).
2 [2004] Lands Tribunal.
3 [2013] UKUT 0134.
4 [2005] EWCA Civ 1305, CA.
5 [2006] 21 EG 132.
6 [2006] 1 EGLR 85, LT.
7 [2007] Ch 335.
8 [2010] UKUY 47, LC.
9 [2010] UKUY 47, LC.
10 [2000] EGCS 108, QBD.
11 (2008) LRX/43/2006, LT.
12 [2001] EWCA Civ 1095, CA.
13 [2015] UKUT 542.
14 [2007] LRX/31/2006, LT.
15 [2011] EWHC 1663 (Ch).
16 [2001] 29 EG 128, LT.
17 [2003] LRX/45/2000, LT.

18 [1999] 2 EGLR 131, LT.

Procedure and costs

2.68 The procedures before the FTT are prescribed by regulations contained in the Tribunal Procedure (First-tier Tribunal) (Property Chamber) Rules 2013, the relevant parts of which are reproduced in **Appendix 2**.

Section 176A of the Commonhold and Leasehold Reform Act 2002 empowers any court to transfer a case to the appropriate tribunal where there are matters falling within the tribunal's jurisdiction. In *Lennon v Ground Rents (Regisport) Ltd*[1], the county court judge ordered a case which involved service charges to be transferred to the FTT only in respect of the issue of the reasonableness of service charges; however, the tribunal decided other matters as well and the Upper Tribunal ruled that the FTT had no jurisdiction under the terms of the transfer to do that. More recently the Upper Tribunal suggested that a transfer order expressed in more general terms should be treated more widely in a practical manner with proper recognition of the expertise of the FTT in relation to residential service charges (*Cain v London Borough of Islington*[2]).

At the Tribunal each party normally bears its own costs. The Tribunal's power to award costs is now derived from s 29 of the Tribunals, Court and Enforcement Act 2007. That section potentially gives tribunals much wider discretion to order costs than the limited power that had been given to LVTs, but it is subject to the Rules, and the 2013 Rules restrict the power of the Tribunal to order one party to pay another's costs; it is limited to cases of wasted costs (costs incurred by improper, unreasonable or negligent acts of legal representatives or advocates) or the unreasonable conduct of a party in bringing, defending or conducting the proceedings. For a recent example of the application of this, see *Willow Court Management Company (1985) Ltd v Alexander*; *Sinclair v 231 Sussex Gardens Right to Manage Limited*; *Stone v 54 Hogarth Road London SW5 Management Limited*[3].

As regards the recovery of the landlord's litigation costs through a service charge, see **2.33**. The Upper Tribunal can be asked to make an order under s 20C that the landlord's costs of the case should not be included in service charges (see for example *Akorita v Marina Heights (St Leonards) Ltd*[4] and **2.33**).

1 [2011] UKUT.
2 [2015] UKUT 117, LC.
3 [2016] UKUT 290, LC.
4 [2011] UKUT 255, LC.

Recovery of overpayments

2.69 The FTT is concerned only with the validity of service charges, not with repayment of sums wrongly paid. If the tenant is successful at the FTT and wishes to recover an overpayment from the landlord, the tenant would have to bring court proceedings against the landlord for repayment and any question of limitation would then be considered by the court (see *R v London Leasehold Valuation Tribunal, ex parte Daejan Properties Ltd*[1], and see **1.98**). Whilst the ambit of the FTT's jurisdiction has been widened since that decision (see **2.67**), the FTT is not given jurisdiction to issue money judgments, but the county court is given power to enforce the FTT's determinations (Commonhold and Leasehold Reform Act 2002, Sch 12, para 11; *Warrior Quay Management Company Ltd v Joachim*[2]).

1 [2000] EGCS 108, QBD.
2 (2008) LRX/43/2006, LT.

RECOVERY OF ARREARS AND OTHER REMEDIES

Abolition of the remedy of distress

2.70 The ancient right to distrain for arrears of rent (and sums reserved as rent, as service charges commonly are) was abolished as from 6 April 2014 by s 71 of the Tribunals, Courts and Enforcement Act 2007. It was replaced, but only for non-residential property, by the commercial rent arrears recovery procedure.

Forfeiture for non-payment of service charges

2.71 If the tenant is in arrears of payments of rent (or sums that the lease states are reserved as rent or recoverable as if rent) or is in breach of a covenant in his lease, the landlord may end the lease by forfeiture (also known as re-entry) if the lease contains a provision to that effect, which most leases do. Forfeiture can generally be carried out by peaceable re-entry (physically entering the property to take it back) or by the landlord issuing and serving court proceedings.

However, in respect of arrears of residential service charges there are a number of limitations imposed on the landlord by statute.

First, no method of forfeiture of a lease of premises let as a dwelling is permissible on the ground of the tenant's failure to pay a service charge unless the amount of the service charge is agreed or admitted by the tenant or has been determined, at least 14 clear days previously, by a court or an arbitral tribunal (Housing Act 1996, s 84(1), (2)). For this purpose, 'service charge' has the same meaning as under s 18(1) of the LTA 1985 (see **2.2**), but does not include a non-variable service charge element of a registered rent (HA 1996, s 77(4)). A service charge is 'determined' on the giving of the decision of the court or an arbitral tribunal, even if that decision is susceptible to appeal or other legal challenge (HA 1996, s 81(3)). The 'court' includes the FFT and its appeal tribunals; determination by an arbitral tribunal (ie arbitration) which satisfies these requirements can only be under an agreement to arbitrate which the parties enter into after the dispute arises; a determination under an arbitration clause in the lease will not count for this purpose.

Secondly, s 168 of the CLRA 2002 follows similar lines and prohibits the service of a forfeiture notice in respect of a residential lease which is a 'long lease' (granted for a term of over 21 years) if the tenant has not admitted the breach of covenant and the landlord had not obtained a court or tribunal final determination that the tenant was in breach of covenant.

Thirdly, it has been held by the Court of Appeal that the above provisions 'require or recognise' that, even where the lease reserves the service charges as rent or provides that the service charge is recoverable as rent, the landlord must serve a notice under s 146 of the Law of Property Act 1925 before forfeiting for unpaid service charges that are within the LTA 1985 (*Freeholders of 69 Marina; Robinson, Simpson and Palmer v Oram and Ghoorun*[1]). The notice under s 146 of the Law of Property Act 1925 must specify the breach of covenant and require its remedy and it must state that s 81 of the HA 1996 applies and must set out the effect of s 81(1). This notification must be no less conspicuous than the remainder of the notice, and the Secretary of State has power to make regulations prescribing a form of words for this purpose. Furthermore, by s 81 of the HA 1996 the landlord must not serve any notice under s 146 of the 1925 Act in respect of arrears of service charge before the amount of the charge has been agreed or determined under the above rules.

These rules equally apply to steps that the landlord might want to take to forfeit a lease on the ground of unpaid 'administration charges' as defined in Sch 11 to the CLRA 2002 (see **2.114**).

Fourthly, by s 167 of the CLRA 2002, no forfeiture will be permitted for small amounts of arrears or where there is only a short period of delay in making payment. The minimum amount of arrears on which forfeiture can be based is currently £350 and the minimum period of delayed payment is currently three years (see the Rights of Re-Entry and Forfeiture (Prescribed Sum and Period) (England) Regulations 2004[2], and the Rights of Re-Entry and Forfeiture (Prescribed Sum and Period) (Wales) Regulations 2005[3]).

Finally, if the landlord is entitled to exercise the right of forfeiture, forfeiting by peaceable re-entry is not lawful in respect of premises which are being occupied as a residence (Protection from Eviction Act 1977). This restriction does not apply if the landlord believes, on reasonable grounds, that the residential occupier had ceased to reside in the property (Protection from Eviction Act 1977, s 1(2)), but a mere temporary absence of the tenant (eg on holiday) would not constitute ceasing to reside. Forfeiture can otherwise be effected by court proceedings, and this is usually a far safer course for the landlord.

Leases often contain a clause under which the tenant must pay the costs incurred by the landlord of and incidental to the preparation of a s 146 notice. If the landlord serves a s 146 notice on the tenant of a dwelling who has failed to pay a service charge that the FTT has ruled is payable, such a clause may require that tenant to pay the costs which the landlord incurred pursuant to HA 1996 in obtaining that FTT decision (see *Freeholders of 69 Marina; Robinson, Simpson and Palmer v Oram and Ghoorun*[4] above).

It was held in *Longmint Ltd v Eggleton*[5]) that the landlord could not enforce the tenant's covenant in the lease to pay the landlord's costs of having a notice prepared under s 146 of the 1925 Act relating to unpaid service charges, because the s 146 notice should not have been served before the LVT hearing due to s 168 of the CLRA 2002. In *Freeholders of 69 Marina* case, the s 146 notice was served after the landlord had obtained an order of the LVT declaring the amount of recoverable service charges, and so the landlord's costs incurred leading up to and including the preparation and service of the s 146 notice were recoverable under the lease covenant.

1 [2011] EWCA Civ 1258, CA.
2 SI 2004/3086.
3 SI 2005/1352.
4 [2011] EWCA Civ 1258, CA.
5 (2009) LON/OOAJ/LSC/2009/115, FTT.

Sums in dispute

2.72 Where s 18 of the LTA 1985 applies, any dispute about whether individual items meet the requirements of s 19 or s 20 of that Act must be settled by the FTT unless the dispute is covered by an arbitration clause or (under the 2002 amendments) by a post-dispute arbitration agreement (see **2.67**).

Preconditions for suing for arrears

2.73 Currently, even if there is no dispute falling within those paragraphs, or such a dispute has been settled or determined, the question arises whether it is a precondition of suing for the arrears that the landlord must have supplied the tenant with a written summary of the costs under s 21 of the LTA 1985. Since the written summary need only be supplied if it is requested in writing by the tenant, it follows that delivery of such a summary cannot be a precondition of suing unless the tenant has made a written request for the summary. Even where the tenant has made such request, it is unclear whether or not this has the effect of precluding the landlord from suing for the service charge until he has supplied the summary; this point was left open by Stuart Smith J in *Woodtrek Ltd v Jezek*[1].

To avoid arguments on this point it is good practice to ensure that the tenant is served with a proper certified summary of costs complying both with s 21 (if it applies) and the terms of the lease itself, before any action is brought against the tenant in respect of non-payment.

If the 2002 amendments on this aspect of the regime come into force, payments of service charges will be incapable of being enforced if the new requirements for notices to accompany service charge demands (see **2.47**) or for statements of accounts and certificates (see **2.55**) have not been followed.

As for preconditions before forfeiture notices can be served, see **2.71**.

1 (1981) 261 EG 571.

CONSULTATION ON APPOINTMENT OF MANAGING AGENTS

Leases to which the statutory rules apply

2.74 The following rules apply to premises where one or more of the tenants are represented by a 'recognised tenants' association', being an association recognised under s 29 of the LTA 1985 (see **2.21**).

Separate legislation provides for a management audit (see **2.85**).

The consultation rules

2.75 Consultation rules are set out in s 30B of the LTA 1985 and provide as set out below:

(1) The association may, at any time, serve notice on the landlord requesting him to consult the association on matters relating to the appointment or employment by the landlord of managing agents.

(2) If, at that time, no managing agents are employed, the landlord must, before appointing any agents, serve notice on the association specifying:
 (a) the name of the proposed managing agent;
 (b) those obligations of the landlord which he proposes to instruct the agents to carry out on his behalf;
 (c) a period of at least one month (beginning with the date of service of the landlord's notice) within which the association may make observations;
 (d) the name and address in the UK of the person to whom the observations are to be sent;

 and the landlord shall have regard to any observations received during the specified period.

(3) If, however, at that time the landlord is employing a managing agent, the landlord must, within one month (beginning with the date of service of the association's notice) serve on the association a notice specifying:
 (a) those obligations of the landlord which he has instructed the agents to carry out on his behalf;
 (b) a reasonable period within which the association may make observations on the manner in which the agents are discharging those obligations and on the desirability of their continuing to discharge them;
 (c) the name and address in the UK of the person to whom the observations are to be sent;

 and the landlord shall have regard to any observations received during that period.

(4) If a notice under (1) above is served, then (in addition to complying with (2) or (3) above, as appropriate) the landlord must:
 (a) at least once every five years, serve notice on the association specifying:
  (i) any changes occurring, since the date of the last notice served by him on the association under s 30B, in the obligations which he has instructed the agents to carry out; and

(ii) a reasonable period within which the association may make observations on the manner in which the agents have discharged those obligations during that period and on the desirability of their continuing to discharge them;

(iii) the name and address in the UK of the person to whom the observations are to be sent;

and the landlord shall have regard to any observations received during that period;

(b) serve a notice complying with (2) above, whenever he proposes to appoint new managing agents, and have regard to any observations received during the specified period;

unless the association gives the landlord notice withdrawing its request to be consulted.

(5) On a change of landlord after service of a notice by the association under (1) above, the notice ceases to have effect but the association may serve a fresh notice on the new landlord.

See also **2.10** in respect of consultation on appointment under management agreements that will operate for over12 months.

VARIATION OF DEFECTIVE SERVICE CHARGE CLAUSES

Statutory framework

2.76 Part IV of the LTA 1987, as amended by s 163 of the Commonhold and Leasehold Reform Act 2002, sets out two separate sets of procedures for seeking orders of the First-tier Tribunal (FTT) to vary long leases of flats which contain allegedly defective provisions. They are subject to different rules.

Sections 35–36 of the LTA 1987 permit an application to be made to the FTT for a variation order in respect of just one lease, whilst s 37 allows an application to be made in respect of a group of leases.

Section 40 of the LTA 1987 applies certain of these provisions to dwellings other than flats (ie houses), in respect of insurance clauses only.

Once a variation has been ordered by the FTT, it is binding not only on the current parties to the lease but also on all other persons, including successors-in-title, predecessors-in-title (LTA 1987, s 39(1)) and sureties (LTA 1987, s 39(2)).

The application of these rules to the Crown is governed by the Commonhold and Leasehold Reform Act 2002, s 172 (see **Appendix 2**).

Leases of flats to which the provisions apply

2.77 These provisions apply to a long lease of a flat. 'Long lease' is defined in s 59(3) of the LTA 1987 to include:

(1) a lease granted for a term certain exceeding 21 years (even if terminable earlier by forfeiture or by a tenant's notice to quit);

(2) a perpetually renewable lease (which, by s 145 of the Law of Property Act 1922, is treated as a lease for 2,000 years) unless granted by subletting out of a lease which is not a long lease; and
(3) a lease granted under the right to buy provisions in Pt V of the Housing Act 1985.

However, by the LTA 1987, s 35(6), these provisions do not apply to a lease:

(a) which demises three or more flats in the same building; or
(b) which constitutes a tenancy to which Pt II of the Landlord and Tenant Act 1954 applies (ie a business tenancy).

Circumstances in (a) might arise, for example, in those cases where a developer of a block of flats grants a headlease of the block to a company which will grant separate underleases of individual flats; the headlease will not fall within these provisions.

The wording of (b) is somewhat unclear as to whether the exclusion relates to premises which at the time of the grant of the lease were premises to which Pt II of the Landlord and Tenant Act 1954 applied or whether the exclusion only applies if the premises are protected by Pt II of that Act at the time of the application for a variation order. The existence of a business tenancy depends not only on the terms of the tenant's lease, but also on his actually occupying the premises for the purposes of a business, or for those and other purposes. Therefore, a lease can, from time to time, move in and out of Pt II of the Landlord and Tenant Act 1954. Furthermore, a business tenancy can exist under Pt II of the Landlord and Tenant Act 1954 even where the terms of the lease prohibit business use (ie if the landlord waives or acquiesces in a breach).

Application to vary an individual lease

2.78 '*Any party*' to the long lease of a flat can apply to the FTT to order that the lease is varied (LTA 1987, s 35(1)). Thus, where the parties to the lease are, for example: (a) the landlord; (b) the tenant; and (c) a management company, any one of those three could make the application. Theoretically, if a guarantor for the tenant were also a party to the lease, he too would be entitled to make an application for a variation order.

Grounds for applying to vary an individual lease

2.79 The grounds for making an application are that the lease '*fails to make satisfactory provision*' for one or more of the matters listed in s 35(2)(a)–(f) of the LTA 1987. Those paragraphs of s 35(2) which relate to service charges (and, thus, fall within the scope of this book) are:

> '(e) the recovery by one party to the lease from another party to it of expenditure incurred or to be incurred by him, or on his behalf, for the benefit of that other party or of a number of persons who include that other party; or
> (f) the computation of a service charge payable under the lease.'

By an amendment inserted by the Commonhold and Leasehold Reform Act 2002, the Secretary of State has power to make regulations adding additional grounds on which applications to vary leases can be made under s 35.

'Service charge' is given the same meaning as under s 18(1) of the LTA 1985 (see **2.2**).

Section 35(4) of the LTA 1987 as amended in 1993 provides that, for the purposes of s 35(2)(f), a lease fails to make satisfactory provision with respect to the computation of a service charge if the lease requires the charge to be a proportion of the service expenditure and this, taken with the contributions payable by other tenants, results in the landlord recovering either less or more than the amount he expended, but see **1.14**. It has been held that this only applies where the tenants' contributions add up to either more than 100 per cent of the cost or less than 100 per cent of the cost and that the FTT does not have jurisdiction to vary the proportion payable by each tenant, however unfair the allocation, if they add up to 100 per cent (*Morgan v Fletcher*[1]).

By a further amendment inserted by s 162 of the Commonhold and Leasehold Reform Act 2002, s 35(3A) provides that, for the purposes of s 35(2)(e), the factors for determining whether the lease makes satisfactory provision can include whether it provides for interest or other amounts to be payable in the event of late payment. This reflects the fact that some older leases do not expressly provide for interest to be paid on late payment.

1 [2009] UKUT 186, LRX/81/2008, LC.

Opposition to variation, and compensation for variation

2.80 The power of the FTT to order the lease to be varied is discretionary; LTA 1987, s 38(1) provides that, where a ground under s 35 is established, the FTT 'may' make an order for the lease to be varied; and s 38(8) enables the FTT to order a variation in terms different from that specified in the application. However, these powers of the FTT are subject to the provisions of s 38(6) and (7), which allow the application to be opposed.

Section 38(6) provides that the FTT shall not make a variation order if it appears to the FTT:

(a) that the variation would be likely substantially to prejudice:
   - (i) the respondent to the application (ie the landlord, if the application is made by the tenant, or vice versa); or
   - (ii) any person who is not a party to the application,

   and that an award of compensation under s 38(10), would not be adequate; or

(b) that for any other reason it would not be reasonable to effect the variation.

These provisions enable a landlord or tenant to oppose a variation on the basis of substantial prejudice or unreasonableness.

Section 38(7) deals expressly with insurance, and provides that the FTT shall not make a variation order:

(a) which would terminate any existing right of the landlord, under the terms of the lease, to nominate the insurer; or
(b) which would require the landlord to nominate a selection of insurers from which the tenant could choose the insurer; or
(c) which, where the lease requires the tenant to insure with a specified insurer, requires the tenant to effect insurance otherwise than with another specified insurer.

If a FTT makes a variation order, it can also order compensation to be paid in respect of any loss or disadvantage which a person is likely to suffer as a result of the variation (LTA 1987, s 38(10)). In view of the provisions of s 38(6), this will apply only where such compensation will be adequate to compensate him; otherwise the variation will be refused.

Consequential variation of other leases

2.81 If an order is made varying the lease of one flat in a block, this may justify other leases being varied. For this reason, there are provisions in the LTA 1987, s 36 under which, if any party to a lease applies to the FTT for a variation order under s 35 of that Act, any other party to that lease can apply to the FTT asking that, if the FTT decides to vary the lease, it should also order the variation of the long leases of other specified flats. Those flats must have the same landlord, but need not be in the same building and need not be in identical terms (LTA 1987, s 36(2)).

By s 36(3), two criteria must be demonstrated to be fulfilled in this respect:

(a) each of those other leases must fail to make satisfactory provision with respect to the same matter or matters as are specified in the original application; and
(b) if a lease variation is made under the original application, it would be in the interests of the party applying under s 36, or in the interests of the other parties to these other leases, to have all the specified leases (including that comprised in the original application) varied *to the same effect*.

The power to make these consequential variations to other leases is discretionary and is limited by the same rights of objection under s 38 as discussed at **2.80** (s 38(2)).

Applications to vary multiple leases

2.82 Section 37 of the LTA 1987 enables a single application to be made requesting the FTT to order the variation of two or more leases, but subject to majority approval of all the parties.

An application under s 37 may be made by either the landlord or any of the tenants, but the following criteria must, in each case, be fulfilled:

(a) the leases must all be long leases of flats under which the landlord is the same person, but they need not be of flats in the same building and need not be in identical terms (s 37(2));

(b) the object to be achieved by the variation must only be achievable satisfactorily if all the specified leases are varied to the same effect (s 37(3));

(c) where the application involves eight or fewer leases, the application must have the consent of all, or all but one, of the parties concerned (s 37(5)(a));

(d) where the application involves nine or more leases, the application must have the consent of at least 75 per cent of the parties concerned, and must not be opposed by more than 10 per cent of them (s 37(5)(b)).

When counting the parties for the majority criteria of (c) or (d) (above), a person who is the tenant of more than one lease is counted as a separate party for each of his leases (s 37(6)(a)). The landlord is counted as one party (s 37(6)(b)).

For criteria (d) above, the tests of whether the consent of the 75 per cent majority has be obtained and whether more than 10 per cent object are to be applied immediately before the application to the Tribunal is made (*Dixon v Wellington Close Management Ltd*[1], *Simon v St Mildreds Court Residents Association Ltd*[2]).

These provisions, unlike those in s 35, do not confine the potential variations to a specified list of matters; the 'object to be achieved' could be any matter contained in (or omitted from) the leases. Presumably, this is justified by the requirements for majority consent to the application – an inappropriate proposed variation is unlikely to command majority support. For an example where an application was made to vary the service charge clauses in the leases of three flats in a converted house, see *Thirlaway v Masculet and others*[3]. (Variations on matters not relating to service charges are outside the scope of this book.)

Because of the 10 per cent provision for objectors, the procedure under s 37 would be a means of forcing a suitable lease variation on all the tenants in a block, notwithstanding a small number of objectors. However, these provisions are equally subject to the rights of opposition contained in s 38 (summarised at **2.80**), and could fail on grounds of substantial prejudice or unreasonableness (LTA 1987, s 38(3)).

1 [2012] UKUT 95, LC.
2 [2015] UKUT 508, LC.
3 [2012] UKUT 302, LC.

Notification and cancellation

2.83 Under s 35(5) of the LTA 1987, rules of FTT have been made requiring notice of any application to be served on all persons likely to be affected by the proposed variation and entitling them to join in the proceedings.

If a person entitled to be served with notice of the proceedings was not served with the notice, he may, under s 39:

(a) sue the person who should have served the notice for damages; and/or
(b) apply to the FTT to cancel or modify the variation (s 39(3)).

Variation of insurance provisions in leases of dwellings other than flats

2.84 Whilst the provisions of LTA 1987, ss 35–39 apply as a whole only to long leases of flats, parts of those provisions are, by s 40, made to apply to long leases of dwellings other than flats (eg houses). This is where the lease fails to make satisfactory provision with respect to '*any matter relating to the insurance of the dwelling, including the recovery of the costs of* such insurance'. Leases of flats are excluded from these provisions (*John Lyon's Charity v Haysport Properties*[1]).

The provisions of s 36 (consequential variation of other leases) and s 38 (FTT discretion, objections, etc) are applied with the appropriate modification. Again the provisions do not apply to a lease consisting of three or more dwellings, or one which constitutes a business tenancy (s 40(4)). Further, a tenant who holds three or more dwellings under two or more separate long leases from the same landlord is also excluded (s 40(4A)) and, for this purpose if the tenant is a body corporate then this exclusion applies even if the other leases are held by associated companies (s 40(4B)).

1 (1995) NPC 165, ChD.

MANAGEMENT AUDIT

Purpose

2.85 The purpose of a management audit under Chapter V of the Leasehold Reform, Housing and Urban Development Act 1993 (LRHUDA 1993) is to ascertain whether the landlord's obligations towards the 'qualifying tenants' in respect of management functions are being discharged in an efficient and effective manner, and service charge monies payable by those tenants are being applied in an efficient and effective manner (LRHUDA 1993, s 78). The audit report may also facilitate an application by the tenants to the FTT for the appointment of a manager under the LTA 1987, s 24 (see **2.95**).

Qualifying tenants

2.86 Only 'qualifying' tenants are entitled to have the audit carried out on their behalf. To qualify, a tenant must hold a dwelling under a 'long lease' or a 'shared ownership lease' under which a service charge is payable. Tenants of business leases (defined in the LRHUDA 1993, s 101 as leases to which Pt II of the Landlord and Tenant Act 1954 applies) are excluded. 'Long lease' is defined in s 7(1) of the LRHUDA 1993; broadly, it is a lease granted for a term of over 21 years. 'Shared ownership lease' is defined in s 7(7) of the LRHUDA 1993 and, broadly, is a lease acquired at a premium equal to a percentage of the value or cost of the dwelling.

If a dwelling is sublet and both the tenant and the subtenant would qualify under these rules, only the subtenant is given the right to demand the audit (LRHUDA 1993, s 77(4)).

Minimum number of qualifying tenants

2.87 If premises contain only one dwelling let to a qualifying tenant, that tenant can require the audit to be carried out (LRHUDA 1993, s 76(4), (5)).

Where premises (which the LRHUDA 1993 calls the 'relevant premises') contain two or more dwellings subject to a 'common service charge' – ie the tenants contribute by way of service charge to the same costs (LRHUDA 1993, s 76(8)) – then:

(a) if the relevant premises contain two dwellings let to qualifying tenants, either or both of them can demand the audit (LRHUDA 1993, s 76(2)(a));
(b) if the relevant premises contain three or more dwellings let to qualifying tenants, the audit has to be required by at least two-thirds of those qualifying tenants (LRHUDA 1993, s 76(2)(b)).

Appointment of auditor

2.88 The auditor is appointed by the qualifying tenants who wish to exercise these rights. Where three or more qualifying tenants demand the audit, the appointment must be made by at least two-thirds of them acting together (LRHUDA 1993, s 78(3)(ii)).

The auditor must be either a qualified accountant as defined in s 28 of the LTA 1985 (see **2.56**) or a qualified surveyor being a fellow or professional associate of the Royal Institution of Chartered Surveyors or of the Incorporated Society of Valuers and Auctioneers or having some other qualification prescribed by regulations (LRHUDA 1993, s 78(5)).

Procedure

2.89 The appointed auditor serves a written notice on the landlord. By s 80 of the LRHUDA 1993, the notice must:

(a) be signed by each of the tenants on whose behalf it is given;
(b) state the names of those tenants and their addresses at the relevant premises;
(c) state the name and address of the appointed auditor;
(d) specify any documents or description of documents which the auditor requires or wishes to inspect (see below);
(e) state the date (if any) on which the auditor wishes to inspect any common parts in the relevant premises or any appurtenant property, being a date between one and two months after the giving of the notice.

In addition to giving the notice to the landlord, the notice must also be given (so far as practical, at the same time) to any other person (the 'relevant person') who carries out the management functions, with a copy of that notice being given to the landlord (LRHUDA 1993, s 79(3)(b)).

The s 80 notice to the landlord may be given to the person who collects rent from the tenants on the landlord's behalf (LRHUDA 1993, s 80(5)).

The documents which the auditor can require to be supplied to him are the costs summaries which the tenants are entitled to require under s 21(1) of the LTA 1985 (see **2.55** and **2.56**). The documents which the auditor can ask to be produced for his inspection are (a) the accounts, receipts and other documents supporting those cost summaries, and (b) any other documents the sight of which is reasonably required by the auditor for the purpose of carrying out his audit (LRHUDA 1993, s 79(2)).

When the provisions as to regular accounts and accountants' certificates under the amended version of s 21 (introduced by the Commonhold and Leasehold Reform Act 2002) come into effect (see **2.55**), those documents will fall within this regime and the auditor will have the choice of inspecting and copying the documents or requiring the landlord to supply copies which (as the auditor decides) are to be sent to the auditor or left for him to collect.

Under s 87 of the LRHUDA 1993, the Secretary of State may approve codes of practice (see **2.92**) to which, under s 78(2), the auditor must have regard when carrying out his audit. Failure by the landlord to comply with an approved code of practice is a ground on which tenants may apply to the court to appoint a manager of the building under the LTA 1987, s 24 as amended by the HA 1996, s 85.

The landlord and any 'relevant person' must comply with the notice, and the auditor can apply to the court under s 81(4) for an order compelling this.

The landlord cannot charge the auditor for providing facilities for him to inspect documents, but can make a reasonable charge for supplying documents to the auditor and for providing copying facilities in respect of other documents (LRHUDA 1993, s 79(5)). If the wording of the tenants' leases allows it, the landlord can include as management costs within the service charges any costs of providing the inspection facilities (LRHUDA 1993, s 79(6)).

If the landlord or relevant person claims that any documents specified by the auditor for production ought not to be inspected by him (presumably on the ground that sight of them is not reasonably required for the purposes of the audit), the landlord can give notice to the auditor to that effect and the matter can, if necessary, be decided by the court (LRHUDA 1993, s 81(1)(b)(ii)).

Section 82 of the LRHUDA 1993 makes provision for an immediate landlord who receives as 80 notice to require relevant information and documents, where appropriate, from a superior landlord. The provisions of ss 81 and 82 of the LRHUDA 1993 have been amended by Sch 10 to the CLRA 2002 to match the amendments mentioned earlier and to clarify the procedures. Section 83 of the LRHUDA 1993 contains provisions dealing with the situation where the landlord, after receiving a notice under s 80, disposes of his interest in the dwellings.

INSURANCE INFORMATION AND CHOICE OF INSURER

Insurance information

2.90 Where the service charge includes an amount payable directly or indirectly for insurance, the tenants have special rights to obtain information about the insurance from the landlord, in addition to any rights contained in their leases. These rights are granted by s 30A of and the Schedule to the LTA 1985, inserted by the LTA 1987. This is in addition to the statutory reasonableness test as to the cost of insurance (see **2.26**).

A request can be served on the landlord (or on an agent collecting the rent) requiring the supply of an insurance summary which must set out, in respect of every relevant policy, the insured amount or amounts, the name of the insurer, and the risks insured. The request for this summary can be made either by the tenant or by a recognised tenants' association. The summary must be supplied within 21 days from the date of the request (in accordance with amendments made by Sch 10 to the Commonhold and Leasehold Reform Act 2002). Where two or more buildings are insured under the same policy, the summary need only be of the tenant's own dwelling and, if it is a flat, the building containing it. Where the tenant's dwelling is a flat, the insured amount specified in the summary must be that relating to the building containing the flat and, if specified in the policy, any amount insured for the flat itself. A full copy of the policy may be supplied instead of a summary.

The tenant, or the secretary of the recognised tenant's association, may request the landlord to give him reasonable facilities for inspecting the insurance policy and any accounts, receipts or other documents evidencing payment of the relevant premiums both for the current insurance period and for the immediately preceding period, and to provide facilities for taking copies or extracts. This right to inspect the insurance policy and related documents is exercisable at any time and the landlord must comply within 21 days of a written request and must provide copying facilities, or supply a copy of the policy and other documents, to the tenant or the association secretary. The landlord can make a reasonable charge to that person for the copying; any costs he incurs in providing inspection facilities can be included in the service charges of the building as management charges if the wording of the lease so allows.

The Schedule to the LTA 1985 contains provisions dealing with the situation where the insurance is effected by a superior landlord. It also contains provisions allowing a tenant to serve directly on the insurer a notice of any damage to the dwelling (and, if a flat, any other affected part of the building) in respect of which a claim could be made under the insurance policy. These provisions will be subject to some minor and consequential amendments to be made by the Commonhold and Leasehold Reform Act 2002, Sch 10, paras 8–13, as from a date to be fixed.

Choice of insurer

2.91 In addition, para 8 of the Schedule to the LTA 1985 (as amended by the HA 1996) contains provisions which apply where the lease requires the tenant (and not the landlord) to insure the building with an insurer nominated by the landlord; these provisions give the tenant the right to challenge the nomination of the insurer on the grounds that the insurance is unsatisfactory or the premiums are excessive. The procedures for challenging the landlord's choice of insurer, by applying to the First-tier Tribunal, are currently set out in The Tribunal Procedure (First-tier Tribunal) (Property Chamber) Rules 2013[1].

These provisions remain in force, but are in effect superseded, in relation to leases of houses (not flats), by provisions in s 164 of the Commonhold and Leasehold Reform Act 2002 which came into effect in 2005. The new provisions (see **Appendix 2**), remove the landlord's right, under the lease, to nominate or approve the insurer of the house, giving the tenant freedom of choice. This will apply even if the landlord's insurer provided satisfactory insurance cover and charged reasonable premiums. The provisions contain safeguards for the landlord, for example by requiring the tenant's insurance to cover the landlord's interests as well as the tenant's, and for the tenant to give written details to the landlord.

More detail on this subject is outside the scope of this book.

1 SI 2013/1169.

APPROVED CODES OF MANAGEMENT PRACTICE

2.92 Under s 87 of the Leasehold Reform, Housing and Urban Development Act 1993, the Secretary of State may by Order approve codes of practice for the management of residential property.

By s 78(2) of the LRHUDA 1993, an auditor must have regard to the landlord's compliance with any relevant approved code when carrying out a management audit (see **2.85**). By s 87 of the LRHUDA 1993, a breach of such a code is admissible in evidence in any civil proceedings, for example in relation to the reasonableness tests (see *Longmint Ltd v Eggleton*[1] and **2.26**). Further, failure by the landlord to comply with an approved code of practice is a ground on which tenants may apply to the court to appoint a manager of the building (see LTA 1987, s 24(2)(ac) and **2.95**).

The latest approval order relating to normal private sector service charge management is The Approval of Code of Management Practice (Residential Management) (Service Charges) (England) Order 2016[2] approving the RICS Service Charge Residential Management Code, third edition, which came into effect on I June 2016.

1 (2009) LON/OOAJ/LSC/2009, LT.
2 SI 2016/516.

DIPLOMATIC AND STATE IMMUNITY

2.93 In addition to the immunity (described at **1.99**) enjoyed by a tenant or occupier which is a foreign state or foreign diplomatic officer, special rules apply to residential premises used as the private residence of a foreign diplomatic officer. Such a residence enjoys the same protection and inviolability as a diplomatic mission, described at **1.102**, namely immunity against entry, execution, etc (Diplomatic Privileges Act 1964, Sch 1, Art 30).

This immunity prevents the landlord from exercising rights to enter the premises or seeking forfeiture of the lease, but would not prevent an action against the tenant for breach of the covenant to pay the service charge (see *Intpro Properties (UK) Ltd v Sauvel*[1]), subject to any personal immunity that the tenant may have (see **1.99** and **1.101**).

1 [1983] 2 All ER 495, CA.

SOCIAL LANDLORDS

2.94 The Secretary of State has power, under ss 219 and 220 of the Housing Act 1996, to give directions to social landlords about service charges in respect of works of repair, maintenance or improvement. The directions may require the waiver or reduction of service charges where a grant or other financial assistance is given to the landlord by the Secretary of State, and may permit the waiver or reduction of service charges in other circumstances which the direction may specify.

'Social landlords' are those landlords (other than housing co-operatives) who can grant secure tenancies under s 80 of the Housing Act 1985, and registered social landlords who are registered under Pt I, Ch 1 of the HA 1996.

The Social Landlords Discretionary Reduction of Service Charges (England) Directions 2014, which took effect on 12 August 2014, allow local authorities and other social landlords to reduce or waive service charges for works of repair, maintenance or improvement by an amount that the landlord considers reasonable in accordance with criteria set out in those Directions.

The Social Landlords Mandatory Reduction of Service Charges (England) Directions 2014 require social landlords to charge no more than £15,000 to a tenant of a property in a London borough or £10,000 outside London, over any five year period for repairs, maintenance or improvements for which financial assistance is received.

It has been held that the jurisdiction of the FTT under LTA 1985 s 27A does not extend to reviewing the exercise of a social landlord's discretion whether or not to reduce service charges under the discretionary regime mentioned above (*Craighead v Homes for Islington Ltd and another*[1]).

As to the application of the LTA 1985 to different types of social landlords, see **2.3**.

As to service charges under leases granted under the right to buy scheme, see **2.44**.

1 [2010] UKUT 47, LC.

MANAGERS AND RIGHT TO MANAGE COMPANIES

Managers

2.95 Part II of the Landlord and Tenant Act 1987 (LTA 1987) gives any tenant a right to apply to the First-tier Tribunal (FTT) to appoint a manager to take over the management of the premises containing his flat. Unlike the establishment of a right to manage ('RTM) company (see **2.98**), this right can only be exercised if the tenant can demonstrate the existence of specific grounds for complaint listed in the LTA 1987, s 24 about the landlord's existing management of the premises. The procedure for such an application is outside the scope of this book.

Certain landlords are exempt from these provisions a 'resident landlord' (defined in the LTA 1987, s 58(2) and (3)) is exempt except where over half the number of flats in his premises are let on long leases, ignoring business tenancies (CLRA 2002 s 102 and Sch 7). Also exempt are the 'exempt landlords' listed in s 58(1) including development corporations, housing action trusts and the Housing Corporation, registered housing associations and fully mutual unregistered housing associations. Certain premises held by charities are also exempt. The application of these provisions to the Crown is set out in the LTA 1987, s 56, which is to be amended by s 172 of the Commonhold and Leasehold Reform Act 2002 as from a date to be fixed (see **Appendix** 2).

The grounds for complaint in the LTA 1987, s 24 include where unreasonable service charges have been made or are proposed or are likely to be made or where there is breach of a relevant approved code of practice (see **2.92**). Here 'service charge' has the same meaning as in the LTA 1985, s 18(1), other than a fixed service charge in a registered rent. A service charge is 'unreasonable' if the amount is unreasonable having regard to the items for which it is payable, or if those items have been provided to an unnecessarily high standard, or if the items are of an insufficient standard with the result that additional service charges are or may be incurred (LTA 1987, s 24(2A)). An auditor's report on the outcome of a management audit can be used in support of an application under s 24 to appoint a manager (see **2.85**).

Manager taking over management

2.96 The order that the FTT can make may include (amongst other things):

(1) provisions with respect to such matters (including incidental or ancillary matters) as the FTT thinks fit in relation to the exercise by the manager of his functions, and the manager can subsequently apply to the FTT for directions with respect to any such matters (LTA 1987, s 24(4));

(2) provisions for the manager to take over from the landlord or other managing person any appropriate contracts (LTA 1987, s 24(5)(a)) and any appropriate contractual or tortious claims accruing before or after the date of the manager's appointment (LTA 1987, s 24(5)(b)); and

(3) provisions for the manager's remuneration to be paid by the landlord or by some or all of the tenants of the premises (LTA 1987, s 24(5)(c)).

The provisions mentioned at (1) might include ordering the landlord to hand over to the manager uncommitted service charge funds and to provide accounts of service costs spent since the last accounts were prepared.

The 'management functions' to which these orders can relate include (but are not limited to) the repair, maintenance or insurance of the premises (LTA 1987, s 24(11)).

Costs of application to appoint a manager

2.97 No order is normally made in connection with FTT proceedings for one party to pay the costs incurred by another party (see **2.68**), but apparently this does not prevent the landlord from seeking to include within the service charges his costs of opposing applications by tenants to the FTT, if the wording of the lease is wide enough to encompass them, although any tenant can ask the FTT for an order prohibiting this under the LTA 1985, s 20C (see the detailed discussion about recovery of costs at **2.33**).

The 'right to manage'

2.98 This regime, created by Pt II of the Commonhold and Leasehold Reform Act 2002 ('CLRA 2002'), gives tenants a collective right to take over the management of their premises. Unlike the appointment of a manager under the LTA 1987, this right can be exercised whether or not the landlord has been guilty of bad management.

The 'right to manage', as the CLRA 2002, s 71 calls it, gives the requisite number of qualifying tenants of flats in a block the right to set up a management company (called an 'RTM company') to take over the management of the building from the landlord.

The relevant provisions of CLRA 2002 are supplemented by the Right to Manage (Prescribed Particulars and Forms) (England) Regulations 2010[1] and the RTM Companies (Memorandum and Articles of Association) (England) Regulations 2010[2]. The main rules are summarised below.

1 SI 2010/825.
2 SI 2010/2767.

Criteria

2.99 In outline, for the right to manage to be exercisable by tenants, those tenants must be 'qualifying tenants' (essentially, holding flats on long leases). Their flats must be in premises to which Chapter 1 of Pt II of the CLRA 2002 applies (essentially, a structurally self-contained building or self-contained section of a building, containing two or more flats let to qualifying tenants, without a resident landlord). At least two-thirds of the flats in the premises must be let to qualifying tenants (if the building has only two flats, both must be let to qualifying tenants). A RTM company must be established with a memorandum and articles of association which meet certain criteria, and the qualifying tenants of at least half the total number of flats in the premises (or, if the premises contain only two flats, the qualifying tenants of both flats) must become members of the RTM company. These requirements are discussed in more detail below.

Qualifying tenants

2.100 A person will be a qualifying tenant for the right to manage if he is the 'tenant' of a 'flat' on a 'long lease' (see below), but subject to certain exceptions described below. The expression 'tenant' covers persons holding a lease or sub-lease or an agreement for a lease or sub-lease (CLRA 2002, s 112(2), (3)). Joint leaseholders are treated together as a single tenant (CLRA 2002, s 75(7)).

Where a flat is let on a long lease and is sublet by the tenant on a long sub-lease, the qualifying tenant will be the person holding the sub-lease (CLRA 2002, s 75(6)). Where a long sub-lease has been granted in breach of covenant out of a superior lease which is not itself a long lease, the subtenant will not be a qualifying tenant unless the superior landlord waived the breach (CLRA 2002, s 75(4)).

A tenant whose tenancy of the flat is a business tenancy protected by Pt II of the Landlord and Tenant Act 1954 will not be a qualifying tenant (CLRA 2002, s 75(3)).

A 'flat' is a separate set of premises, whether or not on the same floor, which forms part of a building, and is constructed or adapted for use as a dwelling, and either the whole or a material part lies above or below some other part of the building (CLRA 2002, s 112(1)). This definition includes flats above shops or garages; maisonettes; duplex apartments, etc.

If the same person holds, from the same landlord, separate leases of two or more parts of a single flat, or separate leases of a single flat or part of one and land or other premises occupied with it (eg a garden, garage or parking space), then such of those leases as are 'long leases' (see below) are together treated as a single long lease (CLRA 2002, s 77(5)). This might apply where, for example, a tenant has been granted separate long leases of a flat and a garage to be used with the flat, or perhaps acquired two adjacent flats under separate leases and converted them into a single flat.

If the qualifying tenant is holding the lease as a trustee, his powers under the trust are deemed to include the right to participate in the right to manage and become a member of a RTM company unless the trust document expressly prohibits it (CLRA 2002, s 111). These provisions also cover cases where the lease is held by a tenant for life or statutory owner under a strict settlement.

Long leases

2.101 A 'long lease' is primarily a lease for a term certain exceeding 21 years, and in most cases whether or not it contains provisions for forfeiture or for early termination (even within the 21 years) either by the tenant or by the landlord (CLRA 2002, s 76(2)(a)). In addition, s 76 provides that the following are also treated as long leases for this purpose:

- a lease for a term not exceeding 21 years but containing provisions for renewal (not perpetually) without requiring payment of a premium, if it has been renewed so as to create a total term exceeding 21 years;
- a perpetually renewable lease, other than one created by sub demise out of a superior lease which is not a long lease;
- a lease for life or for a term determinable on the death or marriage of the tenant, which is deemed by the Law of Property Act 1925, s 149(6) to be a terminable lease for 99 years, but except as mentioned below;

- a lease granted under the right to buy provisions of Pt V of the Housing Act 1985 or under the right under that Act to acquire on rent to mortgage terms or under the provisions of that Act as applied by s 17 of the Housing Act 1996;
- a 'shared ownership lease' – that is, a lease granted at a premium being only a percentage of the cost or value of the flat, but carrying the right for the tenant to acquire further shares in its value – if the tenant's total share has reached 100 per cent.

However, if a lease contains provision for termination by notice given after the death or marriage of the tenant, it will not be a 'long lease' if the notice can be given at any time after the death or marriage, and the notice period is three months or less, and the terms of the lease prohibit both assignment (otherwise than by exchange under the Housing Act 1985, s 92) and subletting of the whole of the flat (CLRA 2002, s 77(1)).

If a tenant who previously had a 'long lease' now has a new tenancy granted (expressly or by implication of law) to him on the expiry of that long lease, his new tenancy is itself deemed to be as a long lease irrespective of its length (CLRA 2002, s 77(2)). Similarly, where a tenant who previously held a 'long lease' remains in occupation by virtue of a deemed continuation of that lease under either Part I of the Landlord and Tenant Act 1954 or Sch 10 of the Local Government and Housing Act 1989 or under the Leasehold Property (Temporary Provisions) Act 1951, it is treated as if the long lease is still running (CLRA 2002, s 77(4)).

Premises to which the right to manage applies

2.102 By the CLRA 2002, s 72, the right to manage applies to premises which are a self-contained building, or a self-contained part of a building, containing two or more flats held by qualifying tenants, where the number of flats held by qualifying tenants is at least two-thirds of the total number of flats in the premises.

'Self-contained' is defined in the legislation. A whole building is self-contained if it is structurally detached (CLRA 2002, s 72(2)). A part of a building is self-contained if it constitutes a vertical division of the building; and the structure of the building is such that the part could be separately redeveloped from the remainder; and the part has independent services (provided by pipes, cables and other fixed installations) or those services could be made independent without significant interruption in the provision of those services to the occupiers of the remainder of the building (CLRA 2002, s 72(3)–(5)). This could, for example, give the right to manage to the tenants of a building forming part of a terrace. An example of a dispute about the extent to which a non-detached building was 'self-contained' is *Minshull Place RTM Company Ltd v Park Rutland Ltd*[1]. Another is in the following example.

EXAMPLE

> *Gala Unity Ltd v Ariadne Road RTM Co Ltd*[2]: An estate comprised two blocks of flats, two coach-houses (flats with parking below), car parking spaces demised with individual flats and various shared areas. Separate RTM claims by the same RTM company were made for each of the two

blocks of flats. Was each block 'self-contained' even if it shared amenities with other buildings and could the 'appurtenant property' mentioned in each claim include the shared areas. **Held:** Yes to both issues. A building could be self-contained even if it shared certain amenities with other buildings and those shared amenities could be treated as 'appurtenant property' even if they do not appertain exclusively to the self-contained building.

However, the right to manage does not apply to premises containing parts which are used (or intended for use) for non-residential purposes where those parts together exceed 25 per cent of the internal floor area of the whole premises; for this purpose, common parts are to be ignored, parts which are ancillary to the flats – such as parking spaces or storage areas – are to be counted as residential, and the internal floors are to be measured as if every floor extended without interruption throughout the inside of the whole of the premises (CLRA 2002, Sch 6, para 1). For a recent case where the detailed measurement of internal floor area for this purpose was disputed, see *Gaingold v WHRA RTM Co Ltd*[3].

Where premises comprise parts in different freehold titles with different freehold owners, the right to manage does not apply to the entirety if any one of those parts is itself a 'self-contained part of a building' within the definition discussed above, but the right to manage can be applied to that part (CLRA 2002, Sch 6, para 2).

Premises with a resident landlord as freeholder are excluded from the right to manage regime if the premises contain not more than four units and are not the whole or part of a purpose-built block of flats. 'Resident landlord' is defined in great detail – in general terms this exemption applies where the freeholder, or an adult member of his family, is at the time occupying a flat owned by the freeholder in the premises as his only or principal home and has so occupied it throughout a period of at least 12 months down to that time, but the provisions also contain detailed rules as to successive ownership by resident landlords, family occupation, trusts, etc (CLRA 2002, Sch 6, para 3).

The right to manage is also excluded when the immediate landlord of any of the qualifying tenants is a local housing authority as defined in the Housing Act 1985, s 1 (CLRA 2002, Sch 6, para 4); when the right to manage is at the time exercisable by a RTM company (CLRA 2002, Sch 6, para 5(1)(a)); and when the right to manage was previously exercisable by a RTM company and this ceased less than four years previously, unless it ceased because the RTM company purchased the freehold or a waiver of this rule is obtained by a RTM company from the FTT on the ground that it would be unreasonable for this rule to apply (CLRA 2002, Sch 6, para 5(1)(b) and (2)).

The right to manage can extend to 'appurtenant property', such as gardens, garages, etc, which belong with, or are usually enjoyed with, the premises (CLRA 2002, ss 72(1)(a), 112(1)). Premises in which the Crown has an interest are not excluded from this legislation (CLRA 2002, s 108).

1 (2004) LON/00AF/LRM/2004/0045, FTT.
2 [2012] EWCA Civ 1372, CA.
3 [2005] 3 EG 122, LT.

Setting up RTM companies

2.103 The company to be set up as a RTM company must conform to a number of conditions listed in the CLRA 2002, ss 73 and 74. It must be a private company limited by guarantee; it must allow all qualifying tenants of flats in the premises to become members; as from the date when it acquires the right to manage the premises, it must also allow landlords of leases of the whole or any part of the premises to become members; and its articles of association must be in the form set out in the Schedule to the RTM Companies (Model Articles) (England) Regulations 2009[1]. The provisions in those forms will automatically override the actual provisions of the articles of the company if different, and no actual provisions will be effective so far as they are inconsistent with the regulations.

A company will not be a RTM company (or, if it has been one, will cease to be one) if it is a commonhold association under Pt I of the CLRA 2002, or it becomes the freeholder of the premises (with or without other premises), or if another company is already the RTM company of the same premises.

1 SI 2009/2767.

Making the claim

2.104 The procedure for acquiring the right to manage is set out in ss 78–89 of the CLRA 2002. A RTM company must be set up in accordance with the rules set out above. If the RTM company needs to obtain relevant information or documentation in connection with making the claim to acquire the right to manage (eg details of the number and ownership of flats, or details of the freehold title), it can serve notice under the CLRA 2002, s 79 on any person requiring him to provide the company with any information in his possession or control which the company reasonably requires for that purpose and requiring him to permit inspection of the relevant documentation by a person authorised by the company and to supply a copy. Service of the notice must be in accordance with CLRA 2002, s 111. The recipient must comply within 28 days of the notice being given. (Obtaining access to different parts of the premises in connection with the claim can only be insisted upon after the claim notice has been served – see below).

At least 14 days before giving its claim notice to the landlord (see below), the RTM company must give written notice to all those qualifying tenants of flats in the premises who have not already become (or agreed to become) members of the RTM company, inviting them to participate (CLRA 2002, ss 78, 80(2)). This notice of invitation to participate must be in the form set out in Sch 1 to the Right to Manage (Prescribed Particulars and Forms) (England) Regulations 2010 (see **2.89**) and must contain the information required by reg 3 of those Regulations. It must be served in accordance with the provisions as to service set out in CLRA 2002, s 111. It must either be accompanied by a copy of the articles of the company, or state where (in England or Wales) and when (for periods of at least two hours on each of at least three days, which can include Saturdays and Sundays) they can be inspected and copies ordered, and specify any fee for providing a copy (not exceeding the reasonable cost of providing it). Failure of the RTM company to allow the inspection or to provide the copy in accordance with that required statement will invalidate the notice to the relevant recipient.

Once 14 days has elapsed after giving all the necessary notices of invitation to participate, and provided that the required minimum number of qualifying tenants have become members (see above), the RTM company must serve notice on the landlord of its claim to acquire the right to manage the premises. This claim notice must be given to each person who is then landlord under a lease of the whole or any part of the premises (this includes the freeholder and any intermediate landlords between the freeholder and the qualifying tenants). It must also be given to each person who is a party to any such lease other than the landlord and the tenant (eg an existing management company), and to any manager appointed under Pt II of the LTA 1987 in relation to all or part of the premises, whether or not together with other premises (see **2.1**); and it must be in the form set out in Sch 2 to the Right to Manage (Prescribed Particulars and Forms) (England) Regulations 2010 (see **2.89**) and must contain the information required by reg 4 of those Regulations.

By a date at least one month after the giving of the claim notice, each recipient of the notice may respond by counter-notice under s 82. The claim notice must specify a date at least three months after the date when it is served, on which the RTM company intends to acquire the right to manage the premises.

The claim notice must be served in accordance with the provisions as to service set out in CLRA 2002, s 111. If any person to be served cannot be found, he need not be given the claim notice (CLRA 2002, s 79(7)), but if this means that no-one would be given the claim notice, the special procedure set out in CLRA 2002, s 85 will apply (see below). A copy of the claim notice must be given to every qualifying tenant in the premises and to any FTT or court that has appointed a manager in respect of the premises

A claim notice will not be invalidated by an inaccuracy in the lease particulars specified in the claim notice. If a member of the RTM company listed in the claim notice was not in fact a qualifying tenant on the date when the claim notice was given, this equally will not invalidate the notice if the required number of qualifying tenants were in fact members at that date. In *Oak Investments RTM Company Ltd v Sinclair Gardens Investments (Kensington) Ltd*[1], the FTT upheld a claim notice which erroneously gave the name of only one of the two persons who were jointly the owners of one of the participating flats, holding that the landlord was not prejudiced by that error or by the participants' failure to give the other joint owner notice of the claim.

Once a claim notice has been given in respect of premises, no other claim notice can be given in relation to the whole or part of those premises (with or without other premises) while it remains in force, which means until it is withdrawn, is deemed to be withdrawn, or ceases to have effect, as mentioned below (CLRA 2002, s 81(3)).

Following the giving of the claim notice, CLRA 2002, s 83 gives various persons the right of access to any part of the premises if that is reasonable in connection with any matter arising out of the claim. These persons are a person authorised by the RTM company to act on its behalf; the landlord of any lease of the whole or any part of the premises and anyone authorised to act on his behalf; any other party to such a lease (other than landlord or tenant) and anyone authorised to act on his behalf; and any manager as mentioned in (4)(c) above and anyone authorised to act on his behalf. To obtain access, at least 10 days' notice must be given (in the manner prescribed in CLRA 2002, s 111) to the occupier of the part to which access is sought or, if it is vacant, to the person entitled to occupy it.

If the RTM company wishes to withdraw the claim notice, it may do so by giving notice of withdrawal to the persons on whom the claim notice had to be served and to the qualifying tenant of every flat in the premises (CLRA 2002, s 86(2)). The notices of withdrawal must be served in accordance with CLRA 2002, s 111. The cost consequences of withdrawal are described below. The RTM company will be deemed, by CLRA 2002, s 87(3), to have withdrawn the claim notice if an order is made for its winding-up or administration, or if it passes a resolution for voluntary winding-up, or if a receiver or manager is appointed over its undertaking, or if possession of any of its property is taken under a floating charge by the holder of a debenture given by the company, or if a voluntary arrangement for the company is approved under Pt I of the Insolvency Act 1986, or if the name of the company is struck off the register of companies under ss 652 or 652A of the Companies Act 1985. Again, the cost consequences are described below.

Where the RTM company is entitled to serve a claim notice but cannot find, or ascertain the identity of, any of the persons to whom the notice would have to be given, then subject to following a specified procedure it may apply to the FTT for an order that it is to acquire the right to manage the premises (see CLRA 2002, s 85).

[1] (2004) LON/OOAE/LOA/0002.

Landlord's counter-notice and subsequent procedures

2.105 The procedures for the landlord and other recipients to respond to a claim notice, and for the RTM company to pursue the claim, are set out in CLRA 2002, ss 84–103. Within the time-limit specified in the claim notice, a recipient of the claim notice may give a counter-notice to the RTM company. The counter-notice must be in the form set out at Sch 3 to the Right to Manage (Prescribed Particulars and Forms) (England) Regulations 2010 (see **2.89**) and can either admit that the RTM company was entitled, at the date of giving the claim notice, to acquire the right to manage the premises, or it can allege that, by reason of some specified provision of the legislation, the RTM company was not so entitled at that date. The counter-notice must be served in accordance with CLRA 2002, s 111.

If the RTM company is given a counter-notice alleging that it was not entitled to acquire the right to manage, the RTM company can apply to the FTT within two months from the giving of that counter-notice (or, where more than one, the last one) to determine the matter. If the RTM company either fails to apply to the FTT within that two-month period, or makes the application but then withdraws it, it is deemed to have withdrawn the claim notice on the expiry of the two-month period or on making the withdrawal of the application, as applicable (CLRA 2002, s 87(1), (2)), in which case the cost consequences described below will apply. If a person who gives a counter-notice alleging that the RTM company was not entitled to acquire the right to manage is subsequently willing to agree that the RTM company was in fact entitled to that right, such agreement can be recorded in writing and the RTM company need then not make or pursue an application to the FTT in relation to that person's counter-notice. If the matter is dealt with by the FTT, any determination of the FTT will be subject to a right of appeal to the Upper Tribunal (Lands Chamber); and then a right of appeal from the Upper Tribunal to the High Court; and then a right of appeal to the Court of Appeal; and then to the House of Lords; but subject to the conditions for appeals imposed by statutes and practice rules. If no appeal against a determination is made within the time-limit for bringing the appeal, the determination becomes final on the expiry of that time-limit. If leave to appeal is required and is sought but is refused, the determination becomes final on the refusal. If an appeal is abandoned, the determination becomes final on the abandonment. If the determination should go to the House of Lords (which is likely to be rare), the determination becomes final on the giving of their judgment.

If a final determination is made to the effect that the RTM company is entitled to acquire the right to manage, then that right, together with related obligations, will be acquired by the RTM company. If the final determination upholds the counter-notice allegation that the RTM company is not entitled to acquire the right to manage the premises, the RTM company will not acquire that right, and the claim notice will cease to have effect (CLRA 2002, s 84(5),(6)). The RTM company, and in certain circumstances its members personally, will be liable to meet certain costs incurred by the landlord and others, as described below.

When the RTM company acquires the right to manage

2.106 Under CLRA 2002, s 90, the date when the RTM company acquires the right to manage the premises depends upon how the claim proceeds. If the RTM company gives a valid claim notice which it does not withdraw, it will acquire the right to manage the premises if it is not, within the specified time-limit mentioned in the claim notice, given any counter-notice alleging that it was not entitled to acquire the right to manage. In such cases the right to manage is acquired immediately on the expiry of that time-limit.

If one or more such counter-notice is given but every person who gives such a counter-notice then agrees in writing that the company is entitled to acquire the right to manage, the right is acquired one month after the date when all such agreements in writing have been made.

If one or more such counter-notice is given by persons who refuse to concede that the company is entitled to acquire the right to manage, the company may make an application to the FTT to decide the matter, and the right to manage will be acquired if there is a determination that the company is entitled to acquire the right to manage the premises. In such situations, the right is acquired one month after the date of the determination becoming final.

There is also a procedure for the RTM company to acquire the right to manage by obtaining a court order to that effect in the case of an untraceable landlord, and in those cases the right to manage is acquired on the date specified in the court order.

Once the right to manage becomes exercisable, the right can be protected by the registration of a caution against the title to the premises at the Land Registry (CLRA 2002, s 102).

Costs of the procedures

2.107 Whatever the outcome of the claim, the RTM company will be liable to pay, in addition to its own costs, the costs reasonably incurred by the landlord and other recipients of the claim notice in consequence of the claim notice being given to them. However, costs which any of them may incur as a party to proceedings before the FTT can only be claimed from the RTM company where the company fails to obtain a determination from the FTT in its favour (CLRA 2002, s 88(1), (3)).

For these purposes, fees which those persons incur for professional services (eg their surveyor's or solicitor's charges) are only recoverable from the RTM company if and to the extent that costs in respect of such professional services might reasonably be expected to have been incurred by the person if the circumstances had been such that he was going to be personally liable for them (CLRA 2002, s 86(2)). This is intended to prevent those persons from incurring professional fees unnecessarily. Any dispute in relation to the amount of any costs payable by the RTM company are to be determined by the FTT (CLRA 2002, s 88(4)).

Where the RTM company, having served a claim notice, fails to acquire the right to manage the premises under the above rules (eg by withdrawing its claim notice, by failing to make an application to the FTT when necessary, by losing such an application, or by being wound up) it is not only the RTM company which will be liable for the costs of the other parties. In this situation the persons who are or have been members of the RTM company will be personally liable, jointly and severally with the company, and with each other, for those costs (CLRA 2002, s 89(3)). This enables the costs to be recovered from the tenants who participate in the attempt to exercise the right to manage, if they fail to provide the RTM company with funds to meet this liability. The expression 'severally' means that any one member could be made to pay the whole of those costs, although ordinarily he would have the right to claim contribution from the other members. The only exception to this personal liability of members is where there has been a transfer or vesting of the lease of a flat from the ownership of a qualifying tenant who was a member of the company into the ownership of a new tenant who has (before the date mentioned above) become a member of the RTM company; in that situation the new member will be liable in place of the former tenant (CLRA 2002, s 89(4), (5)).

Functions acquired by the RTM company

2.108 The RTM company will take over from the landlord (or an existing management company or manager) those obligations in the flat leases which constitute 'management functions', as well as certain other matters outside the scope of this book.

The 'management functions' are defined in the CLRA 2002, s 96. They are the functions of the landlord, management company or manager with respect to services, repairs, maintenance, improvements, insurance and management, but excluding functions relating exclusively to any flats or other units which are not let to qualifying tenants, and also excluding functions relating to re-entry or forfeiture of leases (CLRA 2002, s 96(5) and (6)). Regulations can be made amending both this list and these exclusions.

The RTM company takes responsibility for these matters in place of the persons previously responsible (CLRA 2002, s 96(2) and (3)) and owes this responsibility to the landlords as well as to the tenants (CLRA 2002, s 97(1)). The RTM company also takes over the power to exercise those rights under the leases that relate to these functions (CLRA 2002, s 97(4)), such as the right to collect service charges.

The persons from whom responsibility has been taken no longer have the power to exercise those rights (CLRA 2002, s 97(2)), although this does not prevent the landlord from effecting his own insurance of the premises at his own cost, if he wishes to do so (CLRA 2002, s 97(3)), nor does he lose the right to collect service charges relating to expenditure incurred before the management has passed to the RTM company (CLRA 2002, s 97(5)).

There is no provision in the legislation dealing with matters such as caretakers' accommodation. Where the functions taken over by the RTM company include an obligation to provide a resident caretaker or some other service involving a part of the building retained by the landlord and over which the leases do not give the tenants rights of use, the RTM company may have to negotiate terms with the landlord for using that part of the building, such as renting it. Whether the cost can be recovered through the service charge will depend on the wording of the service charge clauses, but in many cases it will be chargeable as a 'cost' of providing the service so long as the total costs of the relevant service pass the reasonableness test under the 1985 Act.

Statutory obligations affecting the RTM company

2.109 The rules relating to service charges in the LTA 1985, ss 18–30, the obligations under the LTA 1987, ss 42–42B to hold service charge funds on trust, and the restrictions on administration charges imposed by Sch 11 to the CLRA 2002, all apply as if the RTM company were the landlord (CLRA 2002, Sch 7, paras 4 and 11). They will apply even if any of them did not previously apply because the landlord was a local authority or other public body exempted by the LTA 1985, s 26 (see **2.3**). Where the RTM company requires a landlord to pay towards service expenditure (as mentioned at **2.113**), the landlord has the same rights on these matters as if he were a tenant of the relevant flat.

The implied obligations under the LTA 1985, s 11 which require a landlord to carry out, at his own cost, certain repairs and provide certain amenities to flats let on short lettings (see **2.34**) will apply to the RTM company in relation to any flats which are let on such short lettings, but only in respect of those elements as do not relate exclusively to the flat (so, for example, the RTM company would be liable for providing space heating and hot water through a communal system being managed by the RTM company, but would not be responsible if the flat had its own individual heaters), and the RTM company will owe those obligations to all occupiers of such flats as well as to the tenant and, indeed, to the landlord (CLRA 2002, Sch 7, para 3).

The RTM company will be bound by the rights of tenants to seek information about insurance under the LTA 1985, s 30A and the Schedule to that Act (see **2.90**), and where the RTM company requires a landlord to pay towards insurance (as mentioned at **2.113**), the landlord also has these rights (CLRA 2002, Sch 7, para 5). The RTM company will be obliged to consult a recognised tenants' association on the appointment of new managing agents under the LTA 1985, s 30B (see **2.74**) but ignoring s 30B(6) of those provisions (CLRA 2002, Sch 7, para 6). The RTM company will be obliged to furnish tenants with details of names and addresses under the LTA 1987, ss 46–48 (see **2.46**) as if it were the landlord (CLRA 2002, Sch 7, para 12).

The tenants will have the right to impose a management audit on the RTM company under the Leasehold Reform, Housing and Urban Development Act 1993 (see **2.85**); and where the RTM company requires a landlord to pay towards service expenditure (as mentioned at **2.113**), the landlord has the same rights on these matters as if he were a tenant of the relevant flat (CLRA 2002, Sch 7, para 14). The right of a recognised tenants' association to appoint a surveyor to investigate service charge matters under the Housing Act 1996, s 84 and Sch 4 to that Act (see **2.22**) will apply in respect of service charges administered by RTM companies, but excluding Sch 4, para 7 (CLRA 2002, Sch 7, para 1).

Management contracts

2.110 Where contracts are in place with contractors for the provision of services or works falling within the management functions which are to be taken over by the RTM company, the RTM company may wish to try to take over some or all of these contracts. These contracts might include contracts of insurance, contracts with managing agents, cleaners, gardeners, maintenance companies, etc.

To facilitate negotiations concerning these contracts, the CLRA 2002, ss 91–92 contain provisions for various notices to be given to the interested parties in order to create an opportunity in which the parties might be able to negotiate a transfer of some or all of these contracts to the RTM company. However, the RTM company may not want to take them over or the contracting parties may not want that to happen, and there is no compulsion in the legislation for any of these contracts to be transferred.

It is by no means clear that any contracts which are not transferred to the RTM company will end automatically when the RTM company acquires the right to manage the premises. If a contract between the landlord and a contractor does not end in this situation, presumably the landlord will continue to be liable to pay the contractor the amount of the contract payments even though the landlord cannot any longer recover those costs through the service charge. It has been suggested that the ability of the contracting parties to perform the contract will then be frustrated because the landlord will no longer have the power to admit its contractors into the common parts to perform their services, and that such contracts will therefore end by reason of the legal doctrine of 'frustration'. However, that doctrine does not normally apply where the ability of a party to perform his contract is impaired by an event which was within the contemplation of the parties when they entered into the contract. It is arguable that, in relation to contracts made after the enactment of CLRA 2002, the exercise of the right to manage is a foreseeable eventuality which ought to be contemplated by the parties and as such is outside the scope of the legal doctrine of frustration. At the publication date of this book there had been no reported case on this difficult point. Ideally the issue should be covered by an express provision in the contract allowing termination in the event that the right to manage is exercised.

Provision of information to the RTM company

2.111 If the RTM company will be acquiring the right to manage it may need to obtain information and documents in order to take over the management, such as service expenditure records, copies of those flat leases which its members have been unable to provide, etc.

Under the CLRA 2002, s 93, the RTM company can require the landlord or other person currently handling the management to provide the company with any information in his possession or control which the company reasonably requires for this purpose, and requiring him to permit inspection of the relevant documentation by a person authorised by the company and to supply a copy.

Transfer of service charge funds to the RTM company

2.112 If the landlord or other party that has been managing the property has service charge contributions in hand, these must, to the extent that they are not required to meet committed service costs, be paid over to the RTM company on or as soon as practicable after the date when it acquires the right to manage or, if later, by the date four months after the date when the RTM company served notice of its claim to exercise the right to manage (CLRA 2002, s 94(4) and (5)).

The amount to be handed over is to be calculated by aggregating the contributions in hand from all tenants of the premises, including the value of any investments (and accrued interest) and deducting an amount equal to the aggregate amount required to meet costs incurred before the acquisition date and properly chargeable against those contributions (CLRA 2002, s 94(1) and (2)). Any dispute on these matters may be referred to the FTT (CLRA 2002, s 94(3)).

Landlord's liability for ongoing service charges

2.113 If the premises:

(a) contain one or more flats or other units (called an 'excluded unit') not let to qualifying tenants (eg let on short lettings or undemised);

(b) have a service charge regime under the leases of flats held by qualifying tenants by which each such tenant is liable to pay a service charge equal to a proportion of the service costs; and
(c) the aggregate of the service charges payable by those qualifying tenants amounts to less than 100 per cent of the total service costs;

then the amount by which the service charges payable by the qualifying tenants falls short of the total service costs can be recovered by the RTM company from the following 'appropriate person' or persons, under the CLRA 2002, s 103(1) and (2).

The appropriate persons are:

(a) in respect of an excluded unit which is not let, the freeholder;
(b) in respect of an excluded unit which is subject to a lease, the landlord of the lease;
(c) in respect of an excluded unit which is let and sublet, the landlord of the most inferior of such leases (CLRA 2002, s 103(5)).

Where there is more than one excluded unit, the appropriate persons bear the shortfall between themselves in the proportions of the internal floor areas of their excluded units (CLRA 2002, s 103(3) and (4)).

Where the landlord is liable, even though these contributions are not strictly a service charge within the 1985 Act, since they are not payable by a tenant, the reasonableness test in s 19 of that Act applies, because CLRA 2002 s 03 refers to relevant costs within the meaning of the 1985 Act (*Gibbs v Clevedon Court (Dulwich) RTM Co Ltd*[1].)

1 [2017] UKUT 411, LC.

ADMINISTRATION CHARGES

Scope

2.114 This regime, created by Sch 11 to the CLRA 2002 and amended by the Housing Act 2016, s 131, applies a reasonableness test and other protections for tenants of dwellings in relation to charges made by landlords where the charges do not fall within to scope of 'service charge' because they may not directly relate to the provision of services, repairs, maintenance, improvements or insurance or the landlord's costs of management.

The regime applies to 'administration charges', which are defined as amounts payable by a tenant of a dwelling either as part of, or in addition to, rent, and which are payable directly or indirectly:

(1) for or in connection with applications for, or the grant of, approvals under the lease (eg consent for assignment, subletting, alterations or keeping pets);
(2) for or in connection with the provision of information or documents by the landlord or another party to the lease such as a management company (eg insurance or service charge documents);

(3) in respect of the tenant's failure to pay sums on their due date to the landlord or other party to the lease (eg interest on late payment of rent or service charges); or

(4) in connection with an actual or alleged breach of covenant under the lease.

However, it does not include any amount payable by a tenant whose rent is registered under Pt IV of the Rent Act 1977, unless the amount is registered as a variable amount under s 71(4) of that Act (see **2.40**).

The provisions added by the Housing Act 2016 relate to amounts payable in respect of certain litigation costs (see **2.115**).

This regime applies to, amongst other things, the charges of the landlord and its agents and solicitors for dealing with licences and deeds of covenant (*Holding & Management (Solitaire) Ltd v Norton*[1]), charges for collection of arrears (*OM Property Management Ltd*[2]) and similar matters.

The scope of this regime does not extend to charges made by a landlord for entering into a deed of variation of the lease (*Mehson v Pellegrino*[3]).

The scope of the rules can be amended by an order of the appropriate Secretary of State.

1 [2012] UKUT 1, LC.
2 [2012] UKUT 102, LC.
3 [2009] UKUT 119, LC.

Reasonableness tests and reduction of liability

2.115 Where the amount of the administration charge is variable – that is, it is not fixed by the lease, either as a stated sum or by a formula for calculating one – the tenant does not have to pay more than a reasonable amount (CLRA 2002, Sch 11, para 2).

Any party can apply to the FTT under Sch 11, para 4 concerning amounts payable by way of administration charge; and the FTT can be asked to decide whether or not anything is payable and, if it is:

(1) who has to pay;
(2) who is to receive the payment;
(3) how much is payable;
(4) when it has to be paid; and
(5) how it is to be paid.

However, no application can be made to the FTT in respect of anything which:

(a) the tenant has agreed or admitted (but merely paying an amount is not itself an admission or agreement of liability);

(b) has been, or is to be, referred to arbitration under an agreement to arbitrate that the parties in dispute have entered into after the dispute has arisen (arbitration clauses in the lease no longer prevent the FTT deciding the dispute);

(c) has been decided by a court; or

(d) has been decided by an arbitral tribunal under an agreement to arbitrate entered into after the dispute arose.

The jurisdiction of the FTT is not exclusive and the court can also decide the reasonableness of an administration charge (Sch 11, para 4(2)).

Where the administration charge relates to litigation costs (the costs of proceedings at court, the First-tier Tribunal or the Upper Tribunal, or an arbitration) there is a further power under para 5A (inserted by the Housing Act 2016) allowing the relevant court or tribunal to reduce or totally extinguish the tenant's liability to pay that charge, making whatever order the court or tribunal considers to be just and equitable. This enables the court or tribunal to prevent or limit the landlord's recovery of such costs from the tenant with whom the proceedings took place, through a provision in that tenant's lease such as the usual clause allowing recovery of costs incurred in relation to notices of and proceedings for breach of covenant (see for example *Freeholders of 69 Marina, St Leonards-on-Sea v Oram and Ghoorun*[1] at **2.71**) and is akin to the powers given by s 20C of the LTA 1985 in relation to their recovery through service charges.

A tenant's application under para 5A in respect of the cost of court proceedings may be made to the same court during the proceedings or to the county court afterwards. If the proceedings are in the First-tier Tribunal or Upper Tribunal, an application during or after those proceedings must be made to that Tribunal. If the costs relate to arbitration proceedings the tenant's application may be made to the same arbitral tribunal during the proceedings or to the county court afterwards.

In *Norton v Holding & Management (Solitaire) Ltd*[2], the FTT held under this jurisdiction that a landlord was making unreasonable administration charges when its managing agent demanded £105 for dealing with consent for the tenant to sublet and demanded £75 for a deed of direct covenant.

1 [2011] EWCA Civ 1258, CA.
2 [2011] CAM/22UF/LAC/2010/0007.

Varying leases which prescribe charges

2.116 Where the amount of the administration charge is fixed by the lease either as a stated sum or by a formula for calculating one, the tenant will have to pay the sum prescribed by the lease, but either party can apply to the FTT to vary the lease, or to order the parties to vary it, on the grounds that the fixed sum or formula is not reasonable (CLRA 2002, Sch 11, para 3). The variation may be as the applying party requests or such other variation as the FTT thinks fit. The provisions of Sch 11 do not state whether the variation can be backdated.

This jurisdiction is exclusive to the FTT and is not exercisable by a court.

Information to tenants

2.117 The provisions of ss 47 and 48 of the LTA 1987, which prescribe information to be given to tenants (see **2.46** and **2.47**) also apply in connection with the charging of administration charges (CLRA 2002, Sch 11, paras 10 and 11).

Demands for administration charges have to include a statement of the paying party's rights and obligations (CLRA 2002, Sch 11, para 3A), prescribed in regulations.

Chapter 3

VALUE ADDED TAX

BASIC VAT RULES

The basic obligation to charge VAT

3.1 VAT is to be charged, at the reduced rate, standard rate or zero rate, as applicable:

(1) on any supply of goods or services made in the UK;
(2) by a person registered for VAT purposes;
(3) if the supply is in the course or furtherance of any business carried on by that person; and
(4) if the supply is not exempted by the Value Added Tax Act 1994 (VATA 1994), Sch 9.

'Goods and services' covers not only goods and services in the normal sense but also land and buildings.

'Business' is not specifically defined in VATA 1994 but includes any trade, profession or vocation. The EU Council Directive of 28 November 2006 on the Common system of Value Added Tax, Directive 2006/112/EC, Art 9 indicates that VAT is to be charged by a person carrying out any 'economic activity' and defines that term widely so that it includes the exploitation for income of tangible or intangible property. Generally, therefore, any supply of goods or services made by a person registered for VAT purposes can be a taxable supply unless it is specifically exempted.

Subject to some complex rules on deemed consideration which are not relevant for the purpose of this book, VAT is charged at the appropriate rate (zero in certain circumstances – see VATA 1994, Sch 8) on the cash consideration received for the supply.

If the consideration is expressed to be 'exclusive of VAT' the appropriate rate is applied to the cash consideration (ie consideration of £100 exclusive of VAT results in a charge to VAT of £20 at the standard rate of 20 per cent and, thus, a total price of £120). However, if the consideration is expressed to be 'inclusive of VAT' or does not refer to VAT at all, the cash consideration is deemed to include VAT (eg VAT-inclusive price of £100 includes VAT of £16.67 and, thus, incorporates a net consideration of £83.33). It is convenient to use the fraction 1/6 when calculating the VAT element of the VAT-inclusive price.

The right to deduct input tax

3.2 'Input tax' is the VAT paid by a person when paying for goods or services supplied to him. For example, where he pays a VAT-inclusive sum of £120 for cleaning services, he will have paid input tax of £20.

A person is entitled, in principle, to deduct input tax suffered by him against VAT payable by him to HM Revenue and Customs (HMRC) (or obtain a refund of input tax from HMRC if the VAT for which he is accountable in that VAT period is too small) if:

(1) he is registered for VAT purposes;
(2) the input tax relates to supplies made to him of goods or services used or to be used by him for the purposes of a business in which he makes *VAT taxable* supplies to his customers; and
(3) he obtains (subject to one or two minor exceptions) a proper VAT invoice for the input tax.

Having identified input tax in respect of supplies received for the purpose of the business, it is necessary to apportion that input tax between taxable and exempt (if any) supplies made by the business (only the former category being deductible). If all the supplies made by a business are taxable supplies (which, for this purpose, includes supplies which are zero rated and supplies which would be taxable if not outside the scope of VAT because they are made to a person outside the UK), then that business can recover all its input tax. However, many businesses make both taxable and exempt supplies and, therefore, can recover only a proportion of the input tax they have suffered. This is known as 'partial exemption' and is discussed in more detail at **3.3**.

Partial exemption

3.3 As mentioned above, where a person registered for VAT purposes makes both taxable and exempt supplies, he may be able to recover only a proportion of input tax suffered on supplies made to him.

It is necessary for such a person to analyse the supplies of goods and services made to him and to attribute those supplies across the following categories:

(1) taxable supplies made by him (including standard-rated, outside the scope and zero-rated supplies);
(2) exempt supplies made by him; and
(3) 'mixed' supplies which are neither wholly taxable nor wholly exempt (eg annual audit fee, telephone charges, etc).

The input tax attributable to category (1) is wholly deductible and that attributed to category (2) is not deductible. Input tax attributed to category (3) is apportioned to determine the amount deductible ('residual input tax').

The rules concerning the apportionment of input tax falling into category (3) are contained in the Value Added Tax Regulations 1995[1] (VAT Regulations 1995). Input tax is apportioned in accordance with a fraction in which the numerator is the value of taxable supplies made by the person for the VAT period in question and the denominator is the value of total supplies made by that person for that period. The proportion of input tax falling within category (3) as determined by that fraction is deductible.

In determining the amount of total supplies for any period for the purpose of the fraction, certain exempt incidental outputs can be left out of account (see reg 101(3) of the VAT Regulations 1995). The most important of these is *any supply of land or buildings*.

If only small amounts of exempt supplies are made, the registered person may fall within a de minimis limit, applied annually. All input tax is recoverable if any one of the three tests is met. The tests are:

- Less than £625 per month on average of input tax is attributable to exempt supplies made by the registered person, provided that such input tax is no more than 50 per cent of all the input tax incurred per month. Therefore, a registered person may incur VAT-inclusive expenditure relating to exempt supplies made by him of up to £45,000 (at the standard rate of VAT of 20 per cent) in any year without having partial exemption status, but only if further expenditure of at least the same amount is incurred in buying goods or services to be used in making taxable supplies. Persons making wholly or substantially exempt supplies (such as dentists) are likely to fail this test but may pass one of the two simpler tests below.
- Total input tax is less than £625 per month on average *and* exempt supplies are less than 50 per cent of total supplies (ie taxable and exempt supplies combined) made by the registered person.
- The net of total input tax less input tax directly apportioned to taxable supplies (ie effectively input tax apportioned to exempt supplies plus residual input tax) is less than £625 per month on average *and* exempt supplies are less than 50 per cent of total supplies (ie taxable and exempt supplies combined) made by the registered person.

[1] SI 1995/2518.

Commercial lettings and the option to tax

3.4 The letting of commercial and domestic property is exempted for VAT purposes by Group 1 of Sch 9 to VATA 1994. Thus, prima facie the provision of premises by a landlord to a tenant under a lease represents an exempt supply, with the result that:

(1) VAT is not chargeable on the consideration (ie the rent); and
(2) input tax incurred by the landlord in respect of any expenses he incurs in relation to the property (eg VAT he pays on maintenance contractor's charges) is not deductible by the landlord.

However, from 1 April 1989 the UK has adopted provisions allowing a property owner to opt to waive this exempt status for commercial property (the 'option to tax'). If he does so:

(1) any supply of the property (ie its letting or sale) made by the owner will become subject to VAT at the standard rate (currently 20 per cent); and

(2) input tax incurred by the owner in respect of any expenses he incurs in relation to the property will become deductible by him.

This option to tax is made by virtue of VATA 1994, Sch 10, para 2 and is revocable only within its first six months (subject to certain conditions), after no interest has been held in the opted property for at least six years or after 20 years in any case. The option to tax must be notified in writing to HMRC within 30 days of the option being made and in certain circumstances the prior written permission of HMRC must be obtained (see HMRC Notice 742A, paragraph 5). A property owner may make a single option to tax which automatically covers all properties to be acquired in the future (VATA 1994, Sch 10, paras 21 and 22). This is called a 'real estate election'.

The option to tax is capable of being exercised only in respect of commercial property and where a building is only partly commercial (eg a shop with a flat above) the option can apply only to that part of the building which is not residential accommodation. The rent on a letting of such a mixed-use building would have to be apportioned if there are not separate lettings of the commercial and residential parts, and HMRC will accept an apportionment which has an objective basis and gives a fair and reasonable result.

Subject to the above rule concerning buildings with mixed uses, an option to tax must have effect in relation to the whole of a building and all the land within its curtilage. Buildings linked internally or by a covered walkway and 'complexes' (ie units grouped around a fully enclosed concourse) are to be taken as a single building covered by the same option to tax, if they are owned by the same person (or by companies in a single VAT group).

Although the provision of parking facilities is normally standard rated for VAT purposes, a letting of premises including parking space is indivisible and the VAT treatment for the rent follows the treatment of the premises generally (ie standard rated if an option to tax has been made or exempt if no option has been made).

Landlords must take care in deciding whether or not to make an option to tax in respect of any particular building because *any* supply made in connection with that building after the option has taken effect, whether by way of letting or sale, must carry VAT at the standard rate and landlords must remember that certain tenants, such as financial institutions, are able to recover only a small proportion of input tax charged on the rents or purchase consideration. Therefore, the ability of the landlord to deduct input tax (perhaps on a costly refurbishment) must be weighed against the possibility of alienating a species of valuable potential tenant.

Buildings occupied by charities for charitable purposes (other than as offices) are accorded the same status as domestic accommodation and the option to tax is suspended in respect of such buildings, if sold to a charity or whilst a charity is a tenant. A charity using premises for business purposes, for example, as a shop, is not treated as occupying for charitable purposes.

It is, perhaps, unlikely that a building already subject to an option to tax would become used wholly or partly as a dwelling or for charitable purposes. However, if this happens the option is effectively suspended in respect of the appropriate part of the property and supplies revert to being exempt from VAT until commercial use recommences.

Some organisations (eg banks) which are largely VAT exempt were exploiting the option to tax. They were procuring property developers to lease back buildings to them or were funding developers to buy land and lease the land to them after development. Thus, the developer could reclaim VAT on the purchase and construction costs and the VAT-exempt organisation suffered irrecoverable VAT only slowly on periodic rents and service charges. Often, the developer was a company within the VAT exempt company's own group. VATA 1994, Sch 10, para 12 prevents this device. If a lease back is granted to a landlord or a developer grants a lease to a person funding a development and either of them, or anyone connected with them, occupies the land other than wholly or mainly for making taxable supplies, then any option to tax made by the landlord is disabled. No VAT will be chargeable on rent or service charges. At least 80 per cent of supplies made must be taxable to avoid the legislation applying (HMRC Notice 742A, paragraph 13.9.1).

It is important to note that, in a lease back, the developer's option to tax is not affected and he must charge VAT on the rent and service charge payable by the ultimate landlord. However, the ultimate landlord's option to tax is disabled and he can neither recover the VAT charged to him nor charge VAT on the rent and service charge payable by the developer. This legislation is extremely complex and more detailed advice should be sought if it appears likely that these rules may apply.

That statutory anti-avoidance provision has been supported by the decision of the European Court of Justice in *Halifax plc v C & E Commissioners (Case C-255/02)*[1], subsequently followed by the English courts in other cases. Halifax Bank (mostly VAT exempt) sought to recover the VAT incurred on the construction of a new call centre by routing the necessary construction services through several intermediate companies in an attempt to avoid an input tax recovery restriction. The facts were complex (as were the judgments) but the European Court of Justice approved the application to VAT of the principle of 'abuse of rights', ie where the accrual of a tax advantage constitutes the principal aim of a transaction or series of transactions and that tax advantage if obtained would be contrary to the purpose of the relevant legislation. If the principle applies, then the courts can re-categorise the transaction(s) so as to remove the tax advantage sought.

[1] [2006] STC 919.

VAT AND COMMERCIAL LETTINGS

The commercial landlord's VAT position

3.5 Service charges for the general upkeep of the structure and common areas of a tenanted commercial building, or for providing the tenants with the services of a person such as a caretaker, are regarded as part of the consideration for the letting, and the liability of the service charge follows that of the main rent. Therefore:

(1) if the landlord has *not* opted to tax in respect of a property, both the rent and the service charge for the services provided under the terms of the lettings of the property will generally be exempt for VAT purposes; but

(2) if the landlord *has* opted to tax, both the rent and the service charge will generally be subject to VAT at the standard rate.

The word 'generally' is used because the above rules apply only to charges for supplies of services which are inherent in the right of the tenant to occupy the premises, such as maintenance by the landlord of the main structure and common parts of a multi-let building.

Supplies such as heating, lighting or cleaning, etc to the area occupied by a tenant are regarded as separate from any right to occupy the premises, and VAT is chargeable by the landlord at the appropriate rate for the particular supply concerned, irrespective of the VAT status of the letting. Almost all these supplies, such as cleaning, heating and lighting, reception services and telephone switchboard, are liable to VAT at the standard rate.

The treatment of supplies of gas and electricity is more complicated. If the landlord rents or owns secondary credit meters, the charges for the units of gas or electricity supplied through those meters by the landlord are standard rated for VAT purposes. However, if the landlord does not provide secondary credit meters to the tenants and simply makes a fixed charge for unmetered supplies of gas or electricity (as would be normal where the only supply is in respect of the common parts of the building – each tenant arranging for his own direct supply to the let premises) the charge follows the treatment of rent for VAT purposes, as described above.

As explained in **3.2**, the landlord can recover input tax charged to him in respect of services supplied on to the tenant, if the on supply is taxable and not exempt. Therefore:

(1) if the landlord *has* opted to tax, all input tax in respect of supplies made to him for the let property should be deductible; but

(2) if the landlord *has not* opted to tax, input tax deduction is restricted to input tax suffered on those items, if any, which are on charged to the tenant with VAT, for example, cleaning services supplied by the landlord's contractor within the premises let to the tenant.

The deductibility of input tax by the landlord influences the way in which he bills the tenant for the service charges. Thus:

(1) where the landlord *does* recover his input tax, he will on charge the tenant for the net amount, ie excluding the input tax which he can recover from HMRC (but he will have to charge the tenants VAT on top of the total net costs); but

(2) where the landlord does *not* recover his input tax, he will on charge the tenant for the gross amount, ie including the input tax (but not charge further VAT on top of it).

EXAMPLE – COMMUNAL SERVICES

The landlord owns a four-storey office building. Each floor is the same size and is separately let. The landlord can charge each tenant for 25 per cent of the costs of maintaining the communal lift. The landlord pays lift maintenance charges of £1,000 + £200 VAT = £1,200.

*(A) Where the landlord has **not** opted to tax*

The landlord cannot recover the £200 input tax from HMRC. The landlord therefore bills each tenant for 25 per cent of £1,200, ie £300. He does not give them VAT invoices (and they cannot recover the VAT – see **3.6**).

*(B) Where the landlord **has** opted to tax*

The landlord can recover the input VAT of £200 from HMRC. The landlord, therefore, bills each tenant for 25 per cent of £1,000, ie £250. He must charge VAT on top, so he charges them £250 + £50 VAT = £300, and provides them with VAT invoices for this (so that they can recover the VAT – see **3.2.2**).

EXAMPLE – NON-COMMUNAL SERVICES

The same landlord as in the above example provides each tenant with office cleaning carried out by the landlord's contractors. The contractors charge the landlord £2,000 + £400 VAT = £2,400.

*(A) Where the landlord has **not** opted to tax*

Even though the landlord has not opted to tax, so that the supply of the premises remains exempt from VAT, nevertheless the supply of office cleaning is standard rated. The landlord must charge VAT for supplying that service on to the tenants and can, therefore, recover the input tax of £400 from HMRC. The landlord bills each tenant for 25 per cent of £2,000, ie £500. He must charge VAT on top, so he charges them £500 + £100 VAT = £600, and provides them with VAT invoices for this (so that they can recover the VAT – see **3.6**).

*(B) Where the landlord **has** opted to tax*

The fact that the landlord has opted makes no difference in practice except that, as a matter of convenience, the cleaning costs can be dealt with in the same computations as the lift maintenance costs, since their VAT treatment is the same (although for different reasons).

The commercial tenant's VAT position

3.6 A commercial tenant using the let premises for the purpose of a fully taxable business can deduct the whole of any input tax charged to him by a landlord in respect of rent and service charges. If the tenant uses the building for the purpose of a business which is partially exempt (as will be almost all financial institutions etc), a partial deduction can be claimed by the tenant in respect of input tax suffered on the rent and service charges. With some partially exempt businesses, the rate of deduction can be very small. If the tenant uses the building for the purpose of a business which is wholly exempt (as will be almost all medical services), no deduction can be claimed by the tenant in respect of input tax suffered on the rent and service charges.

EXAMPLE – COMMUNAL SERVICES

Using the same example as set out under **3.5**, where the landlord pays lift maintenance charges of £1,000 + £200 VAT = £1,200, and will charge this equally between four tenants. Assume that three of the tenants are traders carrying on businesses which involve making wholly taxable supplies to their customers, but the fourth tenant is a private doctor making wholly VAT-exempt supplies to his patients.

(A) Where the landlord has ***not*** *opted to tax*

The landlord charges each tenant £300 and does not give them VAT invoices. None of the tenants can recover any VAT, even though VAT was part of the sum paid to the lift company. The actual cost to each of them is therefore, £300.

(B) Where the landlord ***has*** *opted to tax*

The landlord charges each tenant £250 + £50 VAT = £300 and provides them with VAT invoices for this. The trading tenants can each recover £50 as input tax in their own VAT returns, so the actual cost to them is only £250 each. The fourth tenant, the doctor, cannot recover any input VAT, so the actual cost to him is the full £300.

EXAMPLE – NON-COMMUNAL SERVICES

The earlier example of the office cleaning services may be taken again, but the same assumption about the four tenants as set out above can also be made.

(A) Where the landlord has ***not*** *opted to tax*

The landlord charges each tenant £500 + £100 VAT = £600 and provides them with VAT invoices for this. The trading tenants can each recover £100 as input tax in their own VAT returns, so the actual cost to them is only £500 each. The fourth tenant, the doctor, cannot recover any input VAT, so the actual cost to him is the full £600.

(B) Where the landlord ***has*** *opted to tax*

The fact that the landlord has opted to tax makes no difference.

If a tenant does not use the property for the purpose of his own commercial activity, but, instead, sublets it to subtenants, the rules indicated in **3.5** will apply to any service charges which he may recharge to his subtenants. The deductibility of input tax by the tenant in respect of service charges made by the landlord will depend on whether or not the tenant has, in turn, opted to tax the supply of the property to the subtenants. If the tenant has so opted, the input tax may be fully deductible but the tenant must charge VAT at the standard rate in respect of the rent and service charges payable by the subtenants.

VAT AND DOMESTIC AND CHARITABLE LETTINGS

The landlord's VAT position

3.7 Domestic (including charitable – see below) lettings have their own peculiar set of rules for VAT purposes and these differ from commercial lettings as follows:

(1) a landlord cannot opt to tax the property and no supplies of domestic lettings can be taxable; and

(2) supplies of basic amenities such as electricity and gas are (as at publication) liable to VAT at a special lower rate of 5 per cent to a domestic tenant or to a landlord for on supply to domestic tenants. This includes supplies of gas or electricity by the landlord through a secondary credit meter and also supplies of heat, ventilation or air conditioning from a central plant operated by the landlord.

Again, it is necessary to examine the basic VAT treatment of rent in connection with domestic letting in order to ascertain the correct treatment of those service charges which follow the treatment of rent and also a landlord's entitlement to deduct input tax charged to him.

The supply by a person constructing a domestic dwelling (or a building to be used for charitable purposes) of a 'major interest' in the building (a lease exceeding 21 years in England and Wales; or 21 years in Scotland) can be zero rated for VAT purposes. Zero-rated status is also offered to a person converting a commercial building to domestic use, providing certain qualifying conditions are met. However, where the consideration is represented by an annual rent rather than an initial premium, only the first payment of rent is zero rated and the remainder of rental payments are exempt for VAT purposes. All rents in respect of a letting of 21 years or less (or, in Scotland, less than 21 years) are exempt. Therefore, the landlord cannot recover input tax charged to him in respect of maintenance expenses incurred after the beginning of the letting, since those expenses will be attributed to exempt supplies.

As the landlord has no ability to opt to tax in respect of the letting of domestic property, rental payments subsequent to the first payment will be exempt from VAT and those service charges which follow the treatment of rent and are made after the initial letting will also be exempt for VAT purposes.

Services for the general upkeep of the structure and common areas of the building, such as janitorial or porterage services, maintenance of communal gardens, and cleaning of the common parts, follow the same VAT treatment as for rent. For the reasons given above, these particular service charges will be exempt for VAT purposes, but this may be of no advantage to the domestic tenant. Unless the landlord uses direct labour, he will usually be charged VAT on the supply of the respective services to him and, since such input VAT will not be deductible by him in his own VAT returns (being attributable to an exempt supply to the tenants), the landlord will almost inevitably pass the cost of that VAT on to the tenants through the service charge by charging on the basis of the gross cost inclusive of the VAT. Thus, the domestic tenant would still bear the cost of the VAT.

Services supplied to the portions of the building occupied by tenants are regarded as supplies separate from the basic right to occupy the premises and, for any supplies other than the basic amenities mentioned above, the landlord must charge VAT at the standard rate on top of the total charges relating to that expenditure. The same rule applies for those basic amenities liable to the special lower rate of 5 per cent. Once again, the landlord can recover the input VAT for costs recharged with VAT, so VAT would be added only to each tenant's share of the basic net costs. Therefore, the tenant may notice little practical difference between charges for services provided in the tenant's premises and charges for services for the communal areas.

It should be noted that where charity tenants are referred to in this paragraph, it is assumed that the premises in question are occupied solely for charitable purposes. If the charity conducts a business on the premises, or part thereof, the comments above concerning commercial lettings apply also to the building. If the business activities are conducted on only part of the premises the service charges are apportioned between the respective parts, and the separate rules for commercial and domestic lettings apply accordingly. An office occupied by a charity is always regarded as occupied for the purposes of business activities and, therefore, 'charitable purposes' are, effectively, restricted to premises used as a home for beneficiaries, schools, etc.

The domestic/charitable tenant's VAT position

3.8 Unless the landlord uses direct labour for the provision of many services, the only costs incurred VAT-free by the domestic tenant (under the present rules) are the basic amenities of water and sewerage services. The other costs, on which the landlord will have been charged VAT at either the standard rate or the lower rate of 5 per cent, will be recharged to the tenant on a VAT-inclusive basis. The domestic tenant can be at a disadvantage compared with most commercial tenants who can be charged VAT directly by the landlord in respect of service charges and who can reclaim the VAT.

Services provided other than by landlords

3.9 The rules explained above apply only if the landlord is providing the services to the tenants. The correct VAT treatment where the services are supplied by a third party (eg the trustee of a maintenance trust, even if the landlord is the trustee) is more complicated and has been the source of much confusion. The House of Lords has laid down guidelines in *Nell Gwynn House Maintenance Trustees v HM Customs & Excise*[1].

1 [1999] STC 79.

The Nell Gwynn House case

3.10 Nell Gwynn House is a block of 435 apartments. Many years ago, the tenants were concerned at the large sum of money held by the headlessee in collected service charges. In order to allay this concern, a fund to pay for the maintenance of the building was established by trust deed to which each tenant contributes under the terms of his or her lease. The independent trustees of the fund employ 17 maintenance staff.

The trustees are paid a fee, agreed by all parties to be VAT standard rated. HMRC accepted that the trustees should not charge VAT on the part of their service charges which recovers the cost to the fund of obtaining maintenance services from third-party contractors, as the trustees had no opportunity of making any profit on this cost. However, HMRC maintained that the trustees should charge the tenants VAT at the standard rate on the balance of the service charges levied (used to pay staff salaries and the trustees' fees out of the fund), arguing that the balance represents consideration for a supply of services. The trustees maintained that VAT is not chargeable on the service charges (except to the extent of their fees), either because the charges represent contributions to a trust fund by the beneficiaries of the trust, or because the service charges are part of an exempt supply of property (ie that the treatment of service charges follows the treatment of the rent for each apartment).

Both grounds were rejected by the VAT Tribunal and the High Court:

(1) the first on the ground that the 'mutuality' principle which has effect for direct tax purposes does not prevent a chargeable supply of services arising for VAT purposes; and

(2) the second on the ground that the trustees could not make a supply of property because they constitute a separate legal entity from the landlord and cannot be equated with the landlord (even if the landlord also acts as the trustee of the maintenance trust).

Undaunted, the trustees appealed to the Court of Appeal with a new argument that no part of the service charge, other than their fee, constitutes consideration under European law because the trustees are not themselves at liberty to deal with the money. This argument was accepted by the Court of Appeal. However, the House of Lords rejected this argument completely and restored the decision of the lower courts. The trustees' application for a reference to the European Court of Justice was refused, although only after the Law Lords deliberated for nine months! The Law Lords brushed aside the trustees' argument that a restoration of the decision of the VAT Tribunal would result in all the service charges being VAT standard rated (whereas HMRC was arguing that only the recharge of salaries and the trustees' fees are standard rated), Lord Slynn stating that any concession by HMRC in respect of this claim cannot affect the true legal position.

The three difficulties with the decision of the House of Lords are as follows:

(1) Their Lordships applied English trust law in deciding that the trustees are not the agents of the beneficiaries. It is submitted that the proper law to apply is European law, in which trusts are hardly known, but mutual funds are recognised. It is likely that on a proper application of European law the trustees would have been regarded as the agent of the beneficiaries and the services as provided by an agent to its principal. This would have removed the liability to VAT on the service charges.

(2) Their Lordships' decision ignored a line of European Court of Justice cases holding that the consideration for a supply is limited to the amount that can be retained by the supplier and any amount that the supplier is mandated to pay away to a third party is to be ignored.

(3) Their Lordships held that the tax point of the supply of staff by the trustees occurs when money is removed from the fund to pay the staff. This decision is difficult to understand because it appears that if the main decision on liability is correct, the only possible tax point is the date of receipt by the trustees of service charges or the date of issue of a tax invoice to a tenant, whichever occurs earlier.

Nevertheless, there is no appeal from the decision of the House of Lords, the European Court of Justice being unable to intervene without a reference from a national court.

The effect of the Nell Gwynn House case – commercial letting

3.11 Service charges for the common parts of a building will be VAT exempt only if:

(1) they are paid to the landlord acting in his capacity as such and not as the trustee of a maintenance trust; and
(2) the landlord has not opted to tax in respect of the property.

The effect of the Nell Gwynn House case – domestic letting

3.12 As all service charges payable under a lease for domestic letting are held in a statutory maintenance fund trust (by virtue of the Landlord and Tenant Act 1987, s 42), then on a strict interpretation of this decision it would appear that all such service charges are VAT standard rated. This is so even if the landlord of the property acts as the trustee of the statutory trust, because when acting as trustee he would be deemed to be a separate legal person for VAT purposes. This was made quite clear in the *Nell Gwynn House* judgment in both the High Court and the House of Lords.

HMRC's view on domestic service charges was set out in Business Brief 3/94 (now paragraph 3.18 of Notice 48), which announced a concession in respect of service charges for the common areas of estates of dwellings and blocks of apartments from 1 April 1994. Paragraph 3.18 of Notice 48 is reproduced below:

> 'The concession exempts from 1 April 1994 all mandatory service charges or similar charges paid by the occupants of residential property towards the upkeep of the dwellings or block of flats in which they reside and towards the provision of a warden, caretakers, and people performing a similar function for those occupants. The concession does not exempt service charges paid in respect of holiday accommodation as defined in VATA 1994 Sch 9 Group 1 Notes 11–13 para 1(e).'

Note that the concession applies only if the service charges are payable mandatorily (eg under the terms of a lease or a statutory trust) to a person other than the landlord (*Devine v C&E Commissioners*[1]). This point was emphasised in 2009 in the European Court of Justice decision in *RLRE Tellmer Property sro v Finanční ředitelství v Ústí nad Labem (Case C-572/07)*[2], where it was held that a service charge for the cleaning of the common parts of an apartment block was a separate taxable supply from the (VAT exempt) letting of the apartments. The tenants were not obliged under their leases to accept these charges and could source cleaning services elsewhere. Subsequent to this decision, HMRC issued Brief 67/09 confirming their previous view that the concession in Paragraph 3.18 of Notice 48 applies only where the provision of services by a landlord is mandatory under a lease or a statutory trust and is not optional.

In contrast, in *Field Fisher Waterhouse LLP v HMRC, ECJ Case C-392/11*[3]; and *HMRC v The Honourable Society of Middle Temple, UT*[4] the Courts held that the supply of services alongside the rent were one indivisible supply of letting so that the charges for the services and the rent attracted the same VAT treatment.

Occupants of an estate may form a tenant-controlled management company. Sometimes that company will purchase the freehold of the estate and engage a service provider to maintain the common areas and provide any necessary warden or housekeepers. The above VAT-exempt treatment can also apply to services provided by such a tenant-controlled management company providing the tenant-controlled management company is bound by the terms of the lease to maintain the common areas of the estate (or provide a warden), and the occupants are invoiced by and pay the service charges directly to the service provider. However, any management fee collected from the occupants is standard rated because it relates to the service provider's supply to the tenant-controlled management company.

1 [1998] BVC 4,057.
2 [2009] STC 2006.
3 [2013] STC 136.
4 [2013] UKUT 250 (TCC), [2013] STC 1998.

Planning point

3.13 The effect appears to be to maintain the pre-*Nell Gwynn House* position with respect to domestic letting, but by concession only! Service charges for compulsory services to the common parts will be VAT exempt. Of course, as demonstrated above, the effective cost to a domestic tenant of service charges does not, in practice, depend on his VAT status, unless the landlord has incurred no VAT in providing such services (as in *Nell Gwynn House*).

Commonholds

3.14 The Commonhold and Leasehold Reform Act 2002 confers upon owners of parts of a building, occupied in common, freehold interests in their respective parts of the property. The freehold interest in the property's common parts is owned by a commonhold association whose membership comprises the owners of the parts.

Charges can be levied by the commonhold association to pay for the upkeep of common parts. These charges are referred to as commonhold assessments and reserve fund levies, and are treated for VAT purposes in the same way as described above for service charges to a long leaseholder or a non-commonhold freeholder. In particular, where the commonhold association is providing the services directly to the holders of dwellings, the charges may be treated as VAT exempt under the paragraph 3.18 of Notice 48 concession (see **3.12**). This treatment is not extended to holiday accommodation.

Alternatively, the commonhold association may engage a service provider to maintain the common parts of an estate. In this case the VAT treatment is similar to that of a tenant-controlled management company (see **3.12**).

VAT AND MIXED-USE BUILDINGS

3.15 Where service charges are made by a landlord to both commercial tenants and domestic tenants in the same property (eg a parade of shops with flats above) and the costs giving rise to the service charges need to be apportioned to arrive at the separate service charges for the commercial tenants and the domestic tenants, HMRC will accept a reasonable apportionment. If the apportionment is not specified in the relevant leases, it may be based on respective floor space, although weighting adjustments will be permitted if floor space alone does not provide a just and reasonable apportionment.

After making the apportionment of the cost, the part apportioned to the commercial tenant is to be dealt with in accordance with **3.5** and that apportioned to the residential tenants is to be dealt with in accordance with **3.7**.

EXAMPLE

A landlord spends £12,000 plus £2,400 VAT, totalling £14,400, on repairing the exterior of a four-storey building containing a retail shop on the ground floor and a residential flat on each of the three upper floors. The shop is let on a ten-year commercial lease and the three flats were sold on long leases. All the leases reserve service charges in equal proportions (25 per cent each) and include the cost of external repairs. The landlord has opted to tax in respect of the building. The position is:

(1) the landlord can recover 25 per cent of the VAT he incurred on the cost of repairing the exterior (ie £600) since that proportion of the cost is attributable to the commercial service charge which is VAT standard rated;
(2) the remaining VAT of £1,800 is not recoverable as it is attributable to the three VAT-exempt domestic service charges;
(3) the commercial tenant's service charge will include 25 per cent of the cost of the works ignoring VAT (ie a charge of £3,000) and the landlord will charge him VAT on that service charge;
(4) the domestic tenants' service charge will each include 25 per cent of the cost of the work inclusive of its irrecoverable VAT (ie a charge of £3,600 each) on which VAT will not be chargeable by the landlord.

VAT AND SHARED PREMISES

General

3.16 Sometimes, a landlord will occupy premises with his tenants, or a tenant will agree to discharge bills for utilities and collect appropriate proportions of the costs from other tenants. This amounts to a sharing of costs and has the following VAT consequences.

Payments collected by one tenant for the landlord

3.17 Tenants may enter into an agreement for one 'lead' tenant to collect payments from the other occupants on behalf of the landlord of their share of the rent, rates and other costs. The collected payments must be passed on in full to the landlord. The 'lead' tenant can treat these collected costs as disbursements and so the other occupiers' shares of these amounts are ignored in determining the VAT position of the 'lead' tenant.

Assuming the landlord has opted to tax the premises, if his business is fully taxable, the 'lead' tenant will be able to claim a deduction for his share of any input tax but not for the other occupiers' shares. He will recoup the other tenants' shares of the total costs from them on a VAT-inclusive basis, and they will not be able to deduct input tax because they will have no tax invoice from the 'lead' tenant to support the claim.

EXAMPLE

Alan, Bill, Colin and Douglas are all tenants in a small building. Alan agrees to collect rent, etc on behalf of the landlord and to recharge the others so that they all share the charges equally. The landlord has opted to tax the building and Alan receives an invoice from the landlord for rent and service charge of £200 + £40 VAT = £240. The position is:

(1) Alan is entitled to recover his one-quarter share of the £40 VAT in his own tax returns, ie £10;
(2) Alan asks each of the others to reimburse him for one-quarter of the total bill of £240, ie £60 each, but he does not give them VAT invoices;
(3) the actual cost to Alan is £60, less his recovered input tax of £10, ie £50. Bill, Colin and Douglas have to pay £60 each and cannot recover any of the VAT.

Generally, therefore, this type of arrangement is suitable only where the landlord has not opted to tax, or where the other tenants are not entitled to reclaim input tax in any event.

Landlord in occupation providing services to tenants

3.18 Where a landlord in occupation provides services to tenants, the costs recharged to tenants by the landlord (including a tenant granting sub-leases) generally follow the basic rules in **3.5** and **3.7**, as appropriate. The additional points to note where the landlord himself occupies the building and shares his own facilities with his tenants are as follows:

(1) *Reception and switchboard*
A charge for part of the cost of operating reception or switchboard facilities (eg based on the wages of the receptionists or telephonist) follows the treatment of rent, and, thus, will be exempt from VAT unless the landlord has opted to tax.
(2) *Office staff and services*
A charge for part of the cost of employing office staff (eg secretaries) *other than staff concerned with maintaining the building* is normally standard rated for VAT purposes, as is the recharge of other office services, such as the provision of photocopying facilities. However, if under the terms of the lease, there is one inclusive charge for office services and accommodation together, and the tenants are expected to pay for the services regardless of whether they actually use them, the liability of the services will follow that of the VAT treatment of the rent (HMRC Notice 742, paragraph 11.7.4).
(3) *Car parking*
A charge of part of the cost of car parking is standard rated.

(4) *Staff facilities*
A compulsory charge for the provision of facilities for use by staff (eg recreation rooms or sports facilities) in the common parts of the building is the same as the VAT treatment for the rents. A charge for the costs of other shared staff facilities (eg canteen, vending machines, sports facilities away from the building) is standard rated for VAT purposes.

A charge for building maintenance staff (mentioned in (2) above) is covered by the normal rules in **3.5** and **3.7**.

Associated companies sharing occupation

3.19 It is not uncommon for a company to take a lease of premises and then to allow associated companies (perhaps companies in the same group) to occupy parts of the premises without themselves entering into arrangements directly with the landlord or entering into formal sub-leases or licences with the actual tenant.

This grant of an informal right to use a part of the premises is a standard-rated supply for VAT purposes and any charge made by the actual tenant is subject to VAT. This applies even if the tenant is simply passing on an appropriate share of costs, such as rent, business rates, insurance, etc (see paragraph 11.8 of HMRC Notice 742). As the actual tenant is making standard-rated supplies, he is able to deduct any input tax charged by the supplier of services in respect of which a recharge with VAT is made to the associated companies.

The necessity for this charge to VAT can be avoided if the tenant and the associated companies can enter into a group VAT registration within the meaning of s 43 of VATA 1994. (The details of that topic are outside the scope of this book.) Alternatively, the tenant could grant a licence of a specified area to its associate (see paragraph 2.5 of HMRC Notice 742).

Serviced offices

3.20 A landlord providing serviced office facilities sometimes separates the charge for facilities from the charge for office space, and sometimes separate contracts are entered into for each of those supplies. The VAT Tribunal has considered the effects of this treatment in the following cases.

EXAMPLES

> *Business Enterprises (UK) Ltd v Commissioners of Customs and Excise*[1]: The appellant company supplied, as a package, serviced office accommodation at a time before the introduction of the option to tax, so that all supplies of property were VAT exempt. The services included furniture, use of a telephone switchboard and cleaning, etc. The company contended that the supplies were taxable at the standard rate (so that it could recover input tax incurred by it in providing the services), but HMRC contended that the company made only supplies of exempt licences to occupy land. The VAT Tribunal held that the company predominantly supplied exempt licences to occupy land and the facilities provided were ancillary and subservient to that predominant supply. The company could not recover any input tax.

Sovereign Street Workspace Ltd v Commissioners of Customs and Excise[2]: *Business Enterprises (UK) Ltd* was distinguished in a subsequent case in which the VAT Tribunal held that a company which supplied serviced office accommodation (and had not opted to tax the building) was making multiple and separate supplies comprising of:

- the grant of exempt licences to occupy land; and
- the supply of the use of facilities including telephone answering services and mail handling which were independent of the land (and taxable at the standard rate of VAT).

The VAT Tribunal held that the consideration paid by the tenants had to be apportioned between the two separate supplies and, accordingly, VAT was chargeable at the standard rate for the use of the facilities.

First Base Properties Ltd v The Commissioners of Customs and Excise[3]: First Base took a lease of office space and then, after partitioning the premises into smaller offices, furnished the offices with business equipment and furniture. The offices were rented to customers as serviced offices but First Base did not opt to tax the building. Customers were charged £15 per square foot for the right to occupy the individual office space allocated to them and £40 per square foot for the services and use of the equipment and furnishings. A customer could rent an unfurnished office without services if he so wished.

First Base attempted to recover the input tax incurred on the equipment and furnishings on the basis that the £40 per square foot rent was a separate taxable supply at the standard rate of VAT. HMRC resisted on the grounds that one single VAT-exempt supply of a licence to occupy the accommodation was being made.

The VAT Tribunal had to decide whether the services and use of the equipment and furnishings was an integral part of the supply of the accommodation or a separate supply for a separate consideration. It distinguished *Business Enterprises (UK) Ltd* on the grounds that First Base specified a separate charge for the services and use of the equipment and furnishings in the rental agreements and there were no supplies of unfurnished offices involved in *Business Enterprises (UK) Ltd*. The fact that First Base offered, and did actually supply, unfurnished accommodation without services appears to have influenced the VAT Tribunal.

Therefore, the VAT Tribunal considered that the charge for the supply of the services and use of the equipment and furnishings was standard rated and that input tax recovery could be made in respect of the purchase of equipment and furnishings. However, First Base was not entirely successful as a charge for cleaning was held to be an integral part of the supply of accommodation and VAT exempt.

Assuming that no option to tax has been made by the landlord (because such an option would render all supplies of both accommodation and facilities liable to VAT at the standard rate), the conclusions to be drawn from these cases are that:

- if a *single* charge is made for the accommodation and the office facilities,

  - then the charge should be exempt from VAT as consideration for a licence to occupy land; unless
  - the office facilities provided are of significant value, in which case an apportionment between exempt accommodation and standard-rated services may be necessary; but
- if a *separate* charge is made for the office facilities, preferably with separate supporting documentation,
  - then that separate charge is most likely to be VAT standard rated and the charge for the accommodation is most likely to be exempt from VAT as consideration for a licence to occupy land; and
  - this treatment is more certain if unfurnished office accommodation, without office facilities, is also let to tenants.

1 (1998) VATTR 160 (3161).
2 MAN/91/403 (9550).
3 LON/93/3122A (11598).

GENERAL POINTS ON VAT

Accounting for VAT on service charges

3.21 VAT becomes chargeable and accountable by reference to a VAT 'tax point'. The basic tax point for rent and for those service charges which follow the treatment of the rent, is the earlier of:

(1) the issue of a VAT invoice (which must conform with particular requirements); or
(2) the receipt by the landlord of payment.

Service charges which do not follow the treatment of the rent (as described above) should, nevertheless, follow the same rule; whilst normally a tax point for an individual item of service will be the date the item of service is completed, service charges are treated as continuing services in respect of which reg 90 of the VAT Regulations 1995 provides that the normal linkage of the tax point to the completion of the service is disapplied.

A landlord is permitted, by the VAT Regulations 1995, to send out a VAT invoice covering a period of up to one year in advance, setting out the payments due from the tenant in that period. The tax point in respect of each payment covered by the VAT invoice is then fixed at the earlier of the due date for, or receipt of, the payment.

However, many landlords do not adopt this procedure because it fixes a tax point at the due date, even if a tenant is late in paying. Instead they send out a 'reminder' for rent and service charges, in a form which does not constitute a VAT invoice, eg by the omission of the VAT number and stating 'This is not a VAT Invoice'. It is important to note that the 'reminder' must not show VAT separately (see VATA 1994, Sch 11, para 5(2)). The tax point is then fixed at the time of receipt of actual payment from the tenant and the landlord sends the tenant a VAT invoice after (but within 30 days of) receiving the payment (as required by reg 13(1) and (5) of the VAT Regulations 1995).

This procedure is not always popular with tenants since they are not entitled to deduct the input tax in their VAT returns until they receive the VAT invoice, and there may be a delay in obtaining a deduction if they make the payment in the last few days of a VAT period and the VAT invoice is not received from the landlord until later. However, as this particular procedure crystallises a tax point only on receipt of payment by the tenant, the tenant cannot, in law, demand a VAT invoice in advance of making payment.

The introduction of the option to tax had the effect of applying VAT to certain rents and service charges which were reserved by leases or other contractual obligations entered into before VAT was generally applied to land and which may, therefore, be silent as to the tenant's liability to pay VAT. Section 89 of VATA 1994 provides that unless the lease or contractual arrangements specify otherwise, the landlord is able to require the tenant to pay VAT in addition to the rents and service charges, as from the date of the option to tax. For this purpose, a lease (but not other contractual arrangements) 'specifies otherwise' only if a specific reference to VAT is made in the clause concerned. Thus, a generally-worded provision that the tenant is not liable to pay tax on the rent will be insufficient to avoid the tenant having to pay VAT on the rent.

It should be noted that s 89 applies only to a lease or contractual arrangement in existence at the time that the option to tax takes effect. If VAT is to be chargeable on rent and service charges reserved by a lease or contractual arrangement granted or entered into after the option, the lease or contract must expressly state that the sums reserved are 'exclusive of VAT' or contain some other express provision for VAT to be paid in addition to the stated amounts. If this is not done the tenant need pay no more than the stated sums, but the receipts by the landlord will be deemed to include VAT for which the landlord must account to HMRC.

Interaction with stamp duty land tax

3.22 HMRC Stamp Taxes maintains that, in respect of the completion of a land transaction return on the grant of a lease, stamp duty land tax is chargeable on the total of rent and VAT where the landlord has opted to tax. It should be noted that if the lease provides for a single inclusive sum for both rent and service charges, stamp duty land tax under para 6 of Sch 17A to the Finance Act 2003 will be chargeable on the sum, including service charges. If, however, the service charges are reserved separately, they will be ignored for stamp duty land tax purposes.

If a lease is granted without an option to tax having being made by the landlord, any hypothetical VAT which would be charged on future rents, if an option were to be made, is ignored for stamp duty land tax purposes. This is a departure from the previous stamp duty treatment, which charged duty on the hypothetical VAT unless the landlord covenanted never to opt the property.

From 1 April 2015 land transactions involving buildings and land in Scotland have fallen under the remit of Land and Buildings Transaction Tax (LBTT), administered by Revenue Scotland rather than under Stamp Duty Land Tax, administered by HMRC. However, LBTT is largely based on Pt 4 of the

Finance Act 2003 and there is no practical difference between the treatment of a land transaction involving a charge to United Kingdom VAT between SDLT and LBTT.

From 1 April 2018 land transactions involving buildings and land wholly or partly in Wales will not be charged to SDLT but to a new Welsh land transactions tax. The treatment of a Welsh land transaction involving a charge to United Kingdom VAT will follow SDLT and LBTT.

VAT procedure for managing agents

3.23 HMRC will not accept a managing agent as being responsible for the landlord's VAT affairs and, therefore, it is not possible for a managing agent to assume sole responsibility for invoicing and accounting for VAT where a landlord has exercised the option to tax and must account for VAT on rents.

However, in the circumstance that VAT is chargeable on rents and/or service charges, it is understood that the following invoicing procedures are acceptable to HMRC:

(1) the landlord issues rent 'reminders' and/or VAT invoices directly to the tenant;

(2) the managing agent invoices the tenant in his own name and using his own VAT registration number. The supply is treated as being made by the landlord to the managing agent and then by the managing agent to the tenant (s 47(3) of VATA 1994). The landlord will issue a VAT invoice to the managing agent and the managing agent will reclaim input tax on it. In turn, the managing agent will issue a VAT invoice to the tenant. However, the involvement of a managing agent cannot change the nature or timing of a supply (which remains that of landlord to tenant in basic law (*Metropolitan Borough of Wirral v C&E*[1])) and the VAT invoices issued by the landlord and the managing agent, therefore, should have the same tax point. This arrangement can make the issue of 'reminders' followed by a VAT invoice after receipt of payment from the tenant somewhat cumbersome;

(3) the managing agent issues a 'reminder' and/or VAT invoice using the landlord's name, address and VAT registration number. In this case the name and address of the managing agent may appear on the documentation only as an instruction to the tenant as to whom the actual payment should be made.

Whichever method of accounting is adopted, the managing agent must ensure that the landlord is kept fully informed as to matters concerning its VAT affairs. In particular, where method (3) (above) is adopted, the landlord must be sent promptly copies of any invoices issued in the name of the landlord to ensure that the VAT charged is appropriately entered in the landlord's VAT return.

In respect of services obtained by the landlord for the premises, the managing agent can either:

(4) arrange for VAT invoices to be issued to him and then himself invoice the landlord accordingly (ensuring that both invoices have the same tax point), the managing agent reclaiming the input tax on the VAT invoice sent to him; or

(5) arrange for contractors to invoice the landlord directly.

It should be noted in option (5) above, that the invoices can still be sent to the managing agent for processing as long as the landlord is shown on the invoice as the recipient of the supply of services and is informed accordingly so that the appropriate reclaim of input tax can be made by the landlord.

Whatever arrangement is adopted, and whether or not 'reminders' are sent before VAT invoices are issued, any failure to operate the chosen procedure correctly may lead to the imposition of a penalty for carelessly or deliberately filing an incorrect return and/or default interest on either or both of the managing agent and the landlord. Where the landlord has a penalty or interest levied against him due to misapplication of procedures by the managing agent, the landlord may seek to hold the agent liable in negligence.

The managing agent should remember to charge VAT at the standard rate on his fees, in all circumstances.

1 [1995] STC 597.

Chapter 4

RESERVE FUNDS AND SINKING FUNDS

DIFFERENT TYPES OF FUNDS

4.1 The creation of a reserve or sinking fund differs from simply making a 'provision' for future expenditure where it may be implied that the provision is to be limited to expenditure that is to be incurred before the expiry of the term of the lease (see *Brown's Operating Systems Ltd v Southwark Roman Catholic Diocesan Corporation*[1], *Court of Appeal and Friends Life Management Services Ltd v A&A Express Building Ltd*[2] and see **1.74**).

Clear wording in the lease is required if the landlord is to have the right to create a true reserve fund or sinking fund, which need only be used when the landlord carries out particular works, even if carried out after the leases expire, and does not need to be refunded to the tenants so far as not spent during the term of their leases.

A mere right for the landlord to make provision (even if called a 'reserve') in one accounting year for expenditure likely to arise in a later accounting year might not be interpreted as allowing him to create that type of reserve fund or sinking fund or even a reserve for specific expenditure; it may instead, depending on the exact wording in the lease, be interpreted as simply aimed at smoothing out the tenant's contributions between years of light and heavy expenditure and carry the implication that the tenant can demand to be credited with his contributions in the accounts of the following accounting years with any continuing surplus carried forward until the end of his lease at which time (whether the term ends by normal expiry or by the exercise of a break clause) any balance of the tenant's contributions must be refunded to the tenant (see *Brown's Operating Systems Ltd v Southwark Roman Catholic Diocesan Corporation*[3] above).

Traditionally, there has been a distinction between reserve funds and sinking funds. Reserve funds were established for the purpose of meeting recurring expenditure (such as periodic redecoration of the exterior and common parts of a building) whilst evening out the annual service costs, whereas sinking funds were to provide for expenditure which might only be incurred once or twice during a lengthy lease term on quite specific items (eg replacement of lifts or reroofing). In recent years, this distinction appears to have become blurred, perhaps because some of the plant and equipment now being manufactured has a much shorter life than was formerly the case or because in many property managers' minds this was a distinction without a practical difference. However, the RICS Professional Statement: Service Charges in Commercial Property (see **7.1**), in paragraph 4.8.4, maintains distinctions between sinking funds and reserve funds and, indeed, depreciation charges.

These funds can be useful to avoid enormous service charges being demanded in the years in which these types of major expenditure take place. However, in the commercial sector they are often resisted by tenants when negotiating leases because they do not want to be subject to enforced savings when they should be able to meet their liabilities in the years when the higher expenditure is actually required. In the case of residential blocks, practice varies even where the leases allow for the establishment of reserve funds; landlords or residents companies do not always exercise their rights for such funds to be established. In the past there have also been cases of funds being 'raided' by managing agents or tenants, to avoid service charges being increased, for expenditure other than that for which the funds had been established.

1 [2007] EWCA Civ 164.
2 [2014] EWHC 1463 (Ch).
3 [2007] EWCA Civ 164, CA.

PRINCIPLES OF OPERATION

Specific purpose clauses

4.2 Some clauses provide for the establishment of a reserve or sinking fund in order to provide for specific types of expenditure, particularly renewals or replacements, but occasionally for more frequently recurring items such as redecoration, for example:

> 'The establishment and maintenance of a sinking fund for the replacement from time to time of the lifts, boilers or other central heating apparatus, hot water supply systems, air conditioning systems appliances, fire-fighting equipment, pumps and all other plant equipment machinery and apparatus serving the Building.'

In the event that the provisions of the lease are specific in this way, the fund can only be established and used in order to provide for the stated items.

Non-specific clauses

4.3 Some reserve or sinking fund clauses are silent or wide-ranging on the types of expenditure for which the fund is to be built up. Others expressly give the landlord or his managing agents discretion on the subject, for example:

> 'To set aside in a reserve fund such sums as the Landlord shall reasonably require to meet such future costs as the Landlord shall reasonably expect to incur in *replacing maintaining and renewing those items which the Landlord has hereby covenanted to replace maintain and renew*.'

This clause limits the purpose for which the fund can be built up to those items of replacement, maintenance and renewal which are within the landlord's covenants, and the landlord would not be entitled to build up the reserve fund for anything which fell outside his covenants. In the above example, the landlord is contractually obliged to act reasonably in estimating and demanding the reserve fund contributions.

If the express reference to a 'fund' is not used, but instead it merely says 'as a reserve', this type of wording might only allow the creating of the type of reserve that must be refunded to the tenant if not spent during the term of his lease (see **4.1**).

Calculation of funds

4.4 Sinking or reserve funds fall into two types and it is recommended that a different approach is taken for each of these, for the purposes of collecting the relevant payments. The two types are:

(1) funds required for regular periodic items, such as redecoration of the exterior; and
(2) funds required for the replacement of major capital items where the anticipated life is in excess of 10 years.

These different types of fund are discussed in the next two sections.

Funds for periodic items

4.5 It should be possible to draw up a five-year plan for any major block under management and to show the incidence of regular, periodic requirements, such as painting of the exterior or interior common parts of a building. The costs involved in this work are generally quantifiable and, under normal circumstances, are not unduly subject to the ravages of inflation. The periods involved are comparatively short, so that interest on the fund is not a major consideration and, consequently, it should be simple to calculate the amount required for the fund to take account of the relevant needs. The five-year plan should be a rolling plan, so that the annual cost can be recalculated in the light of both inflation and interest.

EXAMPLE

In a block of flats the only periodic items are the painting of the exterior every three years and the painting of the interior common parts every five years. Assuming that the current cost of painting the exterior is £20,000 and the current cost of the painting of the interior common parts is £10,000, the five-year cash-flow requirements are as follows:

Year 1 – Nil

Year 2 – Nil

Year 3 – Paint exterior £20,000

Year 4 – Nil

Year 5 – Paint interior £10,000

If interest and inflation are ignored the annual payments to provide sufficient funds for this work amount to £8,666, so that after five years the total income on this simple basis will have been £43,330 and the total expenditure £30,000, leaving £13,330 towards the next exterior painting in

Year 6. However, this is too simple an approach and the reality is shown in Table 4.1 (below), where the following assumptions have been taken:

(1) interest has been added yearly at 4 per cent per annum net of tax, giving an annual rate of 5.13 per cent (for a basic rate taxpayer);
(2) the expenditure has been inflated at 3 per cent per annum compound;
(3) the contributions are received at the beginning but the expenditure is made at the end of each financial year.

Table 4.1

Year	*Income*	*Interest*	*Total*	*Expenditure*	*Balance c/f*
	£	£	£	£	£
Year 1	8,666	347	9,013	—	9,013
Year 2	8,666	707	9,373	—	18,386
Year 3	8,666	1,082	9,748	21,855	6,279
Year 4	8,666	598	9,264	—	15,543
Year 5	8,666	968	9,634	11,593	13,584
Year 6	8,666	890	9,556	23,881	–741

It will be seen that the two expenditures can be met from the balance being held in the account, so that at the end of Year 5 there is a balance of £13,584. However, the expenditure on external painting is due in Year 6 and this produces a deficit at the end of Year 6 of £741. If interest runs ahead of inflation this deficit is not important since the position will rectify by itself at the beginning of Year 7, but this will not be the case if the reverse happens.

Funds for long-term capital expenditure

4.6 Long-term capital expenditure is not radically different from the situation given above, except that the actual expenditure is much more difficult to predict, owing to the long periods involved. It will, therefore, be necessary to check the calculations periodically to see that the sinking fund scheme is on target. Two schemes can be devised:

(1) constant payment scheme; and
(2) increasing annual costs scheme.

A simple example can be used to indicate the two approaches.

EXAMPLE

A fund is required to replace a lift. The current cost of providing a new lift is £25,000 and the anticipated life of the lift is 15 years. Assuming as in the above examples that cost inflation is 3 per cent per annum and that interest on the sinking fund is at 4 per cent per annum compound, the cost of the new lift is 15 years' time will be £25,000 multiplied by the amount of £1 for 15 years at 3 per cent = £35,950.

Constant payment scheme

4.7 In order to find the annual sum with constant payments, the anticipated replacement cost must be divided by the annual sinking fund for 15 years at 4 per cent per annum, making £2,130. The calculation should be tested after five years to check that the sinking fund is on target and no action needs to be taken. If, however, the actual cost is found to be higher, it will be necessary to predict the anticipated replacement cost after a further 10 years and this new cost, minus the balance in the fund to date, must be amortised over the remaining 10 years and the new annual cost found. Of course, the reverse could be true and, therefore, it could be found that the anticipated repayment cost had fallen so that the adjustment would be downwards. The advantage of this scheme is that there is a constancy of payments, but the disadvantage is that the cost is high in the early years and low in the later years, so that the actual percentage of disposable income applicable to this fund is falling. The second method provides for the opposite effect.

Variable annual payments

4.8 Table 4.2 below has been calculated by taking the current cost of a new lift as £25,000 and dividing this by 15, to give a required sinking fund in Year 1 of £1,666. The sinking fund payments should have then been increased by 3 per cent per annum to give the figure shown. It will be seen that, at the end of 15 years, the total amount in the fund is just under £39,000, which compares very favourably with the required amount of £38,650. It is not worth adjusting the percentage increase to allow for the very small difference between the two relevant figures. The advantage of this scheme is that the payments will rise in pace with inflation rises so that the percentage of disposable income should remain constant. Again, the calculations can be tested on a regular basis and recalculations made, if it is found that the anticipated replacement cost is higher or lower than the originally calculated figure. In these examples, it has been assumed that the sinking fund payments will be made yearly in advance and that interest will be credited at the end of each year in arrears. In any sinking fund scheme there must be some assumption about the interest and inflation, and account must also be taken of ability to pay, as well as the actual mathematical calculations. If the Tables are presented to the tenants in advance so that they are aware of the anticipated annual increases, there should be fewer problems in collecting the funds.

Table 4.2

Year	*Income*	*Interest*	*Total*	*Expenditure*	*Balance c/f*
	£	£	£	£	£
Year 1	1,666	67	1,733	—	1,733
Year 2	1,716	138	1,854	—	3,587
Year 3	1,767	214	1,982	—	5,568
Year 4	1,820	296	2,116	—	7,684
Year 5	1,875	382	2,257	—	9,942
Year 6	1,931	475	2,406	—	12,348

Year	*Income*	*Interest*	*Total*	*Expenditure*	*Balance c/f*
Year 7	1,989	573	2,563	—	14,911
Year 8	2,049	678	2,727	—	17,638
Year 9	2,110	790	2,900	—	20,538
Year 10	2,174	908	3,082	—	23,621
Year 11	2,239	1,034	3,273	—	26,894
Year 12	2,306	1,168	3,474	—	30,368
Year 13	2,375	1,310	3,685	—	34,053
Year 14	2,447	1,460	3,907	—	37,960
Year 15	2,520	1,619	4,139	38,650	3,449

Crediting the tenants with reserves

4.9 When funds held in a reserve fund are taken out in order to be applied towards the expenditure for which they have been set aside, it is proper practice for the service charge to be computed by charging each tenant individually with his appropriate share of the costs and crediting him with his share of the funds taken from reserve.

Some surveyors merely credit the total sum taken from reserve against the total amount of the relevant expenditure, and then allocate the net cost among the tenants. However, this will be unfair and inappropriate where tenants have not contributed to the reserve in the same proportions as their current service charge liability; this might arise, for example, where some parts of the building were let to tenants who paid contributions to the reserve fund at a time when other parts were unlet or were let to tenants who had no such liability.

The individual method of crediting tenants is almost certainly obligatory for residential lettings under the statutory trust regime created by s 42 of the Landlord and Tenant Act 1987 (LTA 1987).

Depreciation

4.10 If the lease entitles the landlord to include in the service charge a sum for 'depreciation' in respect of plant and machinery, this is a sum which can be retained by the landlord, although it may be implied that, for the purpose of calculating the service charges if and when the relevant plant is actually replaced during the term of the lease, credit for the depreciation amount is to be given against the actual cost of replacement.

EXAMPLE

> *Secretary of State for the Environment v Possfund (North West) Ltd*[1]: The lease did not entitle the landlord to create a reserve fund, but it did entitle him to charge depreciation in respect of plant and machinery. The landlord obtained payments from the tenant, ostensibly towards the future replacement of the air conditioning system. The system was not replaced by the end of the lease and the tenant sought a refund of the payments. **Held:** The payments were attributable to the depreciation charge and so the amount

contributed by the tenant belonged to the landlord and was not refundable, but the landlord 'would ordinarily be expected' to give credit for the depreciation sum against the cost of new plant and machinery if it was replaced during the term.

This type of provision is not the same as one allowing the creation of a reserve fund or sinking fund (*Brown's Operating Systems Ltd v Southwark Roman Catholic Diocesan Corporation*[2]).

1 [1997] 39 EG 179, ChD.
2 [2007] EWCA Civ 164, CA.

Repayment

4.11 Where tenants pay on-account payments for service charges, generally any unspent surplus belongs to the tenants and a tenant is entitled to a refund of his surplus contribution when the lease ends: *Brown's Operating Systems Ltd v Southwark Roman Catholic Diocesan Corporation*[1], Court of Appeal. That will apply even if the lease refers to the money being held 'in reserve'.

If the lease expressly allow the landlord to charge an annual sum for a 'reserve fund' or 'sinking fund' or for 'depreciation', will the tenants entitled to a refund if it has not been spent by the end of their leases?

In *Brown's Operating Systems Ltd v Southwark Roman Catholic Diocesan Corporation*[2] Lady Justice Smith's judgment implied that the ownership of funds in a reserve fund might be different from ordinary surplus service charge monies and that the landlord might be entitled to retain unspent reserve fund sums if the wording clearly allowed the fund to provide for expenditure likely to be incurred after the end of the term of the lease. However the point was not decided.

In *Secretary of State for the Environment v Possfund (North West) Ltd*[3], one tenant in Bush House, Aldwych, London WC2 paid an annual sum as a separate item of service charge which was set aside by the landlord earmarked for replacing the air conditioning system. These sums amounted to over £600,000 on which interest had accrued bringing the fund to over £1m. No new air conditioning system had been installed by the end of the lease and the tenants sought a full refund. The service charge clause stated that provision for future expenditure was 'by means of depreciation allowance'. Rimer J held that sums for 'depreciation' belonged to the landlord. The concept was justified by the fact that the plant suffered wear and tear resulting in a reduction in its life through usage for the tenants' benefit throughout the term. However, the judge also said that the landlord would 'ordinarily' be expected to give credit to the tenant against the actual expenditure on replacing the relevant plant and machinery if that was incurred during the term, and that if the plant was replaced during the term at lower cost than the sum in the fund, the landlord would be expected to give credit to the tenant for the excess against future depreciation payments.

In *Brown's Operating Systems Ltd v Southwark Roman Catholic Diocesan Corporation*[4], the Court of Appeal held that the *Possfund* case did not lay down any general rule about such matters.

1 [2007] EWCA Civ 164.
2 [2007] EWCA Civ 164.
3 (1997) 39 EG 179, ChD.
4 [2007] EWCA Civ 164.

INVESTMENT OF FUNDS

Basic principles

4.12 The provisions of the lease may expressly require the fund to be invested and the interest earned to be accumulated. The lease may state specifically that the fund is to be held on trust, in which case there is a clear duty to invest the fund in appropriately safe investments, such as in a bank deposit account or building society account. Even in the absence of an express direction to invest or an express trust, there is possibly an implied duty that the fund should be invested so as to earn interest (see *Yorkbrook Investments Ltd v Batten*[1]). It is, in any event, good practice for service charge monies to be held in a separate bank account identified as being the service charge (or sinking or reserve) fund for the particular building and for each tenant where they pay different amounts in to the fund. The RICS Professional Statement: Service Charges in Commercial Property imposes a mandatory requirement on chartered surveyors who manage commercial property for landlords to ensure that service charge monies (including reserve and sinking funds) are held in one or more discrete or virtual bank accounts.

1 (1985) 276 EG 545.

Where LTA 1985 and LTA 1987 apply

4.13 In the case of residential service charges to which s 18 of LTA 1985 applies (see **2.1**), not only does the reasonableness test apply to the amounts that the landlord requires to be contributed to the fund but there is also a statutory requirement for the investment of such monies as trust funds (s 42 of LTA 1987 and Orders made under that section – see **2.62**).

There are also proposed provisions as to designated accounts in which funds are to be held (s 42A of LTA 1987, inserted by the Commonhold and Leasehold Reform Act 2002 but not yet in force) as set out at **2.53**.

SECURITY PROBLEMS WITH RESERVE FUNDS

4.14 If the fund is not held as trust money or identified as being money held for a specific purpose, there is a danger that if the landlord (or its agent) holding the funds in its own name were to become bankrupt or go into liquidation, the fund might form part of the general assets of the landlord (or agent) and the tenants would then have to prove in the bankruptcy or liquidation in order to recover the fund, and rank in priority after preferential creditors.

For these reasons, it is preferable for the funds to be held in a separate, designated bank or building society account and identified as being the reserve or sinking fund for the particular building (see *Re Chelsea Cloisters Ltd*[1]; *National Westminster Bank v Halesowen Presswork*[2]; *Re Arthur Sanders Ltd*[3]).

1 (1980) 41 P&CR 98.
2 [1972] AC 785.
3 (1981) BLR 125.

TAX PROBLEMS WITH RESERVE AND SINKING FUNDS

Introduction

Landlords' tax position

4.15 Service charges levied by a landlord will, in most cases, form part of the landlord's income arising from ownership of land and be charged to income or corporation tax as profits from a property business, either UK or overseas (under Pt 3 of the Income Tax (Trading and Other Income) Act 2005 for income tax purposes and Pt 4 of the Corporation Tax Act 2009 for corporation tax purposes). Such profits were previously taxed under the old, and now abolished, Sch A. Services provided by the landlord for which the charges are made will rarely be sufficiently intensive to form a trading activity from which the service charges comprise trading receipts. It should be noted that references in this section to a 'landlord' refer only to the person holding the freehold or superior interest in the property, unless specific reference is made otherwise.

Service charges are levied to meet specific expenditure incurred by the landlord in providing services to tenants and performing the obligations imposed upon the landlord under the lease. Revenue expenditure so incurred by the landlord will be deductible under the normal rules for a property business. The position with regard to expenditure on plant and machinery (eg provision of a new lift) is more complicated but, generally, capital allowances may be granted to the landlord under ss 11 and 16 of the Capital Allowances Act 2001. However, as capital allowances for plant and machinery used in a property business are given (currently) at a rate of 100 per cent only for the first £200,000 of expenditure and then either 18 per cent per annum or 8 per cent per annum (for long life integral assets, eg lifts, heating systems) on a reducing balance basis, a mismatch can occur between service charge receipts and the capital allowance for any period of assessment, so that a portion of the service charge receipts relating to expenditure on machinery and plant may remain taxable in the year of receipt. Certain plant and machinery for energy or water efficient purposes or in buildings situated in enterprise zones attract higher allowances but are outside the scope of this book.

Expenditure does not qualifying for capital allowances if it is incurred in providing plant or machinery for use in a dwelling.

For this purpose a dwelling includes a flat used as a residence. Plant such as a lift which serves the whole of a block of flats is not let for use in a dwelling and therefore qualifies for capital allowances. A central heating system which serves the whole of a block of flats qualifies for capital allowances so far as it serves the common parts; if it also provides central heating for the individual flats, the expenditure should strictly be apportioned (but HMRC has previously stated that in practice it does not insist on apportionment if the expenditure on the part serving the individual flats is less than 25 per cent of the total expenditure. However, this concession was withdrawn in Autumn 2010 (apparently on the grounds it was given in error originally) so advantage may no longer be taken of it.

Tenants' tax position

4.16 A commercial tenant occupying leased premises for the purpose of his trade or business will be entitled normally to deduct the service charges paid in computing trading profits. This is so whether or not the landlord immediately expends the funds or creates a sinking fund, providing the tenant has divested himself absolutely of the sum in question. A more difficult point is the classification of the payment of a service charge by the tenant into revenue or capital expenditure.

The fact that a service charge is payable at regular intervals and may be reserved as rent in the lease is support for the view that the payment represents revenue expenditure, no matter how the landlord expends the sum in the upkeep of the building. Further, the service charge will usually be levied by the landlord with a view to a mix of anticipated expenditure, both revenue and capital, in the course of upkeep and maintenance. However, this does not prevent the payment of a service charge representing capital expenditure by the tenant if it is to meet specific capital expenditure by the landlord and caution must be taken in drafting clauses providing for the payment of service charges.

If certain payments of service charges are unavoidably classified as capital expenditure by the tenant, it would appear that there is insufficient nexus between the levying of the service charge and the capital expenditure by the landlord, so that the expenditure of the tenant would not be a 'capital contribution' within s 537 of the Capital Allowances Act 2001 entitling the tenant to capital allowances. The provisions of s 183 of the 2001 Act permitting a transfer of capital allowances from a lessor to a lessee will not be of help as the plant and machinery in the common areas of the building will not be subject to any lease but will be retained by the landlord.

The writer once conducted a long argument with HMRC concerning the tax treatment of sizeable service charges paid by a headlessee. The freeholder had instituted a programme of refurbishment to the building which included substantial capital expenditure on the lifts, etc. HMRC argued that a proportion of the headlessee's service charges were disallowable in the headlessee's property business computation because of the capital works on which the freeholder had spent the service charges collected. HMRC also wished to disallow a similar proportion of the service charges levied by the headlessee on its subtenants, so that the disallowance would have been repeated several times over! Of course, this was a nonsense as on a properly constructed lease only the freeholder should have suffered a disallowance in its property business computations for the capital expenditure.

The construction of the relevant leases required the headlessee to pay a single service charge with no direct apportionment to any particular expenditure by the freeholder, over which the headlessee had no control. After referring the matter to the appropriate technical expert at HMRC, the Inspector of Taxes conceded that the service charges were wholly allowable in the headlessee's property business computation.

Sinking funds – problems of timing

4.17 If a landlord is beneficially entitled under the lease (as opposed to a trust arrangement – see below) to a service charge calculated so as to exceed current expenditure, the service charge remains chargeable as profits from a property business. Even though the receipts, or part of them, may be set aside by the landlord into a sinking fund, the landlord will not be able to avoid bringing the receipts into account as income for the purposes of the property business in the relevant chargeable period.

Further, no deduction may be made for tax purposes for sums set aside in the sinking fund as there will have been no *payment* of a deductible expense nor the *incurring* of expenditure on the provision of machinery or plant.

Of course, payments out of the fund will be deductible for tax purposes (except for capital expenditure as above) but if the fund is set aside to meet occasional substantial expenditure (eg the refurbishment of the whole of the outside of the building), the expenditure may exceed the landlord's total letting receipts for the chargeable period in which the expenditure is incurred and therefore tax relief may be delayed until later periods or there may never be sufficient receipts to cover the expenditure. The calculation of service charges over the period of the sinking fund will need to take into account this possible restriction on tax relief available to the landlord when the fund is expended.

Tax problems with trust arrangements

General

4.18 Some leases provide for service charge sinking funds to be held in an express or implied trust for the benefit of the tenants from time to time. It is important that the fund is held for the benefit of the tenants, because for a trust to be validly created there must be one or more beneficiaries in whose favour the court can decree performance. The trust may provide for the fund to be held for the purpose of maintaining the building without being an invalid purpose trust, provided that there is at least one beneficiary who is able to enforce the trust for the purpose of maintaining the building.

Payment into the trust

4.19 The classification of payments of service charges made by tenants to the landlord acting as trustee is complex and there is no specific authority. The main possibilities for classifying the receipts of the trustees are:

(1) income taxable as profits of a property business;
(2) income chargeable under the residual head of Ch 8 of Pt 5 of the Income Tax (Trading and Other Income) Act 2005 (for income tax), Ch 8 of Pt 10 of the Corporation Tax Act 2009 (for corporation tax);
(3) an annual payment chargeable as savings and investment income under Ch 7 of Pt 5 of the Income Tax (Trading and Other Income) Act 2005 (for income tax), Ch 7 of Pt 10 of the Corporation Tax Act 2009 (for corporation tax); or
(4) a capital payment.

It is not thought that the income is chargeable as profits from a property business as the landlord qua trustee does not have any interest in the property from which to derive income. In order to constitute an annual payment the receipt must be 'pure income profit' in the hands of the trustee. In other words, the trustee must receive the sum without any obligation to do anything in return. It is thought that, in the hands of the trustee, the payments from tenants are not pure income from which it then meets incidental expenses but rather that the receipts are one element of the overall determination of income and expenditure. Thus, the receipts would not be annual payments and the tenants would not be entitled to deduct them as a charge on income. However, if the obligation to maintain the building is placed on the landlord and the trust exists simply to reimburse the landlord for the cost of meeting his obligations, the receipts may represent 'pure income profit' in the hands of the trustee because the trust will not actually perform any obligation for the receipt of payment from the tenant. The taxation treatment may depend on whether or not the obligation of maintaining the building is placed on the landlord or the trustee (albeit he is the same person as the landlord).

This leaves the possibility of assessment on the trustee under the residual head of Chapter 8 of Pt 5 of the Income Tax (Trading and Other Income) Act 2005 or Chapter 8 of Pt 10 of the Corporation Tax Act 2009 or the possibility that payments by the tenants represent capital contributions to the trust, in effect sums settled on trust.

Possibility of payments into trust being capital

4.20 There is a strong argument that receipts from the tenant would be chargeable in the hands of the trustee under Chapter 8 of Pt 5 of the Income Tax (Trading and Other Income) Act 2005 or Chapter 8 of Pt 10 of the Corporation Tax Act 2009 and, in that event, there may be a liability to income tax in the early years of the sinking fund from which subsequent expenditure could not be deducted. However, it may be possible to argue that the receipts are capital contributions from the tenants (although that would destroy any possibility of a tax deduction for commercial tenants) following the line of argument in the case of *IRC v The Forth Conservancy Board (No 2)*[1], which concerned the taxability of a surplus of receipts over expenditure of a statutory body charged with the maintenance of the River and Firth of Forth. The argument is that the tenants are both settlors and beneficiaries of the trust and as such the trustee, as custodian of the fund, cannot be chargeable to income tax in respect of surpluses arising. On this basis, the payments by tenants to the trust represent the settling of additional capital sums which do not have the quality of income in the hands of the landlord as trustee.

[1] (1931) 16 TC 103.

Summary of taxation of payments into trust

4.21 It can be seen that there was no one clear line of authority concerning the taxation of the payment of service charges by tenants into a trust. However, in its Tax Bulletin No 37 of 1998 (now published as paragraph 1075 of HMRC's Property Income Manual), HMRC was prompted by the introduction of reforms to the taxation of property businesses to provide its opinion on the taxation of service charge trusts. The opinion (which is not binding and can be retracted at any time) refers specifically to tenant-owned flat management companies but should apply to all service charge and sinking fund trust arrangements. However, it is necessary to be absolutely certain that a trust arrangement actually exists (see **2.62**).

HMRC's view is that service charges received by a trustee ordinarily will be outside the scope of taxation, either as profits from a property business or otherwise. HMRC's reasoning is that, under proper accountancy principles, usually it will not be correct to tax as profits from a property business sums to which the landlord is not beneficially entitled. Consequently, service charges received by a trustee will ordinarily be received as capital in the landlord's capacity as trustee (under either a common law trust or s 42 of LTA 1987 statutory trust). If the trust includes a power to accumulate income, then investment income arising on the fund may be chargeable on the trustee at the income tax rate applicable to trusts (see below). Note that s 42 of LTA 1987 contains an implied power to accumulate in the case of all statutory trusts.

Any rent receivable by a landlord in his capacity as such, rather than as a trustee of a service charge or sinking fund trust, is outside any trust arrangement and remains chargeable on the landlord as profits from a property business.

The opinion published by HMRC in its Property Income Manual paragraph 1075 endorses the view that payments by tenants into a service charge or sinking fund trust are capital in nature. Rent received by a landlord in his capacity as landlord is chargeable to tax as profits from a property business in the usual manner.

HMRC expanded on its view of service charge or sinking fund trusts in its Tax Bulletin No 48 of 2000 (see now paragraphs 5705–5755 of HMRC's Trusts, Settlements and Estates Manual). The paragraphs in the Trusts, Settlements and Estates Manual are more detailed than paragraph 1075 of the Property Income Manual and they reprise the HMRC view of service charge and sinking funds. The reader is referred to them as a very useful summary of its view (https://www.gov.uk/hmrc-internal-manuals/trusts-settlements-and-estates-manual/tsem5700).

The tax rates paid by the trustees on accumulated income earned on the service charge fund depend on whether the trust fund is for commercial property or dwellings. For commercial property, income of the fund over £1,000 per tax year is taxable at the special trust rate of 45 per cent (38.1 per cent for dividends). Income under £1,000 per tax year is taxed as for dwellings. For dwellings, the income of the fund is taxable at the basic rate of 20 per cent (32.5 per cent for dividends).

Up until tax year 2015–16 banks and building societies were required to deduct tax at the basic rate of 20 per cent from payments of interest to trustees. The position has changed from and including tax year 2016–17 onwards and tax is no longer deducted at source by banks and building societies.

Commercial tenants' tax position

4.22 The opinion expressed by HMRC and set out above determines the tax deductibility of a commercial tenant's payments into a service charge or sinking fund trust. Regrettably, as far as the commercial tenant is concerned, the opinion is fatal to the tenant's ability to claim a tax deduction for the payments. This is because the payments are classified as capital contributions to the trust and the payments lack the necessary revenue nature for a tax deduction.

Inheritance tax

4.23 No review of a trust is complete without considering the incidence of inheritance tax. It is arguable that a trust arrangement for a sinking fund is wholly commercial and involves no element of bounty in its creation. However, it is understood that HMRC regards a sinking fund trust as within the inheritance tax provisions and the treatment is that of a discretionary trust. Accordingly, there would be a potential charge to inheritance tax on property leaving the settlement (other than by way of the payment of expenses, eg on the determination of the trust) and on each 10-year anniversary of its creation. This latter, potential charge could have serious effects on a large property with a sinking fund for long-term projects.

Maintenance companies

General

4.24 The landlord may create a company specifically responsible for the upkeep and maintenance of the property, with or without a transfer of the freehold reversion to the company. With residential properties, each tenant may be a shareholder in the company, the landlord having no interest and, in that event, the tenant would transfer his share in the company to an assignee of the lease on a sale.

If the company does not hold the freehold reversion to the building, receipts of service charges cannot be chargeable as profits from a property business and, usually, the company will be regarded as carrying on a trade of providing maintenance services. If the company receives service charges as a trustee of a trust for a sinking fund, the tax considerations set out above will apply. This is particularly relevant in connection with service charges for residential blocks of flats, for which, in most cases, s 42 of LTA 1987 creates, by statute, a trust arrangement for the sinking fund (but see **4.28**).

Mutuality

4.25 Where there is no trust arrangement, it is likely that the principle of mutuality would normally apply if the tenants are the only shareholders. This principle is based on the maxim that a person cannot make a profit from himself and, following *Styles v New York Life Insurance Company*[1], the fact that the mutual activity is carried out through a company does not prevent the mutuality principle applying. Therefore, the principle of mutuality would apply to exempt profits from corporation tax, but only if the maintenance company is carrying on a trade of providing maintenance services.

However, mutuality is specifically to be ignored in a property business for both income tax and corporation tax purposes (Income Tax (Trading and Other Income) Act 2005, s 321; Corporation Tax Act 2009, s 260) so both service charges and interest income arising on the fund would remain chargeable to income tax or corporation tax, despite the element of mutuality involved, if the maintenance company holds the freehold reversion to the business because the property business rules would have precedence.

1 (1889) 2 TC 460.

Tenants' tax position

4.26 A tenant of commercial property should be able to deduct, as a trading expense, the service charges paid, following the principle in *Thomas v Richard Evans & Co Ltd*[1], which concerned a mutual insurance reserve fund and bears strong resemblances to a sinking fund for service charges. However, the comments above concerning the possible identification of a capital element to the service charges should be borne in mind.

If a surplus of funds is returned to members on the liquidation of a maintenance company, the receipts may be subject to tax under Chapter 8 of Pt 5 of the Income Tax (Trading and Other Income) Act 2005 or Chapter 8 of Pt 10 of the Corporation Tax Act 2009, to the extent that the service charges were claimed as trading expenses.

1 (1927) 10 TC 790.

Summary

4.27 In summary, it is likely that service charges paid to maintenance companies will be either payments under trust arrangements, attracting the same difficulties with regard to tax which are outlined above, or the service charges will be taxable and a commercial tenant will receive tax relief on them.

Section 42 of LTA 1987 – perpetuity period

4.28 There is an apparent dichotomy between s 42 of LTA 1987 and the normal rule of trust law which prevents trusts continuing indefinitely. A valid trust must not be capable of continuing beyond the expiry of a 'perpetuity period' of 125 years. A s 42 trust determines on the expiry of the last remaining lease for the property concerned, which can, in extremis, be 999 years from the creation of the trust. Thus, s 42 trusts potentially offend against the perpetuity principle and are invalid.

However, there is a basic presumption that Parliament cannot have intended to legislate for invalid trusts and that the provisions of s 42 are intended to overrule the law on perpetuities. If this presumption is incorrect and a trust is invalid, the fund remains the property of the tenants in the proportions to which they have contributed. Any income arising on the fund is apportioned amongst those tenants and no tax relief is available for commercial tenants in respect of contributions to the fund until the fund is expended.

DRAFTING POINTS

4.29 When drafting leases which have to make provision for such funds, lawyers must not only take account of the tax and security problems associated with reserve and sinking funds, but also the problems which are posed by the law of trusts. A full discourse on the subject is beyond the scope of this book, but a few basic points should be noted.

A 'purpose trust' (a fund for a specific purpose which does not have individuals as beneficiaries) cannot validly be created, except for solely charitable purposes, unless it can be seen, ultimately, to have persons as beneficiaries (*Re Denley's Trust Deed*[1]).

Furthermore, a trust for beneficiaries must vest the fund in them before the expiry of the 'perpetuity period', which is a fixed period of 125 years under the Perpetuities and Accumulations Act 2009, s 5.

However, once trust property becomes vested absolutely in a group of adult beneficiaries, they can put an end to the trust and call for the fund to be distributed amongst themselves (*Saunders v Vautier*[2]). This would be most inconvenient if the vesting of a reserve fund occurred before the end of the leases, when major expenditure on repairs and renewals was still pending.

Some of the questions which arise for the draftsman are, therefore as follows:

(1) Should the lease declare an express trust of the fund or remain silent on the point?
(2) If a trust is expressed, should this be a 'purpose trust' or specify the tenants as beneficiaries?
(3) What perpetuity period should be applied?

It has been suggested that an acceptable formula would be to provide that the landlord will hold the fund on trust to expend it on the specified categories of works during the perpetuity period, and that any surplus at the end of the period would be held for the then tenants in the same proportions as their liability to pay service charges.

The perpetuity period would be as long as possible, unless, perhaps, the existing building had a limited life after which it was to be demolished or reconstructed at the landlord's cost, in which case the period should end prior to that time.

However, the tax problems outlined in **4.15** must be remembered, and there seems to be no simple way to resolve the conflicting factors of tax and trust law. This may explain why many landlords shy away altogether from establishing reserve or sinking funds.

1 [1969] 1 Ch 373.
2 (1841) 4 Beav 115.

Chapter 5

SERVICE CHARGES – FREEHOLD AND COMMONHOLD PROPERTIES

LEGAL ISSUES OF FREEHOLD SERVICE CHARGES

Inability to enforce positive covenants

5.1 Unlike the tenant's covenants in a lease, which are usually automatically binding on (and, thus, enforceable by the landlord against) every assignee of the lease (see **1.83**), positive covenants given by a purchaser of freehold land are not directly enforceable by the covenantee (the person to whom the covenants are given, ie the vendor who imposed them) against a person acquiring the land from the purchaser. The original person giving a positive covenant remains liable to perform it (unless the terms of the covenant free him from liability when he parts with the property) and, often, the person acquiring the property from him will expressly covenant to indemnify him in respect of the liability. Nevertheless, unless further provisions of the types mentioned in **5.2** are used, generally the covenantee cannot sue the new owner in respect of positive covenants.

There is an archaic exception: a covenant to maintain fences on the boundary of the covenantee's land may be treated as a 'fencing easement' that binds the covenantor's successors, but that is definitely a rare exception to the general rule (*Churston Golf Club v Haddock*[1]).

Accordingly, if the freehold of a property is sold and, in the transfer or conveyance, the purchaser simply covenants to pay a service charge towards the cost incurred by the vendor in, for example, maintaining private roads or amenity areas, if the purchaser subsequently resells the property, the vendor cannot sue the new owner for the service charge. He can only sue the original purchaser, if he can find him.

1 [2018] EWHC 347 (Ch).

Possible solutions

5.2 The problem outlined in **5.1** can be tackled in a number of ways:

(1) By providing, in the original transfer or conveyance, a further positive covenant that, when the purchaser sells the property, he will procure that the new owner gives a direct covenant to the covenantee that he will perform the positive covenants in the original transfer or conveyance (including the covenant as to obtaining direct covenants on a further sale).

(2) By providing, in the original transfer or conveyance, that the use of the roads or amenities is conditional on the owner of the property having paid the service charges.

(3) By reserving the service charges as an estate rentcharge under the Rentcharges Act 1977.

(4) By disposing of premises on a commonhold, rather than a freehold, basis (see **5.8**).

Method (1) can break down if, contrary to the covenant, an owner fails to ensure that his successor gives the direct covenant to the covenantee, as occurred in *Thamesmead Town Ltd v Allotey*[1], where the estate company had no right to sue the new house owner for payment of certain estate costs. This can usually be avoided by providing for the registered title of the property to contain a restriction against registration of any transfer without the direct covenant being given by the transferee.

Method (2) is hard to enforce because clearly it is difficult physically to prevent one owner of a property on an estate from using the roads or other amenities without affecting their use by other owners who have paid their service charges. It would be possible to seek an injunction against the defaulting owner but this is a costly and uncertain remedy. The estate rentcharge under method (3) is, in many respects, better, but it has its limitations. These are considered below.

1 [1998] 37 EG 161, CA.

ESTATE RENTCHARGES

The Rentcharges Act 1977

5.3 The Rentcharges Act 1977 enables the vendor of a freehold property to reserve:

(a) a nominal rentcharge for the purpose of making positive covenants given by the purchaser enforceable against the purchaser's successors-in-title (s 2(4)(a)); and/or

(b) a variable rentcharge which will be payable by the purchaser and his successors in title (s 2(4)(b)).

The variable rentcharge can only cover the costs of the performance by the rent owner of covenants for:

(1) the provision of services;
(2) the carrying out of maintenance or repairs;
(3) the effecting of insurance; or
(4) the making of any payment by him for the benefit of the land subjected to the rentcharge (or that and other land).

Item (4) enables the rent owner to include in the rentcharge sums such as rates and similar outgoings levied on common parts which are used by the paying parties (*Orchard Trading Estate Management Ltd v Johnson Security Ltd*[1]).

However, the rentcharge can only be reserved if the transfer or conveyance includes express covenants by the rent owner (usually the vendor, but possibly a management company) to provide the services or other matters for which the charge is to be made.

By s 2(5) of the Rentcharges Act 1977, an estate rentcharge will be valid only if 'it represents a payment for the performance by the rent owner of any such covenant . . . which is reasonable in relation to that covenant'. In *Orchard Trading* (above), the Court of Appeal held that this meant that the clauses of the deed creating the rentcharge had to be reasonable. The court considered that provisions under which the rent owner would recoup his actual expenditure were reasonable (and therefore valid) even if they did not expressly limit the charge to 'reasonable' amounts, whereas provisions which, for example, imposed an excessive fixed payment would not be reasonable (and therefore would be invalid). Having decided that the rentcharge clauses need not contain an express test of reasonableness, the court left open the question whether a reasonableness test would be implied into the actual operation of the clauses.

1 [2002] EWCA Civ 40, CA.

Application

5.4 The scheme under the Rentcharges Act 1977 is extremely useful where a developer is selling the freeholds of houses on a residential estate, or units on an industrial or warehousing estate, and requires to reserve a service charge to cover the cost of maintaining private roads, services or amenities. The estate rentcharge can be created in one of two ways:

(1) by granting the rentcharge to a management company before selling off the units or plots, and selling them subject to the rentcharge; or
(2) by reserving the rentcharge on the sale of each unit or plot.

In either case there should be a separate rentcharge created or reserved in respect of each unit or plot equal to its proper proportion of the total estate costs.

RIGHT TO BUY HOUSES

Introduction

5.5 The sale of freehold houses under the 'right to buy' legislation is governed by ss 118 *et seq* of the Housing Act 1985 and, in relation to 'registered social landlords' such as housing associations, by ss 16 *et seq* of the Housing Act 1996, the details of which are beyond the scope of this book. However, there are provisions which include matters relating to service charges and insurance contributions.

Provisions relating to service charges etc

5.6 Under s 139 of the Housing Act 1985 (which also applies to sales under the 1996 Act) the conveyance must comply with the provisions of Parts I, II and IV of the Sixth Schedule to that Act. These include a number of relevant matters, which can be summarised in outline as follows:

(1) The conveyance can contain such covenants and conditions which are reasonable in the circumstances (para 5 of the Sixth Schedule). Presumably this enables terms to be included for the payment of service charges or maintenance contributions.

(2) The freehold can be conveyed subject to an estate rentcharge (para 21(3) of the Sixth Schedule). The use of estate rentcharges is discussed at 5.3. Under para 21(3)(a) of the Sixth Schedule the transferor must indemnify the transferee if the rentcharge also affects other land; this could be avoided if the transferor created individual rentcharges (eg in favour of a management company) issuing out of each separate house prior to the right to buy being exercised.

Limitation of service charges

5.7 Where the freehold of a house has been conveyed by a 'public sector authority' and the terms of the conveyance enable the vendor to recover from the purchaser a service charge, the service charge is limited by ss 47–51 of the Housing Act 1985, which contains provisions quite similar to some of those applied to tenants' service charges by the LTA 1985 as originally enacted.

The term 'public sector authority' is defined in s 45(2) of that Act as including a local authority, a National Park authority, a new town corporation, an urban development corporation, a housing action trust, the Development Board for Rural Wales, the Housing Corporation, and a registered social landlord.

In such cases, costs can only be taken into account in determining a service charge to the extent that they are reasonably incurred and, where they are incurred on the provision of services or the carrying out of works, only if the services or works are of a reasonable standard (Housing Act 1985, s 47). Further, where sums are payable on account before the relevant costs are incurred, no greater amount than is reasonable is payable and any necessary adjustment must be made by repayment, reduction of subsequent charges or otherwise once the actual costs have been incurred.

Apart from an arbitration agreement, any agreement by the payer will be void so far as it purports to provide for a determination in a particular manner or on particular evidence of any issue as to whether costs have been reasonably incurred, interim charges are of a reasonable amount, or the services or works are of a reasonable standard.

Under s 48, the payer is entitled to request in writing that the payee supplies him with a written summary of the costs which are relevant to the service charges, and the payee must comply with the request within one month or within six months from the end of the relevant accounting period, whichever is later, provided that the accounting period does not exceed 12 months. The summary must set out the costs in a way showing how they are or will be reflected in demands for service charges and they must be certified by a qualified accountant (defined in s 51) as being, in his opinion, a fair summary complying with these requirements and as being sufficiently supported by accounts, receipts and other documents which have been produced to him.

Where the payer has obtained a summary, he may within six months of obtaining it require the payee in writing to give him reasonable facilities for inspecting the accounts, receipts and other documents supporting the summary and taking copies or extracts from them, and the payee must make these facilities available for a period of two months beginning not later than one month after the request is made.

In cases where a grant has been or is to be paid under s 523 of the Housing Act 1985 by way of assistance for the provision of separate service pipes for water supply, or under Ch 1 of Pt 1 of the Housing Grant, Construction and Regeneration Act 1996, any costs summary must state this fact and credit for the relevant grant must be given against the relevant service costs when calculating the service charge.

COMMONHOLD HOUSES AND FLATS

Introduction

5.8 Commonhold is an alternative type of freehold land ownership introduced by the Commonhold and Leasehold Reform Act 2002 (CLRA 2002). Houses, flats and other 'units' can be sold as commonhold units if they are part of a freehold estate (which can be a single building or an estate of buildings) which has been registered by the owner as commonhold land at the Land Registry.

The estate is to be administered by a commonhold association, which must be a company limited by guarantee, and will be regulated by a commonhold community statement ('CCS'). All the purchasers of units, called 'unit-holders', are to be members of the association.

The CCS and the memorandum and articles of the commonhold association must conform to requirements set out in the CLRA 2002, ss 31, 34 and Sch 3 (the details of which are largely outside the scope of this book), and must also conform to requirements to be laid down by regulations made by the Secretary of State under the CLRA 2002, s 32. The current regulations are the Commonhold Regulations 2004[1].

Regulations 9 provides that, except where a unit is an entire self-contained building, the structure and exterior are to be comprised in the common parts. As a result, the common parts, structure and exterior of multi-unit commonhold buildings are to be repaired and maintained by the commonhold association, just like multi-leased buildings where the landlord or management company does so.

Commonhold has not proved popular and at the publication date of this book the regime is under review, but specific amendments have not yet been proposed.

1 SI 2004/1829 as amended by the Commonhold (Amendment) Regulations 2009, SI 2009/2363.

Commonhold assessments and reserve funds

5.9 Section 31(5) of the CLRA 2002 permits the CCS to impose duties on unit-holders which may include the duty to pay money to the commonhold association and to pay interest in the event of late payment. The equivalent of a service charge in the case of commonhold is called the 'commonhold assessment'.

Detailed provisions are contained in the Commonhold Regulations 2004. Regulation 15 requires the CCS to be in a prescribed form which is set out in Sch 3 to the Regulations. The prescribed form of CCS has Annexes into which details applicable to the particular building or estate are to be inserted. Part 3 of the standard form of CCS governs contributions to expenditure incurred by the commonhold association. Paragraph 3.2 of the CCS provides for the allocation to units of the liability to contribute to the commonhold assessment; details of this allocation are to appear in Annex 3 paragraph 1 of the CCS for the particular building or estate. Paragraph 3.3 of the CCS provides for the allocation to units of the liability to contribute to one or more reserve funds and details are to be inserted in Annex 3 paragraph 2 of the CCS.

The CCS provides for the 'expenses' of the commonhold association to form the basis for the commonhold assessment, but it does not define 'expenses', although it defines 'reserve fund' as a fund 'to finance the repair or maintenance of the common parts . . .'. It is not stated that these expressions are mutually exclusive, so it may be assumed that the 'expenses' within the commonhold assessment can include costs of repairs and maintenance as well as the cost of providing services such as gardening and the professional costs of running the association.

The duties of the commonhold association and of the unit-holders are set out in Part 4 of the CCS. Paragraph 4.4 imposes on the commonhold association duties of insurance of the common parts, with details to be inserted in Annex 4 paragraphs 5 and 6. Paragraph 4.5.1 of the CCS imposes on the commonhold association duties to repair the common parts, and paragraph 4.6 imposes restrictions on altering the common parts. Paragraph 4.11 of the CCS provides procedures, including mediation, to be followed by unit-holders who wish to enforce a right or duty against the association, or by the association if it wishes to enforce a right or duty against a unit-holder, and by a unit-holder who wishes to enforce a right or duty against another unit-holder or a tenant – in each case going straight to court is only permitted 'in an emergency'.

Many buildings are constructed or serviced such that a unit ought properly to bear a particular percentage of certain service costs and a different percentage of other service costs. The concept of apportioning service charges into two or more tranches is discussed at **1.58**. However, the wording of s 38 of CLRA 2002 and of paragraph 3.2 and Annex 3 para 1 of the CCS all indicate that there can only be a single commonhold assessment for the whole commonhold, with each unit being liable for a single fixed percentage, so it is doubtful whether the commonhold assessment itself can be divided into different tranches with units contributing different percentages to each tranche. On the other hand, there is express provision in the regulations and the CCS for having more than one reserve fund for the costs of 'repair and maintenance', so it may be possible to adopt the somewhat artificial device of subdividing the costs of repairs and maintenance into a number of separate reserve funds, leaving the commonhold assessment to cover only the other 'expenses' of the association. That device might facilitate a tranched apportionment of some of the service costs, but is unlikely to be able to be used for non-maintenance costs such as electricity charges or employment costs. This may mean that it is not fully possible to separate out those costs which (say) relate to common parts serving only one section of the building from costs which apply only to other parts or to the building as a whole. This could be a significant disadvantage compared with the leasehold system where there is far less prescription as to the detailed provisions that can be built into the legal documents.

Unlike the statutory regime governing residential service charges under leases (see **Chapter 2**), there is no provision in CLRA 2002, the Regulations or the CCS for imposing reasonableness criteria in respect of the charges to be levied by commonhold associations. There are provisions for consultation with unit-holders about the proposed amounts and the government took the view that it is sufficient that the commonhold association is run by the unit-holders through their elected directors who will consult the unit-holders about proposed expenditure; any differences of opinion should then be settled by majority voting, or by voting directors out of office, largely without any external interference by the courts or tribunals under a reasonableness test. If unit-holders could refuse to pay their assessments on the ground that an item of expense had been unreasonably incurred, the association would have insufficient income to meet its expenses and might become insolvent, thereby undermining the regime.

Procedure

5.10 The commonhold association decides upon the 'expenses' to be comprised in the commonhold assessment and upon any sums to be set aside in reserve funds. Under the provisions of the CCS taken together with the prescribed form of articles of association of the commonhold association, this function is largely delegated to the directors.

There is a prescribed process set out in paragraphs 4.2.1–4.2.4 of the CCS for the directors to make an annual estimate of the income they need to raise to meet the 'expenses' of the commonhold association (see **5.9**) and they have the power to make estimates from time to time of any additional income that may be needed. Whenever the directors determine that income must be raised from unit-holders, they must give notice to each unit-holder using prescribed Form 1 as set out in Sch 4 of the 2004 Regulations. This notice informs the unit-holder of the proposed total annual assessment, the percentage allocated to his unit, and the amount he will have to pay. Unit-holders are invited by the notice to make representations to the directors within one month and the directors must consider any such representations when making their decision. Following making their decision, they must use Form 2 to demand the appropriate payment from the unit-holders, giving at least 14 days for payment to be made. If, in 'an emergency', any additional sum has to be demanded from unit-holders in order to meet the expenses, the directors must do so using Form 3.

There is also a prescribed procedure in paragraphs 4.2.6–4.2.14 of the CCS for establishing reserve funds. The directors are obliged to decide at appropriate intervals whether to establish one or more reserve funds. During the first year of the commonhold being set up, they must consider whether or not to commission a reserve study from an appropriately qualified person. Such a study must in any event be obtained once every 10 years. The directors must consider the study when deciding whether to establish or continue any reserve fund. If they decide to do so, they must implement that decision. Alternatively the unit-holders may, by passing an ordinary resolution of the association, instruct the directors to establish a reserve fund. The directors must try to ensure that unnecessary levies are not accumulated.

Notices of proposed levies for reserve funds must be given to unit-holders using Form 4, which invites representations within one month. The directors must consider any such representations when making their decision and, following making their decision, they must use Form 5 to demand payment from the unit-holders, giving at least 14 days for payment to be made.

Non-payment

5.11 Interest at the rate prescribed under the CCS can be charged to any unit-holder who is late in paying his assessment, emergency assessment or levy. The commonhold association also has power to give notice to any tenant or subtenant of a unit-holder to divert his rent payments to the association where the unit-holder's payments are in arrears (CCS, paragraphs 4.2.17–4.2.38).

Alternatively the CCS could sue the unit-holder for payment. The provisions of paragraph 4.11 of the CCS, which require disputes to be dealt with initially by negotiation or alternative dispute resolution, are merely permissive in relation to arrears of payments and do not prevent the immediate use of legal proceedings (CCS, paragraph 4.11.11), although the association might be at risk of not recovering all its legal costs if it institutes court proceedings for payment of arrears without trying to obtain payment by negotiation or mediation.

RESIDENTIAL ESTATE MANAGEMENT SCHEMES

Introduction

5.12 It is common for estate management schemes to require the owners of enfranchised houses and blocks of flats to pay service charges towards the cost of maintaining unadopted roads, communal gardens, private sewers and other shared amenities.

The Commonhold and Leasehold Reform Act 2002 ('CLRA 2002') has introduced reasonableness tests which apply to payments (which are called 'estate charges') which arise under schemes made under the statutory provisions of the Leasehold Reform Act 1967, s 19 and the Leasehold Reform, Housing and Urban Development Act 1993, Pt I, Ch 4. These relate to the purchase of the freeholds of houses and blocks of flats which are located in an estate where the freeholders are required to contribute towards communal expenses. The scope of matters for which the 'payments' arise is not limited and these rules are not therefore confined to repairs, services etc but could cover any types of expenditure.

Reasonableness test for variable estate charges

5.13 Section 159(2) of the CLRA 2002 provides that 'variable estate charges' – those which are not fixed by the scheme as either a specific sum or by a formula for calculating one – are only payable up to a reasonable amount.

Where a scheme specifies a formula for determining the proportions in which variable costs incurred by the estate manager are to be allocated between freeholders, the charges based on those costs appear to fall outside the reasonableness test imposed by s 159(2) – which may be a drafting error in the legislation – but the basis of allocation between freeholders may be reviewed by the FTT under s 159(3) as mentioned in **5.14** (see *Botterill v Hampstead Garden Suburb Trust Ltd*[1]).

Any party can apply to the FTT under s 159(6) to determine whether an estate charge is payable and the FTT can be asked to decide:

(1) who has to pay;
(2) who is to receive the payment;
(3) how much is payable;
(4) when it has to be paid;
(5) how it is to be paid.

However, no application can be made to the FTT under s 159(6) in respect of anything which:

(a) the paying party has agreed or admitted (but merely paying the amount demanded is not itself an admission or agreement of liability);
(b) has been, or is to be, referred to arbitration under an agreement to arbitrate that the parties in dispute have entered into after the dispute has arisen (arbitration clauses in the scheme documents do not prevent the FTT deciding the dispute);
(c) has been decided by a court; or
(d) has been decided by an arbitral tribunal under an agreement to arbitrate entered into after the dispute arose.

The fact that a payment in respect of the charge has been paid does not prevent the FTT determining the matter (CLRA 2002, s 159(7)).

The jurisdiction given to the FTT is in addition to any jurisdiction of a court, so if there are court proceedings as to whether costs are chargeable under the terms of the scheme documents, the court could determine the matter and need not refer it to the FTT.

1 [2007] LRX/135/2007, LT.

Varying schemes which prescribe estate charges

5.14 Where the amount of an estate charge is fixed by the scheme as either a specific sum or by a formula for calculating one, the amount prescribed at any time will be payable, but the paying party can apply to the FTT for an order varying the scheme on the grounds that the amount specified, or the formula, is unreasonable (CLRA 2002, s 159(3)).

This jurisdiction includes varying any formula set out in the scheme specifying how the variable costs incurred by the estate manager are to be allocated between the various freeholders (*Botterill v Hampstead Garden Suburb Trust Ltd*[1]).

The variation may be as the applying party requests or such other variation as the FTT thinks fit. The provisions do not state whether the variation can be backdated to catch sums already payable.

This jurisdiction to vary schemes is exclusive to the FTT and cannot be exercised by the court.

1 [2007] LRX/135/2007, LT.

Chapter 6

STATUTORY OBLIGATIONS

INTRODUCTION

6.1 The emergence of a distinct body of law relating to the environment, both from common law and statute, and the development of areas of statute law relating to health, safety and disability, are increasingly affecting the practice of property management. The pace at which property managers are able to respond to such regulation, or to adopt a wide range of voluntary initiatives, is directly affected by service charge clauses and the ability to recover the additional costs involved. Voluntary initiatives are unlikely to be adopted unless they will produce long-term, economic benefits, such as ongoing running cost savings deriving from installing energy-efficient equipment and making provision for persons with disabilities.

It is becoming more widespread to construct buildings in accordance with good environmental and social practices – at least, where this can be achieved without excessive cost. It therefore makes sense for service charge clauses to contemplate, and require, that parallel requirements be imposed throughout the life of the property.

In relation to work carried out to existing buildings pursuant to statutory obligations, the recovery of the cost from tenants will depend upon the provisions of the legislation and the terms of the tenants' leases (see **1.30** and **6.2**).

In some cases, compliance with these types of legislation will involve professional time being spent on compliance issues. It may be possible to include the fees for this in the service charge where the charge is expressed to cover the cost of compliance with legislation or the cost of proper management and related professional fees.

With regard to the voluntary practices which the property industry is being encouraged to adopt but which are not required by legislation, whether landlords can be required to adopt them, and whether tenants can be required to pay for them, will depend on the relevant provisions of the lease.

RECOVERY OF COSTS

Costs of compliance

6.2 A well-drawn service charge clause will expressly include the costs incurred by the landlord in complying with statutory obligations in respect of such matters as common parts and communal services, and (in relation to multi-occupied buildings) the main structures. In the absence of an express provision, the costs concerned may, nevertheless, be recoverable under a sweeping-up clause (see **1.14**) or be the subject of a specific statutory provision entitling the landlord to apply to the court to order the tenants to contribute towards the costs.

If a landlord has to meet the costs of dealing with a statutory requirement, either directly or by reimbursing the costs expended by an authority (eg local authority's costs of abating a nuisance), and this liability arises because of a tenant's acts or omissions which constitute a breach by him of the covenants in his lease (as will often be the case, for example, under the usual covenant to comply with statutes), the landlord may be able to recoup his expenditure from that tenant in damages for breach of covenant. In addition, many leases contain separate provisions expressly requiring the tenant to meet certain costs of this type, particularly the cost of abating a nuisance from the demised premises.

Risk of prosecution and fines

6.3 Many new environmental offences have been created in the past few years which are often strict offences. There are a number of examples where landlords or property management companies, or the individuals involved in them, could be prosecuted under environmental legislation. Substantial fines could be imposed, even on companies or individuals with few assets. The ability of the management company or landlord to obtain an indemnity from the tenants could, therefore, be crucial to the survival of the company.

The landlord should be wary of failing to comply with a statutory requirement in the belief that he will be able to recoup a fine from the tenants. Even if the lease clearly provided for this, any attempt to recover from the tenants the amount of a fine imposed on the landlord would, in effect, be seeking indemnity against the consequences of a criminal offence. In some circumstances, the common law, for reasons of public policy, renders contractual provisions for that type of indemnity unenforceable. This topic is complex and falls outside the scope of this book, but, briefly, the courts have in some instances distinguished criminal acts involving individual negligence or wilful default from those of strict liability involving no fault on the part of the offender. In the former case, an indemnity against the criminal penalty will almost always be void; in the latter case, it may, in some situations, arguably be valid. Furthermore, however, if the landlord was in breach of a covenant in the lease requiring him to observe statutory requirements or good estate management in relation to common parts, communal services, main structures, etc, and the fine arose as a result of his failure to fulfil his covenant, he might be barred from seeking to recover the fine from his tenants under the principle that one cannot benefit from one's own breach of obligation (see *Alghussein*

Establishment v Eton College[1]).

1 [1991] 1 All ER 267, HL.

EXAMPLES OF STATUTORY DUTIES

6.4 The following is a brief summary of the main elements of those statutory obligations that typically affect landlords of multi-let buildings. Readers requiring more detail should consult the relevant legislation.

Control of asbestos

6.5 The current regime is the set of duties imposed on a 'dutyholder' by the Control of Asbestos Regulations 2006[1], reg 4, by which non-residential premises must be checked for the presence or likely presence of asbestos which, if found or believed likely to be present, must be managed using a written plan of management. Fuller details of these duties are set out in the regulations.

The 'non-residential premises' to which this regime applies include not only commercial properties such as offices and shops but also the service areas of residential buildings such as blocks of flats. In relation to premises which are let, these duties are imposed on every party who is liable to repair or maintain the premises or the means of access and egress to them under the terms of a tenancy or a contract (reg 4(1)(a)). If there is no such person, then it is every party in control of those premises or the access (reg 4(1)(b)).

Accordingly, in relation to a multi-let building, where the landlord is under obligations imposed on him by the tenants' leases for maintaining or repairing common parts, the landlord will be the 'dutyholder' in respect of that building. Where the landlord has entered into a contract which imposes an obligation as to maintenance of the premises or the common parts on an agent or maintenance company, it appears that the existence of that contract may mean that the agent or maintenance company is also a 'dutyholder' who is liable to perform these duties. The landlord or his agent will be liable to perform the duties in respect of the building generally and in particular in respect of those parts having a communal function such as boiler rooms and service areas.

In respect of non-residential parts of buildings demised to tenants, both the landlord and the tenant may be 'dutyholders' and their contributions towards compliance are to reflect the nature and extent of their repair and maintenance obligations under the tenant's lease (reg 4(1)).

1 SI 2006/2739.

Disability provision

6.6 Another example of statutory obligations which may affect landlords is the range of disability duties originally imposed under the Disability Discrimination Acts 1995 and 2005 and now contained in the Equality Act 2010. Many of the provisions of that Act are designed to prevent discrimination in respect of age, disability, gender reassignment, marriage or civil partnership, pregnancy or maternity, race, religion or belief, sex or sexual orientation, but the provisions that relate to works to be carried out to premises focus on persons with a disability.

Briefly, ss 29–31 of the Equality Act 2010 impose on a person who provides 'services', which includes 'facilities', to the public or a section of the public a duty to make certain 'reasonable adjustments' described in Sch 2 of the Act. Where a person is obliged to provide services to another person's employees, those employees may be deemed to be a section of the public (s 31(5)). Consequently the persons who are subject to these duties appear to include landlords who provide and control common parts of buildings which are open to the public, such as the malls and precincts of shopping centres, and those landlords who provide services or facilities for use by the employees of the tenants in the building. The duties so imposed include adopting reasonable alternative management policies or practices or methods of providing services in order to avoid substantially disadvantaging disabled persons, but without changing the nature of the services; taking reasonable steps in relation to physical features that may substantially disadvantage a disabled person compared with persons who are not disabled; and taking reasonable steps to provide any auxiliary aid for disabled persons. For example, staircases and escalators to upper or lower floors might have to be supplemented by lifts; and lift control buttons might need to be marked in Braille and the operations supplemented by recorded announcements, for those with sight disabilities.

In addition, ss 20 and 36 of the Act provide that duties may be imposed on 'a controller of let premises', who could be the landlord or a managing agent, to make certain types of 'reasonable adjustment' described in Sch 4 of the Act in relation to the premises that are let (residential or commercial) and to common parts serving residential (but not commercial) premises, for the benefit of any disabled person who may be the tenant or is otherwise entitled to occupy the premises. The duties have to be triggered by a request from the disabled person. In relation to works to the demised premises, the 'controller' may be required to provide an auxiliary aid for the use and enjoyment of those premises, but this does not include removing or altering any physical feature *apart from* furniture, furnishings, signs, taps, door handles, door bells or entry systems, equipment or decorative matters. In relation to works to the common parts serving residential premises occupied by a disabled person as his only or main home (not common parts serving only commercial premises), the controller may be required to make reasonable adjustments to the physical features of those common parts, but the controller must consult the other users of those common parts and can require the disabled person to enter into an agreement about any costs to be incurred and about reinstatement when the disabled person ceases to live in the building.

By regs 13 and 21 of the Equality Act 2010 (Commencement No 4, Savings, Consequential, Transitional and Incidental Provisions and Revocations) Order 2010[1], certain specified guidance and regulations on disability matters issued under the Disability Discrimination Act 1995 remain in force until new guidance or regulations are issued under the 2010 Act.

1 SI 2010/2317.

Fire safety

6.7 The current fire safety regime is governed by the Regulatory Reform (Fire Safety) Order 2005[1], which came into force on 8 June 2005. Various duties are imposed on the 'responsible person'. The regime applies (with limited exceptions) to all premises apart from individual private dwellings, although the common parts serving two or more dwellings are within the regime.

The 'responsible person' in the case of a workplace is the employer. In relation to other premises, it is the person who has control of the premises in connection with his business, and if none it is the 'owner' (art 3(b)(ii)), which is defined in art 2 as the person receiving the 'rack rent', whether he receives it for his own account or on behalf of another person (or who would receive the rack rent if the premises were let). The 'rack rent' is defined as a rent of not less than two-thirds of the year to year letting value of the premises less the probable cost of maintenance and outgoings. Accordingly, in relation to a multi-let building the 'responsible person' might be the landlord, or a rent-collecting managing agent, or a management company which controls the common parts. A managing agent who does not collect the rent, or a maintenance contractor, might also be a 'responsible person' under the provisions of art 5(4), which provide that any person who, by virtue of any contract, has an obligation of any extent as to the maintenance, repair or safety of premises, is treated as being in control of the premises to the extent of those obligations.

In outline, in relation to the private sector, the 'responsible person' has duties to take general fire precautions (including risk reduction, means of escape, detectors, alarms, training, etc), to carry out risk assessments, to make and maintain fire safety arrangements, to eliminate or reduce risks from dangerous substances, to provide and maintain fire-fighting and detection equipment, to provide and identify emergency routes and exits, and to create and arrange training on fire procedures. Reference should be made to the Order for further detail.

1 SI 2005/1541.

Waste disposal

6.8 Section 34 of the Environmental Protection Act 1990 places a duty of care on any person who produces, stores, transports, treats or disposes of controlled waste or who acts as a broker of controlled waste. 'Controlled waste' covers commercial, industrial and household waste.

An individual residential occupier is not under this duty as regards his own household waste. However, his landlord, if he manages the disposal of the waste, will be under the duty of care. The statutory duty, therefore, applies to any landlord (or management company) which has obligations related to waste, whether in respect of an industrial estate, office block, shopping centre or a block of flats.

Landlords must take reasonable measures to comply with the duty of care as it applies to them in relation to the particular obligations which they are given. The duty of care has the effect of imposing obligations which include:

(1) a duty to prevent the escape of waste from the control of the person subject to the duty of care, or from the control of any other person;
(2) keeping waste safe against corrosion, wind, accidental spillage or leakage, scavenging or thieves;
(3) storing waste in containers which are suitable, given the nature of the waste;
(4) segregating categories of waste which are incompatible (for example because they react with one another) and to label waste containers appropriately;
(5) ensuring that the waste is transferred only to an authorised person (as defined in s 34 of the Environmental Protection Act 1990 as amended by Sch 22 to the Environment Act 1995) or to a person for authorised transport purposes, and completing a transfer note on transfer of the waste.

Additional regulations apply to certain specific wastes, such as 'special' or hazardous wastes. Breach of the duty of care is a criminal offence which carries a maximum penalty of an unlimited fine if convicted.

Section 59 of the Environmental Protection Act 1990, as amended by the Clean Neighbourhoods and Environment Act 2005, gives waste regulation and collection authorities the power, in certain circumstances, to take remedial measures in respect of controlled waste which has been deposited illegally. The cost of compliance principally falls upon any person who deposited or knowingly caused or knowingly permitted the deposit of any of the waste but in certain circumstances it will fall upon the owner.

Section 33(1)(c) of the Environmental Protection Act 1990 provides that it is an offence to treat, keep or dispose of controlled waste in a manner likely to cause pollution of the environment or harm to human health. The maximum penalty on conviction on indictment is imprisonment for a term not exceeding two years or a fine or both. Stiffer penalties apply to an offence committed in relation to 'special' waste.

Effluent and pollution

6.9 Section 85 of the Water Resources Act 1991 provides that it is an offence for any person to 'cause or knowingly permit any poisonous, noxious or polluting matter or any solid waste matter to enter any controlled waters'. Most watercourses come within the definition of 'controlled waters'. It is also an offence to cause or knowingly permit any trade or sewage effluent to be discharged into any controlled waters in contravention of a relevant consent. On conviction on indictment, the maximum penalty for an offence under s 85 is imprisonment for a term not exceeding two years or a fine or both.

Section 118 of the Water Industry Act 1991 makes it an offence for the 'occupier' of premises to discharge 'trade effluent' into public sewers without a consent. 'Trade effluent' is defined in s 141 of that Act, as amended by the Water Act 2003, and includes liquid (with or without particles of matter in suspension) produced in the course of any trade or industry carried on at trade premises. 'Occupier' is likely to include any person having a degree of control over the activities of persons on the premises. In the case of effluent emanating from the communal drainage system of an industrial estate, the occupier might be the landlord or management company.

By s 161 of the Water Resources Act 1991, as amended, the Environment Agency has power to carry out certain anti-pollution works and operations where it appears to it that any poisonous, noxious or polluting matter is likely to enter any controlled waters or to have been present in controlled waters. The reasonable costs of carrying out the works can be recovered from any person who caused or knowingly permitted the matter in question to be present in the relevant place.

These provisions could lead to substantial liabilities being incurred by landlords and other property managers. It is, for example, relatively commonplace for the landlord of an industrial estate or a management company to be responsible for operating and maintaining private sewage or effluent treatment works. Those landlords should ensure that they seek to obtain trade effluent discharge consents, and should install and maintain treatment plant which is able to cope with the nature and volume of effluents emanating from the tenants' units. Whilst many leases of industrial premises impose obligations on the tenants not to discharge corrosive or pollutant substances into the drains or sewers, this is not universal and many industrial tenants expect the communal drainage system to be able to cope with a wide range of effluent.

Statutory nuisances

6.10 Section 79 of the Environmental Protection Act 1990, as amended by the Environment Act 1995 and by the Clean Neighbourhoods and Environment Act 2005, defines those matters which constitute a 'statutory nuisance'. They are wide ranging and include:

(1) premises in such a state as to be prejudicial to health or a nuisance;
(2) emission of smoke, fumes, gases or noise from premises so as to be prejudicial to health or a nuisance;
(3) dust, steam, smell or other effluvia arising on industrial, trade or business premises and being prejudicial to health or a nuisance,

but do not include land contamination which is covered by separate provisions of the LT(C)A 1995.

Local authorities can prohibit, restrict or require the abatement of, a statutory nuisance, by serving an abatement notice under s 80 of the Environmental Protection Act 1990 as amended by the Clean Neighbourhoods and Environment Act 2005. The notice can require the execution of works where they are necessary for the prohibition, restriction or abatement of the statutory nuisance. If the nuisance arises out of a defect of a structural nature, the notice is served on the owner of the premises. If the person responsible for the nuisance cannot be found or the nuisance has not yet occurred, the notice is served on the owner or occupier of the premises. Failure without reasonable excuse to comply with the notice is an offence, rendering the person liable to a fine, and it also enables the local authority to take steps to abate the nuisance and do whatever may be necessary in execution of the notice. Section 81(4) provides that the local authority may recover any expenses reasonably incurred in abating or preventing the recurrence of a statutory nuisance from the person by whose acts or defaults the nuisance arose. If that person is the owner of the premises, reasonable expenses may be recovered from any person who is the owner for the time being.

Air conditioning systems

6.11 Cooling towers which form part of an air conditioning system can harbour legionella, as, indeed, can water systems generally. In 2001 the Health and Safety Executive and the Local Authorities Enforcement Liaison Committee issued an Approved Code of Practice ('ACoP') and Guidance on the prevention or control of legionellosis (including legionnaire's disease) which included reference to the Management of Health and Safety at Work Regulations 1999[1], made under the Health and Safety at Work Act 1974. Subsequently the Control of Substances Hazardous to Health Regulations 2002[2], ('COSHH 2002'), have come into force. It is not an offence, as such, to fail to comply with the provisions of the ACoP, but failure to comply can be taken into account by a court in criminal proceedings for breach of the Health and Safety at Work Act 1974 or of COSHH 2002.

The Notification of Cooling Towers and Evaporative Condensers Regulations 1992[3], require any person who has, to any extent, control of non-domestic premises containing wet cooling towers and/or evaporative condensers to notify their local authority's Environmental Health Department that they have that equipment.

1 SI 1999/2677.
2 SI 2002/2677.
3 SI 1992/2225.

Contaminated land

6.12 Part 2 of the Environment Act 1995 inserted ss 78A–78YC into the Environmental Protection Act 1990 in respect of contaminated land.

This is defined as land having substances in, on or under it, and as a result significant harm is being caused (or there is a significant possibility of such significant harm being caused) to the health of living organisms, the ecological system, or property, or pollution of controlled waters is being caused or is likely to be caused.

Part 2A has been extended to include radioactivity originating from nuclear installations. In December 2007 the Pt 2A regime was modified to cover unacceptable risks to human health from radioactivity originating from nuclear licensed sites. However it is said that it is unlikely that any sites meeting the relevant criteria will be found.

The procedure under these provisions is that the local authority will inspect land in its area, identify contaminated land, and notify the Environment Agency and also the 'owner' of the land, its occupier, and any 'appropriate person'. After a consultation period of at least three months, a Remediation Notice is to be served by the local authority on the 'appropriate person' and an entry made on a register. If land is believed to fall into the category of a 'special site' (as designated by regulations), the steps towards securing remediation will be taken by the Environment Agency instead of the local authority. The statutory framework is currently supplemented, in relation to England, by the Contaminated Land (England) Regulations 2006[1], and the DEFRA Contaminated Land Statutory Guidance, April 2012. The Scottish Executive and the National Assembly for Wales are responsible for the contaminated land regime in Scotland and Wales respectively.

The 'appropriate person' is the person who caused or knowingly permitted the substance to be present. 'Knowingly permitted' is not defined but case law indicates that it means having knowledge of the presence of the substance, having power to procure its remediation (eg its removal, treatment or encapsulation) and the elapse of adequate time to do this. If there is no person liable under the foregoing, the Remediation Notice is served on the 'owner'. The 'owner' is the person entitled to receive the rack rent of the land (or would be if the land were let) and so will normally exclude a tenant who is paying a market rent. 'Owner' does not include a mortgagee unless he is in possession.

In the DEFRA Guidance, which has statutory force, the person who caused the substance to be present and the person who knowingly permitted the substance to be present are termed Class A persons and those who are neither but are simply owners or occupiers are termed Class B persons. Under the Environmental Protection Act 1990, s 78F and section 7 of the Guidance, no person in Class B (*owner or occupier*) is to be liable for remediation if a person is found within Class A (*causing or knowingly permitting*). A person's potential liability as 'owner' or 'occupier' in Class B may arise if the enforcing authority cannot find anyone liable within Class A. In that case, as between the owner and the occupier within Class B, a tenant will not be an 'owner' if he pays a full rent; a tenant as 'occupier' will be excluded under para 7.78(a) of the DEFRA Circular if he is a mere licensee and will be excluded under para 7.78(b) if he pays a full rent and has no beneficial interest in the land beyond his tenancy; and thus it may leave the landlord (as owner) carrying the liability.

Where substances escape from one person's land onto another's, the Remediation Notice may be served on the person who caused or knowingly permitted the substance to be on the source land as well as being served on any person who caused or knowingly permitted it to be on the affected land.

An appeal against a Remediation Notice is possible to the Secretary of State. If properly required remediation work is not done, an offence is committed by the recipient of the notice. Furthermore, the local authority or Environment Agency can carry out the work and the costs incurred, plus interest, can be recovered from him.

1 SI 2006/1380.

Energy efficiency certification

6.13 The Energy Performance of Buildings (Certificates and Inspections) (England and Wales) Regulations 2007, as amended, require landlords of most residential and commercial buildings in England or Wales to provide prospective tenants with energy performance certificates (EPCs). The certificate is to be accompanied by a Recommendation Report identifying possible steps to improve the energy efficiency rating of the property. An EPC is only required on an intended disposal of premises to which the regulations apply and, once produced, is valid for 10 years.

EPCs are also required for freehold sales, and Minimum Energy Efficiency Standards need to be achieved before certain premises may be let, but they are outside the scope of this book.

EPCs are required when a dwelling is being let by the landlord on a long lease or on a short letting. In the non-residential sectors, the EPC regime applies on the letting of most buildings (having roofs and walls) which use energy for conditioning their indoor climate – which presumably means that they have electric, gas or oil heating and/or cooling – but it does not apply to industrial sites, workshops, low energy-consuming agricultural buildings or stand-alone buildings of less than 50m2. A part of a building is subject to the regime if it has been designed or altered to be used separately; this will probably encompass most flats and individual retail and leisure units and office suites as well as whole buildings. Consequently it will apply not only where the landlord of the whole building intends to let the whole building or a unit in it, but also where the tenant of a single unit intends to sublet his unit.

Where a unit benefits from air-conditioning controlled centrally, the regulations appear to provide that, in the case of a subletting, the duty to provide the EPC to a prospective subtenant of the unit is imposed on the tenant's landlord so far as the air-conditioning aspect is concerned, but this is not absolutely clear from the wording and it is also unclear why the regulations do not deal with central heating on a similar basis.

The regulations also impose separate requirements for public buildings. Public authorities and institutions providing public services to a large number of people and frequently visited by those persons and who occupy space in a building with a total useful floor area greater than 1,000m2 will have to prominently display a Display Energy Certificate ('DEC') and hold a valid advisory report (similar to a recommendation report). 'Institutions providing public services to a large number of people' are defined in the Guidance as 'those providing services traditionally associated with local or national Government'. Examples include state schools, leisure centres (not private clubs), public libraries, hospitals (not private hospitals unless NHS patients are admitted), golf courses open to the public, and museums and art galleries sponsored by public authorities. A DEC is to show the actual energy consumption of a building and its operation rating and is intended to provide information to the public about the energy efficiency of buildings regularly used by them. DECs must be renewed annually and must also be displayed at all times in a prominent position clearly visible to the public. The advisory report which accompanies it must be renewed every seven years.

Where a building is partly occupied by a public authority or relevant institution and partly by a private organisation, a DEC and advisory report is only needed in respect of the part occupied by the public body.

The regulations contain requirements for landlords and tenants to co-operate with each other where necessary to facilitate compliance with the EPC and

DEC obligations, but the regulations do not address the question how the costs incurred (such as the costs of engaging an approved energy assessor) are to be borne between landlords and tenants. It will therefore depend on the exact wording of the service charge provisions in the leases of units in a building or complex in order to determine whether a landlord who obtains EPCs for, say, the purpose of letting vacant units in that building or complex can recover all or part of the cost through the service charges.

CRC Energy efficiency scheme

6.14 The Carbon Reduction Commitment Energy Efficiency Scheme is a compulsory emissions trading scheme managed by the Environment Agency affecting large businesses and public sector organisations.

The Government has announced that the Scheme it is to be abolished and that organisations will report under the Scheme for the last time by the end of July 2019 and surrender allowances (see below) for emissions from energy supplied in the 2018–2019 compliance year by the end of October 2019.

Under the scheme, groups of companies and other organisations consuming large amounts of energy have to purchase 'allowances' under the CRC Energy Efficiency Scheme Order 2013 as amended by the CRC Energy Efficiency Scheme (Amendment) Order 2014.

Qualification for the scheme is based on electricity usage. For the current Phase 2, organisations will qualify if, during the qualification year, they consumed over 6,000 megawatt-hours (MWh) of qualifying electricity through settled half-hourly meters. Organisations that meet the qualification threshold must register using the on-line CRC Registry, which is administered by the Environment Agency. Qualifying organisations have to comply legally with the scheme or face financial and other penalties.

Organisations which participate within the CRC are required to monitor their energy use, and report their energy supplies annually. The Environment Agency's reporting system applies emissions factors to calculate participants' carbon dioxide (CO2) emissions on the basis of this information.

Participants must purchase and surrender allowances to offset their emissions. Allowances can either be bought at annual fixed-price sales, or traded on the secondary market. One allowance must be surrendered for each tonne of CO2 emitted. The allowance price in Phase 1 was £12 per tonne of CO2.

In the current phase, participants have the option of buying allowances in advance in the cheaper 'forecast sale' at the start of a compliance year, or in a more expensive 'compliance sale' after the end of the year. For the current phase, the following prices apply:

CRC Scheme Year	*Forecast Sale Price*	*Compliance Sale Price*
2017/18	£16.60	£17.10
2018/19	£17.20	£18.30

An issue for landlords is how much of the costs incurred under the scheme (whether just the cost of buying allowances or also administration costs) are to be recoverable from tenants. The simplistic view is that, for service charge purposes, those costs are merely part of the expenditure incurred by the landlord in obtaining the energy required to provide services such as heating, lighting, lifts etc and that the Scheme costs can be included in the service charge on the basis that it is part of the cost of providing those services (see the discussion about the meaning of 'cost' at **1.36** and **1.41**). However there are arguments to the contrary and it remains to be seen how the courts might decide these matters if they are disputed. It might be argued that Scheme payments are not sufficiently closely connected to the actual cost of energy to fall within the 'cost' of providing the energy-consuming service.

Further, since the Scheme operates at group organisation level, the Scheme payments may not be made by the actual landlord company. Since the reported energy usage is of the total across all the organisation's premises, the allowances are not directly allocated to individual buildings and to enable the costs to be recovered from tenants it may be necessary for the leases to specify how such costs are to be apportioned between all the relevant buildings. It has been held by tribunals on residential service charges that where the lease of a unit contains a service charge clause that refers (as is quite common) to costs incurred in respect of the building containing the unit, but makes no reference to apportioning costs incurred on that building together with other buildings, this has the effect that the landlord cannot unilaterally apportion to that building undivided costs it has incurred on that and other buildings, so those types of costs cannot be included in such a service charge without express provision (*Norwich City Council v Redford*[1]; *Kelsall v LB of Islington*[2]).

Accordingly, express provisions allowing and governing the apportionment of Scheme costs across the buildings owned by entities within that member organisation are likely to be necessary. A fair apportionment might be pro rata to the energy consumption of each building.

How the Scheme costs so attributed to a building are then to be allocated between the tenants is another issue; the latest multi-let buildings often have sophisticated systems to measure the relative energy consumption of each unit and that might be an appropriate basis for those buildings.

In addition to payments made under the Scheme, participants are likely to incur internal administration costs. As for the charging of such overheads within service charges, see **1.41**.

The RICS Professional Statement: Service Charges in Commercial Property (see **7.1**) in paragraph 4.8.2 states that best practice is for landlords to absorb their costs of managing and administering their involvement in the Scheme and to apportion any payments made under the Scheme across their group companies and between buildings on a fair and reasonable basis which is applied consistently.

1 [2015] UKUT 30, LC.
2 [2006] LVT.

GREEN LEASES

6.15 A number of practice guidelines have been promulgated to encourage the landlords and tenants to comply with recommended practices and standards for energy saving and environmental protection.

One example is the concept of 'green leases', which are leases containing provisions intended to further environmentally-friendly initiatives such as energy efficiency and the recycling of waste. Where these might require improvements to existing buildings, views vary as to whether they should be legally binding obligations or merely initiatives that the parties are encouraged to adopt voluntarily from time to time during a tenancy, perhaps by landlords entering into 'memoranda of understandings' with each new tenant or assignee. The cost of some such initiatives can be considerable, such as the replacement of boilers or the installation of solar panels, and any return in the form of saved operating costs can take a long time to be recovered, so in a difficult letting market such expenditure is unlikely to be supported by those tenants who do not see corporate social responsibility as important for their businesses.

The RICS Professional Statement: Service Charges in Commercial Property (see **7.1**) comments on these issues at paragraph 4.10.

Chapter 7

COMMERCIAL CODES OF PRACTICE

RICS PROFESSIONAL STATEMENT – SERVICE CHARGES IN COMMERCIAL PROPERTY

7.1 A new RICS Professional Statement: Service Charges in Commercial Property, first edition, has been published by the Royal Institution of Chartered Surveyors to take effect on 1 April 2019 and it replaces (and is largely derived from) the third edition of the RICS Code of Practice on that subject.

It is set out in three parts: Part 1 sets out its aims and objectives and various mandatory requirements, Part 2 contains core principles and Part 3 prescribes best practice to support the core principles.

Chartered surveyors are obliged to comply with the Professional Statement, which sets out obligations that 'must' be observed as well as those that 'should' be observed. The RICS advises chartered surveyors that sections within its Professional Statements that use the word 'must' set mandatory professional, behavioural, competence and/or technical requirements, from which their members must not depart. As for sections that use the word 'should', these constitute areas of good practice and the RICS recognises that there may be exceptional circumstances in which it is appropriate for a member to depart from those provisions – but in such situations the RICS may require the member to justify their decisions and actions.

The RICS will take account of relevant Professional Statements in deciding whether a member acted professionally, appropriately and with reasonable competence. It is also likely that during any legal proceedings relating to a chartered surveyor's conduct on matters covered by a RICS Professional Statement, a judge, adjudicator or equivalent will take the provisions of that Professional Statement into account. The RICS recognises that there may be legislative requirements or regional, national or international standards that have precedence over a RICS Professional Statement.

This Statement encourages transparency, communication, the monitoring and reviewing of the quality of management and the cost and standard of services, and provides straightforward guidelines covering a variety of matters including the bearing of initial capital costs, providing value for money, apportioning costs between tenants, consulting with tenants, preparing estimates, and producing accounts. It also explains a benchmarking system for cost analysis.

Model service charge provisions reflecting the 3rd edition of the Code (with which the new Statement is similar in many respects) have been published by the City of London Law Society and can be accessed from its website: www.citysolicitors.org.uk.

CODE FOR LEASING BUSINESS PREMISES IN ENGLAND AND WALES

7.2 This was first published in 1995, and the current Code was issued in 2007. A new Code is currently in preparation.

Prepared by a joint working group (chaired by one of the authors of this book) which comprised delegates from bodies representing property occupiers, owners, investors and funders as well as property professionals (both surveyors and lawyers), the 2007 Code is a response to the government's pressure on landlords to provide tenants with more flexible lease terms. The Code aims to promote fairness in commercial leases, and recognises a need to increase awareness of property issues, especially among small businesses, ensuring that occupiers of business premises have the information necessary to negotiate the best deal available to them. The Code consists of three parts, a 10 point Landlord Code of requirements for landlords in order for their lease to be Code-compliant; an Occupiers Guide, explaining terms and providing tips; and a set of model Heads of Terms.

Recommendation 6 of the Landlord Code states that: 'Landlords must, during negotiations, provide best estimates of service charges, insurance payments and any other outgoings that tenants will incur under their leases. Landlords must disclose known irregular events that would have a significant impact on the amount of future service charges. Landlords should be aware of the RICS 2006 Code of Practice on Service charges in Commercial Property and seek to observe its guidance in drafting new leases and on renewals.'

The Occupiers Guide gives prospective tenants tips about service charge information to request when negotiating a new commercial lease.

Appendix 1

SPECIMEN NOTICES, DEMANDS, ACCOUNTS AND CERTIFICATES

Notice under section 48 of the Landlord and Tenant Act 1987

A1.1

(Name of tenant) To:

. . . . *(address of tenant)*

being the tenant of premises known as *(address of premises)*.

We (*name and address of landlord's solicitors or agents*), on behalf of your landlord (*name of landlord*), give you notice pursuant to section 48(1) of the Landlord and Tenant Act 1987 that the address of your landlord for service of notices (including notices of proceedings) is:

(*landlord's address for service*)

Signed: . . . .

Date: . . . . 20. . . . . .

Specimen summary of service costs

A1.2

[Issued under paras 5.1 to 5.4 of the specimen service charge clause in the form set out in APPENDIX 1.*]*

Re: ABC House, Alphabet Street, Anytown

Certificate of Service Costs for the Accounting Year ended 30 June 2011

	£
Cleaning of common parts	1,005.70
Gardening	500.00
Boiler fuel and maintenance	4,705.60
Lift maintenance	520.34
Security	299.17
Porters and other staff	4,074.81
Telephone and entryphone	198.33
Window cleaning	360.00
Internal maintenance	264.66
Fire equipment hire	111.74
External redecoration	19,828.42
External repairs	4,222.52
Management fees	4,120.82
	40,212.11
Less taken from reserve	22,000.00
	18,212.11
Add provision for reserve fund	4,500.00
TOTAL EXPENDITURE	22,712.11
Reserve fund at 1 July 2010	27,715.25
Interest accrued	1,247.19
Sums taken as above	22,000.00
	6,962.44
Reserve fund provision	4,500.00
Reserve fund at 30 June 2011	11,462.44

All the above sums are [inclusive] [exclusive] of value added tax.

(Landlord's, agent's or accountant's certificate of correctness to be added – see Specimens 3 and 4 below.)

Specimen certificate of service charge under terms of lease

A1.3

[Issued under para 5.4 of the specimen service charge in the form set out in **APPENDIX 1**.*]*

[Issued under para 5.4 of the specimen service charge in the form set out in **APPENDIX 1**.*]*

[This form represents the certificate of the landlord or managing agent under the first of the alternative provisions set out in para 5.4 of the specimen clauses contained in **APPENDIX 1**. *It will be observed that the wording below closely follows that contained in the part of the service charge clause or schedule which provides for the issue of the certificate. This is the proper basis for drafting any certificate to be issued under the express terms of a lease: the wording of the relevant clause should be followed as closely as possible.]*

We hereby certify that the above is a true and accurate account of the service] of the leases of the] [Schedule costs referred to in [clause]. above-mentioned property in respect of the accounting period ended [

Signed: . . . .

Date: . . . . 20 . . . . . .

Specimen certificate of service charge under the Landlord and Tenant Act 1985

A1.4

[To conform with s 21 of the Landlord and Tenant Act 1985 until the amendments made by the Commonhold and Leasehold Reform Act 2002 come into effect. After that time, this certificate would have to be redrafted so as to comply with the new s 21(3) and regulations made under the new s 21(4)(b) and (c).]

I hereby certify that in my opinion the above is a fair summary complying with Section 21(5) of the Landlord and Tenant Act 1985 of the costs incurred by or on behalf of . . . . (*landlord*) . . . . in connection with the matters for which the service charge is payable, and is sufficiently supported by accounts, receipts and other documents which have been produced to me.

Signed: . . . . Accountant

Date: . . . . 20 . . . . . .

Specimen statement of service charge

A1.5

[Issued under para 5.5 of the specimen service charge in the form set out in APPENDIX 1.*]*

ABC LANDLORDS LIMITED . . . . (*landlord's address*)

RE: ABC HOUSE, ALPHABET STREET, ANYTOWN

To:

STATEMENT OF SERVICE CHARGES DUE FROM YOU AS TENANT OF OFFICE SUITE X FOR THE ACCOUNTING YEAR ENDED 30 JUNE 2010

	£	£
Total Expenditure as per attached Accounts		22,712.11
(14.3% Total service charge payable of £22,712.11)		3,247.83
Less interim charges	£750	
24.6.2010	£750	
25.3.2010	£750	
25.12.2009	£750	
29.9.2009 received:		–3,000.00
BALANCE DUE		247.83

All sums are [inclusive] [exclusive] of value added tax.

Service charges: summary of tenants' rights and obligations

A1.6

1 This summary, which briefly sets out your rights and obligations in relation to variable service charges, must by law accompany a demand for service charges. Unless a summary is sent to you with a demand, you may withhold the service charge. The summary does not give a full interpretation of the law and if you are in any doubt about your rights and obligations you should seek independent advice.

2 Your lease sets out your obligations to pay service charges to your landlord in addition to your rent. Service charges are amounts payable for services, repairs, maintenance, improvements, insurance or the landlord's costs of management, to the extent that the costs have been reasonably incurred.

3 You have the right to ask a leasehold valuation tribunal to determine whether you are liable to pay service charges for services, repairs, maintenance, improvements, insurance or management. You may make a request before or after you have paid the service charge. If the tribunal determines that the service charge is payable, the tribunal may also determine:

- who should pay the service charge and who it should be paid to;
- the amount;
- the date it should be paid by; and
- how it should be paid.

However, you do not have these rights where:

- a matter has been agreed or admitted by you;
- a matter has already been, or is to be, referred to arbitration or has been determined by arbitration and you agreed to go to arbitration after the disagreement about the service charge or costs arose; or
- a matter has been decided by a court.

4 If your lease allows your landlord to recover costs incurred or that may be incurred in legal proceedings as service charges, you may ask the court or tribunal, before which those proceedings were brought, to rule that your landlord may not do so.

5 Where you seek a determination from a leasehold valuation tribunal, you will have to pay an application fee and, where the matter proceeds to a hearing, a hearing fee, unless you qualify for a waiver or reduction. The total fees payable will not exceed £500, but making an application may incur additional costs, such as professional fees, which you may also have to pay.

6 A leasehold valuation tribunal has the power to award costs, not exceeding £500, against a party to any proceedings where:

- it dismisses a matter because it is frivolous, vexatious or an abuse of process; or
- it considers a party has acted frivolously, vexatiously, abusively, disruptively or unreasonably.

The Upper Tribunal has similar powers when hearing an appeal against a decision of a leasehold valuation tribunal.

7 If your landlord:

- proposes works on a building or any other premises that will cost you or any other tenant more than £250; or
- proposes to enter into an agreement for works or services which will last for more than 12 months and will cost you or any other tenant more than £100 in any 12 month accounting period,
- your contribution will be limited to these amounts unless your landlord has properly consulted on the proposed works or agreement or a leasehold valuation tribunal has agreed that consultation is not required.

8 You have the right to apply to a leasehold valuation tribunal to ask it to determine whether your lease should be varied on the grounds that it does not make satisfactory provision in respect of the calculation of a service charge payable under the lease.

9 You have the right to write to your landlord to request a written summary of the costs which make up the service charges. The summary must:

- cover the last 12-month period used for making up the accounts relating to the service charge ending no later than the date of your request, where the accounts are made up for 12-month periods; or
- cover the 12-month period ending with the date of your request, where the accounts are not made up for 12-month periods.

The summary must be given to you within one month of your request or 6 months of the end of the period to which the summary relates whichever is the later.

10 You have the right, within 6 months of receiving a written summary of costs, to require the landlord to provide you with reasonable facilities to inspect the accounts, receipts and other documents supporting the summary and for taking copies or extracts from them.

11 You have the right to ask an accountant or surveyor to carry out an audit of the financial management of the premises containing your dwelling, to establish the obligations of your landlord and the extent to which the service charges you pay are being used efficiently. It will depend on your circumstances whether you can exercise this right alone or only with the support of others living in the premises. You are strongly advised to seek independent advice before exercising this right.

12 Your lease may give your landlord a right of re-entry or forfeiture where you have failed to pay charges which are properly due under the lease. However, to exercise this right, the landlord must meet all the legal requirements and obtain a court order. A court order will only be granted if you have admitted you are liable to pay the amount or it is finally determined by a court, tribunal or by arbitration that the amount is due. The court has a wide discretion in granting such an order and it will take into account all the circumstances of the case.

Specimen prescribed notice under the Landlord and Tenant (Covenants) Act 1995

Landlord and Tenant (Covenants) Act 1995 (Notices) Regulations 1995 Form 1

Landlord and Tenant (Covenants) Act 1995
Section 17

A1.7

Notice to Former Tenant or Guarantor of Intention to Recover Fixed Charge

To

IMPORTANT – The person giving this notice is protecting the right to recover the amount(s) specified from you now or at some time in the future. There may be action which you can take to protect your position. Read the notice and all the notes overleaf carefully. If you are in any doubt about the action you should take, seek advice immediately, for instance from a solicitor or citizens advice bureau.

1 This notice is given under section 17 of the Landlord and Tenant (Covenants) Act 1995.

2 It relates to

let under a lease dated and made between

[of which you were formerly a tenant].

3 We as landlord hereby give you notice that the fixed charges of which details are set out in the attached Schedule are now due and unpaid, and that we intend to recover from you the amounts specified in the Schedule [and interest from the date and calculated on the basis specified in the Schedule].

4 There is a possibility that your liability in respect of the fixed charges detailed in the Schedule will subsequently be determined to be for a greater amount.

5 All correspondence about this notice should be sent to the landlord's agent at the address given below.

Dated the day of 20

Signature . . . . of landlord's agent

Name and address of landlord:

[Name and address of landlord's agent:

Notes

1 The person giving you this notice alleges that you are still liable for the performance of the tenant's obligations under the tenancy to which this notice relates, either as a previous tenant bound by privity of contract or an authorised guarantee agreement, or because you are the guarantor of a previous tenant. By giving you this notice, the landlord (or other person entitled to enforce payment, such as a management company) is protecting his right to require you to pay the amount specified in the notice. There may be other sums not covered by the notice which the landlord can also recover

because they are not fixed charges (for example, in respect of repairs or costs if legal proceedings have to be brought). If you pay the amount specified in this notice in full, you will have the right to call on the landlord to grant you an 'overriding lease', which puts you in the position of landlord to the present tenant. There are both advantages and drawbacks to doing this, and you should take advice before coming to a decision.

Validity of notice

2 The landlord is required to give this notice within six months of the date on which the charge or charges in question became due (or, if it became due before 1 January 1996, within six months of that date). If the notice has been given late, it is not valid and the amount in the notice cannot be recovered from you. The date of the giving of the notice may not be the date written on the notice or the date on which you actually saw it. It may, for instance, be the date on which the notice was delivered through the post to your last address known to the landlord. If you are in any doubt, you should seek advice immediately.

Interest

3 If interest is payable on the amount due, the landlord does not have to state the precise amount of interest, but he must state the basis on which interest is calculated to enable you to work out the likely amount, or he will not be able to claim interest at all. This does not include interest which may be payable under rules of court if legal proceedings are brought.

Change in amount due

4 Apart from interest, the landlord is not entitled to recover an amount which is more than he has specified in the notice with one exception. This is where the amount cannot be finally determined within six months after it is due (for example, if there is a dispute concerning an outstanding rent review or if the charge is a service charge collected on account and adjusted following final determination). In such a case, if the amount due is eventually determined to be more than originally notified, the landlord may claim the larger amount if and only if he completes the paragraph giving notice of the possibility that the amount may change, and gives a further notice specifying the larger amount within three months of the final determination.

Appendix 2

EXTRACTS FROM LEGISLATION

Amendments not yet in force are denoted in the following way: words in *italics* (other than headings) are to be repealed and words in square brackets are to be inserted.

LANDLORD AND TENANT ACT 1985

INFORMATION TO BE GIVEN TO TENANT

A2.1

1 Disclosure of landlord's identity

(1) If the tenant of premises occupied as a dwelling makes a written request for the landlord's name and address to—

- (a) any person who demands, or the last person who received, rent payable under the tenancy, or
- (b) any other person for the time being acting as agent for the landlord, in relation to the tenancy,

that person shall supply the tenant with a written statement of the landlord's name and address within the period of 21 days beginning with the day on which he receives the request.

(2) A person who, without reasonable excuse, fails to comply with subsection (1) commits a summary offence and is liable on conviction to a fine not exceeding level 4 on the standard scale.

(3) In this section and section 2—

- (a) 'tenant' includes a statutory tenant; and
- (b) 'landlord' means the immediate landlord.

2 Disclosure of directors, etc of corporate landlord

(1) Where a tenant is supplied under section 1 with the name and address of his landlord and the landlord is a body corporate, he may make a further written request to the landlord for the name and address of every director and of the secretary of the landlord.

(2) The landlord shall supply the tenant with a written statement of the information requested within the period of 21 days beginning with the day on which he receives the request.

(3) A request under this section is duly made to the landlord if it is made to—

- (a) an agent of the landlord, or
- (b) a person who demands the rent of the premises concerned;

and any such agent or person to whom such a request is made shall forward it to the landlord as soon as may be.

(4) A landlord who, without reasonable excuse, fails to comply with a request under this section, and a person who, without reasonable excuse, fails to comply with a requirement imposed on him by subsection (3), commits a summary offence and is liable on conviction to a fine not exceeding level 4 on the standard scale.

3 Duty to inform tenant of assignment of landlord's interest

(1) If the interest of the landlord under a tenancy of premises which consist of or include a dwelling is assigned, the new landlord shall give notice in writing of the assignment, and of his name and address, to the tenant not later than the next day on which rent is payable under the tenancy or, if that is within two months of the assignment, the end of that period of two months.

(2) If trustees constitute the new landlord, a collective description of the trustees as the trustees of the trust in question may be given as the name of the landlord, and where such a collective description is given—

- (a) the address of the new landlord may be given as the address from which the affairs of the trust are conducted, and
- (b) a change in the persons who are for the time being the trustees of the trust shall not be treated as an assignment of the interest of the landlord.

(3) A person who is the new landlord under a tenancy falling within subsection (1) and who fails, without reasonable excuse, to give the notice required by that subsection, commits a summary offence and is liable on conviction to a fine not exceeding level 4 on the standard scale.

(3A) The person who was the landlord under the tenancy immediately before the assignment ('the old landlord') shall be liable to the tenant in respect of any breach of any covenant, condition or agreement under the tenancy occurring before the end of the relevant period in like manner as if the interest assigned were still vested in him; and where the new landlord is also liable to the tenant in respect of any such breach occurring within that period, he and the old landlord shall be jointly and severally liable in respect of it.

(3B) In subsection (3A) 'the relevant period' means the period beginning with the date of the assignment and ending with the date when—

- (a) notice in writing of the assignment, and of the new landlord's name and address is given to tenant by the new landlord (whether in accordance with subsection (1) or not),
- (b) notice in writing of the assignment, and of the new landlord's name and last-known address, is given to the tenant by the old landlord,

whichever happens first.

(4) In this section—

- (a) 'tenancy' includes a statutory tenancy, and
- (b) references to the assignment of the landlord's interest include any conveyance or mortgage or charge.

3A Duty to inform tenant of possible right to acquire landlord's interest

(1) Where a new landlord is required by section 3(1) to give notice to a tenant of an assignment to him, then if—

- (a) the tenant is a qualifying tenant within the meaning of Part 1 of the Landlord and Tenant Act 1987 (tenants' rights of first refusal), and
- (b) the assignment was a relevant disposal within the meaning of that Part affecting premises to which at the time of the disposal that Part applied,

the landlord shall give also notice in writing to the tenant to the following effect.

(2) The notice shall state—

- (a) that the disposal to the landlord was one to which Part 1 of the Landlord and Tenant Act 1987 applied;
- (b) that the tenant (together with other qualifying tenants) may have the right under that Part—
  - (i) to obtain information about the disposal, and
  - (ii) to acquire the landlord's interest in the whole or part of the premises in which the tenant's flat is situated; and

(c) the time within which any such right must be exercised, and the fact that the time would run from the date of receipt of notice under this section by the requisite majority of qualifying tenants (within the meaning of that Part).

(3) A person who is required to give notice under this section and who fails, without reasonable excuse, to do so within the time allowed for giving notice under section 3(1) commits a summary offence and is liable on conviction to a fine not exceeding level 4 on the standard scale.

. . .

8 Implied terms as to fitness for human habitation

(1) In a contract to which this section applies for the letting of a house for human habitation there is implied, notwithstanding any stipulation to the contrary—

(a) a condition that the house is fit for human habitation at the commencement of the tenancy, and

(b) an undertaking that the house will be kept by the landlord fit for human habitation during the tenancy.

(2) . . .

(3) This section applies to a contract if—

(a) the rent does not exceed the figure applicable in accordance with subsection (4), and

(b) the letting is not on such terms as to the tenant's responsibility as are mentioned in subsection (5).

(4) The rent limit for the application of this section is shown by the following Table, by reference to the date of making of the contract and the situation of the premises;

Date of making of contract	Rent limit
Before 31st July 1923.	In London: £40. Elsewhere: £26 or £16 (see Note 1).
On or after 31st July 1923 and before 6th July 1957.	In London: £40. Elsewhere: £26.
On or after 6th July 1957.	In London: £80. Elsewhere: £52.

NOTES

(1) The applicable figure for contracts made before 31st July 1923 is £26 in the case of premises situated in a borough or urban district which at the date of the contract had according to the last published census a population of 50,000 or more. In the case of a house situated elsewhere, the figure is £16.

(2) The references to 'London' are, in relation to contracts made before 1st April 1965, to the administrative county of London and, in relation to contracts made on or after that date, to Greater London exclusive of the outer London boroughs.

(5) This section does not apply where a house is let for a term of three years or more (the lease not being determinable at the option of either party before the expiration of three years) upon terms that the tenant puts the premises into a condition reasonably fit for human habitation.

(6) In this section 'house' includes—

(a) a part of a house, and

(b) any yard, garden, outhouses and appurtenances belonging to the house or usually enjoyed with it.

9 Application of s 8 to certain houses occupied by agricultural workers

(1) Where under the contract of employment of a worker employed in agriculture the provision of a house for his occupation forms part of his remuneration and the

provisions of section 8 (implied terms as to fitness for human habitation) are inapplicable by reason only of the house not being let to him—

(a) there are implied as part of the contract of employment, notwithstanding any stipulation to the contrary, the like condition and undertaking as would be implied under that section if the house were so let, and

(b) the provisions of that section apply accordingly, with the substitution of 'employer' for 'landlord' and such other modifications as may be necessary.

(2) This section does not affect any obligation of a person other than the employer to repair a house to which this section applies, or any remedy for enforcing such an obligation.

(3) In this section 'house' includes—

(a) a part of a house, and

(b) any yard, garden, outhouses and appurtenances belonging to the house or usually enjoyed with it.

10 Fitness for human habitation

In determining for the purposes of this Act whether a house is unfit for human habitation, regard shall be had to its condition in respect of the following matters—

repair,
stability,
freedom from damp,
internal arrangement,
natural lighting,
ventilation,
water supply,
drainage and sanitary conveniences,
facilities for preparation and cooking of food and for the disposal of waste water;

and the house shall be regarded as unfit for human habitation if, and only if, it is so far defective in one or more of those matters that it is not reasonably suitable for occupation in that condition.

REPAIRING OBLIGATIONS

11 Repairing obligations in short leases

(1) In a lease to which this section applies (as to which, see sections 13 and 14) there is implied a covenant by the lessor—

(a) to keep in repair the structure and exterior of the dwelling-house (including drains, gutters and external pipes),

(b) to keep in repair and proper working order the installations in the dwelling-house for the supply of water, gas and electricity and for sanitation (including basins, sinks, baths and sanitary conveniences, but not other fixtures, fittings and appliances for making use of the supply of water, gas or electricity), and

(c) to keep in repair and proper working order the installations in the dwelling-house for space heating and heating water.

(1A) If a lease to which this section applies is a lease of a dwelling-house which forms part only of a building, then, subject to subsection (1B), the covenant implied by subsection (1) shall have effect as if—

(a) the reference in paragraph (a) of that subsection to the dwelling-house included a reference to any part of the building in which the lessor has an estate or interest; and

(b) any reference in paragraphs (b) and (c) of that subsection to an installation in the dwelling-house included a reference to an installation which, directly or indirectly, serves the dwelling-house and which either—

(i) forms part of any part of a building in which the lessor has an estate or interest; or

(ii) is owned by the lessor or under his control.

(1B) Nothing in subsection (1A) shall be construed as requiring the lessor to carry out any works or repairs unless the disrepair (or failure to maintain in working order) is such as to affect the lessee's enjoyment of the dwelling-house or of any common parts, as defined in section 60(1) of the Landlord and Tenant Act 1987, which the lessee, as such, is entitled to use.

(2) The covenant implied by subsection (1) ('the lessor's repairing covenant') shall not be construed as requiring the lessor—

(a) to carry out works or repairs for which the lessee is liable by virtue of his duty to use the premises in a tenant-like manner, or would be so liable but for an express covenant on his part,

(b) to rebuild or reinstate the premises in the case of destruction or damage by fire, or by tempest, flood or other inevitable accident, or

(c) to keep in repair or maintain anything which the lessee is entitled to remove from the dwelling-house.

(3) In determining the standard of repair required by the lessor's repairing covenant, regard shall be had to the age, character and the dwelling-house and the locality in which it is situated.

(3A) In any case where—

(a) the lessor's repairing covenant has effect as mentioned in subsection (1A), and

(b) in order to comply with the covenant the lessor needs to carry out works or repairs otherwise than in, or to an installation in the dwelling-house, and

(c) the lessor does not have a sufficient right in the part of the building or the installation concerned to enable him to carry out the required works or repairs,

then, in any proceedings relating to a failure to comply with the lessor's repairing covenant, so far as it requires the lessor to carry out the works or repairs in question, it shall be a defence for the lessor to prove that he used all reasonable endeavours to obtain, but was unable to obtain, such rights as would be adequate to enable him to carry out the works or repairs.

(4) A covenant by the lessee for the repair of the premises is of no effect so far as it relates to the matters mentioned in subsection (1)(a) to (c), except so far as it imposes on the lessee any of the requirements mentioned in subsection (2)(a) or (c).

(5) The reference in subsection (4) to a covenant by the lessee for the repair of the premises includes a covenant—

(a) to put in repair or deliver up in repair,

(b) to paint, point or render,

(c) to pay money in lieu of repairs by the lessee, or

(d) to pay money on account of repairs by the lessor.

(6) In a case in which the lessor's repairing covenant is implied there is also implied a covenant by the lessee that the lessor, or any person authorised by him in writing, may at reasonable times of the day and on giving 24 hours' notice in writing to the occupier, enter the premises comprised in the lease for the purpose of viewing their condition and state of repair.

12 Restriction on contracting out of s 11

(1) A covenant or agreement, whether contained in a lease to which section 11 applies or in an agreement collateral to such a lease, is void in so far as it purports—

(a) to exclude or limit the obligations of the lessor or the immunities of the lessee under that section, or

(b) to authorise any forfeiture or impose on the lessee any penalty, disability or obligation in the event of his enforcing or relying upon those obligations or immunities,

unless the inclusion of the provision was authorised by the county court.

(2) The county court may, by order made with the consent of the parties, authorise the inclusion in a lease, or in an agreement collateral to a lease, of provisions excluding or modifying in relation to the lease, the provisions of section 11 with respect to the repairing obligations of the parties if it appears to the court that it is reasonable to do so, having regard to all the circumstances of the case, including the other terms and conditions of the lease.

13 Leases to which s 11 applies: general rule

(1) Section 11 (repairing obligations) applies to a lease of a dwelling-house granted on or after 24th October 1961 for a term of less than seven years.

(1A) Section 11 also applies to a lease of a dwelling-house in England granted on or after the day on which section 166 of the Localism Act 2011 came into force which is—

(a) a secure tenancy for a fixed term of seven years or more granted by a person within section 80(1) of the Housing Act 1985 (secure tenancies: the landlord condition), or

(b) an assured tenancy for a fixed term of seven years or more that—

(i) is not a shared ownership lease, and

(ii) is granted by a private registered provider of social housing.]

[(1B) In subsection (1A)—

"assured tenancy" has the same meaning as in Part 1 of the Housing Act 1988;

"secure tenancy" has the meaning given by section 79 of the Housing Act 1985; and

"shared ownership lease" means a lease—

(a) granted on payment of a premium calculated by reference to a percentage of the value of the dwelling-house or of the cost of providing it, or

(b) under which the lessee (or the lessee's personal representatives) will or may be entitled to a sum calculated by reference, directly or indirectly, to the value of the dwelling-house.

(2) In determining whether a lease is one to which section 11 applies—

(a) any part of the term which falls before the grant shall be left out of account and the lease shall be treated as a lease for a term commencing with the grant,

(b) a lease which is determinable at the option of the lessor before the expiration of seven years from the commencement of the term shall be treated as a lease for a term of less than seven years, and

(c) a lease (other than a lease to which paragraph (b) applies) shall not be treated as a lease for a term of less than seven years if it confers on the lessee an option for renewal for a term which, together with the original term, amounts to seven years or more.

(3) This section has effect subject to—

(a) section 14 (leases to which section 11 applies: exceptions), and

(b) section 32(2) (provisions not applying to tenancies within Part II of the Landlord and Tenant Act 1954).

14 Leases to which s 11 applies: exceptions

(1) Section 11 (repairing obligations) does not apply to a new lease granted to an existing tenant, or to a former tenant still in possession, if the previous lease was not a lease to which section 11 applied (and, in the case of a lease granted before 24th October 1961, would not have been if it had been granted on or after that date).

(2) In subsection (1)—

'existing tenant' means a person who is when, or immediately before, the new lease is granted, the lessee under another lease of the dwelling-house;

'former tenant still in possession' means a person who—

(a) was the lessee under another lease of the dwelling-house which terminated at some time before the new lease was granted, and

(b) between the termination of that other lease and the grant of the new lease was continuously in possession of the dwelling-house or of the rents and profits of the dwelling-house; and

'the previous lease' means the other lease referred to in the above definitions.

(3) Section 11 does not apply to a lease of a dwelling-house which is a tenancy of an agricultural holding within the meaning of the Agricultural Holdings Act 1986 and in relation to which that Act applies or to a farm business tenancy within the meaning of the Agricultural Tenancies Act 1995.

(4) Section 11 does not apply to a lease granted on or after 3rd October 1980 to—

a local authority,

a National Park authority,

a new town corporation,

an urban development corporation,

a Mayoral development corporation,

the Development Board for Rural Wales,

a non-profit registered provider of social housing,

a registered social landlord,

a co-operative housing association,

an educational institution or other body specified, or of a class specified, by regulations under section 8 of the Rent Act 1977 or paragraph 8 of Schedule 1 to the Housing Act 1988 (bodies making student lettings), or

a housing action trust established under Part III of the Housing Act 1988.

(5) Section 11 does not apply to a lease granted on or after 3rd October 1980 to—

(a) Her Majesty in right of the Crown (unless the lease is under the management of the Crown Estate Commissioners), or

(b) a government department or a person holding in trust for Her Majesty for the purposes of a government department.

15 Jurisdiction of county court

The county court has jurisdiction to make a declaration that section 11 (repairing covenants) applies, or does not apply, to a lease—

(a) whatever the net annual value of the property in question, and

(b) notwithstanding that no other relief is sought than a declaration.

16 Meaning of 'lease' and related expressions

In sections 11 to 15 (repairing obligations in short leases)—

(a) 'lease' does not include a mortgage term;

(b) 'lease of a dwelling-house' means a lease by which a building or part of a building is let wholly or mainly as a private residence, and 'dwelling-house' means that building or part of a building;

(c) 'lessee' and 'lessor' mean, respectively, the person for the time being entitled to the term of a lease and to the reversion expectant on it.

17 Specific performance of landlord's repairing obligations

(1) In proceedings in which a tenant of a dwelling alleges a breach on the part of his landlord of a repairing covenant relating to any part of the premises in which the dwelling is comprised, the court may order specific performance of the covenant whether or not the breach relates to a part of the premises let to the tenant and notwithstanding any equitable rule restricting the scope of the remedy, whether on the basis of a lack of mutuality or otherwise.

(2) In this section—

(a) 'tenant' includes a statutory tenant,

(b) in relation to a statutory tenant the reference to the premises let to him is to the premises of which he is a statutory tenant,

(c) 'landlord', in relation to a tenant, includes any person against whom the tenant has a right to enforce a repairing covenant, and

(d) 'repairing covenant' means a covenant to repair, maintain, renew, construct or replace any property.

SERVICE CHARGES

18 Meaning of 'service charge' and 'relevant costs'

(1) In the following provisions of this Act 'service charge' means an amount payable by a tenant of a dwelling as part of or in addition to the rent—

(a) which is payable, directly or indirectly, for services, repairs, maintenance, improvements or insurance or the landlord's costs of management, and

(b) the whole or part of which varies or may vary according to the relevant costs.

(2) The relevant costs are the costs or estimated costs incurred or to be incurred by or on behalf of the landlord, or a superior landlord, in connection with the matters for which the service charge is payable.

(3) For this purpose—

(a) 'costs' includes overheads, and

(b) costs are relevant costs in relation to a service charge whether they are incurred, or to be incurred, in the period for which the service charge is payable or in an earlier or later period.

19 Limitation of service charges: reasonableness

(1) Relevant costs shall be taken into account in determining the amount of a service charge payable for a period—

(a) only to the extent that they are reasonably incurred, and

(b) where they are incurred on the provision of services or the carrying out of works, only if the services or works are of a reasonable standard;

and the amount payable shall be limited accordingly.

(2) Where a service charge is payable before the relevant costs are incurred, no greater amount than is reasonable is so payable, and after the relevant costs have been incurred any necessary adjustment shall be made by repayment, reduction or subsequent charges or otherwise.

(5) If a person takes any proceedings in the High Court in pursuance of any of the provisions of this Act relating to service charges and he could have taken those proceedings in the county court, he shall not be entitled to recover any costs.

20 Limitation of service charges: consultation requirements

(1) Where this section applies to any qualifying works or qualifying long term agreement, the relevant contributions of tenants are limited in accordance with subsection (6) or (7) (or both) unless the consultation requirements have been either—

(a) complied with in relation to the works on agreement, or

(b) dispensed with in relation to the works or agreement by (or on appeal from) the appropriate tribunal.

(2) In this section 'relevant contribution', in relation to a tenant and any works or agreement, is the amount which he may be required under the terms of his lease to contribute (by the payment of service charges) to relevant costs incurred on carrying out the works or under the agreement.

(3) This section applies to qualifying works if relevant costs incurred on carrying out the works exceed an appropriate amount.

(4) The Secretary of State may by regulations provide that this section applies to a qualifying long term agreement—

(a) if relevant costs incurred under the agreement exceed an appropriate amount, or

(b) if relevant costs incurred under the agreement during a period prescribed by the regulations exceed an appropriate amount.

(5) An appropriate amount is an amount set by regulations made by the Secretary of State; and the regulations may make provision for either or both of the following to be an appropriate amount—

(a) an amount prescribed by, or determined in accordance with, the regulations, and

(b) an amount which results in the relevant contribution of any one or more tenants being an amount prescribed by, or determined in accordance with, the regulations.

(6) Where an appropriate amount is set by virtue of paragraph (a) of subsection (5), the amount of the relevant costs incurred on carrying out the works or under the agreement which may be taken into account in determining the relevant contributions of tenants is limited to the appropriate amount.

(7) Where an appropriate amount is set by virtue of paragraph (b) of that subsection, the amount of the relevant contribution of the tenant, or each of the tenants, whose relevant contribution would otherwise exceed the amount prescribed by, or determined in accordance with, the regulations is limited to the amount so prescribed or determined.

20ZA Consultation requirements: supplementary

(1) Where an application is made to the appropriate tribunal for a determination to dispense with all or any of the consultation requirements in relation to any qualifying works or qualifying long term agreement, the tribunal may make the determination if satisfied that it is reasonable to dispense with the requirements.

(2) In section 20 and this section—

'qualifying works' means works on a building or any other premises, and

'qualifying long term agreement' means (subject to subsection (3)) an agreement entered into, by or on behalf of the landlord or a superior landlord, for a term of more than twelve months.

(3) The Secretary of State may by regulations provide that an agreement is not a qualifying long term agreement—

(a) if it is an agreement of a description prescribed by the regulations, or

(b) in any circumstances so prescribed.

(4) In section 20 and this section 'the consultation requirements' means requirements prescribed by regulations made by the Secretary of State.

(5) Regulations under subsection (4) may in particular include provision requiring the landlord—

- (a) to provide details of proposed works or agreements to tenants or the recognised tenants' association representing them,
- (b) to obtain estimates for proposed works or agreements,
- (c) to invite tenants or the recognised tenants' association to propose the names of persons from whom the landlord should try to obtain other estimates,
- (d) to have regard to observations made by tenants or the recognised tenants' association in relation to proposed works or agreements and estimates, and
- (e) to give reasons in prescribed circumstances for carrying out works or entering into agreements.

(6) Regulations under section 20 or this section—

- (a) may make provision generally or only in relation to specific cases, and
- (b) may make different provision for different purposes.

(7) Regulations under section 20 or this section shall be made by statutory instrument which shall be subject to annulment in pursuance of a resolution of either House of Parliament.

20A Limitation of service charges: grant-aided works

(1) Where relevant costs are incurred or to be incurred on the carrying out of works in respect of which a grant has been or is to be paid under section 523 of the Housing Act 1985 (assistance for provision of separate service pipe for water supply) or any provision of Part I of the Housing Grants, Construction and Regeneration Act 1996 (grants, etc for renewal of private sector housing) or any corresponding earlier enactment or article 3 of the Regulatory Reform (Housing Assistance) (England and Wales) Order 2002 (power of local housing authorities to provide assistance), the amount of the grant shall be deducted from the costs and the amount of the service charge payable shall be reduced accordingly.

(2) In any case where—

- (a) relevant costs are incurred or to be incurred on the carrying out of works which are included in the external works specified in a group repair scheme, within the meaning of Part I of the Housing Grants, Construction and Regeneration Act 1996, and
- (b) the landlord participated or is participating in that scheme as an assisted participant,

the amount which, in relation to the landlord, is the balance of the cost determined in accordance with section 69(3) of the Housing Grants, Construction and Regeneration Act 1996 shall be deducted from the costs, and the amount of the service charge payable shall be reduced accordingly.

20B Limitation of service charges: time limit on making demands

(1) If any of the relevant costs taken into account in determining the amount of any service charge were incurred more than 18 months before a demand for payment of the service charge is served on the tenant, then (subject to subsection (2)), the tenant shall not be liable to pay so much of the service charge as reflects the costs so incurred.

(2) Subsection (1) shall not apply if, within the period of 18 months beginning with the date when the relevant costs in question were incurred, the tenant was notified in writing that those costs had been incurred and that he would subsequently be required under the terms of his lease to contribute to them by the payment of a service charge.

20C Limitation of service charges: costs of proceedings

(1) A tenant may make an application for an order that all or any of the costs incurred, or to be incurred, by the landlord in connection with proceedings before a

court, residential property tribunal or leasehold valuation tribunal or the First-tier Tribunal, or the Upper Tribunal, or in connection with arbitration proceedings, are not to be regarded as relevant costs to be taken into account in determining the amount of any service charge payable by the tenant or any other person or persons specified in the application.

(2) The application shall be made—

- (a) in the case of court proceedings, to the court before which the proceedings are taking place or, if the application is made after the proceedings are concluded, to the county court;
- (aa) in the case of proceedings before a residential property tribunal, to a leasehold valuation tribunal;
- (b) in the case of proceedings before a leasehold valuation tribunal, to the tribunal before which the proceedings are taking place or, if the application is made after the proceedings are concluded, to any leasehold valuation tribunal;
- (ba) in the case of proceedings before the First-tier Tribunal, to the tribunal;
- (c) in the case of proceedings before the Upper Tribunal, to the tribunal;
- (d) in the case of arbitration proceedings, to the arbitral tribunal or, if the application is made after the proceedings are concluded, to the county court.

(3) The court or tribunal to which the application is made may make such order on the application as it considers just and equitable in the circumstances.

21 Request for summary of relevant costs

(1) A tenant may required the landlord in writing to supply him with a written summary of the costs incurred—

- *(a) if the relevant accounts are made up for periods of twelve months, in the last such period ending not later than the date of the request, or*
- *(b) if the accounts are not so made up, in the period of twelve months ending with the date of the request,*

and which are relevant costs in relation to the service charges payable or demanded as payable in that or any other period.

(2) If the tenant is represented by a recognised tenants' association and he consents, the request may be made by the secretary of the association instead of by the tenant and may then be for the supply of the summary to the Secretary.

(3) A request is duly served on the landlord if it is served on—

- *(a) an agent of the landlord named as such in the rent book or similar document, or*
- *(b) the person who receives the rent on behalf of the landlord;*

and a person on whom a request is so served shall forward it as soon as may be to the landlord.

(4) The landlord shall comply with the request within one month of the request or within six months of the end of the period referred to in subsection (1)(a) or (b) whichever is the later.

(5) The summary shall state whether any of the costs relate to works in respect of which a grant has been or is to be paid under section 523 of the Housing Act 1985 (assistance for provision of separate service pipe for water supply) or any provision of Part I of the Housing Grants, Construction and Regeneration Act 1996 (grants, &c. for renewal of private sector housing) or any corresponding earlier enactment and set out the costs in a way showing how they have been or will be reflected in demands for service charges and, in addition, shall summarise each of the following items, namely—

- *(a) any of the costs in respect of which no demand for payment was received by the landlord within the period referred to in subsection (1)(a) or (b),*

- *(b)* *any of the costs in respect of which—*
  - *(i)* *a demand for payment was so received, but*
  - *(ii)* *no payment was made by the landlord within that period, and*
- *(c)* *any of the costs in respect of which—*
  - *(i)* *a demand for payment was so received, and*
  - *(ii)* *payment was made by the landlord within that period,*

and specify the aggregate of any amounts received by the landlord down to the end of that period on account of service charges in respect of relevant dwellings and still standing to the credit of the tenants of those dwellings at the end of that period

(5A) In subsection (5)"relevant dwelling" means a dwelling whose tenant is either—

- *(a)* *the person by or with the consent of whom the request was made, or*
- *(b)* *a person whose obligations under the terms of his lease as regards contributing to relevant costs relate to the same costs as the corresponding obligations of the person mentioned in paragraph (a) above relate to.*

(5B) The summary shall state whether any of the costs relate to works which are included in the external works specified in a group repair scheme, within the meaning of Chapter II of Part I of the Housing Grants, Construction and Regeneration Act 1996 or any corresponding earlier enactment,, in which the landlord participated or is participating as an assisted participant.

(6) If the service charges in relation to which the costs are relevant costs as mentioned in subsection (1) are payable by the tenants of more than four dwellings, the summary shall be certified by a qualified accountant as—

- *(a)* *in his opinion a fair summary complying with the requirements of subsection (5), and*
- *(b)* *being sufficiently supported by accounts, receipts and other documents which have been produced to him.*

[21 Service charge information

(1) The appropriate national authority may make regulations about the provision, by landlords of dwellings to each tenant by whom service charges are payable, of information about service charges.

(2) The regulations must, subject to any exceptions provided for in the regulations, require the landlord to provide information about—

- (a) the service charges of the tenant,
- (b) any associated service charges, and
- (c) relevant costs relating to service charges falling within paragraph (a) or (b).

(3) The regulations must, subject to any exceptions provided for in the regulations, require the landlord to provide the tenant with a report by a qualified person on information which the landlord is required to provide by virtue of this section.

(4) The regulations may make provision about—

- (a) information to be provided by virtue of subsection (2),
- (b) other information to be provided (whether in pursuance of a requirement or otherwise),
- (c) reports of the kind mentioned in subsection (3),
- (d) the period or periods in relation to which information or reports are to be provided,
- (e) the times at or by which information or reports are to be provided,
- (f) the form and manner in which information or reports are to be provided (including in particular whether information is to be contained in a statement of account),
- (g) the descriptions of persons who are to be qualified persons for the purposes of subsection (3).

(5) Subsections (2) to (4) do not limit the scope of the power conferred by subsection (1).

(6) Regulations under this section may—

(a) make different provision for different cases or descriptions of case or for different purposes,

(b) contain such supplementary, incidental, consequential, transitional, transitory or saving provision as the appropriate national authority considers appropriate.

(7) Regulations under this section are to be made by statutory instrument which, subject to subsections (8) and (9)—

(a) in the case of regulations made by the Secretary of State, is to be subject to annulment in pursuance of a resolution of either House of Parliament, and

(b) in the case of regulations made by the Welsh Ministers, is to be subject to annulment in pursuance of a resolution of the National Assembly for Wales.

(8) The Secretary of State may not make a statutory instrument containing the first regulations made by the Secretary of State under this section unless a draft of the instrument has been laid before, and approved by a resolution of, each House of Parliament.

(9) The Welsh Ministers may not make a statutory instrument containing the first regulations made by the Welsh Ministers under this section unless a draft of the instrument has been laid before, and approved by a resolution of, the National Assembly for Wales.

(10) In this section—

'the appropriate national authority'—

(a) in relation to England, means the Secretary of State, and

(b) in relation to Wales, means the Welsh Ministers,

'associated service charges', in relation to a tenant by whom a contribution to relevant costs is payable as a service charge, means service charges of other tenants so far as relating to the same costs.]

[21A Withholding of service charges

(1) A tenant may withhold payment of a service charge if—

(a) the landlord has not supplied a document to him by the time by which he is required to supply it under section 21, or

(b) the form or content of a document which the landlord has supplied to him under that section (at any time) does not conform exactly or substantially with the requirements prescribed by regulations under subsection (4) of that section.

(2) The maximum amount which the tenant may withhold is an amount equal to the aggregate of—

(a) the service charges paid by him in the accounting period to which the document concerned would or does relate, and

(b) so much of the aggregate amount required to be dealt with in the statement of account for that accounting period by section 21(1)(c)(i) as stood to his credit.

(3) An amount may not be withheld under this section—

(a) in a case within paragraph (a) of subsection (1), after the document concerned has been supplied to the tenant by the landlord, or

(b) in a case within paragraph (b) of that subsection, after a document conforming exactly or substantially with the requirements prescribed by regulations under section 21(4) has been supplied to the tenant by the landlord by way of replacement of the one previously supplied.

(4) If, on an application made by the landlord to the appropriate tribunal, the tribunal determines that the landlord has a reasonable excuse for a failure giving rise to the right of a tenant to withhold an amount under this section, the tenant may not withhold the amount after the determination is made.

(5) Where a tenant withholds a service charge under this section, any provisions of the tenancy relating to non-payment or late payment of service charges do not have effect in relation to the period for which he so withholds it.]

21B Notice to accompany demands for service charges

(1) A demand for the payment of a service charge must be accompanied by a summary of the rights and obligations of tenants of dwellings in relation to service charges.

(2) The Secretary of State may make regulations prescribing requirements as to the form and content of such summaries of rights and obligations.

(3) A tenant may withhold payment of a service charge which has been demanded from him if subsection (1) is not complied with in relation to the demand.

(4) Where a tenant withholds a service charge under this section, any provisions of the lease relating to non-payment or late payment of service charges do not have effect in relation to the period for which he so withholds it.

(5) Regulations under subsection (2) may make different provision for different purposes.

(6) Regulations under subsection (2) shall be made by statutory instrument which shall be subject to annulment in pursuance of a resolution of either House of Parliament.

22 Request to inspect supporting accounts, etc

(1) This section applies where a tenant, or the secretary of a recognised tenants' association, has obtained such a summary as is referred to in section 21(1) (summary of relevant costs), whether in pursuance of that section or otherwise.

(2) The tenant, or the secretary with the consent of the tenant, may within six months of obtaining the summary require the landlord in writing to afford him reasonable facilities—

- *(a) for inspecting the accounts, receipts and other documents supporting the summary, and*
- *(b) for taking copies or extracts from them.*

(3) A request under this section is duly served on the landlord if it is served on—

- *(a) an agent of the landlord named as such in the rent book or similar document, or*
- *(b) the person who receives the rent on behalf of the landlord;*

and a person on whom a request is so served shall forward it as soon as may be to the landlord.

(4) The landlord shall make such facilities available to the tenant or secretary for a period of two months beginning not later than one month after the request is made.

(5) The landlord shall—

- *(a) where such facilities are for the inspection of any documents, make them so available free of charge;*
- *(b) where such facilities are for the taking of copies or extracts, be entitled to make them so available on payment of such reasonable charge as he may determine.*

(6) The requirement imposed on the landlord by subsection (5)(a) to make any facilities available to a person free of charge shall not be construed as precluding the landlord from treating as part of his costs of management any costs incurred by him in connection with making those facilities so available.

[22 Inspection, etc of documents

(1) A tenant may by notice in writing require the landlord—

(a) to afford him reasonable facilities for inspecting accounts, receipts or other documents relevant to *the matters which must be dealt with in a statement of account required to be supplied to him under*[information required to be provided to him by virtue of] section 21 and for taking copies of or extracts from them, or

(b) to take copies of or extracts from any such accounts, receipts or other documents and either send them to him or afford him reasonable facilities for collecting them (as he specifies).

(2) If the tenant is represented by a recognised tenants' association and he consents, the notice may be served by the secretary of the association instead of by the tenant (and in that case any requirement imposed by it is to afford reasonable facilities, or to send copies or extracts, to the secretary).

(3) A notice under this section may not be served after the end of the period of six months beginning with the date by which the tenant is required to be *supplied with the statement of account under*[provided with the information concerned by virtue of] section 21.

(4) But if—

(a) the *statement of account*[information] is not *supplied*[provided] to the tenant on or before that date, or

(b) the *statement of account*[information] so *supplied*[provided] does not conform exactly or substantially with the requirements prescribed by regulations under section *21(4)*[21],

the six month period mentioned in subsection (3) does not begin until any later date on which the *statement of account*[information] (conforming exactly or substantially with those requirements) is *supplied*[provided] to him.

(5) A notice under this section is duly served on the landlord if it is served on—

(a) an agent of the landlord named as such in the rent book or similar document, or

(b) the person who receives the rent on behalf of the landlord;

and a person on whom such a notice is so served must forward it as soon as may be to the landlord.

(6) The landlord must comply with a requirement imposed by a notice under this section within the period of twenty-one days beginning with the day on which he receives the notice.

(7) To the extent that a notice under this section requires the landlord to afford facilities for inspecting documents—

(a) he must do so free of charge, but

(b) he may treat as part of his costs of management any costs incurred by him in doing so.

(8) The landlord may make a reasonable charge for doing anything else in compliance with a requirement imposed by a notice under this section.]

23 Request relating to information held by superior landlord

(1) If a request under section 21 (request for summary of relevant costs) relates in whole or in part to relevant costs incurred by or on behalf of a superior landlord, and the landlord to whom the request is made is not in possession of the relevant information—

(a) he shall in turn make a written request for the relevant information to the person who is his landlord (and so on, if that person is not himself the superior landlord),

(b) the superior landlord shall comply with that request within a reasonable time, and

(c) *the immediate landlord shall then comply with the tenant's or secretary's request, or that part of it which relates to the relevant costs incurred by or on behalf of the superior landlord, within the time allowed by section 21 or such further time, if any, as is reasonable in the circumstances.*

(2) If a request under section 22 (request for facilities to inspect supporting accounts, etc) relates to a summary of costs incurred by or on behalf of a superior landlord—

(a) *the landlord to whom the request is made shall forthwith inform the tenant or secretary of that fact and of the name and address of the superior landlord, and*

(b) *section 22 shall then apply to the superior landlord as it applies to the immediate landlord.*

[23 Information held by superior landlord

(1) *If a statement of account which the landlord is required to supply under*[information which the landlord is required to provide by virtue of] section 21 relates to matters concerning a superior landlord and the landlord is not in possession of the relevant information [which relates to those matters]—

(a) he may by notice in writing require the person who is his landlord to give him the relevant information (and so on, if that person is not himself the superior landlord), and

(b) the superior landlord must comply with the requirement within a reasonable time.

(2) If a notice under section 22 imposes a requirement in relation to documents held by a superior landlord—

(a) the landlord shall immediately inform the tenant or secretary of that fact and of the name and address of the superior landlord, and

(b) section 22 then applies in relation to the superior landlord (as in relation to the landlord).]

[23A Effect of change of landlord

(1) This section applies where, at a time when a duty imposed on the landlord or a superior landlord by or by virtue of any of sections 21 to 23 remains to be discharged by him, he disposes of the whole or part of his interest as landlord or superior landlord to another person.

(2) If the landlord or superior landlord is, despite the disposal, still in a position to discharge the duty to any extent, he remains responsible for discharging it to that extent.

(3) If the other person is in a position to discharge the duty to any extent, he is responsible for discharging it to that extent.

(4) Where the other person is responsible for discharging the duty to any extent (whether or not the landlord or superior landlord is also responsible for discharging it to that or any other extent)—

(a) references to the landlord or superior landlord in sections 21 to 23[and any regulations under section 21] are to, or include, the other person so far as is appropriate to reflect his responsibility for discharging the duty to that extent, but

(b) in connection with its discharge by the other person, section 22(6) applies as if the reference to the day on which the landlord receives the notice were to the date of the disposal referred to in subsection (1)[; and

(c) any regulations under section 21 apply subject to any modifications contained in the regulations].]

24 Effect of assignment on request

The assignment of a tenancy does not affect the validity of a request made under section 21, 22 or 23 before the assignment; but a person is not obliged to provide a summary or make facilities available more than once for the same dwelling and for the same period.

[24 Effect of assignment

The assignment of a tenancy does not affect any duty imposed by or by virtue of any of sections 21 to 23A; but a person is not required to comply with more than a reasonable number of requirements imposed by any one person.]

25 Failure to comply with ss 21, 22 or 23 an offence

(1) It is a summary offence for a person to fail, without reasonable excuse, to perform a duty imposed on him *by section 21, 22 or 23* [by or by virtue of any of sections 21 to 23A].

(2) A person committing such an offence is liable on conviction to a fine not exceeding level 4 on the standard scale.

[(3) Subsection (1) does not apply where the person is-

(a) a local authority for an area in Wales, or

(b) a registered social landlord.][1]

1 Applicable only in Wales.

26 Exception: tenants of certain public authorities

(1) Sections 18 to 25 (limitation on service charges *and requests for information about costs* [, *statements of account* [service charge information, reports on such information] and inspection etc of documents]) do not apply to a service charge payable by a tenant of—

a local authority,

a National Park authority, or

a new town corporation,

unless the tenancy is a long tenancy, in which case sections 18 to 24 apply but section 25 (offence of failure to comply) does not.

(2) The following are long tenancies for the purposes of subsection (1), subject to subsection (3)—

(a) a tenancy granted for a term certain exceeding 21 years, whether or not it is (or may become) terminable before the end of that term by notice given by the tenant or by re-entry or forfeiture;

(b) a tenancy for a term fixed by law under a grant with a covenant or obligation for perpetual renewal, other than a tenancy by sub-demise from one which is not a long tenancy;

(c) any tenancy granted in pursuance of Part V of the Housing Act 1985 (the right to buy), including any tenancy granted in pursuance of that Part as it has effect by virtue of section 17 of the Housing Act 1996 (the right to acquire).

(3) A tenancy granted so as to become terminable by notice after a death is not a long tenancy for the purposes of subsection (1), unless—

(a) it is granted by a housing association which at the time of the grant is[a private registered provider of social housing or] a registered social landlord,

(b) it is granted at a premium calculated by reference to a percentage of the value of the dwelling-house or the cost of providing it, and

(c) at the time it is granted it complies with the requirements of the regulations then in force under section 140(4)(b) of the Housing Act 1980 or paragraph 4(2)(b) of Schedule 4A to the Leasehold Reform Act

1967 (conditions for exclusion of shared ownership leases from Part I of the Leasehold Reform Act 1967) or, in the case of a tenancy granted before any such regulations were brought into force, with the first such regulations to be in force.

27 Exception: rent registered and not entered as variable

Sections 18 and 25 (limitation on service charges *and requests for information about costs* [, *statements of account*[service charge information, reports on such information] and inspection etc of documents]) do not apply to a service charge payable by the tenant of a dwelling the rent of which is registered under Part IV of the Rent Act 1977, unless the amount registered is, in pursuance of section 71(4) of that Act, entered as a variable amount.

27A Liability to pay service charges: jurisdiction

(1) An application may be made to a leasehold valuation tribunal for a determination whether a service charge is payable and, if it is, as to—

- (a) the person by whom it is payable,
- (b) the person to whom it is payable,
- (c) the amount which is payable,
- (d) the date at or by which it is payable, and
- (e) the manner in which it is payable.

(2) Subsection (1) applies whether or not any payment has been made.

(3) An application may also be made to a leasehold valuation tribunal for a determination whether, if costs were incurred for services, repairs, maintenance, improvements, insurance or management of any specified description, a service charge would be payable for the costs and, if it would, as to—

- (a) the person by whom it would be payable,
- (b) the person to whom it would be payable,
- (c) the amount which would be payable,
- (d) the date at or by which it would be payable, and
- (e) the manner in which it would be payable.

(4) application under subsection (1) or (3) may be made in respect of a matter which—

- (a) has been agreed or admitted by the tenant,
- (b) has been, or is to be, referred to arbitration pursuant to a post-dispute arbitration agreement to which the tenant is a party,
- (c) has been the subject of determination by a court, or
- (d) has been the subject of determination by an arbitral tribunal pursuant to a post-dispute arbitration agreement.

(5) But the tenant is not to be taken to have agreed or admitted any matter by reason only of having made any payment.

(6) An agreement by the tenant of a dwelling (other than a post-dispute arbitration agreement) is void in so far as it purports to provide for a determination—

- (a) in a particular manner, or
- (b) on particular evidence,

of any question which may be the subject of an application under subsection (1) or (3).

(7) The jurisdiction conferred on the appropriate tribunal in respect of any matter by virtue of this section is in addition to any jurisdiction of a court in respect of the matter.

28 Meaning of 'qualified accountant'

(1) The reference to a 'qualified accountant' in section 21(6) (certification of summary of information about relevant costs) [section 21(3)(a) (certification of

statements of account)] is to a person who, in accordance with the following provisions, has the necessary qualification and is not disqualified from acting.

(2) A person has the necessary qualification if he is eligible for appointment as a [statutory auditor under Part 42 of the Companies Act 2006..

(4) The following are disqualified from acting—

- (b) an officer, employee or partner of the landlord or, where the landlord is a company, of an associated company;
- (c) a person who is a partner or employee of any such officer or employee;
- (d) an agent of the landlord who is a managing agent for any premises to which any of the costs covered by the summary in question relate [the statement of account in question relates];
- (e) an employee or partner of any such agent.

(5) For the purposes of subsection (4)(b) a company is associated with a landlord company if it is (within the meaning of section 1159 of the Companies Act 2006) the landlord's holding company, a subsidiary of the landlord or another subsidiary of the landlord's holding company.

(5A) For the purposes of subsection (4)(d) a person is a managing agent for any premises to which any costs relate [any statement of account relates] if he has been appointed to discharge any of the landlord's obligations relating to the management by him of the premises and owed to the tenants who may be required under the terms of their leases to contribute to those costs [costs covered by the statement of account] by the payment of service charges.

(6) Where the landlord is [an emanation of the Crown,] a local authority, National Park authority or a new town corporation—

- (a) the persons who have the necessary qualification include members of the Chartered Institute of Public Finance and Accountancy, and
- (b) subsection (4)(b) (disqualification of officers and employees of landlord) does not apply.

29 Meaning of 'recognised tenants' association'

(1) A recognised tenants' association is an association of qualifying tenants (whether with or without other tenants) which is recognised for the purposes of the provisions of this Act relating to service charges either—

- (a) by notice in writing given by the landlord to the secretary of the association, or
- (b) by a certificate-
  - (i) in relation to dwellings in England, of the First-tier Tribunal; and
  - (ii) in relation to dwellings in Wales, a a member of the local rent assessment committee panel.

(2) A notice given under subsection (1)(a) may be withdrawn by the landlord by notice in writing given to the secretary of the association not less than six months before the date on which it is to be withdrawn.

(3) A certificate given under subsection (1)(b)(i) may be cancelled by the First-tier Tribunal and a certificate given under subsection (1)(b)(ii) may be cancelled any member of the local rent assessment committee panel.

(4) In this section the 'local rent assessment committee panel' means the persons appointed by the Lord Chancellor under the Rent Act 1977 to the panel of persons to act as members of a rent assessment committee for the registration area in Wales in which the dwellings let to the qualifying tenants are situated, and for the purposes of this section a number of tenants are qualifying tenants if each of them may be required under the terms of his lease to contribute to the same costs by the payment of a service charge.

(5) The Secretary of State may by regulations specify—

(a) the procedure which is to be followed in connection with an application for, or for the cancellation of, a certificate under subsection (1)(b)(ii);

(b) the matters to which regard is to be had in giving or cancelling a certificate under subsection (1)(b);

(c) the duration of such a certificate; and

(d) any circumstances in which a certificate is not to be given under subsection (1)(b).

(6) Regulations under subsection (5)—

(a) may make different provisions with respect to different cases or descriptions of case, including different provision for different areas, and

(b) shall be made by statutory instrument which shall be subject to annulment in pursuance of a resolution of either House of Parliament.

29A Tenants' associations: power to request information about tenants

(1) The Secretary of State may by regulations impose duties on a landlord to provide the secretary of a relevant tenants' association with information about relevant qualifying tenants.

(2) The regulations may—

(a) make provision about the tenants about whom information must be provided and what information must be provided;

(b) require a landlord to seek the consent of a tenant to the provision of information about that tenant;

(c) require a landlord to identify how many tenants have not consented.

(3) The regulations may—

(a) authorise a landlord to charge costs specified in or determined in accordance with the regulations;

(b) impose time limits on a landlord for the taking of any steps under the regulations;

(c) make provision about the form or content of any notices under the regulations (including provision permitting or requiring a person to design the form of a notice);

(d) make other provision as to the procedure in connection with anything authorised or required by the regulations.

(4) The regulations may confer power on a court or tribunal to make an order remedying a failure by a landlord to comply with the regulations.

(5) The regulations may include supplementary, incidental, transitional or saving provision.

(6) Regulations under this section are to be made by statutory instrument.

(7) A statutory instrument containing regulations under this section is subject to annulment in pursuance of a resolution of either House of Parliament.

(8) In this section—

"relevant tenants' association", in relation to a landlord, means an association of tenants of the landlord at least one of whom is a qualifying tenant of a dwelling in England;

"relevant qualifying tenant" means—

(a) a person who is a qualifying tenant of a dwelling in England and a member of the relevant tenants' association, or

(b) a person who is a qualifying tenant of a dwelling in England by virtue of being required to contribute to the same costs as a qualifying tenant who is a member of the relevant tenants' association;

"qualifying tenant" means a tenant who, under the terms of the lease, is required to contribute to the same costs as another tenant by the payment of a service charge.

30 Meaning of 'flat', 'landlord' and 'tenant'

In the provisions of this Act relating to service charges—

'landlord' includes any person who has a right to enforce payment of a service charge;

'tenant' includes:

(a) a statutory tenant, and

(b) where the dwelling or part of it is sub-let, the sub-tenant.

INSURANCE

30A Rights of tenants with respect to insurance

The Schedule to this Act (which confers on tenants certain rights with respect to the insurance of their dwellings) shall have effect.

MANAGING AGENTS

30B Recognised tenants' associations to be consulted about managing agents

(1) A recognised tenants' association may at any time serve a notice on the landlord requesting him to consult the association in accordance with this section on matters relating to the appointment or employment by him of a managing agent for any relevant premises.

(2) Where, at the time when any such notice is served by a recognised tenants' association, the landlord does not employ any managing agent for any relevant premises, the landlord shall, before appointing such a managing agent, serve on the association a notice specifying—

(a) the name of the proposed managing agent;

(b) the landlord's obligations to the tenants represented by the association which it is proposed that the managing agent should be required to discharge on his behalf; and

(c) a period of not less than one month beginning with the date of service of the notice within which the association may make observations on the proposed appointment.

(3) Where, at the time when a notice is served under subsection (1) by a recognised tenants' association, the landlord employs a managing agent for any relevant premises, the landlord shall, within the period of one month beginning with the date of service of that notice serve on the association a notice specifying—

(a) the landlord's obligations to the tenants represented by the association which the managing agent is required to discharge on his behalf; and

(b) a reasonable period within which the association may make observations on the manner in which the managing agent has been discharging those obligations, and on the desirability of his continuing to discharge them.

(4) Subject to subsection (5), a landlord who has been served with a notice by an association under subsection (1) shall, so long as he employs a managing agent for any relevant premises—

(a) serve on that association at least once in every five years a notice specifying—

(i) any change occurring since the date of the last notice served by him on the association under this section in the obligations which the managing agent has been required to discharge on his behalf; and

(ii) a reasonable period within which the association may make observations on the manner in which the managing agent has discharged those obligations since that date, and on the desirability of his continuing to discharge them;

(b) serve on that association, whenever he proposes to appoint a new managing agent for any relevant premises, a notice specifying the matters mentioned in paragraphs (a) to (c) of subsection (2).

(5) A landlord shall not, by virtue of a notice served by an association under subsection (1), be required to serve on the association a notice under subsection (4)(a) or (b) if the association subsequently serves on the landlord a notice withdrawing its request under subsection (1) to be consulted by him.

(6) Where—

(a) a recognised tenants' association has served a notice under subsection (1) with respect to any relevant premises, and

(b) the interest of the landlord in those premises becomes vested in a new landlord,

that notice shall cease to have effect with respect to those premises (without prejudice to the service by the association on the new landlord of a fresh notice under that subsection with respect to those premises).

(7) Any notice served by a landlord under this section shall specify the name and the address in the United Kingdom of the person to whom any observations made in pursuance of the notice are to be sent; and the landlord shall have regard to any such observations that are received by that person within the period specified in the notice.

(8) In this section—

'landlord', in relation to a recognised tenants' association, means the immediate landlord of the tenants represented by the association or a person who has a right to enforce payment of service charges payable by any of those tenants;

'managing agent', in relation to any relevant premises, means an agent of the landlord appointed to discharge any of the landlord's obligations to the tenants represented by the recognised tenants' association in question which relate to the management by him of those premises; and

'tenant' includes a statutory tenant;

and for the purposes of this section any premises (whether a building or not) are relevant premises in relation to a recognised tenants' association if any of the tenants represented by the association may be required under the terms of their leases to contribute by the payment of service charges to costs relating to those premises.

31 Reserve power to limit rents

(1) The Secretary of State may by order provide for—

(a) restricting or preventing increases of rent for dwellings which would otherwise take place, or

(b) restricting the amount of rent which would otherwise be payable on new lettings of dwellings;

and may so provide either generally or in relation to any specified description of dwelling.

(2) An order may contain supplementary or incidental provisions, including provisions excluding, adapting or modifying any provision made by or under an enactment (whenever passed) relating to rent or the recovery of overpaid rent.

(3) In this section—

'new letting' includes any grant of a tenancy, whether or not the premises were previously let, and any grant of a licence;

'rent' includes a sum payable under a licence, but does not include a sum attributable to rates or council tax or, in the case of dwellings of local authorities, National Park authorities or new town corporations, to the use of furniture, or the provision of services;

and for the purposes of this section an increase in rent takes place at the beginning of the rental period for which the increased rent is payable.

(4) An order under this section shall be made by statutory instrument which shall be subject to annulment in pursuance of a resolution of either House of Parliament.

SUPPLEMENTARY PROVISIONS

32 Provisions not applying to tenancies within Part II of the Landlord and Tenant Act 1954

(1) The following provisions do not apply to a tenancy to which Part II of the Landlord and Tenant Act 1954 (business tenancies) applies—

sections 1 to 3A (information to be given to tenant),

section 17 (specific performance of landlord's repairing obligations).

(2) Section 11 (repairing obligations) does not apply to a new lease granted to an existing tenant, or to a former tenant still in possession, if the new lease is a tenancy to which Part II of the Landlord and Tenant Act 1954 applies and the previous lease either is such a tenancy or would be but for section 28 of that Act (tenancy not within Part II if renewal agreed between the parties).

In this subsection 'existing tenant', 'former tenant still in possession' and 'previous lease' have the same meaning as in section 14(2).

(3) Section 31 (reserve power to limit rents) does not apply to a dwelling forming part of a property subject to a tenancy to which Part II of the Landlord and Tenant Act 1954 applies; but without prejudice to the application of that section in relation to a sub-tenancy of a part of the premises comprised in such a tenancy.

33 Liability of directors, etc for offences by body corporate

(1) Where an offence under this Act which has been committed by a body corporate is proved—

(a) to have been committed with the consent or connivance of a director, manager, secretary or other similar officer of the body corporate, or a person purporting to act in any such capacity, or

(b) to be attributable to any neglect on the part of such an officer or person,

he, as well as the body corporate, is guilty of an offence and liable to be proceeded against and punished accordingly.

(2) Where the affairs of a body corporate are managed by its members, subsection (1) applies in relation to the acts and defaults of a member in connection with his functions of management as if he were a director of the body corporate.

. . .

36 Meaning of 'lease' and 'tenancy' and related expressions

(1) In this Act 'lease' and 'tenancy' have the same meaning.

(2) Both expressions include—

(a) a sub-lease or sub-tenancy, and

(b) an agreement for a lease or tenancy (or sub-lease or sub-tenancy).

(3) The expressions 'lessor' and 'lessee' and 'landlord' and 'tenant', and references to letting, to the grant of a lease or to covenants or terms, shall be construed accordingly.

37 Meaning of 'statutory tenant' and related expressions

In this Act—

(a) 'statutory tenancy' and 'statutory tenant' mean a statutory tenancy or statutory tenant within the meaning of the Rent Act 1977 or the Rent (Agriculture) Act 1976; and

(b) 'landlord', in relation to a statutory tenant, means the person who, apart from the statutory tenancy, would be entitled to possession of the premises.

38 Minor definitions

In this Act—

'address' means a person's place of abode or place of business or, in the case of a company, its registered office;

'appropriate tribunal' means—

(a) in relation to a dwelling in England the First-tier Tribunal or, where determined by or under Tribunal Procedure Rules, the Upper Tribunal; and

(b) in relation to a dwelling in Wales, a leasehold valuation tribunal;

'arbitration agreement', 'arbitration proceedings' and 'arbitral tribunal' have the same meaning as in Part I of the Arbitration Act 1996 and 'post-dispute arbitration agreement', in relation to any matter, means an arbitration agreement made after a dispute about the matter has arisen;

'co-operative housing association' has the same meaning as in the Housing Associations Act 1985;

'dwelling' means a building or part of a building occupied or intended to be occupied as a separate dwelling, together with any yard, garden, outhouses and appurtenances belonging to it or usually enjoyed with it;

'housing association' has the same meaning as in the Housing Associations Act 1985;

'local authority' means a district, county, county borough or London borough council, the Common Council of the City of London or the Council of the Isles of Scilly and in sections 14(4), 26(1) and 28(6) includes the Broads Authority, a police and crime commissioner, the Mayor's Office for Policing and Crime, , a joint authority established by Part IV of the Local Government Act 1985, an economic prosperity board established under section 88 of the Local Democracy, Economic Development and Construction Act 2009, a combined authority established under section 103 of that Act, a fire and rescue authority created by an order under section 4A of the Fire and Rescue Services Act 2004 and the London Fire Commissioner;

'local housing authority' has the meaning given by section 1 of the Housing Act 1985;

'new town corporation' means—

(a) a development corporation established by an order made, or treated as made, under the New Towns Act 1981, or

(b) the Homes and Communities Agency so far as exercising functions in relation to anything transferred (or to be transferred) to it as mentioned in section 52(1)(a) to (d) of the Housing and Regeneration Act 2008, or

(c) the Welsh Ministers so far as exercising functions in relation to anything transferred (or to be transferred) to them as mentioned in section 36(1)(a)(i) to (iii) of the New Towns Act 1981;

'protected tenancy' has the same meaning as in the Rent Act 1977;

'registered social landlord' has the same meaning as in the Housing Act 1985 (see section 5(4) and (5) of that Act);

'restricted contract' has the same meanng as in the Rent Act 1977;

'urban development corporation' has the same meaning as in Part XVI of the Local Government, Planning and Land Act 1980.

39 Index of defined expressions

The following Table shows provisions defining or otherwise explaining expressions used in this Act (other than provisions defining or explaining an expression in the same section):

Address	section 38
arbitration agreement, arbitration proceedings, arbitral tribunal and post-dispute arbitration agreement	section 38
co-operative housing association	section 38
Dwelling	section 38
dwelling-house (in the provisions relating to repairing obligations)	section 16
fit for human habitation	section 10
housing association	section 38
landlord— (generally)	section 36(3)
(in sections 1 and 2)	section 1(3)
(in the provisions relating to rent books)	section 4(3)
(in the provisions relating to service charges)	section 30
(in relation to a statutory tenancy)	section 37(b)
lease, lessee and lessor— (generally)	section 36
(in the provisions relating to repairing obligations)	section 16
local authority	section 38
local housing authority	section 38
new town corporation	section 38
protected tenancy	section 38
qualified accountant (for the purposes of section *21(6)* [21(3)(a)]	section 28
registered social landlord	section 38
recognised tenants' association	section 29
relevant costs (in relation to a service charge)	section 18(2)
restricted contract	section 38
service charge	section 18(1)
statutory tenant	section 37(a)
tenancy and tenant— (generally)	section 36
(in sections 1 and 2)	section 1(3)
(in the provisions relating to rent books)	section 4(3)
(in the provisions relating to service charges)	section 30
urban development corporation	section 38

40 Short title, commencement and extent

(1) This Act may be cited as the Landlord and Tenant Act 1985.

(2) This Act comes into force on 1st April 1986.

(3) This Act extends to England and Wales.

SCHEDULE

RIGHTS OF TENANTS WITH RESPECT TO INSURANCE

Section 30A

1 Construction

In this Schedule—

'landlord', in relation to a tenant by whom a service charge is payable which includes an amount payable directly or indirectly for insurance, includes any person who has a right to enforce payment of that service charge;
'relevant policy', in relation to a dwelling, means any policy of insurance under which the dwelling is insured (being, in the case of a flat, a policy covering the building containing it); and
'tenant' includes a statutory tenant.

2 Summary of insurance cover

(1) Where a service charge is payable by the tenant of a dwelling which consists of or includes an amount payable directly or indirectly for insurance, the tenant may by notice in writing require the landlord to supply by him with a written summary of the insurance for the time being effected in relation to the dwelling.

(2) If the tenant is represented by a recognised tenants' association and he consents, the notice may be served by the secretary of the association instead of by the tenant and may then be for the supply of the summary to the secretary.

(3) A notice under this paragraph is duly served on the landlord if it is served on—

(a) an agent of the landlord named as such in the rent book or similar document, or

(b) the person who receives the rent on behalf of the landlord;

and a person on whom such a notice is so served shall forward it as soon as may be to the landlord.

(4) The landlord shall, within the period of twenty-one days beginning with the day on which he receives the notice, comply with it by supplying to the tenant or the secretary of the recognised tenants' association (as the case may require) such a summary as is mentioned in sub-paragraph (1), which shall include—

(a) the insured amount or amounts under any relevant policy, and

(b) the name of the insurer under any such policy, and

(c) the risks in respect of which the dwelling or (as the case may be) the building containing it is insured under any such policy.

(5) In sub-paragraph (4)(a) 'the insured amount or amounts', in relation to a relevant policy, means—

(a) in the case of a dwelling other than a flat, the amount for which the dwelling is insured under the policy; and

(b) in the case of a flat, the amount for which the building containing it is insured under the policy and, if specified in the policy, the amount for which the flat is insured under it.

(6) The landlord shall be taken to have complied with the notice if, within the period mentioned in sub-paragraph (4), he instead supplies to the tenant or the secretary (as the case may require) a copy of every relevant policy.

(7) In a case where two or more buildings are insured under any relevant policy, the summary or copy supplied under sub-paragraph (4) or (6) so far as relating to that policy need only be of such parts of the policy as relate—

(a) to the dwelling, and

(b) if the dwelling is a flat, to the building containing it.

3 Inspection of insurance policy, etc

(1) Where a service charge is payable by the tenant of a dwelling which consists of or includes an amount payable directly or indirectly for insurance, the tenant may by notice in writing require the landlord—

(a) to afford him reasonable facilities for inspecting any relevant policy or associated documents and for taking copies of or extracts from them, or

(b) to take copies of or extracts from any such policy or documents and either send them to him or afford him reasonable facilities for collecting them (as he specifies).

(2) If the tenant is represented by a recognised tenants' association and he consents, the notice may be served by the secretary of the association instead of by the tenant (and in that case any requirement imposed by it is to afford reasonable facilities, or to send copies or extracts, to the secretary).

(3) A notice under this paragraph is duly served on the landlord if it is served on—

(a) an agent of the landlord named as such in the rent book or similar document, or

(b) the person who receives the rent on behalf of the landlord;

and a person on whom such a notice is so served shall forward it as soon as may be to the landlord.

(4) The landlord shall comply with a requirement imposed by a notice under this paragraph within the period of twenty-one days beginning with the day on which he receives the notice.

(5) To the extent that a notice under this paragraph requires the landlord to afford facilities for inspecting documents—

(a) he shall do so free of charge, but

(b) he may treat as part of his costs of management any costs incurred by him in doing so.

(6) The landlord may make a reasonable charge for doing anything else in compliance with a requirement imposed by a notice under this paragraph.

(7) In this paragraph—

'relevant policy' includes a policy of insurance under which the dwelling was insured for the period of insurance immediately preceding that current when the notice is served (being, in the case of a flat, a policy covering the building containing it), and

'associated documents' means accounts, receipts or other documents which provide evidence of payment of any premiums due under a relevant policy in respect of the period of insurance which is current when the notice is served or the period of insurance immediately preceding that period.

4 Insurance effected by superior landlord

(1) If a notice is served under paragraph 2 in a case where a superior landlord has effected, in whole or in part, the insurance of the dwelling in question and the landlord on whom the notice is served is not in possession of the relevant information—

(a) he shall in turn by notice in writing require the person who is his landlord to give him the relevant information (and so on, if that person is not himself the superior landlord),

(b) the superior landlord shall comply with the notice within a reasonable time, and

(c) the immediate landlord shall then comply with the tenant's or secretary's notice in the manner provided by sub-paragraphs (4) to (7) of paragraph 2 within the time allowed by that paragraph or such further time, if any, as is reasonable in the circumstances.

(2) If, in a case where a superior landlord has effected, in whole or in part, the insurance of the dwelling in question, notice under paragraph 3 imposes a requirement relating to any policy of insurance effected by the superior landlord—

(a) the landlord on whom the notice is served shall forthwith inform the tenant or secretary of that fact and of the name and address of the superior landlord, and

(b) that paragraph shall then apply to the superior landlord in relation to that policy as it applies to the immediate landlord.

4A Effect of change of landlord

(1) This paragraph applies where, at a time when a duty imposed on the landlord or a superior landlord by virtue of any of paragraphs 2 to 4 remains to be discharged by him, he disposes of the whole or part of his interest as landlord or superior landlord).

(2) If the landlord or superior landlord is, despite the disposal, still in a position to discharge the duty to any extent, he remains responsible for discharging it to that extent.

(3) If the other person is in a position to discharge the duty to any extent, he is responsible for discharging it to that extent.

(4) Where the other person is responsible for discharging the duty to any extent (whether or not the landlord or superior landlord is also responsible for discharging it to that or any other extent)—

- (a) references to the landlord or superior landlord in paragraphs 2 to 4 are to, or include, the other person so far as is appropriate to reflect his responsibility for discharging the duty to that extent, but
- (b) in connection with its discharge by that person, paragraphs 2(4) and 3(4) apply as if the reference to the day on which the landlord receives the notice were to the date of the disposal referred to in sub-paragraph (1).

5 Effect of assignment

The assignment of a tenancy does not affect any duty imposed by virtue of any of paragraphs 2 to 4A; but a person is not required to comply with more than a reasonable number of requirements imposed by any one person.

6 Offence of failure to comply

(1) It is a summary offence for a person to fail, without reasonable excuse, to perform a duty imposed on him by or by virtue of any of paragraphs 2 to 4A.

(2) A person committing such an offence is liable on conviction to a fine not exceeding level 4 on the standard scale.

7 Tenant's right to notify insurers of possible claim

(1) This paragraph applies to any dwelling in respect of which the tenant pays to the landlord a service charge consisting of or including an amount payable directly or indirectly for insurance.

(2) Where—

- (a) it appears to the tenant of any such dwelling that damage has been caused—
  - (i) to the dwelling, or
  - (ii) if the dwelling is a flat, to the dwelling or to any other part of the building containing it,

in respect of which a claim could be made under the terms of a policy of insurance, and

- (b) it is a term of that policy that the person insured under the policy should give notice of any claim under it to the insurer within a specified period,

the tenant may, within that specified period, serve on the insurer a notice in writing stating that it appears to him that damage has been caused as mentioned in paragraph (a) and describing briefly the nature of the damage.

(3) Where—

- (a) any such notice is served on an insurer by a tenant in relation to any such damage, and
- (b) the specified period referred to in sub-paragraph (2)(b) would expire earlier than the period of six months beginning with the date on which the notice is served,

the policy in question shall have effect as regards any claim subsequently made in respect of that damage by the person insured under the policy as if for the specified period there were substituted that period of six months.

(4) Where the tenency of a dwelling to which this paragraph applies is held by joint tenants, a single notice under this paragraph may be given by any one or more of those tenants.

(5) The Secretary of State may by regulations prescribe the form of notices under this paragraph and the particulars which such notices must contain.

(6) Any such regulations—

(a) may make different provision with respect to different cases of descriptions of case, including different provision for different areas, and

(b) shall be made by statutory instrument.

8 Right to challenge landlord's choice of insurers

(1) This paragraph applies where a tenancy of a dwelling requires the tenant to insure the dwelling with an insurer nominated or approved by the landlord.

(2) The tenant or landlord may apply to the county court or the appropriate tribunal for a determination whether—

(a) the insurance which is available from the nominated or approved insurer for insuring the tenant's dwelling is unsatisfactory in any respect, or

(b) the premiums payable in respect of any such insurance are excessive.

(3) No such application may be made in respect of a matter which—

(a) has been agreed or admitted by the tenant,

(b) under an arbitration agreement to which the tenant is a party is to be referred to arbitration, or

(c) has been the subject of determination by a court or arbitral tribunal.

(4) On an application under this paragraph the court or tribunal may make—

(a) an order requiring the landlord to nominate or approve such other insurer as is specified in the order, or

(b) an order requiring him to nominate or approve another insurer who satisfies such requirements in relation to the insurance of the dwelling as are specified in the order.

(6) An agreement by the tenant of a dwelling (other than an arbitration agreement) is void in so far as it purports to provide for a determination in a particular manner, or on particular evidence, of any question which may be the subject of an application under this paragraph.

9 Exception for tenants of certain public authorities

(1) Paragraphs 2 to 8 do not apply to a tenant of—

a local authority,

a National Park authority, or

a new town corporation;

unless the tenancy is a long tenancy, in which case paragraphs 2 to 5 and 7 and 8 apply but paragraph 6 does not.

(2) Subsections (2) and (3) of section 26 shall apply for the purposes of sub-paragraph (1) as they apply for the purposes of subsection (1) of that section.

LANDLORD AND TENANT ACT 1987

. . .

PART IV
VARIATION OF LEASE

Applications relating to flats

A2.2

35 Application by party to lease for variation of lease

(1) Any party to a long lease of a flat may make an application to the appropriate tribunal for an order varying the lease in such manner as is specified in the application.

(2) The grounds on which any such application may be made are that the lease fails to make satisfactory provision with respect to one or more of the following matters, namely—

- (a) the repair or maintenance of—
  - (i) the flat in question, or
  - (ii) the building containing the flat, or
  - (iii) any land or building which is let to the tenant under the lease or in respect of which rights are conferred on him under it;
- (b) the insurance of the building containing the flat or of any such land or building as is mentioned in paragraph (a)(iii);
- (c) the repair or maintenance of any installations (whether they are in the same building as the flat or not) which are reasonably necessary to ensure that occupiers of the flat enjoy a reasonable standard of accommodation;
- (d) the provision or maintenance of any services which are reasonably necessary to ensure that occupiers of the flat enjoy a reasonable standard of accommodation (whether they are services connected with any such installations or not, and whether they are services provided for the benefit of those occupiers or services provided for the benefit of the occupiers of a number of flats including that flat);
- (e) the recovery by one party to the lease from another party to it of expenditure incurred or to be incurred by him, or on his behalf, for the benefit of that other party or of a number of persons who include that other party;
- (f) the computation of a service charge payable under the lease.
- (g) such other matters as may be prescribed by regulations made by the Secretary of State.

(3) For the purposes of subsection (2)(c) and (d) the factors for determining, in relation to the occupiers of a flat, what is a reasonable standard of accommodation may include—

- (a) factors relating to the safety and security of the flat and its occupiers and of any common parts of the building containing the flat; and
- (b) other factors relating to the condition of any such common parts.

(3A) For the purposes of subsection (2)(e) the factors for determining, in relation to a service charge payable under a lease, whether the lease makes satisfactory provision include whether it makes provision for an amount to be payable (by way of interest or otherwise) in respect of a failure to pay the service charge by the due date.

(4) For the purposes of subsection (2)(f) a lease fails to make satisfactory provision with respect to the computation of a service charge payable under it if—

(a) it provides for any such charge to be a proportion of expenditure incurred, or to be incurred, by or on behalf of the landlord or a superior landlord; and

(b) other tenants of the landlord are also liable under their leases to pay by way of service charges proportions of any such expenditure; and

(c) the aggregate of the amounts that would, in any particular case, be payable by reference to the proportions referred to in paragraphs (a) and (b) would either exceed or be less than the whole of any such expenditure.

(5) Procedure regulations under Schedule 12 to the Commonhold and Leasehold Reform Act 2002 and the Tribunal Procedure Rules shall make provision—

(a) for requiring notice of any application under this Part to be served by the person making the application, and by any respondent to the application, on any person who the applicant, or (as the case may be) the respondent, knows or has reason to believe is likely to be affected by any variation specified in the application, and

(b) for enabling persons served with any such notice to be joined as parties to the proceedings.

(6) For the purposes of this Part a long lease shall not be regarded as a long lease of a flat if—

(a) the demised premises consist of or include three or more flats contained in the same building; or

(b) the lease constitutes a tenancy to which Part II of the Landlord and Tenant Act 1954 applies.

(8) In this section 'service charge' has the meaning given by section 18(1) of the 1985 Act.

(9) For the purposes of this section and sections 36 to 39, "appropriate tribunal" means—

(a) if one or more of the long leases concerned relates to property in England, the First-tier Tribunal or, where determined by or under Tribunal Procedure Rules, the Upper Tribunal; and

(b) if one or more of the long leases concerned relates to property in Wales, a leasehold valuation tribunal.

36 Application by respondent for variation of other leases

(1) Where an application ('the original application') is made under section 35 by any party to a lease, any other party to the lease may make an application to the tribunal asking it, in the event of its deciding to make an order effecting any variation of the lease in pursuance of the original application, to make an order which effects a corresponding variation of each of such one or more other leases as are specified in the application.

(2) Any lease so specified—

(a) must be a long lease of a flat under which the landlord is the same person as the landlord under the lease specified in the original application; but

(b) need not be a lease of a flat which is in the same building as the flat let under that lease, nor a lease drafted in terms identical to those of that lease.

(3) The grounds on which an application may be made under this section are—

(a) that each of the leases specified in the application fails to make satisfactory provision with respect to the matter or matters specified in the original application; and

(b) that, if any variation is effected in pursuance of the original application, it would be in the interests of the person making the application under this section, or in the interests of the other persons who are parties to the leases specified in that application, to have all of the leases in question (that is to say, the ones specified in that application together with the one specified in the original application) varied to the same effect.

37 Application by majority of parties for variation of leases

(1) Subject to the following provisions of this section, an application may be made to the appropriate tribunal in respect of two or more leases for an order varying each of those leases in such manner as is specified in the application.

(2) Those leases must be long leases of flats under which the landlord is the same person, but they need not be leases of flats which are in the same building, nor leases which are drafted in identical terms.

(3) The grounds on which an application may be made under this section are that the object to be achieved by the variation cannot be satisfactorily achieved unless all the leases are varied to the same effect.

(4) An application under this section in respect of any leases may be made by the landlord or any of the tenants under the leases.

(5) Any such application shall only be made if—

(a) in a case where the application is in respect of less than nine leases, or all but one, of the parties concerned consent to it; or

(b) in a case where the application is in respect of more than eight leases, it is not opposed for any reason by more than 10 per cent of the total number of the parties concerned and at least 75 per cent of that number consent to it.

(6) For the purposes of subsection (5)—

(a) in the case of each lease in respect of which the application is made, the tenant under the lease shall constitute one of the parties concerned (so that in determining the total number of the parties concerned a person who is the tenant under a number of such leases shall be regarded as constituting a corresponding number of the parties concerned); and

(b) the landlord shall also constitute one of the parties concerned.

Orders varying leases

38 Orders varying leases

(1) If, on an application under section 35, the grounds on which the application was made are established to the satisfaction of the tribunal, the tribunal may (subject to subsections (6) and (7)) make an order varying the lease specified in the application in such manner as is specified in the order.

(2) If—

(a) an application under section 36 was made in connection with that application, and

(b) the grounds set out in subsection (3) of that section are established to the satisfaction of the tribunal with respect to the leases specified in the application under section 36,

the tribunal may (subject to subsections (6) and (7)) also make an order varying each of those leases in such manner as is specified in the order.

(3) If, on an application under section 37, the grounds set out in subsection (3) of that section are established to the satisfaction of the tribunal with respect to the leases specified in the application, the tribunal may (subject to subsections (6) and (7)) make an order varying each of those leases in such manner as is specified in the order.

(4) The variation specified in an order under subsection (1) or (2) may be either the variation specified in the relevant application under section 35 or 36 or such other variation as the tribunal thinks fit.

(5) If the grounds referred to in subsection (2) or (3) (as the case may be) are established to the satisfaction of the tribunal with respect to some but not all the leases

specified in the application, the power to make an order under that subsection shall extend to those leases only.

(6) A tribunal shall not make an order under this section effecting any variation of a lease if it appears to the tribunal—

- (a) that the variation would be likely substantially to prejudice—
  - (i) any respondent to the application, or
  - (ii) any person who is not a party to the application,

  and that an award under subsection (10) would not afford him adequate compensation, or
- (b) that for any other reason it would not be reasonable in the circumstances for the variation to be effected.

(7) A tribunal shall not, on an application relating to the provision to be made by a lease with respect to insurance, make an order under this section effecting any variation of the lease—

- (a) which terminates any existing right of the landlord under its terms to nominate an insurer for insurance purposes; or
- (b) which requires the landlord to nominate a number of insurers from which the tenant would be entitled to select an insurer for those purposes; or
- (c) which, in a case where the lease requires the tenant to effect insurance with a specified insurer, requires the tenant to effect insurance otherwise than with another specified insurer.

(8) A tribunal may, instead of making an order varying a lease in such manner as is specified in the order, make an order directing the parties to the lease to vary it in such manner as is so specified; and accordingly any reference in this Part (however expressed) to an order which effects any variation of a lease or to any variation effected by an order shall include a reference to an order which directs the parties to a lease to effect a variation of it or (as the case may be) a reference to any variation effected in pursuance of such an order.

(9) A tribunal may by order direct that a memorandum of any variation of a lease effected by an order under this section shall be endorsed on such documents as are specified in the order.

(10) Where a tribunal makes an order under this section varying a lease the tribunal may, if it thinks fit, make an order providing for any party to the lease to pay, to any other party to the lease or to any other person, compensation in respect of any loss or disadvantage that the tribunal considers he is likely to suffer as a result of the variation.

39 Effect of orders varying leases: applications by third parties

(1) Any variation effected by an order under section 38 shall be binding not only on the parties to the lease for the time being but also on other persons (including any predecessors in title of those parties), whether or not they were parties to the proceedings in which the order was made or were served with a notice by virtue of section 35(5).

(2) Without prejudice to the generality of subsection (1), any variation effected by any such order shall be binding on any surety who has guaranteed the performance of any obligation varied by the order; and the surety shall accordingly be taken to have guaranteed the performance of that obligation as so varied.

(3) Where any such order has been made and a person was, by virtue of section 35(5), required to be served with a notice relating to the proceedings in which it was made, but he was not so served, he may—

- (a) bring an action for damages for breach of statutory duty against the person by whom any such notice was so required to be served in respect of that person's failure to serve it;
- (b) apply to the appropriate tribunal for the cancellation or modification of the variation in question.

(4) A tribunal may on an application under subsection (3)(b) with respect to any variation of a lease—

(a) by order cancel that variation or modify it in such manner as is specified in the order, or

(b) make such an order as is mentioned in section 38(10) in favour of the person making the application,

as it thinks fit.

(5) Where a variation is cancelled or modified under paragraph (a) of subsection (4)—

(a) the cancellation of modification shall take effect as from the date of the making of the order under that paragraph or as from such later date as may be specified in the order, and

(b) the tribunal may by order direct that a memorandum of the cancellation or modification shall be endorsed on such documents as are specified in the order;

and, in a case where a variation is so modified, subsections (1) and (2) above shall, as from the date when the modification takes effect, apply to the variation as modified.

Applications relating to dwellings other than flats

40 Application for variation of insurance provisions of lease of dwelling other than a flat

(1) Any party to a long lease of a dwelling may make an application to the appropriate tribunal for an order varying the lease, in such manner as is specified in the application, on the grounds that the lease fails to make satisfactory provision with respect to any matter relating to the insurance of the dwelling, including the recovery of the costs of such insurance.

(2) Sections 36 and 38 shall apply to an application under subsection (1) subject to the modifications specified in subsection (3).

(3) Those modifications are as follows—

(a) in section 36—

(i) in subsection (1), the reference to section 35 shall be read as a reference to subsection (1) above, and

(ii) in subsection (2), any reference to a flat shall be read as a reference to a dwelling; and

(b) in section 38—

(i) any reference to an application under section 35 shall be read as a reference to an application under subsection (1) above, and

(ii) any reference to an application under section 36 shall be read as a reference to an application under section 36 as applied by subsection (2) above.

(4) For the purposes of this section, a long lease shall not be regarded as a long lease of a dwelling if—

(a) the demised premises consist of three or more dwellings; or

(b) the lease constitutes a tenancy to which Part II of the Landlord and Tenant Act 1954 applies.

(4A) Without prejudice to subsection (4), an application under subsection (1) may not be made by a person who is a tenant under a long lease of a dwelling if, by virtue of that lease and one or more other long leases of dwellings, he is also a tenant from the same landlord of at least two other dwellings.

(4B) For the purposes of subsection (4A), any tenant of a dwelling who is a body corporate shall be treated as a tenant of any other dwelling held from the same landlord which is let under a long lease to an associated company, as defined in section 20(1).

(5) In this section, 'dwelling' means a dwelling other than a flat.

(6) For the purposes of subsection (1), "appropriate tribunal" means—

- (a) if one or more of the dwellings concerned is in England, the First-tier Tribunal or, where determined by or under Tribunal Procedure Rules, the Upper Tribunal; and
- (b) if one or more of the dwellings concerned is in Wales, a leasehold valuation tribunal.

. . .

PART V
MANAGEMENT OF LEASEHOLD PROPERTY

SERVICE CHARGES

. . .

42 Service charge contributions to be held in trust

(1) This section applies where the tenants of two or more dwellings may be required under the terms of their leases to contribute to the same costs or the tenant of a dwelling may be required under the terms of his lease to contribute to costs to which no other tenant of a dwelling may be required to contribute, by the payment of service charges; and in this section—

'the contributing tenants' means those tenants and 'the sole contributing tenant' means that tenant;

'the payee' means the landlord or other person to whom any such charges are payable by those tenants, or that tenant, under the terms of their leases, or his lease;

'relevant service charges' means any such charges;

'service charge' has the meaning given by section 18(1) of the 1985 Act, except that it does not include a service charge payable by the tenant of a dwelling the rent of which is registered under Part IV of the Rent Act 1977, unless the amount registered is, in pursuance of section 71(4) of that Act, entered as a variable amount;

'tenant' does not include a tenant of an exempt landlord; and

'trust fund' means the fund, or (as the case may be) any of the funds, mentioned in subsection (2) below.

(2) Any sums paid to the payee by the contributing tenants, or the sole contributing tenant by way of relevant service charges, *and any investments representing those sums*, shall (together with any income accruing thereon) be held by the payee either as a single fund or, if he thinks fit, in two or more separate funds.

(3) The payee shall hold any trust fund—

- (a) on trust to defray costs incurred in connection with the matters for which the relevant service charges were payable (whether incurred by himself or by any other person), and
- (b) subject to that, on trust for the persons who are the contributing tenants for the time being, or the person who is the sole contributing tenant for the time being.

(4) Subject to subsections (6) to (8), the contributing tenants shall be treated as entitled by virtue of subsection (3)(b) to such shares in the residue of any such fund as are proportionate to their respective liabilities to pay relevant service charges or the sole contributing tenant shall be treated as so entitled to the residue of any such fund.

(5) If the Secretary of State by order so provides, any sums standing to the credit of any trust fund may, instead of being invested in any other manner authorised by law, be invested in such manner as may be specified in the order; and any such order may contain such incidental, supplemental or transitional provisions as the Secretary of State considers appropriate in connection with the order.

(6) On the termination of the lease of any of the contributing tenants the tenant shall not be entitled to any part of any trust fund, and (except where subsection (7) applies) any part of any such fund which is attributable to relevant service charges paid under the lease shall accordingly continue to be held on the trusts referred to in subsection (3).

(7) On the termination of the lease of the last of the contributing tenants, or of the lease of the sole contributing tenant, any trust fund shall be dissolved as at the date of the termination of the lease, and any assets comprised in the fund immediately before its dissolution shall—

- (a) if the payee is the landlord, be retained by him for his own use and benefit, and
- (b) in any other case, be transferred to the landlord by the payee.

(8) Subsections (4), (6) and (7) shall have effect in relation to any of the contributing tenants, or the sole contributing tenant, subject to any express terms of his lease (whenever it was granted) which relate to the distribution, either before or (as the case may be) at the termination of the lease, of amounts attributable to relevant service charges paid under its terms *(whether the lease was granted before or after the commencement of this section).*

(9) Subject to subsection (8), the provisions of this section shall prevail over the terms of any express or implied trust created by a lease so far as inconsistent with those provisions, other than an express trust so created, in the case of a lease of any of the contributing tenants, before the commencement of this section or, in the case of the lease of a sole contributing tenant, before the commencement of paragraph 15 of Schedule 10 to the Commonhold and Leasehold Reform Act 2002.

[42A Service charge contributions to be held in designated account

(1) The payee must hold any sums standing to the credit of any trust fund in a designated account at a relevant financial institution.

(2) An account is a designated account in relation to sums standing to the credit of a trust fund if—

- (a) the relevant financial institution has been notified in writing that sums standing to the credit of the trust fund are to be (or are) held in it, and
- *(b) no other funds are held in the account,*
- [(b) any other sums held in the account are sums standing to the credit of one or more other trust funds,]

and the account is an account of a description specified in regulations made by the *Secretary of State*[appropriate national authority].

[(2A) The appropriate national authority may by regulations ensure that a payee who holds more than one trust fund in the same designated account cannot move any of those funds to another designated account unless conditions specified in the regulations are met.]

(3) Any of the contributing tenants, or the sole contributing tenant, may by notice in writing require the payee—

- (a) to afford him reasonable facilities for inspecting documents evidencing that subsection (1) is[, or regulations under subsection (2A) are,] complied with and for taking copies of or extracts from *them*[such documents], or
- (b) to take copies of or extracts from any such documents and either send them to him or afford him reasonable facilities for collecting them (as he specifies).

(4) If the tenant is represented by a recognised tenants' association and he consents, the notice may be served by the secretary of the association instead of by the tenant (and in that case any requirement imposed by it is to afford reasonable facilities, or to send copies or extracts, to the secretary).

(5) A notice under *this section* [subsection (3)] is duly served on the payee if it is served on—

(a) an agent of the payee named as such in the rent book or similar document, or

(b) the person who receives the rent on behalf of the payee;

and a person on whom such a notice is so served must forward it as soon as may be to the payee.

(6) The payee must comply with a requirement imposed by a notice under *this section* [subsection (3)] within the period of twenty-one days beginning with the day on which he receives the notice.

(7) To the extent that a notice under *this section* [subsection (3)] requires the payee to afford facilities for inspecting documents—

(a) he must do so free of charge, but

(b) he may treat as part of his costs of management any costs incurred by him in doing so.

(8) The payee may make a reasonable charge for doing anything else in compliance with a requirement imposed by a notice under *this section* [subsection (3)].

(9) Any of the contributing tenants, or the sole contributing tenant, may withhold payment of a service charge if he has reasonable grounds for believing that the payee has failed to comply with the duty imposed on him by subsection (1); and any provisions of his tenancy relating to non-payment or late payment of service charges do not have effect in relation to the period for which he so withholds it.

[(9A) Regulations under subsection (2A) may include provision about—

(a) the circumstances in which a contributing tenant who has reasonable grounds for believing that the payee has not complied with a duty imposed on him by the regulations may withhold payment of a service charge,

(b) the period for which payment may be so withheld,

(c) the amount of service charge that may be so withheld;

and the regulations may provide that any provisions of the contributing tenant's tenancy relating to non-payment or late payment of service charge do not have effect in relation to the period for which the payment is so withheld.]

(10) Nothing in this section [or in regulations under subsection (2A)]applies to the payee if the circumstances are such as are specified in regulations made by the *Secretary of State*[appropriate national authority].

[(10A) Regulations under this section may—

(a) make different provision for different cases, including different provision for different areas,

(b) contain such supplementary, incidental, consequential, transitional, transitory or saving provision as the appropriate national authority considers appropriate.

(10B) Regulations under this section are to be made by statutory instrument which—

(a) in the case of regulations made by the Secretary of State, is to be subject to annulment in pursuance of a resolution of either House of Parliament, and

(b) in the case of regulations made by the Welsh Ministers, is to be subject to annulment in pursuance of a resolution of the National Assembly for Wales.]

(11) In this section—

['the appropriate national authority'—

(a) in relation to England, means the Secretary of State, and

(b) in relation to Wales, means the Welsh Ministers,]

'recognised tenants' association' has the same meaning as in the 1985 Act, and 'relevant financial institution' has the meaning given by regulations made by the *Secretary of State*[appropriate national authority];

and expressions used both in section 42 and this section have the same meaning as in that section.]

[42B Failure to comply with section 42A

(1) If a person fails, without reasonable excuse, to comply with a duty imposed on him by or by virtue of section 42A he commits an offence.

(2) A person guilty of an offence under this section is liable on summary conviction to a fine not exceeding level 4 on the standard scale.

(3) Where an offence under this section committed by a body corporate is proved—

(a) to have been committed with the consent or connivance of a director, manager, secretary or other similar officer of the body corporate, or a person purporting to act in such a capacity, or

(b) to be due to any neglect on the part of such an officer or person,

he, as well as the body corporate, is guilty of the offence and liable to be proceeded against and punished accordingly.

(4) Where the affairs of a body corporate are managed by its members, subsection (3) applies in relation to the acts and defaults of a member in connection with his functions of management as if he were a director of the body corporate.

(5) Proceedings for an offence under this section may be brought by a local housing authority (within the meaning of section 1 of the Housing Act 1985).]

. . .

PART VI
INFORMATION TO BE FURNISHED TO TENANTS

46 Application of Part VI, etc

(1) This Part applies to premises which consist of or include a dwelling and are not held under a tenancy to which Part II of the Landlord and Tenant Act 1954 applies.

(2) In this Part 'service charge' has the meaning given by section 18(1) of the 1985 Act.

(3) In this Part 'administration charge' has the meaning given by paragraph 1 of Schedule 11 to the Commonhold and Leasehold Reform Act 2002.

47 Landlord's name and address to be contained in demands for rent, etc

(1) Where any written demand is given to a tenant of premises to which this Part applies, the demand must contain the following information, namely—

(a) the name and address of the Landlord, and

(b) if that address is not in England and Wales, an address in England and Wales at which notices (including notices in proceedings) may be served on the landlord by the tenant.

(2) Where—

(a) a tenant of any such premises is given such a demand, but

(b) it does not contain any information required to be contained in it by virtue of subsection (1),

then (subject to subsection (3)) any part of the amount demanded which consists of a service charge or an administration charge ('the relevant amount') shall be treated for all purposes as not being due from the tenant to the landlord at any time before that information is furnished by the landlord by notice given to the tenant.

(3) The relevant amount shall not be so treated in relation to any time when, by virtue of an order of any court or tribunal, there is in force an appointment of a receiver or manager whose functions include the receiving of service charges or (as the case may be) administration charges from the tenant.

(4) In this section 'demand' means a demand for rent or other sums payable to the landlord under the terms of the tenancy.

48 Notification by landlord of address for service of notices

(1) A landlord of premises to which this Part applies shall by notice furnish the tenant with an address in England and Wales at which notices (including notices in proceedings) may be served on him by the tenant.

(2) Where a landlord of any such premises fails to comply with subsection (1), any rent, service charge or administration charge otherwise due from the tenant to the landlord shall (subject to subsection (3)) be treated for all purposes as not being due from the tenant to the landlord at any time before the landlord does comply with that subsection.

(3) Any such rent, service charge or administration charge shall not be so treated in relation to any time when, by virtue of an order of any court or tribunal, there is in force an appointment of a receiver or manager whose functions include the receiving of rent, service charges or (as the case may be) administration charges from the tenant.

. . .

53 Regulations and orders

(1) Any power of the Secretary of State to make an order or regulations under this Act shall be exercisable by statutory instrument and may be exercised so as to make different provision for different cases, including different provision for different areas.

(2) A statutory instrument containing—

(a) an order made under section 1(5), 25(6), *42(5)* or 55, or

(b) any regulations made under section 20(4) or 35(2)(g)[*or 42A*],

shall be subject to annulment in pursuance of a resolution of either House of Parliament.

[(3) This section does not apply to any power to make regulations under section 42A.]

54 Notices

(1) Any notice required or authorised to be served under this Act—

(a) shall be in writing; and

(b) may be sent by post.

(2) Any notice purporting to be a notice served under any provision of Part I or III by the requisite majority of any qualifying tenants (as defined for the purposes of that provision) shall specify the names of all of the persons by whom it is served and the addresses of the flats of which they are qualifying tenants.

(3) The Secretary of State may by regulations prescribe—

(a) the form of any notices required or authorised to be served under or in pursuance of any provision of Parts I to III, and

(b) the particulars which any such notices must contain (whether in addition to, or in substitution for, any particulars required by virtue of the provision in question).

(4) Subsection (3)(b) shall not be construed as authorising the Secretary of State to make regulations under subsection (3) varying any of the periods specified in section 5A(4) or (5), 5B(5) or (6), 5C(4) or (5), 5D(4) or (5) or 5E(3) (which accordingly can only be varied by regulations under section 20(4)).

55 Application to Isles of Scilly

This Act shall apply to the Isles of Scilly subject to such exceptions, adaptations and modifications as the Secretary of State may by order direct.

56 Crown land

(1) *This Act* [Parts 1 and 3 and sections 42 to 42B (and so much of this Part as relates to those provisions)] shall apply to a tenancy from the Crown if there has ceased to be a Crown interest in the land subject to it.

(3) Where there exists a Crown interest in any land subject to a tenancy from the Crown and the person holding that tenancy is himself the landlord under any other tenancy whose subject-matter comprises the whole or part of that land, *this Act* [the provisions mentioned in subsection (1)] shall apply to that other tenancy, and to any derivative sub-tenancy, notwithstanding the existence of that interest.

(4) For the purposes of this section 'tenancy from the Crown' means a tenancy of land in which there is, or has during the subsistence of the tenancy been, a Crown interest superior to the tenancy, and 'Crown interest' means—

- (a) an interest comprised in the Crown Estate;
- (b) an interest belonging to Her Majesty in right of the Duchy of Lancaster;
- (c) an interest belonging to the Duchy of Cornwall;
- (d) any other interest belonging to a government department or held on behalf of Her Majesty for the purposes of a government department.

57 Financial provision

There shall be paid out of money provided by Parliament any increase attributable to this Act in the sums payable out of money so provided under any other Act.

58 Exempt landlords and resident landlords

(1) In this Act 'exempt landlord' means a landlord who is one of the following bodies, namely—

- (a) a district, county , county borough or London borough council, the Common Council of the City of London, a fire and rescue authority created by an order under section 4A of the Fire and Rescue Services Act 2004, the London Fire Commissioner, the Council of the Isles of Scilly, a police and crime commissioner, the Mayor's Office for Policing and Crime, a joint authority established by Part 4 of the Local Government Act 1985, an economic prosperity board established under section 88 of the Local Democracy, Economic Development and Construction Act 2009 or a combined authority established under section 103 of that Act;
- (b) a development corporation established by an order made (or having effect as if made) under the New Towns Act 1981;
- (ba) a Mayoral development corporation;
- (c) an urban development corporation within the meaning of Part XVI of the Local Government, Planning and Land Act 1980;
- (ca) a housing action trust established under Part III of the Housing Act 1988;
- (dd) the Broads Authority;
- (de) a National Park authority;
- (df) the Homes and Communities Agency;
- (dg) the Greater London Authority so far as exercising its housing or regeneration functions or its new towns and urban development functions;
- (e) the Regulator of Social Housing;
- (f) a housing trust (as defined in section 6 of the Housing Act 1985) which is a charity;
- (g) a non-profit private registered provider of social housing;
- (ga) a registered social landlord;
- (gb) a fully mutual housing association which is neither a private registered provider of social housing nor a registered social landlord; or

(h) an authority established under section 10 of the Local Government Act 1985 (joint arrangements for waste disposal functions).

(1ZA) In this Act "exempt landlord", in relation to social housing (within the meaning of Part 2 of the Housing and Regeneration Act 2008), includes a landlord which is a profit-making private registered provider of social housing.

(1A) In subsection (1)(ga) "registered social landlord" has the same meaning as in the Housing Act 1985 (see section 5(4) and (5) of that Act).

(1B) In subsection (1)(gb) "fully mutual housing association" has the same meaning as in the Housing Associations Act 1985 (see section 1(1) and (2) of that Act).

(2) For the purposes of this Act the landlord of any premises consisting of the whole or part of a building is a resident landlord of those premises at any time if—

(a) the premises are not, and do not form part of, a purpose-built block of flats; and

(b) at that time the landlord occupies a flat contained in the premises as his only or principal residence; and

(c) he has so occupied such a flat throughout a period of not less than 12 months ending with that time.

(3) In subsection (2) "purpose-built block of flats" means a building which contained as constructed, and contains, two or more flats.

59 Meaning of 'lease', 'long lease' and related expressions

(1) In this Act 'lease' and 'tenancy' have the same meaning; and both expressions include—

(a) a sub-lease or sub-tenancy, and

(b) an agreement for a lease or tenancy (or for a sub-lease or sub-tenancy).

(2) The expressions 'landlord' and 'tenant', and references to letting, to the grant of a lease or to covenants or the terms of a lease shall be construed accordingly.

(3) In this Act 'long lease' means—

(a) a lease granted for a term certain exceeding 21 years, whether or not it is (or may become) terminable before the end of that by notice given by the tenant or by re-entry or forfeiture;

(b) a lease for a term fixed by law under a grant with a covenant or obligation for perpetual renewal, other than a lease by sub-demise from one which is not a long lease; or

(c) a lease granted in pursuance of Part V of the Housing Act 1985 (the right to buy), including a lease granted in pursuance of that Part as it has effect by virtue of section 17 of the Housing Act 1996 (the right to acquire).

60 General interpretation

(1) In this Act—

'the 1985 Act' means the Landlord and Tenant Act 1985;

'charitable purposes', in relation to a charity, means charitable purposes whether of that charity or of that charity and other charities;

'common parts', in relation to any building or part of a building, includes the structure and exterior of that building or part and any common facilities within it;

'the court' means the High Court or the county court;

'dwelling' means a building or part of a building occupied or intended to be occupied as a separate dwelling, together with any yard, garden, outhouses and appurtenances belonging to it or usually enjoyed with it;

'exempt landlord' has the meaning given by section 58(1);

'flat' means a separate set of premises, whether or not on the same floor, which—

(a) forms part of a building, and

(b) is divided horizontally from some other part of that building, and
(c) is constructed or adapted for use for the purposes of a dwelling;

'functional land', in relation to a charity, means land occupied by the charity, or by trustees for it, and wholly or mainly used for charitable purposes;

'landlord' (except for the purposes of Part I) means the immediate landlord or, in relation to a statutory tenant, the person who, apart from the statutory tenancy, would be entitled to possession of the premises subject to the tenancy;

'lease' and related expressions shall be construed in accordance with section 59(1) and (2);

'long lease' has the meaning given by section 59(3);

'mortgage' includes any charge or lien, and references to a mortgagee shall be construed accordingly;

'notices in proceedings' means notices or other documents served in, or in connection with, any legal proceedings;

'resident landlord' shall be construed in accordance with section 58(2);

'statutory tenancy' and 'statutory tenant' mean a statutory tenancy or statutory tenant within the meaning of the Rent Act 1977 or the Rent (Agriculture) Act 1976;

'tenancy' includes a statutory tenancy.

(1A) In this Act a reference to the Welsh Ministers in their new towns residuary capacity means the Welsh Ministers so far as exercising functions in relation to anything transferred (or to be transferred) to them as mentioned in section 36(1)(a)(i) to (iii) of the New Towns Act 1981.

LEASEHOLD REFORM, HOUSING AND URBAN DEVELOPMENT ACT 1993

...

CHAPTER V
TENANTS' RIGHT TO MANAGEMENT AUDIT

A2.3

76 Right to audit management by landlord

(1) This Chapter has effect to confer on two or more qualifying tenants of dwellings held on leases from the same landlord the right, exercisable subject to and in accordance with this Chapter, to have an audit carried out on their behalf which relates to the management of the relevant premises and any appurtenant property by or on behalf of the landlord.

(2) That right shall be exercisable—

- (a) where the relevant premises consist of or include two dwellings let to qualifying tenants of the same landlord, by either or both of those tenants; and
- (b) where the relevant premises consist of or include three or more dwellings let to qualifying tenants of the same landlord, by not less than two-thirds of those tenants;

and in this Chapter the dwellings let to those qualifying tenants are referred to as 'the constituent dwellings'.

(3) In relation to an audit on behalf of two or more qualifying tenants—

- (a) 'the relevant premises' means so much of—
  - (i) the building or buildings containing the dwellings let to those tenants, and
  - (ii) any other building or buildings,

  as constitutes premises in relation to which management functions are discharged in respect of the costs of which common service charge contributions are payable under the leases of those qualifying tenants; and
- (b) 'appurtenant property' means so much of any property not contained in the relevant premises as constitutes property in relation to which any such management functions are discharged.

(4) This Chapter also has effect to confer on a single qualifying tenant of a dwelling the right, exercisable subject to and in accordance with this Chapter, to have an audit carried out on his behalf which relates to the management of the relevant premises and any appurtenant property by or on behalf of the landlord.

(5) That right shall be exercisable by a single qualifying tenant of a dwelling where the relevant premises contain no other dwelling let to a qualifying tenant apart from that let to him.

(6) In relation to an audit on behalf of a single qualifying tenant—

- (a) 'the relevant premises' means so much of—
  - (i) the building containing the dwelling let to him, and
  - (ii) any other building or buildings,

  as constitutes premises in relation to which management functions are discharged in respect of the costs of which a service charge is payable under his lease (whether as a common service charge contribution or otherwise); and
- (b) 'appurtenant property' means so much of any property not contained in the relevant premises as constitutes property in relation to which any such management functions are discharged.

(7) The provisions of sections 78 to 83 shall, with any necessary modifications, have effect in relation to an audit on behalf of a single qualifying tenant as they have effect in relation to an audit on behalf of two or more qualifying tenants.

(8) For the purposes of this section common service charge contributions are payable by two or more persons under their leases if they may be required under the terms of those leases to contribute to the same costs by the payment of service charges.

77 Qualifying tenants

(1) Subject to the following provisions of this section, a tenant is a qualifying tenant of a dwelling for the purposes of this Chapter if—

- (a) he is a tenant of the dwelling under a long lease other than a business lease; and
- (b) any service charge is payable under the lease.

(2) For the purposes of subsection (1) a lease is a long lease if—

- (a) it is a lease falling within any of paragraphs (a) to (c) of subsection (1) of section 7; or
- (b) it is a shared ownership lease (within the meaning of that section), whether granted in pursuance of Part V of the Housing Act 1985 or otherwise and whatever the share of the tenant under it.

(3) No dwelling shall have more than one qualifying tenant at any one time.

(4) Accordingly—

- (a) where a dwelling is for the time being let under two or more leases falling within subsection (1), any tenant under any of those leases which is superior to that held by any other such tenant shall not be a qualifying tenant of the dwelling for the purposes of this Chapter, and
- (b) where a dwelling is for the time being let to joint tenants under a lease falling within subsection (1), the joint tenants shall (subject to paragraph (a)) be regarded for the purposes of this Chapter as jointly constituting the qualifying tenant of the dwelling.

(5) A person can, however, be (or be among those constituting) the qualifying tenant of each of two or more dwellings at the same time, whether he is tenant of those dwellings under one lease or under two or more separate leases.

(6) Where two or more persons constitute the qualifying tenant of a dwelling in accordance with subsection (4)(b), any one or more of those persons may sign a notice under section 80 on behalf of both or all of them.

78 Management audits

(1) The audit referred to in section 76(1) is an audit carried out for the purpose of ascertaining—

- (a) the extent to which the obligations of the landlord which—
  - (i) are owed to the qualifying tenants of the constituent dwellings, and
  - (ii) involve the discharge of management functions in relation to the relevant premises or any appurtenant property,

  are being discharged in an efficient and effective manner; and
- (b) the extent to which sums payable by those tenants by way of service charges are being applied in an efficient and effective manner;

and in this Chapter any such audit is referred to as a 'management audit'.

(2) In determining whether any such obligations as are mentioned in subsection (1)(a) are being discharged in an efficient and effective manner, regard shall be had to any applicable provisions of any code of practice for the time being approved by the Secretary of State under section 87.

(3) A management audit shall be carried out by a person who—

- (a) is qualified for appointment by virtue of subsection (4); and

(b) is appointed—
(i) in the circumstances mentioned in section 76(2)(a), by either or both of the qualifying tenants of the constituent dwellings, or
(ii) in the circumstances mentioned in section 76(2)(b), by not less than two-thirds of the qualifying tenants of the constituent dwellings;

and in this Chapter any such person is referred to as 'the auditor'.

(4) A person is qualified for appointment for the purposes of subsection (3) above if—

(a) he has the necessary qualification (within the meaning of subsection (1) of section 28 of the 1985 Act (meaning of 'qualified accountant')) or is a qualified surveyor;
(b) he is not disqualified from acting (within the meaning of that subsection); and
[(a) he is—
(i) a member of a body which is a recognised supervisory body for the purposes of Part 42 of the Companies Act 2006;
(ii) a qualified surveyor; or
(iii) where the landlord is a relevant landlord, a member of the Chartered Institute of Public Finance and Accountancy;
(b) he is not any of the following—
(i) an officer, employee or partner of the landlord or, where the landlord is a company, of an associated company;
(ii) a person who is a partner or employee of any such officer or employee;
(iii) an agent of the landlord who is a managing agent for any premises to which the audit in question relates; or
(iv) an employee or partner of any such agent; and]
(c) he is not a tenant of any premises contained in the relevant premises.

(5) For the purposes of subsection (4)(a) above a person is a qualified surveyor if he is a fellow or professional associate of the Royal Institution of Chartered Surveyors or of the Incorporated Society of Valuers and Auctioneers or satisfies such other requirement or requirements as may be prescribed by regulations made by the Secretary of State.

[(5A) For the purposes of subsection (4)(b)(i) above a company is associated with a landlord company if it is the landlord's holding company, a subsidiary of the landlord or another subsidiary of the landlord's holding company.

(5B) Subsection (4)(b)(i) does not apply where the landlord is a relevant landlord.

(5C) For the purposes of subsection (4)(b)(iii) above a person is a managing agent for any premises if he has been appointed to discharge any of the landlord's obligations relating to the management by the landlord of the premises.]

(6) The auditor may appoint such persons to assist him in carrying out the audit as he thinks fit.

[(7) In this section—

'holding company' and 'subsidiary' have the meanings given by section 1159 of the Companies Act 2006;

'relevant landlord' means—
(a) a local authority (within the meaning of the Landlord and Tenant Act 1985);
(b) a National Park authority; or
(c) a new town corporation (within the meaning of the Act of 1985).]

79 Rights exercisable in connection with management audits

(1) Where the qualifying tenants of any dwellings exercise under section 80 their right to have a management audit carried out on their behalf, the rights conferred on the auditor by *subsection (2)* [subsections (2) and (2A)] below shall be exercisable by him in connection with the audit.

(2) The rights conferred on the auditor by this subsection are—

(a) a right to require the landlord—

(i) to supply him with such a summary as is referred to in section 21(1) of the 1985 Act (request for summary of relevant costs) in connection with any service charges payable by the qualifying tenants of the constituent dwellings, and

(ii) to afford him reasonable facilities for inspecting, or taking copies of, or extracts from, the accounts, receipts and other documents supporting any such summary;

(b) a right to require the landlord or any relevant person to afford him reasonable facilities for inspecting any other documents sight of which is reasonably required by him for the purpose of carrying out the audit; and

(c) a right to require the landlord or any relevant person to afford him reasonable facilities for taking copies of or extracts from any documents falling within paragraph (b).

[(2) The right conferred on the auditor by this subsection is a right to require the landlord—

(a) to afford him reasonable facilities for inspecting accounts, receipts or other documents relevant to *the matters which must be shown in any statement of account required to be supplied* [information required to be provided] to the qualifying tenants of the constituent dwellings *under*[by virtue of] section 21 of the 1985 Act and for taking copies of or extracts from them, or

(b) to take copies of or extracts from any such accounts, receipts or other documents and either send them to him or afford him reasonable facilities for collecting them (as he specifies).]

(2A) The right conferred on the auditor by this subsection is a right to require the landlord or any relevant person—

(a) to afford him reasonable facilities for inspecting any other documents sight of which is reasonably required by him for the purpose of carrying out the audit and for taking copies of or extracts from them, or

(b) to take copies of or extracts from any such documents and either send them to him or afford him reasonable facilities for collecting them (as the auditor specifies).]

(3) The rights conferred on the auditor by *subsection (2)* [subsections (2) and (2A)] shall be exercisable by him—

(a) in relation to the landlord, by means of a notice under section 80; and

(b) in relation to any relevant person, by means of a notice given to that person at (so far as is reasonably practicable) the same time as a notice under section 80 is given to the landlord;

and, where a notice is given to any relevant person in accordance with paragraph (b) above, a copy of that notice shall be given to the landlord by the auditor.

(4) The auditor shall also be entitled, on giving notice in accordance with section 80, to carry out an inspection of any common parts comprised in the relevant premises or any appurtenant property.

(5) The landlord or (as the case may be) any relevant person shall—

(a) *where facilities for the inspection of any documents are required under subsection (2)(a)(ii) or (b), make those facilities available free of charge;*

(b) *where any documents are required to be supplied under subsection (2)(a)(i) or facilities for the taking of copies or extracts are required under subsection (2)(a)(ii) or (c), be entitled to supply those documents or (as the case may be) make those facilities available on payment of such reasonable charge as he may determine.*

(6) The requirement imposed on the landlord by subsection (5)(a) to make any facilities available free of charge shall not be construed as precluding the landlord from treating as part of his costs of management any costs incurred by him in connection with making those facilities so available.

[(5) To the extent that a requirement imposed under this section on the landlord or any relevant person requires him to afford facilities for inspecting documents, he shall do so free of charge; but the landlord may treat as part of his costs of management any costs incurred by him in doing so.

(6) The landlord or a relevant person may make a reasonable charge for doing anything else in compliance with such a requirement.]

(7) In this Chapter 'relevant person' means a person (other than the landlord) who—

(a) is charged with responsibility—

(i) for the discharge of any such obligations as are mentioned in section 78(1)(a), or

(ii) for the application of any such service charges as are mentioned in section 78(1)(b); or

(b) has a right to enforce payment of any such service charges.

(8) In this Chapter references to the auditor in the context of—

(a) *being afforded any such facilities as are mentioned in subsection (2)* [a requirement imposed under subsection (2) or (2A)], or

(b) the carrying out of any inspection under subsection (4)

shall be read as including a person appointed by the auditor under section 78(6).

80 Exercise of right to have a management audit

(1) The right of any qualifying tenants to have a management audit carried out on their behalf shall be exercisable by the giving of a notice under this section.

(2) A notice given under this section—

(a) must be given to the landlord by the auditor, and

(b) must be signed by each of the tenants on whose behalf it is given.

(3) Any such notice must—

(a) state the full name of each of those tenants and the address of the dwelling of which he is a qualifying tenant;

(b) state the name and address of the auditor;

(c) *specify any documents or description of documents—*

(i) *which the landlord is required to supply to the auditor under section 79(2)(a)(i), or*

(ii) *in respect of which he is required to afford the auditor facilities for inspection or for taking copies or extracts under any other provision of section 79(2); and*

[(c) specify any documents or description of documents in respect of which a requirement is imposed on him under section 79(2) or (2A); and]

(d) if the auditor proposes to carry out an inspection under section 79(4), state the date on which he proposes to carry out the inspection.

(4) The date specified under subsection (3)(d) must be a date falling not less than one month nor more than two months after the date of the giving of the notice.

(5) A notice is duly given under this section to the landlord of any qualifying tenants if it is given to a person who receives on behalf of the landlord the rent payable by any such tenants; and a person to whom such a notice is so given shall forward it as soon as may be to the landlord.

81 Procedure following giving of notice under s 80

(1) Where the landlord is given a notice under section 80, then within the period of one month beginning with the date of the giving of the notice, he shall—

- *(a)* *supply the auditor with any document specified under subsection (3)(c)(i) of that section, and afford him, in respect of any document falling within section 79(2)(a)(ii), any facilities specified in relation to it under subsection (3)(c)(ii) of section 80;*
- *(b)* *in the case of every other document or description of documents specified in the notice under subsection (3)(c)(ii) of that section, either—*
  - *(i)* *afford the auditor facilities for inspection or (as the case may be) taking copies or extracts in respect of that document or those documents, or*
  - *(ii)* *give the auditor a notice stating that he objects to doing so for such reasons as are specified in the notice; and*
- [(a) comply with it so far as it relates to documents within section 79(2);
- (b) either—
  - (i) comply with it, or
  - (ii) give the auditor a notice stating that he objects to doing so for such reasons as are specified in the notice,

  so far as it relates to documents within section 79(2A); and]
- (c) if a date is specified in the notice under subsection (3)(d) of that section, either approve the date or propose another date for the carrying out of an inspection under section 79(4).

(2) Any date proposed by the landlord under subsection (1)(c) must be a date falling not later than the end of the period of two months beginning with the date of the giving of the notice under section 80.

(3) Where a relevant person is given a notice under section 79 *requiring him to afford the auditor facilities for inspection or taking copies or extracts in respect of any documents or description of documents specified in the notice, then within the period of one month beginning with the date of the giving of the notice, he shall, in the case of every such document or description of documents, either—*

- *(a)* *afford the auditor the facilities required by him; or*
- *(b)* *give the auditor a notice stating that he objects to doing so for such reasons as are specified in the notice.*

[, then within the period of one month beginning with the date of the giving of the notice, he shall either—

- (a) comply with it, or
- (b) give the auditor a notice stating that he objects to doing so for such reasons as are specified in the notice,

in the case of every document or description or document specified in the notice.]

(4) If by the end of the period of two months beginning with—

- (a) the date of the giving of the notice under section 80, or
- (b) the date of the giving of such a notice under section 79 as is mentioned in subsection (3) above,

the landlord or (as the case may be) a relevant person has failed to comply with any requirement of the notice, the court may, on the application of the auditor, make an order requiring the landlord or (as the case may be) the relevant person to comply with that requirement within such period as is specified in the order.

(5) The court shall not make an order under subsection (4) in respect of any document or documents unless it is satisfied that the document or documents falls or fall within *paragraph (a) or (b) of section 79(2)* [section 79(2) or (2A)].

(6) If by the end of the period of two months specified in subsection (2) no inspection under section 79(4) has been carried out by the auditor, the court may, on the application of the auditor, make an order providing for such an inspection to be carried out on such date as is specified in the order.

(7) Any application for an order under subsection (4) or (6) must be made before the end of the period of four months beginning with—

- (a) in the case of an application made in connection with a notice given under section 80, the date of the giving of that notice; or
- (b) in the case of an application made in connection with such a notice under section 79 as is mentioned in subsection (3) above, the date of the giving of that notice.

82 Requirement relating to information etc held by superior landlord

(1) Where the landlord is required by a notice under section 80 to supply any summary falling within section 79(2)(a), and any information necessary for complying with the notice so far as relating to any such summary is in the possession of a superior landlord—

- *(a) the landlord shall make a written request for the relevant information to the person who is his landlord (and so on, if that person is himself not the superior landlord);*
- *(b) the superior landlord shall comply with that request within the period of one month beginning with the date of the making of the request; and*
- *(c) the landlord who received the notice shall then comply with it so far as relating to any such summary within the time allowed by section 81(1) or such further time, if any, as is reasonable.*

(2) Where—

- *(a) the landlord is required by a notice under section 80 to afford the auditor facilities for inspection or taking copies or extracts in respect of any documents or description of documents specified in the notice, and*
- *(b) any of the documents in question is in the custody or under the control of a superior landlord,*

the landlord shall on receiving the notice inform the auditor as soon as may be of that fact and of the name and address of the superior landlord, and the auditor may then give the superior landlord a notice requiring him to afford the facilities in question in respect of the document.

[(1) Where the landlord is given a notice under section 80 imposing on him a requirement relating to any documents which are held by a superior landlord, he shall inform the auditor as soon as may be of that fact and of the name and address of the superior landlord.

(2) The auditor may then give the superior landlord a notice requiring him to comply with the requirement.]

(3) Subsections (3) to (5) and (7) of section 81 shall, with any necessary modifications, have effect in relation to a notice given to a superior landlord under subsection (2) above as they have effect in relation to any such notice given to a relevant person as is mentioned in subsection (3) of that section.

83 Supplementary provisions

(1) Where—

- (a) a notice has been given to a landlord under section 80, and
- (b) at a time when any obligations arising out of the notice remain to be discharged by him—

(i) he disposes of the whole or part of his interest as landlord of the qualifying tenants of the constituent dwellings, and

(ii) the person acquiring any such interest of the landlord is in a position to discharge any of those obligations to any extent,

that person shall be responsible for discharging those obligations to that extent, as if he had been given the notice under that section.

(2) If the landlord is, despite any such disposal, still in a position to discharge those obligations to the extent referred to in subsection (1), he shall remain responsible for so discharging them; but otherwise the person referred to in that subsection shall be responsible for so discharging them to the exclusion of the landlord.

(3) Where a person is so responsible for discharging any such obligations (whether with the landlord or otherwise):

(a) references to the landlord in section 81 shall be read as including, or as, references to that person to such extent as is appropriate to reflect his responsibility for discharging those obligations; but

(b) in connection with the discharge of any such obligations by that person, that section shall apply as if any reference to the date of the giving of the notice under section 80 were a reference to the date of the disposal referred to in subsection (1).

(4) Where—

(a) a notice has been given to a relevant person under section 79, and

(b) at a time when any obligations arising out of the notice remain to be discharged by him, he ceases to be a relevant person, but

(c) he is, despite ceasing to be a relevant person, still in a position to discharge those obligations to any extent,

he shall nevertheless remain responsible for discharging those obligations to that extent; and section 81 shall accordingly continue to apply to him as if he were still a relevant person.

(5) Where—

(a) a notice has been given to a landlord under section 80, or

(b) a notice has been given to a relevant person under section 79,

then during the period of twelve months beginning with the date of that notice, no subsequent such notice may be given to the landlord or (as the case may be) that person on behalf of any persons who, in relation to the earlier notice, were qualifying tenants of the constituent dwellings.

84 Interpretation of Chapter V

In this Chapter—

'the 1985 Act' means the Landlord and Tenant Act 1985;

'appurtenant property' shall be construed in accordance with section 76(3) or (6);

'the auditor', in relation to a management audit, means such a person as is mentioned in section 78(3);

'the constituent dwellings' means the dwellings referred to in section 76(2)(a) or (b) (as the case may be);

'landlord' means immediate landlord;

'management audit' means such an audit as is mentioned in section 78(1);

'management functions' includes functions with respect to the provision of services or the repair, maintenance, improvement or insurance of property;

'relevant person' has the meaning given by section 79(7);

'the relevant premises' shall be construed in accordance with section 76(3) or (6);

'service charge' has the meaning given by section 18(1) of the 1985 Act.

CHAPTER VI
MISCELLANEOUS
CODES OF PRACTICE

. . .

87 Approval by Secretary of State of codes of management practice

(1) The Secretary of State may, if he considers it appropriate to do so, by order—

- (a) approve any code of practice—
  - (i) which appears to him to be designed to promote desirable practices in relation to any matter or matters directly or indirectly concerned with the management of residential property by relevant persons; and
  - (ii) which has been submitted to him for his approval;
- (b) approve any modifications of any such code which have been so submitted; or
- (c) withdraw his approval for any such code or modifications.

(2) The Secretary of State shall not approve any such code or any modifications of any such code unless he is satisfied that arrangements have been made for the text of the code or the modifications to be published in such manner as he considers appropriate for bringing the provisions of the code or the modifications to the notice of those likely to be affected by them (which, in the case of modifications of a code, may include publication of a text of the code incorporating the modifications).

(3) The power of the Secretary of State under this section to approve a code of practice which has been submitted to him for his approval includes power to approve a part of any such code; and references in this section to a code of practice may accordingly be read as including a reference to a part of a code of practice.

(4) At any one time there may be two or more codes of practice for the time being approved under this section.

(5) A code of practice approved under this section may make different provision with respect to different cases or descriptions of cases, including different provision for different areas.

(6) Without prejudice to the generality of subsections (1) and (5)—

- (a) a code of practice approved under this section may, in relation to any such matter as is referred to in subsection (1), make provision in respect of relevant persons who are under an obligation to discharge any function in connection with that matter as well as in respect of relevant persons who are not under such an obligation; and
- (b) any such code may make provision with respect to—
  - (i) the resolution of disputes with respect to residential property between relevant persons and the tenants of such property;
  - (ii) competitive tendering for works in connection with such property; and
  - (iii) the administration of trusts in respect of amounts paid by tenants by way of service charges.

(7) A failure on the part of any person to comply with any provision of a code of practice for the time being approved under this section shall not of itself render him liable to any proceedings; but in any proceedings before a court or tribunal—

- (a) any code of practice approved under this section shall be admissible in evidence; and
- (b) any provision of any such code which appears to the court or tribunal to be relevant to any question arising in the proceedings shall be taken into account in determining that question.

(8) For the purposes of this section—

(a) 'relevant person' means any landlord of residential property or any person who discharges management functions in respect of such property, and for this purpose 'management functions' includes functions with respect to the provision of services or the repair, maintenance, improvement or insurance of such property;

(b) 'residential property' means any building or part of a building which consists of one or more dwellings let on leases, but references to residential property include—

  (i) any garage, outhouse, garden, yard and appurtenances belonging to or usually enjoyed with such dwellings,

  (ii) any common parts of any such building or part, and

  (iii) any common facilities which are not within any such building or part; and

(c) 'service charge' means an amount payable by a tenant of a dwelling as part of or in addition to the rent—

  (i) which is payable, directly or indirectly, for services, repairs, maintenance, improvements or insurance or any relevant person's costs of management, and

  (ii) the whole or part of which varies or may vary according to the costs or estimated costs incurred or to be incurred by any relevant person in connection with the matters mentioned in sub-paragraph (i).

(9) This section applies in relation to dwellings let on licences to occupy as it applies in relation to dwellings let on leases, and references in this section to landlords and tenants of residential property accordingly include references to licensors and licensees of such property.

HOUSING ACT 1996

. . .

PART III
LANDLORD AND TENANT

CHAPTER I

TENANTS' RIGHTS
FORFEITURE

A2.4

81 Restriction on termination of tenancy for failure to pay service charge

(1) A landlord may not, in relation to premises let as a dwelling, exercise a right of re-entry or forfeiture for failure by a tenant to pay a service charge or administration charge unless—

(a) it is finally determined by (or on appeal from) the appropriate tribunal or by a court, or by an arbitral tribunal in proceedings pursuant to a post-dispute arbitration agreement, that the amount of the service charge or administration charge is payable by him, or

(b) the tenant has admitted that it is so payable.

(2) The landlord may not exercise a right of re-entry or forfeiture by virtue of subsection (1)(a) until after the end of the period of 14 days beginning with the day after that on which the final determination is made.

(3) For the purposes of this section it is finally determined that the amount of a service charge or administration charge is payable—

(a) if a decision that it is payable is not appealed against or otherwise challenged, at the end of the time for bringing an appeal or other challenge, or

(b) if such a decision is appealed against or otherwise challenged and not set aside in consequence of the appeal or other challenge, at the time specified in subsection (3A).

(3A) The time referred to in subsection (3)(b) is the time when the appeal or other challenge is disposed of–

(a) by the determination of the appeal or other challenge and the expiry of the time for bringing a subsequent appeal (if any), or

(b) by its being abandoned or otherwise ceasing to have effect.

(4) The reference in subsection (1) to premises let as a dwelling does not include premises let on—

(a) a tenancy to which Part II of the Landlord and Tenant Act 1954 applies (business tenancies),

(b) a tenancy of an agricultural holding within the meaning of the Agricultural Holdings Act 1986 in relation to which that Act applies, or

(c) a farm business tenancy within the meaning of the Agricultural Tenancies Act 1995.

(4A) References in this section to the exercise of a right of re-entry or forfeiture include the service of a notice under section 146(1) of the Law of Property Act 1925 (restriction on re-entry or forfeiture).

(5) In this section –

(a) 'administration charge' has the meaning given by Part 1 of Schedule 11 to the Commonhold and Leasehold Reform Act 2002,

(b) 'arbitration agreement' and 'arbitral tribunal' have the same meaning as in Part 1 of the Arbitration Act 1996 and 'post-dispute arbitration agreement', in relation to any matter, means an arbitration agreement made after a dispute about the matter has arisen,

(c) 'dwelling' has the same meaning as in the Landlord and Tenant Act 1985, and

(d) 'service charge' means a service charge within the meaning of section 18(1) of the Landlord and Tenant Act 1985, other than one excluded from that section by section 27 of that Act (rent of dwelling registered and not entered as variable).

(5A) Any order of a court to give effect to a determination of the appropriate tribunal shall be treated as a determination by the court for the purposes of this section.

(6) Nothing in this section affects the exercise of a right of re-entry or forfeiture on other grounds.

(7) For the purposes of this section, "appropriate tribunal" means—

(a) in relation to premises in England, the First-tier Tribunal or, where determined by or under Tribunal Procedure Rules, the Upper Tribunal; and

(b) in relation to premises in Wales, a leasehold valuation tribunal.

. . .

84 Right to appoint surveyor to advise on matters relating to service charges

(1) A recognised tenants' association may appoint a surveyor for the purposes of this section to advise on any matters relating to, or which may give rise to, service charges payable to a landlord by one or more members of the association.

The provisions of Schedule 4 have effect for conferring on a surveyor so appointed rights of access to documents and premises.

(2) A person shall not be so appointed unless he is a qualified surveyor. For this purpose 'qualified surveyor' has the same meaning as in section 78(4)(a) of the Leasehold Reform, Housing and Urban Development Act 1993 (persons qualified for appointment to carry out management audit).

(3) The appointment shall take effect for the purposes of this section upon notice in writing being given to the landlord by the association stating the name and address of the surveyor, the duration of his appointment and the matters in respect of which he is appointed.

(4) An appointment shall cease to have effect for the purposes of this section if the association gives notice in writing to the landlord to that effect or if the association ceases to exist.

(5) A notice is duly given under this section to a landlord of any tenants if it is given to a person who receives on behalf of the landlord the rent payable by those tenants; and a person to whom such a notice is so given shall forward it as soon as may be to the landlord.

(6) In this section—

'recognised tenants' association' has the same meaning as in the provisions of the Landlord and Tenant Act 1985 relating to service charges (see section 29 of that Act); and

'service charge' means a service charge within the meaning of section 18(1) of that Act other than one excluded from that section by section 27 of that Act (rent of dwelling registered and not entered as variable).

. . .

SCHEDULE 4

RIGHTS EXERCISABLE BY SURVEYOR APPOINTED BY TENANTS' ASSOCIATION

Section 84

1 Introductory

(1) A surveyor appointed for the purposes of section 84 has the rights conferred by this Schedule.

(2) In this Schedule—

- (a) 'the tenants' association' means the association by whom the surveyor was appointed, and
- (b) the surveyor's 'functions' are his functions in connection with the matters in respect of which he was appointed.

2 Appointment of assistants

(1) The surveyor may appoint such persons as he thinks fit to assist him in carrying out his functions.

(2) References in this Schedule to the surveyor in the context of—

- (a) being afforded any such facilities as are mentioned in paragraph 3, or
- (b) carrying out an inspection under paragraph 4,

include a person so appointed.

3 Right to inspect documents, etc

(1) The surveyor has a right to require the landlord or any other relevant person—

- (a) to afford him reasonable facilities for inspecting any document sight of which is reasonably required by him for the purposes of his functions, and
- (b) to afford him reasonable facilities for taking copies of or extracts from any such documents.

(2) In sub-paragraph (1) 'other relevant person' means a person other than the landlord who is or, in relation to a future service charge, will be—

- (a) responsible for applying the proceeds of the service charge, or
- (b) under an obligation to a tenant who pays the service charge in respect of any matter to which the charge relates.

(3) The rights conferred on the surveyor by this paragraph are extricable by him by notice in writing given by him to the landlord or other person concerned.

Where a notice is given to a person other than the landlord, the surveyor shall give a copy of the notice to the landlord.

(4) The landlord or other person to whom notice is given shall, within the period of one week beginning with the date of the giving of the notice or as soon as reasonably practicable thereafter, either—

- (a) afford the surveyor the facilities required by him for inspecting and taking copies or extracts of the documents to which the notice relates, or
- (b) give the surveyor a notice stating that he objects to doing so for reasons specified in the notice.

(5) Facilities for the inspection of any documents required under sub-paragraph (1)(a) shall be made available free of charge.

This does not mean that the landlord cannot treat as part of his costs of management any costs incurred by him in connection with making the facilities available.

(6) A reasonable charge may be made for facilities for the taking of copies or extracts required under sub-paragraph (1)(b).

(7) A notice is duly given under this paragraph to the landlord of a tenant if it is given to a person who receives on behalf of the landlord the rent payable by that tenant.

A person to whom such a notice is so given shall forward it as soon as may be to the landlord.

4 Right to inspect premises

(1) The surveyor also has the right to inspect any common parts comprised in relevant premises or any appurtenant property.

(2) In sub-paragraph (1)—

'common parts', in relation to a building or part of a building, includes the structure and exterior of the building or part and any common facilities within it;

'relevant premises' means so much of—

(i) the building or buildings containing the dwellings let to members of the tenants' association, and

(ii) any other building or buildings,

as constitute premises in relation to which management functions are discharged in respect of the costs of which service charges are payable by members of the association; and

'appurtenant property' means so much of any property not contained in relevant premises as constitutes property in relation to which any such management functions are discharged.

For the purposes of the above definitions 'management functions' includes functions with respect to the provision of services, or the repair, maintenance, improvement or insurance of property.

(3) On being requested to do so, the landlord shall afford the surveyor reasonable access for the purposes of carrying out an inspection under this paragraph.

(4) Such reasonable access shall be afforded to the surveyor free of charge. This does not mean that the landlord cannot treat as part of his costs of management any costs incurred by him in connection with affording reasonable access to the surveyor.

(5) A request is duly made under this paragraph to the landlord of a tenant if it is made to a person appointed by the landlord to deal with such requests or, if no such person has been appointed, to a person who receives on behalf of the landlord the rent payable by that tenant. A person to whom such a request is made shall notify the landlord of the request as soon as may be.

5 Enforcement of rights by the court

(1) If the landlord or other person to whom notice was given under paragraph 3 has not, by the end of the period of one month beginning with the date on which notice was given, complied with the notice, the court may, on the application of the surveyor, make an order requiring him to do so within such period as is specified in the order.

(2) If the landlord does not, within a reasonable period after the making of a request under paragraph 4, afford the surveyor reasonable access for the purposes of carrying out an inspection under that paragraph, the court may, on the application of the surveyor, make an order requiring the landlord to do so on such date as is specified in the order.

(3) An application for an order under this paragraph must be made before the end of the period of four months beginning with the date on which notice was given under paragraph 3 or the request was made under paragraph 4.

(4) An order under this paragraph may be made in general terms or may require the landlord or other person to do specific things, as the court thinks fit.

6 Documents held by superior landlord

(1) Where a landlord is required by a notice under paragraph 3 to afford the surveyor facilities for inspection or taking copies or extracts in respect of any document which is in the custody or under the control of a superior landlord—

(a) the landlord shall on receiving the notice inform the surveyor as soon as may be of the name and address of the superior landlord, and

(b) the surveyor may then give the superior landlord notice in writing requiring him facilities in question in respect of the document.

(2) Paragraphs 3 and 5(1) and (3) have effect, with any necessary modifications, in relation to a notice given to a superior landlord under this paragraph.

7 Effect of disposal by landlord

(1) Where a notice under paragraph 3 has been given or a request under paragraph 4 has been made to a landlord, and at a time when any obligations arising out of the notice or request remain to be discharged by him—

(a) he disposes of the whole or part of his interest as landlord of any member of the association, and

(b) the person acquiring that interest ('the transferee') is in a position to discharge obligations to any extent,

that person shall be responsible for discharging those obligations to that extent, as if he had been given the notice under paragraph 3 or had received the request under paragraph 4.

(2) If the landlord is, despite the disposal, still in a position to discharge those obligations, he remains responsible for doing so. Otherwise, the transferee is responsible for discharging them to the exclusion of the landlord.

(3) In connection with the discharge of such obligations by the transferee, paragraphs 3 to 6 apply with the substitution for any reference to the date on which notice was given under paragraph 3 or the request was made under paragraph 4 of a reference to the date of the disposal.

(4) In this paragraph 'disposal' means a disposal whether by the creation or transfer of an estate or interest, and includes the surrender of a tenancy; and references to the transferee shall be construed accordingly.

8 Effect of person ceasing to be a relevant person

Where a notice under paragraph 3 has been given to a person other than the landlord and, at a time when any obligations arising out of the notice remain to be discharged by him, he ceases to be such a person as is mentioned in paragraph 3(2), then, if he is still in a position to discharge those obligations to any extent he remains responsible for discharging those obligations, and the provisions of this Schedule continue to apply to him, to that extent.

COMMONHOLD AND LEASEHOLD REFORM ACT 2002

. . .

A2.5

159 Charges under estate management schemes

(1) This section applies where a scheme under—

(a) section 19 of the 1967 Act (estate management schemes in connection with enfranchisement under that Act),

(b) Chapter 4 of Part 1 of the 1993 Act (estate management schemes in connection with enfranchisement under the 1967 Act or Chapter 1 of Part 1 of the 1993 Act), or

(c) section 94(6) of the 1993 Act (corresponding schemes in relation to areas occupied under leases from Crown),

includes provision imposing on persons occupying or interested in property an obligation to make payments ('estate charges').

(2) A variable estate charge is payable only to the extent that the amount of the charge is reasonable; and 'variable estate charge' means an estate charge which is neither—

(a) specified in the scheme, nor

(b) calculated in accordance with a formula specified in the scheme.

(3) Any person on whom an obligation to pay an estate charge is imposed by the scheme may apply to the appropriate tribunal for an order varying the scheme in such manner as is specified in the application on the grounds that—

(a) any estate charge specified in the scheme is unreasonable, or

(b) any formula specified in the scheme in accordance with which any estate charge is calculated is unreasonable.

(4) If the grounds on which the application was made are established to the satisfaction of the tribunal, it may make an order varying the scheme in such manner as is specified in the order.

(5) The variation specified in the order may be—

(a) the variation specified in the application, or

(b) such other variation as the tribunal thinks fit.

(6) An application may be made to the appropriate tribunal for a determination whether an estate charge is payable by a person and, if it is, as to—

(a) the person by whom it is payable,

(b) the person to whom it is payable,

(c) the amount which is payable,

(d) the date at or by which it is payable, and

(e) the manner in which it is payable.

(7) Subsection (6) applies whether or not any payment has been made.

(8) The jurisdiction conferred on the appropriate tribunal in respect of any matter by virtue of subsection (6) is in addition to any jurisdiction of a court in respect of the matter.

(9) No application under subsection (6) may be made in respect of a matter which—

(a) has been agreed or admitted by the person concerned,

(b) has been, or is to be, referred to arbitration pursuant to a post-dispute arbitration agreement to which that person is a party,

(c) has been the subject of determination by a court, or

(d) has been the subject of determination by an arbitral tribunal pursuant to a post-dispute arbitration agreement.

(10) But the person is not to be taken to have agreed or admitted any matter by reason only of having made any payment.

(11) An agreement (other than a post-dispute arbitration agreement) is void in so far as it purports to provide for a determination—

(a) in a particular manner, or

(b) on particular evidence,

of any question which may be the subject matter of an application under subsection (6).

(12) In this section—

'post-dispute arbitration agreement' in relation to any matter, means an arbitration agreement made after a dispute about the matter has arisen, and 'arbitration agreement' and 'arbitral tribunal' have the same meanings as in Part 1 of the Arbitration Act 1996 (c. 23).

(13) For the purposes of this section, "appropriate tribunal" means—

(a) in relation to premises in England, the First-tier Tribunal or, where determined by or under Tribunal Procedure Rules, the Upper Tribunal; and

(b) in relation to premises in Wales, a leasehold valuation tribunal.

. . .

164 Insurance otherwise than with landlord's insurer

(1) This section applies where a long lease of a house requires the tenant to insure the house with an insurer nominated or approved by the landlord ('the landlord's insurer').

(2) The tenant is not required to effect the insurance with the landlord's insurer if—

(a) the house is insured under a policy of insurance issued by an authorised insurer,

(b) the policy covers the interests of both the landlord and the tenant,

(c) the policy covers all the risks which the lease requires be covered by insurance provided by the landlord's insurer,

(d) the amount of the cover is not less than that which the lease requires to be provided by such insurance, and

(e) the tenant satisfies subsection (3).

(3) To satisfy this subsection the tenant—

(a) must have given a notice of cover to the landlord before the end of the period of fourteen days beginning with the relevant date, and

(b) if (after that date) he has been requested to do so by a new landlord, must have given a notice of cover to him within the period of fourteen days beginning with the day on which the request was given.

(4) For the purposes of subsection (3)—

(a) if the policy has not been renewed the relevant date is the day on which it took effect and if it has been renewed it is the day from which it was last renewed, and

(b) a person is a new landlord on any day if he acquired the interest of the previous landlord under the lease on a disposal made by him during the period of one month ending with that day.

(5) A notice of cover is a notice specifying—

(a) the name of the insurer,

(b) the risks covered by the policy,

(c) the amount and period of the cover, and

(d) such further information as may be prescribed.

(6) A notice of cover—

(a) must be in the prescribed form, and

(b) may be sent by post.

(7) If a notice of cover is sent by post, it may be addressed to the landlord at the address specified in subsection (8).

(8) That address is—

(a) the address last furnished to the tenant as the landlord's address for service in accordance with section 48 of the 1987 Act (notification of address for service of notices on landlord), or

(b) if no such address has been so furnished, the address last furnished to the tenant as the landlord's address in accordance with section 47 of the 1987 Act (landlord's name and address to be contained in demands for rent).

(9) But the tenant may not give a notice of cover to the landlord at the address specified in subsection (8) if he has been notified by the landlord of a different address in England and Wales at which he wishes to be given any such notice.

(10) In this section—

'authorised insurer', in relation to a policy of insurance, means a person who may carry on in the United Kingdom the business of effecting or carrying out contracts of insurance of the sort provided under the policy without contravening the prohibition imposed by section 19 of the Financial Services and Markets Act 2000 (c. 8),

'house' has the same meaning as for the purposes of Part 1 of the 1967 Act,

'landlord' and 'tenant' have the same meanings as in Chapter 1 of this Part,

'long lease' has the meaning given by sections 74 and 75 of this Act, and

'prescribed' means prescribed by regulations made by the appropriate national authority.

. . .

167 Failure to pay small amount for short period

(1) A landlord under a long lease of a dwelling may not exercise a right of re-entry or forfeiture for failure by a tenant to pay an amount consisting of rent, service charges or administration charges (or a combination of them) ('the unpaid amount') unless the unpaid amount—

(a) exceeds the prescribed sum, or

(b) consists of or includes an amount which has been payable for more than a prescribed period.

(2) The sum prescribed under subsection (1)(a) must not exceed £500.

(3) If the unpaid amount includes a default charge, it is to be treated for the purposes of subsection (1)(a) as reduced by the amount of the charge; and for this purpose 'default charge' means an administration charge payable in respect of the tenant's failure to pay any part of the unpaid amount.

(4) In this section 'long lease of a dwelling' does not include—

(a) a tenancy to which Part 2 of the Landlord and Tenant Act 1954 (c. 56) (business tenancies) applies,

(c) a tenancy of an agricultural holding within the meaning of the Agricultural Holdings Act 1986 (c. 5) in relation to which that Act applies, or

(d) a farm business tenancy within the meaning of the Agricultural Tenancies Act 1995 (c. 8).

(5) In this section—

'administration charge' has the same meaning as in Part 1 of Schedule 11,

'dwelling' has the same meaning as in the 1985 Act,

'landlord' and 'tenant' have the same meaning as in Chapter 1 of this Part, 'long lease' has the same meaning given by sections 74 and 75 of this Act, except that a shared ownership lease is a long lease whatever the tenant's total share,

'prescribed' means prescribed by regulations made by the appropriate national authority, and

'service charge' has the meaning given by section 18(1) of the 1985 Act.

. . .

CROWN APPLICATION

172 Application to Crown

(1) The following provisions apply in relation to Crown land (as in relation to other land)—

- (a) sections 18 to 30B of (and the Schedule to) the 1985 Act (service charges, insurance and managing agents),
- (b) Part 2 of the 1987 Act (appointment of manager by the appropriate tribunal),
- (c) Part 4 of the 1987 Act (variation of leases),
- (d) sections 46 to 49 of the 1987 Act (information to be furnished to tenants),
- (e) Chapter 5 of Part 1 of the 1993 Act (management audit),
- (f) section 81 of the Housing Act 1996 (c. 52) (restriction on termination of tenancy for failure to pay service charge etc),
- (g) section 84 of (and Schedule 4 to) that Act (right to appoint surveyor), and
- (h) in this Chapter, the provisions relating to any of the provisions within paragraphs (a) to (g), Part 1 of Schedule 11 and sections 162 to 165 and sections 167 and 171.

(2) Land is Crown land if there is or has at any time been an interest or estate in the land—

- (a) comprised in the Crown Estate,
- (b) belonging to Her Majesty in right of the Duchy of Lancaster,
- (c) belonging to the Duchy of Cornwall, or
- (d) belonging to a government department or held on behalf of Her Majesty for the purposes of a government department.

(3) No failure by the Crown to perform a duty imposed by or by virtue of any of sections 21 to 23A of, or any of paragraphs 2 to 4A of the Schedule to, the 1985 Act makes the Crown criminally liable; but the High Court may declare any such failure without reasonable excuse to be unlawful.

(4) Any sum payable under any of the provisions mentioned in subsection (1) by the Chancellor of the Duchy of Lancaster may be raised and paid under section 25 of the Duchy of Lancaster Act 1817 (c. 97) as an expense incurred in improvement of land belonging to Her Majesty in right of the Duchy.

(5) Any sum payable under such provision by the Duke of Cornwall (or any other possessor for the time being of the Duchy of Cornwall) may be raised and paid under section 8 of the Duchy of Cornwall Management Act 1863 (c. 49) as an expense incurred in permanently improving the possessions of the Duchy.

(6) In section 56 of the 1987 Act (Crown land)—

- (a) in subsection (1), for 'This Act' substitute 'Parts 1 and 3 and sections 42 to 42B (and so much of this Part as relates to those provisions)', and
- (b) in subsection (3), for 'this Act' substitute 'the provisions mentioned in subsection (1)'.

(9) And no case may be stated for the opinion of the High Court in respect of such a decision by virtue of that provision.

. . .

SCHEDULE 11
ADMINISTRATION CHARGES

Section 158

PART 1
REASONABLENESS OF ADMINISTRATION CHARGES

1 Meaning of 'administration charge'

(1) In this Part of this Schedule 'administration charge' means an amount payable by a tenant of a dwelling as part of or in addition to the rent which is payable, directly or indirectly—

- (a) for or in connection with the grant of approvals under his lease, or applications for such approvals,
- (b) for or in connection with the provision of information or documents by or on behalf of the landlord or a person who is party to his lease otherwise than as landlord or tenant,
- (c) in respect of a failure by the tenant to make a payment by the due date to the landlord or a person who is party to his lease otherwise than as landlord or tenant, or
- (d) in connection with a breach (or alleged breach) of a covenant or condition in his lease.

(2) But an amount payable by the tenant of a dwelling the rent of which is registered under Part 4 of the Rent Act 1977 (c. 42) is not an administration charge, unless the amount registered is entered as a variable amount in pursuance of section 71(4) of that Act.

(3) In this Part of this Schedule 'variable administration charge' means an administration charge payable by a tenant which is neither—

- (a) specified in his lease, nor
- (b) calculated in accordance with a formula specified in his lease.

(4) An order amending sub-paragraph (1) may be made by the appropriate national authority.

2 Reasonableness of administration charges

A variable administration charge is payable only to the extent that the amount of the charge is reasonable.

3

(1) Any party to a lease of a dwelling may apply to the appropriate tribunal for an order varying the lease in such manner as is specified in the application on the grounds that—

- (a) any administration charge specified in the lease is unreasonable, or
- (b) any formula specified in the lease in accordance with which any administration charge is calculated is unreasonable.

(2) If the grounds on which the application was made are established to the satisfaction of the tribunal, it may make an order varying the lease in such manner as is specified in the order.

(3) The variation specified in the order may be—

- (a) the variation specified in the application, or
- (b) such other variation as the tribunal thinks fit.

(4) The tribunal may, instead of making an order varying the lease in such manner as is specified in the order, make an order directing the parties to the lease to vary it in such manner as is so specified.

(5) The tribunal may by order direct that a memorandum of any variation of a lease effected by virtue of this paragraph be endorsed on such documents as are specified in the order.

(6) Any such variation of a lease shall be binding not only on the parties to the lease for the time being but also on other persons (including any predecessors in title), whether or not they were parties to the proceedings in which the order was made.

4 Notice in connection with demands for administration charges

(1) A demand for the payment of an administration charge must be accompanied by a summary of the rights and obligations of tenants in dwellings in relation to administration charges.

(2) The appropriate national authority may make regulations prescribing requirements as to the form and content of such summaries of rights and obligations.

(3) A tenant may withhold payment of an administration charge which has been demanded from him if sub-paragraph (1) is not complied with in relation to the demand.

(4) Where a tenant withholds an administration charge under this paragraph, any provisions of the lease relating to non-payment or late payment of administration charges do not have effect in relation to the period for which he so withholds it.

5 Liability to pay administration charges

(1) An application may be made to the appropriate tribunal for a determination whether an administration charge is payable and, if it is, as to—

- (a) the person by whom it is payable,
- (b) the person to whom it is payable,
- (c) the amount which is payable,
- (d) the date at or by which it is payable, and
- (e) the manner in which it is payable.

(2) Sub-paragraph (1) applies whether or not any payment has been made.

(3) The jurisdiction conferred on the appropriate tribunal in respect of any matter by virtue of sub-paragraph (1) is in addition to any jurisdiction of a court in respect of the matter.

(4) No application under sub-paragraph (1) may be made in respect of a matter which—

- (a) has been agreed or admitted by the tenant,
- (b) has been, or is to be, referred to arbitration pursuant to a post-dispute arbitration agreement to which the tenant is a party,
- (c) has been the subject of determination by a court, or
- (d) has been the subject of determination by an arbitral tribunal pursuant to a post-dispute arbitration agreement.

(5) But the tenant is not to be taken to have agreed or admitted any matter by reason only of having made any payment.

(6) An agreement by the tenant of a dwelling (other than a post-dispute arbitration agreement) is void in so far as it purports to provide for a determination—

- (a) in a particular manner, or
- (b) on particular evidence,

of any question which may be the subject matter of an application under sub-paragraph (1).

6 Interpretation

(1) This paragraph applies for the purposes of this Part of this Schedule.

(2) 'Tenant' includes a statutory tenant.

(3) 'Dwelling' and 'statutory tenant' (and 'landlord' in relation to a statutory tenant) have the same meanings as in the 1985 Act.

(4) 'Post-dispute arbitration agreement', in relation to any matter, means an arbitration agreement made after a dispute about the matter has arisen.

(5) 'Arbitration agreement' and 'arbitral tribunal' have the same meanings as in Part 1 of the Arbitration Act 1996.

(6) 'Appropriate tribunal' means—

- (a) in relation to premises in England, the First-tier Tribunal or, where determined by or under Tribunal Procedure Rules, the Upper Tribunal; and
- (b) in relation to premises in Wales, a leasehold valuation tribunal.

SERVICE CHARGES (CONSULTATION REQUIREMENTS) (ENGLAND) REGULATIONS 2003

(SI 2003/1987)

A2.6

1 Citation, commencement and application

(1) These Regulations may be cited as the Service Charges (Consultation Requirements) (England) Regulations 2003 and shall come into force on 31st October 2003.

(2) These Regulations apply in relation to England only.

(3) These Regulations apply where a landlord—

(a) intends to enter into a qualifying long term agreement to which section 20 of the Landlord and Tenant Act 1985 applies on or after the date on which these Regulations come into force; or

(b) intends to carry out qualifying works to which that section applies on or after that date.

2 Interpretation

(1) In these Regulations—

'the 1985 Act' means the Landlord and Tenant Act 1985;

'close relative', in relation to a person, means a spouse or cohabitee, a parent, parent-in-law, son, son-in-law, daughter, daughter-in-law, brother, brother-in-law, sister, sister-in-law, step-parent, step-son or step-daughter of that person;

'cohabitee', in relation to a person, means—

(a) a person of the opposite sex who is living with that person as husband or wife; or

(b) a person of the same sex living with that person in a relationship which has the characteristics of the relationship between husband and wife;

'nominated person' means a person whose name is proposed in response to an invitation made as mentioned in paragraph 1(3) of Schedule 1 or paragraph 1(3) of Part 2 of Schedule 4; and 'nomination' means any such proposal;

'public notice' means notice published by the Publications Office of the EU pursuant to the Public Contracts Regulations 2015;

'relevant period', in relation to a notice, means the period of 30 days beginning with the date of the notice;

'RTB tenancy' means the tenancy of an RTB tenant;

'RTB tenant', in relation to a landlord, means a person who has become a tenant of the landlord by virtue of section 138 of the Housing Act 1985 (duty of landlord to convey freehold or grant lease), section 171A of that Act (cases in which right to buy is preserved), section 180 of the Housing and Regeneration Act 2008 or section 16 of the Housing Act 1996 (right of tenant to acquire dwelling) under a lease whose terms include a requirement that the tenant shall bear a reasonable part of such costs incurred by the landlord as are mentioned in paragraphs 16A to 16D of Schedule 6 to that Act (service charges and other contributions payable by the tenant);

'section 20' means section 20 (limitation of service charges: consultation requirements) of the 1985 Act;

'section 20ZA' means section 20ZA (consultation requirements: supplementary) of that Act;

'the relevant matters', in relation to a proposed agreement, means the goods or services to be provided or the works to be carried out (as the case may be) under the agreement.

(2) For the purposes of any estimate required by any provision of these Regulations to be made by the landlord—

(a) value added tax shall be included where applicable; and

(b) where the estimate relates to a proposed agreement, it shall be assumed that the agreement will terminate only by effluxion of time.

3 Agreements that are not qualifying long term agreements

(1) An agreement is not a qualifying long term agreement—

(a) if it is a contract of employment; or

(b) if it is a management agreement made by a local housing authority and—

(i) a tenant management organisation; or

(ii) a body established under section 2 of the Local Government Act 2000 or section 1 of the Localism Act 2011;

(c) if the parties to the agreement are—

(i) a holding company and one or more of its subsidiaries; or

(ii) two or more subsidiaries of the same holding company;

(d) if—

(i) when the agreement is entered into, there are no tenants of the building or other premises to which the agreement relates; and

(ii) the agreement is for a term not exceeding five years.

(2) An agreement entered into, by or on behalf of the landlord or a superior landlord—

(a) before the coming into force of these Regulations; and

(b) for a term of more than twelve months,

is not a qualifying long term agreement, notwithstanding that more than twelve months of the term remain unexpired on the coming into force of these Regulations.

(3) An agreement for a term of more than twelve months entered into, by or on behalf of the landlord or a superior landlord, which provides for the carrying out of qualifying works for which public notice has been given before the date on which these Regulations come into force, is not a qualifying long term agreement.

(4) In paragraph (1)—

'holding company' and 'subsidiaries' have the same meaning as in the Companies Act 1985;

'management agreement' has the meaning given by section 27(2) of the Housing Act 1985; and

'tenant management organisation' has the meaning given by section 27AB(8) of the Housing Act 1985.

4 Application of section 20 to qualifying long term agreements

(1) Section 20 shall apply to a qualifying long term agreement if relevant costs incurred under the agreement in any accounting period exceed an amount which results in the relevant contribution of any tenant, in respect of that period, being more than £100.

(2) In paragraph (1), 'accounting period' means the period—

(a) beginning with the relevant date, and

(b) ending with the date that falls twelve months after the relevant date.

(3) [Subject to paragraph (3A), in] the case of the first accounting period, the relevant date is—

- (a) if the relevant accounts are made up for periods of twelve months, the date on which the period that includes the date on which these Regulations come into force ends, or
- (b) if the accounts are not so made up, the date on which these Regulations come into force.

[(3A) Where—

- (a) a landlord intends to enter into a qualifying long term agreement on or after 12th November 2004; and
- (b) he has not at any time between 31st October 2003 and 12th November 2004 made up accounts relating to service charges referable to a qualifying long term agreement and payable in respect of the dwellings to which the intended agreement is to relate,

the relevant date is the date on which begins the first period for which service charges referable to that intended agreement are payable under the terms of the leases of those dwellings.]

(4) In the case of subsequent accounting periods, the relevant date is the date immediately following the end of the previous accounting period.

5 The consultation requirements: qualifying long term agreements

(1) Subject to paragraphs (2) and (3), in relation to qualifying long term agreements to which section 20 applies, the consultation requirements for the purposes of that section and section 20ZA are the requirements specified in Schedule 1.

(2) Where public notice is required to be given of the relevant matters to which a qualifying long term agreement relates, the consultation requirements for the purposes of sections 20 and 20ZA, as regards the agreement, are the requirements specified in Schedule 2.

(3) In relation to a RTB tenant and a particular qualifying long term agreement, nothing in paragraph (1) or (2) requires a landlord to comply with any of the consultation requirements applicable to that agreement that arise before the thirty-first day of the RTB tenancy.

6 Application of section 20 to qualifying works

For the purposes of subsection (3) of section 20 the appropriate amount is an amount which results in the relevant contribution of any tenant being more than £250.

7 The consultation requirements: qualifying works

(1) Subject to paragraph (5), where qualifying works are the subject (whether alone or with other matters) of a qualifying long term agreement to which section 20 applies, the consultation requirements for the purposes of that section and section 20ZA, as regards those works, are the requirements specified in Schedule 3.

(2) Subject to paragraph (5), in a case to which paragraph (3) applies the consultation requirements for the purposes of sections 20 and 20ZA, as regards qualifying works referred to in that paragraph, are those specified in Schedule 3.

(3) This paragraph applies where—

- (a) under an agreement entered into, by or on behalf of the landlord or a superior landlord, before the coming into force of these Regulations, qualifying works are carried out at any time on or after the date that falls two months after the date on which these Regulations come into force; or
- (b) under an agreement for a term of more than twelve months entered into, by or on behalf of the landlord or a superior landlord, qualifying works for which public notice has been given before the date on which these Regulations come into force are carried out at any time on or after the date.

(4) Except in a case to which paragraph (3) applies, and subject to paragraph (5), where qualifying works are not the subject of a qualifying long term agreement to which section 20 applies, the consultation requirements for the purposes of that section and section 20ZA, as regards those works—

(a) in a case where public notice of those works is required to be given, are those specified in Part 1 of Schedule 4;

(b) in any other case, are those specified in Part 2 of that Schedule.

(5) In relation to a RTB tenant and particular qualifying works, nothing in paragraph (1), (2) or (4) requires a landlord to comply with any of the consultation requirements applicable to that agreement that arise before the thirty-first day of the RTB tenancy.

SCHEDULE 1

CONSULTATION REQUIREMENTS FOR QUALIFYING LONG TERM AGREEMENTS OTHER THAN THOSE FOR WHICH PUBLIC NOTICE IS REQUIRED

Regulation 5(1)

1 Notice of intention

(1) The landlord shall give notice in writing of his intention to enter into the agreement—

(a) to each tenant; and

(b) where a recognised tenants' association represents some or all of the tenants, to the association.

(2) The notice shall—

(a) describe, in general terms, the relevant matters or specify the place and hours at which a description of the relevant matters may be inspected;

(b) state the landlord's reasons for considering it necessary to enter into the agreement;

(c) where the relevant matters consist of or include qualifying works, state the landlord's reasons for considering it necessary to carry out those works;

(d) invite the making, in writing, of observations in relation to the proposed agreement; and

(e) specify—

(i) the address to which such observations may be sent;

(ii) that they must be delivered within the relevant period; and

(iii) the date on which the relevant period ends.

(3) The notice shall also invite each tenant and the association (if any) to propose, within the relevant period, the name of a person from whom the landlord should try to obtain an estimate in respect of the relevant matters.

2 Inspection of description of relevant matters

(1) Where a notice under paragraph 1 specifies a place and hours for inspection—

(a) the place and hours so specified must be reasonable; and

(b) a description of the relevant matters must be available for inspection, free of charge, at that place and during those hours.

(2) If facilities to enable copies to be taken are not made available at the times at which the description may be inspected, the landlord shall provide to any tenant, on request and free of charge, a copy of the description.

3 Duty to have regard to observations in relation to proposed agreement

Where, within the relevant period, observations are made in relation to the proposed agreement by any tenant or recognised tenants' association, the landlord shall have regard to those observations.

4 Estimates

(1) Where, within the relevant period, a single nomination is made by a recognised tenants' association (whether or not a nomination is made by any tenant), the landlord shall try to obtain an estimate from the nominated person.

(2) Where, within the relevant period, a single nomination is made by only one of the tenants (whether or not a nomination is made by a recognised tenants' association), the landlord shall try to obtain an estimate from the nominated person.

(3) Where, within the relevant period, a single nomination is made by more than one tenant (whether or not a nomination is made by a recognised tenants' association), the landlord shall try to obtain an estimate—

- (a) from the person who received the most nominations; or
- (b) if there is no such person, but two (or more) persons received the same number of nominations, being a number in excess of the nominations received by any other person, from one of those two (or more) persons; or
- (c) in any other case, from any nominated person.

(4) Where, within the relevant period, more than one nomination is made by any tenant and more than one nomination is made by a recognised tenants' association, the landlord shall try to obtain an estimate—

- (a) from at least one person nominated by a tenant; and
- (b) from at least one person nominated by the association, other than a person from whom an estimate is sought as mentioned in paragraph (a).

5 Preparation of landlord's proposals

(1) The landlord shall prepare, in accordance with the following provisions of this paragraph, at least two proposals in respect of the relevant matters.

(2) At least one of the proposals must propose that goods or services are provided, or works are carried out (as the case may be), by a person wholly unconnected with the landlord.

(3) Where an estimate has been obtained from a nominated person, the landlord must prepare a proposal based on that estimate.

(4) Each proposal shall contain a statement of the relevant matters.

(5) Each proposal shall contain a statement, as regards each party to the proposed agreement other than the landlord—

- (a) of the party's name and address; and
- (b) of any connection (apart from the proposed agreement) between the party and the landlord.

(6) For the purposes of sub-paragraphs (2) and (5)(b), it shall be assumed that there is a connection between a party (as the case may be) and the landlord—

- (a) where the landlord is a company, if the party is, or is to be, a director or manager of the company or is a close relative of any such director or manager;
- (b) where the landlord is a company, and the party is a partner in a partnership, if any partner in that partnership is, or is to be, a director or manager of the company or is a close relative of any such director or manager;
- (c) where both the landlord and the party are companies, if any director or manager of one company is, or is to be, a director or manager of the other company;

(d) where the party is a company, if the landlord is a director or manager of the company or is a close relative of any such director or manager; or

(e) where the party is a company and the landlord is a partner in a partnership, if any partner in that partnership is a director or manager of the company or is a close relative of any such director or manager.

(7) Where, as regards each tenant's unit of occupation and the relevant matters, it is reasonably practicable for the landlord to estimate the relevant contribution attributable to the relevant matters to which the proposed agreement relates, each proposal shall contain a statement of that estimated contribution.

(8) Where—

(a) it is not reasonably practicable for the landlord to make the estimate mentioned in sub-paragraph (7); and

(b) it is reasonably practicable for the landlord to estimate, as regards the building or other premises to which the proposed agreement relates, the total amount of his expenditure under the proposed agreement,

each proposal shall contain a statement of that estimated expenditure.

(9) Where—

(a) it is not reasonably practicable for the landlord to make the estimate mentioned in sub-paragraph (7) or (8)(b); and

(b) it is reasonably practicable for the landlord to ascertain the current unit cost or hourly or daily rate applicable to the relevant matters,

each proposal shall contain a statement of that cost or rate.

(10) Where the relevant matters comprise or include the proposed appointment by the landlord of an agent to discharge any of the landlord's obligations to the tenants which relate to the management by him of premises to which the agreement relates, each proposal shall contain a statement—

(a) that the person whose appointment is proposed—

(i) is or, as the case may be, is not, a member of a professional body or trade association; and

(ii) subscribes or, as the case may be, does not subscribe, to any code of practice or voluntary accreditation scheme relevant to the functions of managing agents; and

(b) if the person is a member of a professional body trade association, of the name of the body or association.

(11) Each proposal shall contain a statement as to the provisions (if any) for variation of any amount specified in, or to be determined under, the proposed agreement.

(12) Each proposal shall contain a statement of the intended duration of the proposed agreement.

(13) Where the landlord has received observations to which (in accordance with paragraph 3) he is required to have regard, each proposal shall contain a statement summarising the observations and setting out the landlord's response to them.

6 Notification of landlord's proposals

(1) The landlord shall give notice in writing of proposals prepared under paragraph 5—

(a) to each tenant; and

(b) where a recognised tenants' association represents some or all of the tenants, to the association.

(2) The notice shall—

(a) be accompanied by a copy of each proposal or specify the place and hours at which the proposals may be inspected;

(b) invite the making, in writing, of observations in relation to the proposals; and

(c) specify—
  (i) the address to which such observations may be sent;
  (ii) that they must be delivered within the relevant period; and
  (iii) the date on which the relevant period ends.

(3) Paragraph 2 shall apply to proposals made available for inspection under this paragraph as it applies to a description of the relevant matters made available for inspection under that paragraph.

7 Duty to have regard to observations in relation to proposals

Where, within the relevant period, observations are made in relation to the landlord's proposals by any tenant or recognised tenants' association, the landlord shall have regard to those observations.

8 Duty on entering into agreement

(1) Subject to sub-paragraph (2), where the landlord enters into an agreement relating to relevant matters, he shall, within 21 days of entering into the agreement, by notice in writing to each tenant and the recognised tenants' association (if any)—

(a) state his reasons for making that agreement or specify the place and hours at which a statement of those reasons may be inspected; and

(b) where he has received observations to which (in accordance with paragraph 7) he is required to have regard, summarise the observations and respond to them or specify the place and hours at which that summary and response may be inspected.

(2) The requirements of sub-paragraph (1) do not apply where the person with whom the agreement is made is a nominated person or submitted the lowest estimate.

(3) Paragraph 2 shall apply to a statement, summary and response made available for inspection under this paragraph as it applies to a description of the relevant matters made available for inspection under that paragraph.

SCHEDULE 2

CONSULTATION REQUIREMENTS FOR QUALIFYING LONG TERM AGREEMENTS FOR WHICH PUBLIC NOTICE IS REQUIRED

1 Notice of intention

(1) The landlord shall give notice in writing of his intention to enter into the agreement—

(a) to each tenant; and

(b) where a recognised tenants' association represents some or all of the tenants, to the association.

(2) The notice shall—

(a) describe, in general terms, the relevant matters or specify the place and hours at which a description of the relevant matters may be inspected;

(b) state the landlord's reasons for considering it necessary to enter into the agreement;

(c) where the relevant matters consist of or include qualifying works, state the landlord's reasons for considering it necessary to carry out those works;

(d) state that the reason why the landlord is not inviting recipients of the notice to nominate persons from whom he should try to obtain an estimate for the relevant matters is that public notice of the relevant matters is to be given;

(e) invite the making, in writing, of observations in relation to the relevant matters; and

(f) specify—

(i) the address to which such observations may be sent;
(ii) that they must be delivered within the relevant period; and
(iii) the date on which the relevant period ends.

2 Inspection of description of relevant matters

(1) Where a notice under paragraph 1 specifies a place and hours for inspection—

(a) the place and hours so specified must be reasonable; and
(b) a description of the relevant matters must be available for inspection, free of charge, at that place and during those hours.

(2) If facilities to enable copies to be taken are not made available at the times at which the description may be inspected, the landlord shall provide to any tenant, on request and free of charge, a copy of the description.

3 Duty to have regard to observations in relation to relevant matters

Where, within the relevant period, observations are made, in relation to the relevant matters by any tenant or recognised tenants' association, the landlord shall have regard to those observations.

4 Preparation of landlord's proposal

(1) The landlord shall prepare, in accordance with the following provisions of this paragraph, a proposal in respect of the proposed agreement.

(2) The proposal shall contain a statement—

(a) of the name and address of every party to the proposed agreement (other than the landlord); and
(b) of any connection (apart from the proposed agreement) between the landlord and any other party.

(3) For the purpose of sub-paragraph (2)(b), it shall be assumed that there is a connection between the landlord and a party—

(a) where the landlord is a company, if the party is, or is to be, a director or manager of the company or is a close relative of any such director or manager;
(b) where the landlord is a company, and the party is a partner in a partnership, if any partner in that partnership is, or is to be, a director or manager of the company or is a close relative of any such director or manager;
(c) where both the landlord and the party are companies, if any director or manager of one company is, or is to be, a director or manager of the other company;
(d) where the party is a company, if the landlord is a director or manager of the company or is a close relative of any such director or manager; or
(e) where the party is a company and the landlord is a partner in a partnership, if any partner in that partnership is a director or manager of the company or is a close relative of any such director or manager.

(4) Where, as regards each tenant's unit of occupation, it is reasonably practicable for the landlord to estimate the relevant contribution to be incurred by the tenant attributable to the relevant matters to which the proposed agreement relates, the proposal shall contain a statement of that contribution.

(5) Where—

(a) it is not reasonably practicable for the landlord to make the estimate mentioned in sub-paragraph (4); and
(b) it is reasonably practicable for the landlord to estimate, as regards the building or other premises to which the proposed agreement relates, the total amount of his expenditure under the proposed agreement,

the proposal shall contain a statement of the amount of that estimated expenditure.

(6) Where—

(a) it is not reasonably practicable for the landlord to make the estimate mentioned in sub-paragraph (4) or (5)(b); and

(b) it is reasonably practicable for the landlord to ascertain the current unit cost or hourly or daily rate applicable to the relevant matters to which the proposed agreement relates,

the proposal shall contain a statement of that cost or rate.

(7) Where it is not reasonably practicable for the landlord to make the estimate mentioned in sub-paragraph (6)(b), the proposal shall contain a statement of the reasons why he cannot comply and the date by which he expects to be able to provide an estimate, cost or rate.

(8) Where the relevant matters comprise or include the proposed appointment by the landlord of an agent to discharge any of the landlord's obligations to the tenants which relate to the management by him of premises to which the agreement relates, each proposal shall contain a statement—

(a) that the person whose appointment is proposed—

(i) is or, as the case may be, is not, a member of a professional body or trade association; and

(ii) subscribes or, as the case may be, does not subscribe, to any code of practice or voluntary accreditation scheme relevant to the functions of managing agents; and

(b) if the person is a member of a professional body trade association, of the name of the body or association.

(9) Each proposal shall contain a statement of the intended duration of the proposed agreement.

(10) Where the landlord has received observations to which (in accordance with paragraph 3) he is required to have regard, the proposal shall contain a statement summarising the observations and setting out the landlord's response to them.

5 Notification of landlord's proposal

(1) The landlord shall give notice in writing of the proposal prepared under paragraph 4—

(a) to each tenant; and

(b) where a recognised tenants' association represents some or all of the tenants, to the association.

(2) The notice shall—

(a) be accompanied by a copy of the proposal or specify the place and hours at which the proposal may be inspected;

(b) invite the making, in writing, of observations in relation to the proposal; and

(c) specify—

(i) the address to which such observations may be sent;

(ii) that they must be delivered within the relevant period; and

(iii) the date on which the relevant period ends.

(3) Paragraph 2 shall apply to a proposal made available for inspection under this paragraph as it applies to a description made available for inspection under that paragraph.

6 Duty to have regard to observations in relation to proposal

Where, within the relevant period, observations are made in relation to the landlord's proposal by any tenant or recognised tenants' association, the landlord shall have regard to those observations.

7 Landlord's response to observations

Where the landlord receives observations to which (in accordance with paragraph 6) he is required to have regard, he shall, within 21 days of their receipt, by notice in writing to the person by whom the observations were made, state his response to the observations.

8 Supplementary information

Where a proposal prepared under paragraph 4 contains such a statement as is mentioned in sub-paragraph (7) of that paragraph, the landlord shall, within 21 days of receiving sufficient information to enable him to estimate the amount, cost or rate referred to in sub-paragraph (4), (5) or (6) of that paragraph, give notice in writing of the estimated amount, cost or rate (as the case may be)—

- (a) to each tenant; and
- (b) where a recognised tenants' association represents some or all of the tenants, to the association.

SCHEDULE 3

CONSULTATION REQUIREMENTS FOR QUALIFYING WORKS UNDER QUALIFYING LONG TERM AGREEMENTS AND AGREEMENTS TO WHICH REGULATION 7(3) APPLIES

1 Notice of intention

(1) The landlord shall give notice in writing of his intention to carry out qualifying works—

- (a) to each tenant; and
- (b) where a recognised tenants' association represents some or all of the tenants, to the association.

(2) The notice shall—

- (a) describe, in general terms, the works proposed to be carried out or specify the place and hours at which a description of the proposed works may be inspected;
- (b) state the landlord's reasons for considering it necessary to carry out the proposed works;
- (c) contain a statement of the total amount of the expenditure estimated by the landlord as likely to be incurred by him on and in connection with the proposed works;
- (d) invite the making, in writing, of observations in relation to the proposed works or the landlord's estimated expenditure;
- (e) specify—
    - (i) the address to which such observations may be sent;
    - (ii) that they must be delivered within the relevant period; and
    - (iii) the date on which the relevant period ends.

2 Inspection of description of proposed works

(1) Where a notice under paragraph 1 specifies a place and hours for inspection—

- (a) the place and hours so specified must be reasonable; and
- (b) a description of the proposed works must be available for inspection, free of charge, at that place and during those hours.

(2) f facilities to enable copies to be taken are not made available at the times at which the description may be inspected, the landlord shall provide to any tenant, on request and free of charge, a copy of the description.

3 Duty to have regard to observations in relation to proposed works and estimated expenditure

Where, within the relevant period, observations are made in relation to the proposed works or the landlord's estimated expenditure by any tenant or the recognised tenants' association, the landlord shall have regard to those observations.

4 Landlord's response to observations

Where the landlord receives observations to which (in accordance with paragraph 3) he is required to have regard, he shall, within 21 days of their receipt, by notice in writing to the person by whom the observations were made, state his response to the observations.

SCHEDULE 4

CONSULTATION REQUIREMENTS FOR QUALIFYING WORKS OTHER THAN WORKS UNDER QUALIFYING LONG TERM OR AGREEMENTS TO WHICH REGULATION 7(3) APPLIES

Regulation 7(4)

PART 1

CONSULTATION REQUIREMENTS FOR QUALIFYING WORKS FOR WHICH PUBLIC NOTICE IS REQUIRED

1 Notice of intention

(1) The landlord shall give notice in writing of his intention to carry out qualifying works—

- (a) to each tenant; and
- (b) where a recognised tenants' association represents some or all of the tenants, to the association.

(2) The notice shall—

- (a) describe, in general terms, the works proposed to be carried out or specify the place and hours at which a description of the proposed works may be inspected;
- (b) state the landlord's reasons for considering it necessary to carry out the proposed works;
- (c) state that the reason why the landlord is not inviting recipients of the notice to nominate persons from whom he should try to obtain an estimate for carrying out the works is that public notice of the works is to be given;
- (d) invite the making, in writing, of observations in relation to the proposed works; and
- (e) specify—
  - (i) the address to which such observations may be sent;
  - (ii) that they must be delivered within the relevant period; and
  - (iii) the date on which the relevant period ends.

2 Inspection of description of proposed works

(1) Where a notice under paragraph 1 specifies a place and hours for inspection—

- (a) the place and hours so specified must be reasonable; and
- (b) a description of the proposed works must be available for inspection, free of charge, at that place and during those hours.

(2) If facilities to enable copies to be taken are not made available at the times at which the description may be inspected, the landlord shall provide to any tenant, on request and free of charge, a copy of the description.

3 Duty to have regard to observations in relation to proposed works

Where, within the relevant period, observations are made in relation to the proposed works by any tenant or the recognised tenants' association, the landlord shall have regard to those observations.

4 Preparation of landlord's contract statement

(1) The landlord shall prepare, in accordance with the following provisions of this paragraph, a statement in respect of the proposed contract under which the proposed works are to be carried out.

(2) The statement shall set out—

- (a) the name and address of the person with whom the landlord proposes to contract; and
- (b) particulars of any connection between them (apart from the proposed contract).

(3) For the purpose of sub-paragraph (2)(b) it shall be assumed that there is a connection between a person and the landlord—

- (a) where the landlord is a company, if the person, or is to be, a director or manager of the company or is a close relative of any such director or manager;
- (b) where the landlord is a company, and the person is a partner in a partnership, if any partner in that partnership is, or is to be, a director or manager of the company or is a close relative of any such director or manager;
- (c) where both the landlord and the person are companies, if any director or manager of one company is, or is to be, a director or manager of the other company;
- (d) where the person is a company, if the landlord is a director or manager of the company or is a close relative of any such director or manager; or
- (e) where the person is a company and the landlord is a partner in a partnership, if any partner in that partnership is a director or manager of the company or is a close relative of any such director or manager.

(4) Where, as regards each tenant's unit of occupation, it is reasonably practicable for the landlord to estimate the amount of the relevant contribution to be incurred by the tenant attributable to the works to which the proposed contract relates, that estimated amount shall be specified in the statement.

(5) Where—

- (a) it is not reasonably practicable for the landlord to make the estimate mentioned in sub-paragraph (4); and
- (b) it is reasonably practicable for the landlord to estimate, as regards the building or other premises to which the proposed contract relates, the total amount of his expenditure under the proposed contract,

that estimated amount shall be specified in the statement.

(6) Where—

- (a) it is not reasonably practicable for the landlord to make the estimate mentioned in sub-paragraph (4) or (5)(b); and
- (b) it is reasonably practicable for the landlord to ascertain the current unit cost or hourly or daily rate applicable to the works to which the proposed contract relates,

that cost or rate shall be specified in the statement.

(7) Where it is not reasonably practicable for the landlord to make the estimate mentioned in sub-paragraph (6)(b), the reasons why he cannot comply and the date by which he expects to be able to provide an estimated amount, cost or rate shall be specified in the statement.

(8) Where the landlord has received observations to which (in accordance with paragraph 3) he is required to have regard, the statement shall summarise the observations and set out his response to them.

5 Notification of proposed contract

(1) The landlord shall give notice in writing of his intention to enter into the proposed contract—

- (a) to each tenant; and
- (b) where a recognised tenants' association represents some or all of the tenants, to the association.

(2) The notice shall—

- (a) comprise, or be accompanied by, the statement prepared in accordance with paragraph 4 ('the paragraph 4 statement') or specify the place and hours at which that statement may be inspected;
- (b) invite the making, in writing, of observations in relation to any matter mentioned in the paragraph 4 statement;
- (c) specify—
  - (i) the address to which such observations may be sent;
  - (ii) that they must be delivered within the relevant period; and
  - (iii) the date on which the relevant period ends.

(3) Where the paragraph 4 statement is made available for inspection, paragraph 2 shall apply in relation to that statement as it applies in relation to a description of proposed works made available for inspection under that paragraph.

6 Landlord's response to observations

Where, within the relevant period, the landlord receives observations in response to the invitation in the notice under paragraph 5, he shall, within 21 days of their receipt, by notice in writing to the person by whom the observations were made, state his response to the observations.

7 Supplementary information

Where a statement prepared under paragraph 4 sets out the landlord's reasons for being unable to comply with sub-paragraph (6) of that paragraph, the landlord shall, within 21 days of receiving sufficient information to enable him to estimate the amount, cost or rate referred to in sub-paragraph (4), (5) or (6) of that paragraph, give notice in writing of the estimated amount, cost or rate (as the case may be)—

- (a) to each tenant; and
- (b) where a recognised tenants' association represents some or all of the tenants, to the association.

PART 2
CONSULTATION REQUIREMENTS FOR QUALIFYING WORKS FOR WHICH PUBLIC NOTICE IS NOT REQUIRED

8 Notice of intention

(1) The landlord shall give notice in writing of his intention to carry out qualifying works—

- (a) to each tenant; and
- (b) where a recognised tenants' association represents some or all of the tenants, to the association.

(2) The notice shall—

- (a) describe, in general terms, the works proposed to be carried out or specify the place and hours at which a description of the proposed works may be inspected;
- (b) state the landlord's reasons for considering it necessary to carry out the proposed works;
- (c) invite the making, in writing, of observations in relation to the proposed works; and
- (d) specify—

(i) the address to which such observations may be sent;
(ii) that they must be delivered within the relevant period; and
(iii) the date on which the relevant period ends.

(3) The notice shall also invite each tenant and the association (if any) to propose, within the relevant period, the name of a person from whom the landlord should try to obtain an estimate for the carrying out of the proposed works.

9 Inspection of description of proposed works

(1) Where a notice under paragraph 1 specifies a place and hours for inspection—
(a) the place and hours so specified must be reasonable; and
(b) a description of the proposed works must be available for inspection, free of charge, at that place and during those hours.

(2) If facilities to enable copies to be taken are not made available at the times at which the description may be inspected, the landlord shall provide to any tenant, on request and free of charge, a copy of the description.

10 Duty to have regard to observations in relation to proposed works

Where, within the relevant period, observations are made, in relation to the proposed works by any tenant or recognised tenants' association, the landlord shall have regard to those observations.

11 Estimates and response to observations

(1) Where, within the relevant period, a nomination is made by a recognised tenants' association (whether or not a nomination is made by any tenant), the landlord shall try to obtain an estimate from the nominated person.

(2) Where, within the relevant period, a nomination is made by only one of the tenants (whether or not a nomination is made by a recognised tenants' association), the landlord shall try to obtain an estimate from the nominated person.

(3) Where, within the relevant period, a single nomination is made by more than one tenant (whether or not a nomination is made by a recognised tenants' association), the landlord shall try to obtain an estimate—
(a) from the person who received the most nominations; or
(b) if there is no such person, but two (or more) persons received the same number of nominations, being a number in excess of the nominations received by any other person, from one of those two (or more) persons; or
(c) in any other case, from any nominated person.

(4) Where, within the relevant period, more than one nomination is made by any tenant and more than one nomination is made by a recognised tenants' association, the landlord shall try to obtain an estimate—
(a) from at least one person nominated by a tenant; and
(b) from at least one person nominated by the association, other than a person from whom an estimate is sought as mentioned in paragraph (a).

(5) The landlord shall, in accordance with this sub-paragraph and sub-paragraphs (6) to (9)—
(a) obtain estimates for the carrying out of the proposed works;
(b) supply, free of charge, a statement ('the paragraph (b) statement') setting out—
 (i) as regards at least two of the estimates, the amount specified in the estimate as the estimated cost of the proposed works; and
 (ii) where the landlord has received observations to which (in accordance with paragraph 3) he is required to have regard, a summary of the observations and his response to them; and
(c) make all of the estimates available for inspection.

(6) At least one of the estimates must be that of a person wholly unconnected with the landlord.

(7) For the purpose of paragraph (6), it shall be assumed that there is a connection between a person and the landlord—

- (a) where the landlord is a company, if the person is, or is to be, a director or manager of the company or is a close relative of any such director or manager;
- (b) where the landlord is a company, and the person is a partner in a partnership, if any partner in that partnership is, or is to be, a director or manager of the company or is a close relative of any such director or manager;
- (c) where both the landlord and the person are companies, if any director or manager of one company is, or is to be, a director or manager of the other company;
- (d) where the person is a company, if the landlord is a director or manager of the company or is a close relative of any such director or manager; or
- (e) where the person is a company and the landlord is a partner in a partnership, if any partner in that partnership is a director or manager of the company or is a close relative of any such director or manager.

(8) Where the landlord has obtained an estimate from a nominated person, that estimate must be one of those to which the paragraph (b) statement relates.

(9) The paragraph (b) statement shall be supplied to, and the estimates made available for inspection by—

- (a) each tenant; and
- (b) the secretary of the recognised tenants' association (if any).

(10) The landlord shall, by notice in writing to each tenant and the association (if any)—

- (a) specify the place and hours at which the estimates may be inspected;
- (b) invite the making, in writing, of observations in relation to those estimates;
- (c) specify—
  - (i) the address to which such observations may be sent;
  - (ii) that they must be delivered within the relevant period; and
  - (iii) the date on which the relevant period ends.

(11) Paragraph 2 shall apply to estimates made available for inspection under this paragraph as it applies to a description of proposed works made available for inspection under that paragraph.

12 Duty to have regard to observations in relation to estimates

Where, within the relevant period, observations are made in relation to the estimates by a recognised tenants' association or, as the case may be, any tenant, the landlord shall have regard to those observations.

13 Duty on entering into contract

(1) Subject to sub-paragraph (2), where the landlord enters into a contract for the carrying out of qualifying works, he shall, within 21 days of entering into the contract, by notice in writing to each tenant and the recognised tenants' association (if any)—

- (a) state his reasons for awarding the contract or specify the place and hours at which a statement of those reasons may be inspected; and
- (b) there he received observations to which (in accordance with paragraph 5) he was required to have regard, summarise the observations and set out his response to them.

(2) The requirements of sub-paragraph (1) do not apply where the person with whom the contract is made is a nominated person or submitted the lowest estimate.

(3) Paragraph 2 shall apply to a statement made available for inspection under this paragraph as it applies to a description of proposed works made available for inspection under that paragraph.

TRIBUNAL PROCEDURE (FIRST-TIER TRIBUNAL) (PROPERTY CHAMBER) RULES 2013

SI 2013/1169

PART 1
INTRODUCTION

A2.7

1 Citation, commencement and interpretation

(1) These Rules may be cited as the Tribunal Procedure (First-tier Tribunal) (Property Chamber) Rules 2013 and come into force on 1st July 2013.

(2) These Rules apply to proceedings before the Property Chamber of the First-tier Tribunal.

(3) In these Rules—

"the 1983 Act" means the Mobile Homes Act 1983;

"the 1986 Act" means the Agricultural Holdings Act 1986;

"the 1991 Act" means the Land Drainage Act 1991;

"the 2002 LR Act" means the Land Registration Act 2002;

"the 2004 Act" means the Housing Act 2004;

"the 2007 Act" means the Tribunals, Courts and Enforcement Act 2007.

"agricultural land and drainage case" means any case in respect of which the Tribunal has jurisdiction conferred—

(a) by or under any enactment specified in section 6A(2) of the Agriculture (Miscellaneous Provisions) Act 1954; or

(b) by the Hill Farming Act 1946;

"applicant" means—

(a) the person who commences Tribunal proceedings, whether by making an appeal, an application, an objection or otherwise;

(b) where an issue in proceedings before a court is transferred by order of the court to the Tribunal, the claimant or applicant in those proceedings;

(c) where proceedings before another tribunal are transferred to the Tribunal, the claimant or applicant in those proceedings;

(d) in a land registration case, the party which the Tribunal has specified as applicant under rule 28(3)(c);

(e) a person who is added or substituted as an applicant under rule 10;

and "application" bears a corresponding meaning;

"designated applicant" in relation to agricultural land and drainage cases means a person who is validly designated by the deceased in the deceased's will in accordance with section 39(4) of the 1986 Act;

"document" means anything in which information is recorded in any form, and an obligation under these Rules or any practice direction or direction to provide or allow access to a document or a copy of a document for any purpose means, unless the Tribunal directs otherwise, an obligation to provide or allow access to such document or copy in a legible form or in a form which can be readily made into a legible form;

"hearing" means an oral hearing and includes a hearing conducted in whole or in part by video link, telephone or other means of instantaneous two-way electronic communication;

"holding" means land (including a ditch) in respect of which an application under the 1986 Act is made;

"IMO authorisation application" means an application for authorisation to make an interim management order under section 102(4) or (7) of the 2004 Act, and "IMO" bears a corresponding meaning;

"interested person"—

- (a) in relation to an agricultural land and drainage case under section 39 of the 1986 Act, includes—
  - (i) any other applicant under that section or any other person eligible to be such an applicant;
  - (ii) any personal representative of the deceased tenant, any person eligible to apply to be the personal representative of the deceased tenant or any person administering the estate of the deceased tenant;
- (b) in relation to a residential property case, means—
  - (i) a person other than the applicant who would have been entitled under the 2004 Act or the Housing Act 1985 to make the application;
  - (ii) a person to whom notice of the application must be given in accordance with the following provisions of the 2004 Act—
    - (aa) paragraph 11(2) of Schedule 1; or
    - (bb) paragraph 14(2) of Schedule 3;
  - (iii) a person to whom the Tribunal must give the opportunity of being heard in accordance with the following provisions—
    - (aa) section 34(4) of the 2004 Act; or
    - (bb) section 317(2) of the Housing Act 1985;
  - (iv) except in relation to an application made under the 1983 Act, the local housing authority, where it is not a party to the application;
  - (v) the person to whom the occupier wants to sell or gift a mobile home under paragraph 7B or 8B of Chapter 2 of Part 1 of Schedule 1 to the 1983 Act;
  - (vi) a qualifying residents' association;

"land registration case" means a case in respect of which the Tribunal has jurisdiction under the 2002 LR Act;

"leasehold case" means a case in respect of which the Tribunal has jurisdiction under any of the enactments specified in section 176A(2) of the Commonhold and Leasehold Reform Act 2002;

"official expert" means a person who for agricultural, drainage or similar expertise is engaged by the Secretary of State to report or act on behalf of the Secretary of State in connection with an application in an agricultural land case;

"original application" means the application originally made to the registrar under the 2002 LR Act that resulted in a reference;

"party" means a person who is, or if the proceedings have been concluded, a person who was, an applicant or respondent when the Tribunal finally disposed of all issues in the proceedings;

"practice direction" means a direction given under section 23 of the 2007 Act;

"qualifying residents' association" means an association that meets the requirements set out in Part 1 of Schedule 1 to the 1983 Act;

"rectification application" means an application to rectify or set aside a document under section 108(2) of the 2002 LR Act;

"registrar" means the Chief Land Registrar;

"residential property case" means a case in respect of which the Tribunal has jurisdiction conferred by or under the Caravan Sites and Control of Development Act 1960, the 1983 Act, the Housing Act 1985, the 2004 Act or the Housing and Planning Act 2016;

"respondent" means—

(a) in an appeal against a decision, direction or order, the person who made the decision, direction or order appealed against;

(b) a person against whom an applicant otherwise brings proceedings;

(c) in a case referred to the Tribunal by a rent officer who has registered a rent under the Rent Act 1977, the landlord or the tenant, as the case may be, who has not objected to the rent which has been registered;

(d) where an issue in proceedings before a court is transferred by order of the court to the Tribunal, the person who was the defendant or respondent in the court proceedings;

(e) in relation to residential property cases or leasehold cases listed in a Schedule to a practice direction, the person or persons, or one of the persons, identified as the respondent in the relevant Schedule to the practice direction;

(f) in a land registration case—

(i) in a reference by the registrar, the party or parties which the Tribunal has specified as respondent under rule 28(3)(c);

(ii) in proceedings under section 108(2) of the 2002 LR Act, the party or parties making an objection to a rectification application;

(iii) in an appeal under paragraph 4 of Schedule 5 to the 2002 LR Act, the registrar;

(g) a person added or substituted as a respondent under rule 10;

"Tribunal" means the First-tier Tribunal.

2 Rules not overriding enactments

Nothing in these Rules overrides any specific provision that is contained in an enactment which confers jurisdiction on the Tribunal.

3 Overriding objective and parties' obligation to co-operate with the Tribunal

(1) The overriding objective of these Rules is to enable the Tribunal to deal with cases fairly and justly.

(2) Dealing with a case fairly and justly includes—

(a) dealing with the case in ways which are proportionate to the importance of the case, the complexity of the issues, the anticipated costs and the resources of the parties and of the Tribunal;

(b) avoiding unnecessary formality and seeking flexibility in the proceedings;

(c) ensuring, so far as practicable, that the parties are able to participate fully in the proceedings;

(d) using any special expertise of the Tribunal effectively; and

(e) avoiding delay, so far as compatible with proper consideration of the issues.

(3) The Tribunal must seek to give effect to the overriding objective when it—

(a) exercises any power under these Rules; or

(b) interprets any rule or practice direction.

(4) Parties must—
- (a) help the Tribunal to further the overriding objective; and
- (b) co-operate with the Tribunal generally.

4 Alternative dispute resolution and arbitration

(1) The Tribunal should seek, where appropriate—
- (a) to bring to the attention of the parties the availability of any appropriate alternative procedure for the resolution of the dispute; and
- (b) if the parties wish, and provided that it is compatible with the overriding objective, to facilitate the use of the procedure.

(2) Part 1 of the Arbitration Act 1996 does not apply to proceedings before the Tribunal.

PART 2
GENERAL POWERS AND PROVISIONS

5 Delegation to staff

(1) Staff appointed under section 40(1) of the 2007 Act (tribunal staff and services) may, with the approval of the Senior President of Tribunals, carry out functions of a judicial nature permitted or required to be done by the Tribunal.

(2) The approval referred to at paragraph (1) may apply generally to the carrying out of specified functions by members of staff of a specified description in specified circumstances.

(3) Within 14 days after the date that the Tribunal sends notice of a decision made by a member of staff pursuant to an approval under paragraph (1) to a party, that party may apply in writing to the Tribunal for that decision to be considered afresh by a judge.

6 Case management powers

(1) Subject to the provisions of the 2007 Act and any other enactment, the Tribunal may regulate its own procedure.

(2) The Tribunal may give a direction in relation to the conduct or disposal of proceedings at any time, including a direction amending, suspending or setting aside an earlier direction.

(3) In particular, and without restricting the general powers in paragraphs (1) and (2), the Tribunal may—
- (a) extend or shorten the time for complying with any rule, practice direction or direction, even if the application for an extension is not made until after the time limit has expired;
- (b) consolidate or hear together two or more sets of proceedings or parts of proceedings raising common issues, or treat a case as a lead case (whether under rule 23 or otherwise);
- (c) permit or require a party to amend a document;
- (d) permit or require a party or another person to provide or produce documents, information or submissions to any or all of the following—
  - (i) the Tribunal;
  - (ii) a party;
  - (iii) in land registration cases, the registrar;
- (e) direct that enquiries be made of any person;
- (f) require a party to state whether that party intends to—
  - (i) attend,
  - (ii) be represented, or
  - (iii) call witnesses,

  at the hearing;
- (g) deal with an issue in the proceedings as a preliminary issue;

(h) hold a hearing to consider any matter, including a case management issue;
(i) decide the form of any hearing;
(j) adjourn or postpone a hearing;
(k) require a party to produce a bundle for a hearing;
(l) require a party to provide an estimate of the length of the hearing;
(m) stay proceedings;
(n) transfer proceedings to another court or tribunal if that other court or tribunal has jurisdiction in relation to the proceedings and
   (i) because of a change of circumstances since the proceedings were started, the Tribunal no longer has jurisdiction in relation to the proceedings; or
   (ii) the Tribunal considers that the other court or tribunal is a more appropriate forum for the determination of the case;
(o) suspend the effect of its own decision pending the determination by the Tribunal or the Upper Tribunal of an application for permission to appeal against, and any appeal or review of, that decision.

7 Procedure for applying for and giving directions

(1) The Tribunal may give a direction on the application of one or more of the parties or on its own initiative.

(2) An application for a direction may be made—
   (a) by sending or delivering a written application to the Tribunal; or
   (b) orally during the course of a hearing.

(3) An application for a direction must include the reason for making that application.

(4) Except with the permission of the Tribunal, if a written application for a direction is made without the consent of every party the applicant must provide—
   (a) a copy of the proposed application to every other party before it is made; and
   (b) confirmation to the Tribunal that the other parties have been notified that any objection they wish to make to the application must be provided in accordance with paragraph (5).

(5) A party who wishes to object to a written application that has been made to the Tribunal for a direction must send written notice of the objection to the Tribunal and the applicant for the direction.

(6) Unless the Tribunal considers that there is good reason not to do so, the Tribunal must send written notice of any direction made by the Tribunal to every party and to any other person affected by the direction.

(7) If a party or any other person sent notice under paragraph (6) of the direction made by the Tribunal wishes to challenge that direction, they may do so by applying for another direction which amends, suspends or sets aside the first direction.

8 Failure to comply with rules, practice directions or Tribunal directions

(1) An irregularity resulting from a failure to comply with any provision of these Rules, a practice direction or a direction does not of itself render void the proceedings or any step taken in the proceedings.

(2) If a party has failed to comply with a requirement in these Rules, a practice direction or a direction, the Tribunal may take such action as the Tribunal considers just, which may include—
   (a) waiving the requirement;
   (b) requiring the failure to be remedied;
   (c) exercising its power under rule 9 (striking out a party's case);
   (d) exercising its power under paragraph (5); or
   (e) barring or restricting a party's participation in the proceedings.

(3) In land registration cases, the action that the Tribunal may take includes—

(a) where the party who failed to comply was the person who made (or has been substituted for or added to the party who made) the original application, directing the registrar to cancel the original application in whole or in part;

(b) where the party who failed to comply was an objector to (or was substituted for or added as an objector to) the original application, directing the registrar to give effect to that application in whole or in part as if that objection had not been made.

(4) In land registration cases, the Tribunal must, if the action taken does not include either of the requirements referred to in paragraph (3), send written notice to the parties of the Tribunal's decision as to what action is taken (if any) and give any consequential directions.

(5) The Tribunal may refer to the Upper Tribunal, and ask the Upper Tribunal to exercise its power under section 25 of the 2007 Act in relation to, any failure by a person to comply with a requirement imposed by the Tribunal—

(a) to attend at any place for the purpose of giving evidence;

(b) otherwise to make themselves available to give evidence;

(c) to swear an oath in connection with the giving of evidence;

(d) to give evidence as a witness;

(e) to produce a document; or

(f) to facilitate the inspection of a document or any other thing (including any premises).

9 Striking out a party's case

(1) The proceedings or case, or the appropriate part of them, will automatically be struck out if the applicant has failed to comply with a direction that stated that failure by the applicant to comply with the direction by a stated date would lead to the striking out of the proceedings or that part of them.

(2) The Tribunal must strike out the whole or a part of the proceedings or case if the Tribunal—

(a) does not have jurisdiction in relation to the proceedings or case or that part of them; and

(b) does not exercise any power under rule 6(3)(n)(i) (transfer to another court or tribunal) in relation to the proceedings or case or that part of them.

(3) The Tribunal may strike out the whole or a part of the proceedings or case if—

(a) the applicant has failed to comply with a direction which stated that failure by the applicant to comply with the direction could lead to the striking out of the proceedings or case or that part of it;

(b) the applicant has failed to co-operate with the Tribunal such that the Tribunal cannot deal with the proceedings fairly and justly;

(c) the proceedings or case are between the same parties and arise out of facts which are similar or substantially the same as those contained in a proceedings or case which has been decided by the Tribunal;

(d) the Tribunal considers the proceedings or case (or a part of them), or the manner in which they are being conducted, to be frivolous or vexatious or otherwise an abuse of the process of the Tribunal; or

(e) the Tribunal considers there is no reasonable prospect of the applicant's proceedings or case, or part of it, succeeding.

(4) The Tribunal may not strike out the whole or a part of the proceedings or case under paragraph (2) or paragraph (3)(b) to (e) without first giving the parties an opportunity to make representations in relation to the proposed striking out.

(5) If the proceedings or case, or part of them, have been struck out under paragraph (1) or (3)(a), the applicant may apply for the proceedings or case, or part of it, to be reinstated.

(6) An application under paragraph (5) must be made in writing and received by the Tribunal within 28 days after the date on which the Tribunal sent notification of the striking out to that party.

(7) This rule applies to a respondent as it applies to an applicant except that—

- (a) a reference to the striking out of the proceedings or case or part of them is to be read as a reference to the barring of the respondent from taking further part in the proceedings or part of them; and
- (b) a reference to an application for the reinstatement of proceedings or case or part of them which have been struck out is to be read as a reference to an application for the lifting of the bar on the respondent from taking further part in the proceedings, or part of them.

(8) If a respondent has been barred from taking further part in proceedings under this rule and that bar has not been lifted, the Tribunal need not consider any response or other submission made by that respondent, and may summarily determine any or all issues against that respondent.

10 Addition, substitution and removal of parties

(1) The Tribunal may give a direction adding, substituting or removing a person as an applicant or a respondent.

(2) If the Tribunal gives a direction under paragraph (1) it may give such consequential directions as it considers appropriate.

(3) A person who is not a party may apply to the Tribunal to be added or substituted as a party.

11 Fees: non-payment

(1) In any case where a fee is payable under an order made under section 42 of the 2007 Act (fees), the Tribunal must not proceed further with the case until the fee is paid.

(2) Where a fee remains unpaid for a period of 14 days after the date on which the fee is payable, the case, if not already started, must not be started.

(3) Where the case has started, it shall be deemed to be withdrawn 14 days after the date on which the Tribunal sends or delivers to the party liable to make payment a written notification that the fee has not been paid.

12 Security for costs

(1) In a land registration case, a respondent may apply for security for the respondent's costs of the proceedings in the Tribunal.

(2) Paragraph (1) does not apply where the Tribunal has directed a party under section 110(1) of the 2002 LR Act to commence court proceedings for the court's decision on the whole or part of a matter.

(3) An application for security for costs must be supported by written evidence and copies of the application and supporting evidence must be provided by the respondent to the applicant in the proceedings.

(4) The Tribunal may make an order for security for costs if it is satisfied that—

- (a) one or more of the conditions subject to which security for costs might be ordered in proceedings in a court to which the Civil Procedure Rules 1998 apply exists;
- (b) it is just to make such an order; and
- (c) the applicant in the proceedings has the ability to comply with the order.

(5) Where the Tribunal decides to order security for costs, it must—

- (a) determine the amount of security; and

(b) direct the manner in which, and the time within which, the security must be given.

13 Orders for costs, reimbursement of fees and interest on costs

(1) The Tribunal may make an order in respect of costs only—

- (a) under section 29(4) of the 2007 Act (wasted costs) and the costs incurred in applying for such costs;
- (b) if a person has acted unreasonably in bringing, defending or conducting proceedings in—
  - (i) an agricultural land and drainage case,
  - (ii) a residential property case, or
  - (iii) a leasehold case; or
- (c) in a land registration case.

(2) The Tribunal may make an order requiring a party to reimburse to any other party the whole or part of the amount of any fee paid by the other party which has not been remitted by the Lord Chancellor.

(3) The Tribunal may make an order under this rule on an application or on its own initiative.

(4) A person making an application for an order for costs—

- (a) must, unless the application is made orally at a hearing, send or deliver an application to the Tribunal and to the person against whom the order is sought to be made; and
- (b) may send or deliver together with the application a schedule of the costs claimed in sufficient detail to allow summary assessment of such costs by the Tribunal.

(5) An application for an order for costs may be made at any time during the proceedings but must be made within 28 days after the date on which the Tribunal sends—

- (a) a decision notice recording the decision which finally disposes of all issues in the proceedings; or
- (b) notice of consent to a withdrawal under rule 22 (withdrawal) which ends the proceedings.

(6) The Tribunal may not make an order for costs against a person (the "paying person") without first giving that person an opportunity to make representations.

(7) The amount of costs to be paid under an order under this rule may be determined by—

- (a) summary assessment by the Tribunal;
- (b) agreement of a specified sum by the paying person and the person entitled to receive the costs (the "receiving person");
- (c) detailed assessment of the whole or a specified part of the costs (including the costs of the assessment) incurred by the receiving person by the Tribunal or, if it so directs, on an application to a county court; and such assessment is to be on the standard basis or, if specified in the costs order, on the indemnity basis.

(8) The Civil Procedure Rules 1998, section 74 (interest on judgment debts, etc) of the County Courts Act 1984 and the County Court (Interest on Judgment Debts) Order 1991 shall apply, with necessary modifications, to a detailed assessment carried out under paragraph (7)(c) as if the proceedings in the Tribunal had been proceedings in a court to which the Civil Procedure Rules 1998 apply.

(9) The Tribunal may order an amount to be paid on account before the costs or expenses are assessed.

14 Representatives

(1) A party may appoint a representative (whether legally qualified or not) to represent that party in the proceedings.

(2) If a party appoints a representative, that party must send or deliver to the Tribunal and to each other party written notice of the representative's name and address.

(3) Anything permitted or required to be done by or provided to a party under these Rules, a practice direction or a direction may be done by or provided to the representative of that party except—

- (a) signing a witness statement; or
- (b) sending or delivering a notice under paragraph (2), if the representative is not a person who, for the purposes of the Legal Services Act 2007, is an authorised person in relation to an activity which constitutes the exercise of a right of audience or the conduct of litigation within the meaning of that Act.

(4) A person who receives due notice of the appointment of a representative—

- (a) must thereafter provide to the representative any document which is required to be sent to the represented party, and need not provide that document to the represented party; and
- (b) may assume that the representative is and remains authorised until receiving written notification to the contrary and an alternative address for communications from the representative or the represented party.

(5) At a hearing a party may be accompanied by another person whose name and address has not been notified under paragraph (2) but who, with the permission of the Tribunal, may act as a representative or otherwise assist in presenting the party's case at the hearing.

(6) Paragraphs (2) to (4) do not apply to a person who accompanies a party under paragraph (5).

15 Calculating time

(1) An act required by these Rules, a practice direction or a direction to be done on or by a particular day must be done before 5pm on that day.

(2) If the time specified by these Rules, a practice direction or a direction for doing any act ends on a day other than a working day, the act is done in time if it is done on the next working day.

(3) In this rule "working day" means any day except a Saturday or Sunday, Christmas Day, Good Friday or a bank holiday under section 1 of the Banking and Financial Dealings Act 1971.

16 Provision of documents

(1) Any document to be provided under these Rules, a practice direction or a direction must be—

- (a) sent by prepaid post or by document exchange, or delivered by hand to the address specified in paragraph (5);
- (b) sent by fax to the number specified for the proceedings;
- (c) as regards any document sent or delivered to or by the Tribunal, by such other method as the Tribunal may permit; or
- (d) as regards any document to be sent or delivered by a method other than one provided for by sub-paragraphs (a), (b) or (c) or another paragraph in this rule, by such other method as the recipient may permit.

(2) The Tribunal may provide any document (including any notice or summons or other information) under these Rules by—

- (a) itself sending or delivering the document; or
- (b) requiring a party to do so.

(3) In any case to which section 39, 41 or 53 of the 1986 Act applies, the applicant, not the Tribunal, must send or deliver a copy of the application and accompanying documents to the landlord of the agricultural holding to which the application relates and to any other person known to the applicant to be interested in the outcome of the application.

(4) If the Tribunal permits or directs documents to be provided to it by email, any requirement in these Rules for a signature on a document may be satisfied by a typed instead of a handwritten signature.

(5) Subject to paragraph (6), the address for the purposes of paragraph (1)(a) is—

- (a) in the case of the Tribunal, the address of the office of the Tribunal;
- (b) in the case of an incorporated company or other body registered in the United Kingdom, the address of the registered or principal office of the company or body or any alternative address notified by that company or body to the Tribunal and all other parties for the purposes of provision of documents;
- (c) in the case of any other person, body or authority, the usual or last known address of that person, body or authority.

(6) The Tribunal and each party may assume that the address provided by a party or its representative or, in a reference, by the registrar is and remains the address to which documents should be sent or delivered until receiving written notification to the contrary and an alternative address for communications.

(7) Subject to paragraph (8), if a party provides a fax number, email address or other details for the electronic transmission of documents to them, that party must accept delivery of documents by that method.

(8) If a party informs the Tribunal and all other parties that a particular form of communication, other than pre-paid post or delivery by hand, should not be used to provide documents to that party, that form of communication must not be used.

(9) If the Tribunal or a party sends a document to another party or to the Tribunal by email or any other electronic means of communication, the recipient may request that the sender provide a hard copy of the document to the recipient. The recipient must make such a request as soon as reasonably practicable after receiving the document electronically.

(10) Unless the Tribunal otherwise permits, where a document is provided for the purposes of the proceedings is or contains a map, plan, drawing or photograph, any copy provided of that map, plan or drawing must be in the same colours as the map, plan, drawing or photograph of which it is a copy, and in agricultural land and drainage cases, maps of any holding or land must be to a scale of 1:10,000 or larger.

(11) The Tribunal may waive a requirement under these Rules to send or deliver a notice or other document to a person or make an order for provision by alternative method (whether by advertisement in a newspaper or otherwise) as the Tribunal may think fit if that person—

- (a) cannot be found after all diligent enquiries have been made;
- (b) has died and has no personal representative;
- (c) is out of the United Kingdom; or
- (d) for any other reason a notice or other document cannot readily be sent or delivered to that person in accordance with these Rules.

(12) Where an enactment requires evidence that a party has supplied any person with a document, that party may satisfy the requirement by providing a certificate signed by the party confirming that the document was provided in accordance with the requirements of this rule.

17 Prevention of disclosure or publication of documents and information

(1) The Tribunal may make an order prohibiting the disclosure or publication of—

- (a) specified documents or information relating to the proceedings; or

(b) any matter likely to lead members of the public to identify any person whom the Tribunal considers should not be identified.

(2) The Tribunal may give a direction prohibiting the disclosure of a document or information to a person if—

(a) the Tribunal is satisfied that such disclosure would be likely to cause that person or some other person serious harm; and

(b) the Tribunal is satisfied, having regard to the interests of justice, that it is proportionate to give such a direction.

(3) If a party (the first party) considers that the Tribunal should give a direction under paragraph (2) prohibiting the disclosure of a document or information to another party (the second party), the first party must—

(a) exclude the relevant document or information from any documents that will be provided to the second party; and

(b) provide to the Tribunal the excluded document or information, and the reason for its exclusion, so that the Tribunal may decide whether the document or information should be disclosed to the second party or should be the subject of a direction under paragraph (2).

(4) The Tribunal may give a direction that certain documents or information must or may be disclosed to the Tribunal on the basis that the Tribunal will not disclose such documents or information to other persons, or specified other persons.

(5) A party making an application for a direction under paragraph (4) may withhold the relevant documents or information from other persons, or the specified other persons, until the Tribunal has made a decision on the application.

(6) Unless the Tribunal considers that there is good reason not to do so, the Tribunal must send notice that a party has made an application for a direction under paragraph (4) to each other party.

(7) In a case involving matters relating to national security, the Tribunal must ensure that information is not disclosed contrary to the interests of national security.

(8) The Tribunal must conduct proceedings and record its decision and reasons appropriately so as not to undermine the effect of an order made under paragraph (1), a direction given under paragraph (2) or (4) or the duty imposed by paragraph (7).

18 Disclosure, evidence and submissions

(1) Without restriction on the general powers in rule 6(1) and (2) (case management powers), the Tribunal may give directions as to—

(a) the exchange between parties of lists of documents which are relevant to the application, or relevant to particular issues, and the inspection of such documents;

(b) the provision by parties of statements of agreed matters;

(c) issues on which it requires evidence or submissions;

(d) the nature of the evidence or submissions it requires;

(e) whether the parties are permitted or required to provide expert evidence, and if so whether the parties must jointly appoint a single expert to provide such evidence;

(f) any limit on the number of witnesses whose evidence a party may put forward, whether in relation to a particular issue or generally;

(g) the manner in which any evidence or submissions are to be provided, which may include a direction for them to be given—

   (i) orally at a hearing; or

   (ii) by written submissions or witness statement; and

(h) the time at which any evidence or submissions are to be provided.

(2) Instead of giving directions under paragraph (1)(a), the Tribunal may provide for the disclosure and inspection of documents to any extent which it considers relevant to the issues in dispute, including—

(a) taking all reasonable steps to ensure that each of the parties is given a copy of any document which has been received from any other party or former party; or
(b) supplying the parties with a copy of any document which embodies the results of any relevant enquiries made by or for the Tribunal for the purposes of the proceedings.

(3) A party to whom a document has been disclosed may use the document only for the purpose of the proceedings in which it is disclosed except where—
(a) the document has been read to or by the Tribunal, or referred to, at a hearing which has been held in public;
(b) the Tribunal gives permission; or
(c) the party who disclosed the document and the person to whom the document belongs agree.

(4) The Tribunal may make an order restricting or prohibiting the use of a document which has been disclosed, even where the document has been read to or by the Tribunal, or referred to, at a hearing which has been held in public.

(5) An application for such an order may be made—
(a) by a party; or
(b) by any person to whom the document belongs.

(6) The Tribunal may—
(a) admit evidence whether or not it—
(i) would be admissible in a civil trial in England and Wales; or
(ii) was available to a previous decision maker; or
(b) exclude evidence that would otherwise be admissible where—
(i) the evidence was not provided within the time allowed by a direction or a practice direction;
(ii) the evidence was otherwise provided in a manner that did not comply with a direction or a practice direction; or
(iii) it would otherwise be unfair to admit the evidence.

(7) The Tribunal may consent to a witness giving, or require any witness to give, evidence on oath, and may administer an oath for that purpose.

(8) A party cannot be directed to produce any document which a party could not be compelled to produce on the trial of an action in a court of law.

(9) On receipt of written notice from the Tribunal of an application under the 1991 Act, the Secretary of State must provide the Tribunal with a report on the matters to which the application relates.

19 Expert evidence

(1) It is the duty of an expert to help the Tribunal on matters within the expert's expertise and this duty overrides any obligation to the person from whom the expert has received instructions or by whom the expert is paid.

(2) No party may adduce expert evidence without the permission of the Tribunal.

(3) Expert evidence is to be given in a written report unless the Tribunal directs otherwise.

(4) Subject to paragraph (6), each party must provide a copy of the written report of any expert witness to the Tribunal and each other party at least 7 days before—
(a) the date of the hearing; or
(b) the date notified upon which the issue to which the expert evidence relates will be determined without a hearing.

(5) A written report of an expert must—
(a) contain a statement that the expert understands the duty in paragraph (1) and has complied with it;
(b) contain the words "I believe that the facts stated in this report are true and that the opinions expressed are correct";

- (c) be addressed to the Tribunal;
- (d) include details of the expert's qualifications and relevant experience;
- (e) contain a summary of the instructions the expert has received for the making of the report; and
- (f) be signed by the expert.

(6) The Tribunal may direct that—

- (a) the expert's evidence must be limited to such matters as the Tribunal directs;
- (b) the expert must attend a hearing to give oral evidence; or
- (c) the parties must jointly instruct the expert.

20 Summoning of witnesses and orders to answer questions or produce documents

(1) On the application of a party or on its own initiative, the Tribunal may—

- (a) by summons require any person to attend as a witness at a hearing at the time and place specified in the summons; or
- (b) order any person to answer any questions or produce any documents in that person's pos-session or control which relate to any issue in the proceedings.

(2) A summons under paragraph (1)(a) must—

- (a) give the person required to attend not less than 14 days' notice of the hearing or such shorter period as the Tribunal may direct; and
- (b) where the person is not a party, make provision for the person's necessary expenses of attendance to be paid, and state who is to pay them.

(3) No person may be compelled to give any evidence or produce any document that the person could not be compelled to give or produce on a trial of an action in a court of law.

(4) A summons or order under this rule must—

- (a) state that the person on whom the requirement is imposed may apply to the Tribunal to vary or set aside the summons or order, if they have not had an opportunity to object to it; and
- (b) state the consequences of failure to comply with the summons or order.

21 Site inspections

(1) Subject to paragraph (2), the Tribunal may inspect—

- (a) the land, property or premises which is the subject of the application;
- (b) any other land, property or premises inspection of which may assist the Tribunal in determining the application;
- (c) the locality of the land, property or premises.

(2) The making of and attendance at an inspection is subject to the Tribunal obtaining all appropriate consents to its request for entry.

(3) The Tribunal must give reasonable written notice of the date and time proposed for the inspection.

(4) The Tribunal may include in its request for entry a request to be accompanied by one or more of—

- (a) the parties (and any party's representative);
- (b) in an agricultural land and drainage case, the official expert;
- (c) if the Tribunal considers necessary—
  - (i) any party's witness;
  - (ii) one or more members of the Tribunal's staff;
- (d) any other person, if the Tribunal considers it appropriate.

(5) In an agricultural land and drainage case, the condition of consent referred to in paragraph (2) does not apply, but the exercise of the right of entry under this paragraph or paragraph (6) is subject to the Tribunal making a direction requiring the person who is the owner or occupier to permit entry to the land, property or premises.

(6) In an agricultural land and drainage case, the Tribunal may direct any person who owns or occupies any land or premises which are relevant to the proceedings to permit the official expert to enter and inspect the land or premises for the purposes for which the official expert was appointed.
(7) Every direction under paragraph (5) or (6) must, unless the occupier was present when the direction was made, contain a statement that the occupier may apply to the Tribunal to vary or set aside the direction.
(8) Where a direction has been made under paragraph (5) or (6), the occupier of the land, property or premises must be given at least 7 days' notice of any inspection.
(9) Rule 19 also applies to the report and evidence of the official expert.

22 Withdrawal

(1) Subject to paragraph (2), a party may give notice of the withdrawal of its case, or any part of it—
- (a) orally at a hearing; or
- (b) by sending or delivering to the Tribunal a written notice of withdrawal.

(2) A written notice of withdrawal must—
- (a) be signed and dated;
- (b) identify the case or part of the case which is withdrawn;
- (c) state whether any part of the case, and if so what, remains to be determined;
- (d) confirm that a copy of the notice of the withdrawal has been provided to all other parties and state the date on which this was done;
- (e) include the written consent of any of the other parties who have consented to the withdrawal.

(3) Notice of withdrawal will not take effect unless the Tribunal consents to the withdrawal.
(4) The Tribunal may make such directions or impose such conditions on withdrawal as it considers appropriate.
(5) A party which has withdrawn its case may apply to the Tribunal for the case to be reinstated.
(6) An application under paragraph (5) must be made in writing and be received by the Tribunal within 28 days after—
- (a) the date of the hearing at which the case was withdrawn orally under paragraph (1)(a); or
- (b) the date on which the Tribunal received the notice under paragraph (1)(b).

(7) The Tribunal must notify each party in writing of a withdrawal under this rule.
(8) Any party may, within 28 days after the date of receipt of notification by the Tribunal under paragraph (7), apply for a case, or part of a case, which has been withdrawn under this rule to be re-instated.

23 Lead cases

(1) This rule applies if—
- (a) two or more cases have been started before the Tribunal;
- (b) in each such case the Tribunal has not made a decision disposing of the proceedings; and
- (c) the cases give rise to common or related issues.

(2) The Tribunal may direct that one or more such cases be specified as a lead case, and stay the other cases ("the related cases").
(3) The Tribunal must send a copy of any direction given under paragraph (2) to each party in a lead case and in the related cases.
(4) A party in a related case referred to in paragraph (3) may apply for the related case to be substituted as the lead case (or added as a lead case) within 28 days after the

date of receipt of notification from the Tribunal of a direction made under paragraph (2).

(5) Where the Tribunal makes a decision in a lead case or cases in respect of the common or related issues—

- (a) the Tribunal must send a copy of the decision to each party in each of the related cases; and
- (b) subject to paragraph (6), the decision will be binding on each of those parties in relation to the common or related issues.

(6) Within 28 days after the date on which the Tribunal sent a copy of the decision to a party under paragraph (5)(a), that party may apply in writing for a direction that the decision is not binding on the parties to a particular related case.

(7) The Tribunal must give directions in respect of cases which are stayed under paragraph (2), providing for the disposal of or further directions in those cases.

(8) If a lead case is withdrawn before the Tribunal makes a decision in respect of the common or related issues, the Tribunal must give directions as to—

- (a) whether another case or other cases are to be specified as a lead case or lead cases; and
- (b) whether any direction affecting the related cases should be set aside or amended.

24 Subsequent applications related to lead case

(1) This rule applies where a decision has been given in a lead case in accordance with rule 23 and a subsequent application is made which includes any of the common or related issues.

(2) The Tribunal may send written notice to the parties to the subsequent application of—

- (a) the matters which it appears to the Tribunal are the common or related issues in the subsequent application and the previously decided lead case;
- (b) the decision recorded in respect of the common or related issues in the lead case;
- (c) the Tribunal's proposal to record its decision on the common or related issues in the subsequent application in materially identical terms to the decision in the lead case;
- (d) the date (being not less than 21 days after the date that the notice was sent) by which any objection to this proposal must be received by the Tribunal; and
- (e) a requirement that any objection must include the grounds on which it is made.

(3) Where no objection is received on or before the date specified in the notice—

- (a) the Tribunal need not determine the matters mentioned in paragraph (2)(a); and
- (b) the decision of the Tribunal in respect of the common or related issues in the lead case must be recorded as the decision of the Tribunal in respect of the common or related issues in the subsequent application.

(4) Where an objection is delivered to the Tribunal's proposal on or before the date specified in the notice the Tribunal must determine the application in accordance with the other provisions of these Rules.

25 Transfer of case to the Upper Tribunal

(1) The Tribunal may refer a case to the President of the Property Chamber with a request that the case be considered for transfer to the Upper Tribunal.

(2) If a case has been referred under paragraph (1), the President of the Property Chamber may, with the concurrence of the President of the Lands Chamber, direct that the case be transferred to and determined by the Upper Tribunal.

(3) The President of the Property Chamber may only direct a transfer under paragraph (2) if the President of the Property Chamber considers that the issues in dispute are likely to be further appealed to the Upper Tribunal and—

- (a) will require lengthy or complex evidence or a lengthy hearing; or
- (b) involve a complex or important principle or issue; or
- (c) involve a large financial sum.

(4) This rule does not apply to a land registration case or an agricultural land and drainage case.

PART 3
WRITTEN DOCUMENTATION, TIME LIMITS ETC

26 Starting proceedings

(1) An applicant must start proceedings before the Tribunal by sending or delivering to the Tribunal a notice of application.

(2) Such an application must be signed and dated and, unless a practice direction makes different provision, include—

- (a) the name and address of the applicant;
- (b) the name and address of the applicant's representative (if any);
- (c) an address where documents for the applicant may be sent or delivered;
- (d) the name and address of each respondent;
- (e) the address of the premises or property to which the application relates;
- (f) the applicant's connection with the premises or property;
- (g) the name and address of any landlord or tenant of the premises to which the application relates;
- (h) the result the applicant is seeking;
- (i) the applicant's reasons for making the application;
- (j) a statement that the applicant believes that the facts stated in the application are true;
- (k) the name and address of every person who appears to the applicant to be an interested person, with reasons for that person's interest;
- (l) in agricultural land and drainage cases, a description of all the land or holding to which the application relates;
- (m) in agricultural land and drainage cases relating to succession under section 39, 41 or 53 of the 1986 Act—
    - (i) confirmation that the applicant has given prior written notice of the application to the landlord of the holding and has brought the application to the notice of other persons interested in the outcome of the application; and
    - (ii) the names and addresses of each person to whom the applicant has provided such notice;
- (n) all further information or documents required by a practice direction.

(3) Where an application is made to which a paragraph in a practice direction relating to residential property cases or leasehold cases applies, it must be accompanied by the particulars and documents specified in the relevant paragraph.

(4) In proceedings to appeal a decision to the Tribunal, the application must be accompanied by a copy of any written record of that decision and any statement of reasons for that decision that the applicant has or can reasonably obtain.

(5) The applicant must provide with the notice of application any fee payable to the Tribunal.

(6) This rule does not apply to the extent that rule 28 applies.

(7) This rule does not apply where a form is prescribed for the purposes of starting proceedings in the Tribunal under Part V of the Rent Act 1977 (rents under restricted

contracts) or Part 1 of the Housing Act 1988 (assured tenancies, shorthold and non-shorthold).

27 Time limits

(1) This rule applies where no time limit for starting proceedings is prescribed by or under another enactment.

(2) Where the notice of application relates to a right to appeal from any decision (including any notice, order or licence), the applicant must provide the notice of application to the Tribunal within 28 days after the date on which notice of the decision to which the appeal relates was sent to the applicant.

(3) In a land registration case to which rule 28(3)(c) applies (references by the registrar), the person directed to be the applicant must provide the statement of case to the Tribunal within 28 days after the date on which written notice of receipt by the Tribunal of the reference by the registrar was sent to the applicant.

(4) In an agricultural land and drainage case—

- (a) a notice of application under section 67(5) of the 1986 Act (compensation for long-term improvements: consent needed) must be made within 28 days after the date on which notice in writing of the Tribunal's decision approving the carrying out of the improvement was sent to the landlord;
- (b) in proceedings under section 26(1) or 28(2) of the 1986 Act (restriction on operation of notices to quit) for the Tribunal's consent to the operation of a notice to quit, made by a landlord after service on the landlord by the tenant of a counter-notice, the notice of application must be made within two months after the date of service of the counter-notice;
- (c) where, at the expiry of the period specified in section 39(1) of the 1986 Act (application for tenancy of holding), only one application under that section in respect of the holding has been made, any application by the landlord under section 44(1) of that Act (opportunity for landlord to seek Tribunal's consent to serve notice to quit) must be made before the expiry of two months after the end of that period;
- (d) where, at the expiry of the period specified in section 39(1) of the 1986 Act (application for tenancy of holding), more than one application under section 39 of the 1986 Act has been made, any application by the landlord under section 44(1) of that Act must be made before the expiry of two months after the Tribunal notifies the landlord that the number of applications under section 39 of the 1986 Act is reduced to one.

28 Referred and transferred cases

(1) This rule applies where a matter is referred, sent or transferred to the Tribunal by—

- (a) a rent officer under paragraph 6 of Schedule 11 to the Rent Act 1977;
- (b) the registrar under section 73(7) of the 2002 LR Act;
- (c) another tribunal, or
- (d) a court.

(2) The requirement to start proceedings in accordance with rule 26(1) does not apply.

(3) Upon receipt of a matter to which this rule relates, the Tribunal must provide to the parties written notice specifying—

- (a) the date when the Tribunal received the matter;
- (b) the names and any known addresses of the parties to the proceedings; and

(c) in a case referred by the registrar, which party or parties will be the applicant or applicants for the purposes of the proceedings and which party or parties will be the respondent or respondents.

(4) Each party whom the Tribunal directs in accordance with paragraph (3)(c) to act as an applicant for the purposes of the Tribunal proceedings, must send or deliver to the Tribunal a statement of case—

(a) containing any information referred to in rule 26(2) which the Tribunal requires;

(b) stating the applicant's reasons for supporting or objecting to the original application to the registrar;

(c) accompanied by copies of any documents available to the applicant which—

(i) are important to the applicant's case; or

(ii) the Tribunal or any other party to the proceedings will require in order properly to understand the applicant's case.

(5) Where a matter has been transferred by a court, the Tribunal may require any party to provide it with a copy of the court order by which the matter was transferred.

29 Notice to respondents, interested persons and other persons

(1) When the Tribunal receives a notice of application in accordance with rule 26(1) or a statement of case in accordance with rule 28(4), the Tribunal must provide a copy of the application and any accompanying documents to the respondent.

(2) The Tribunal must also provide to the respondent a written notice informing the respondent of the requirements of rule 30.

(3) On being notified of the name and address of an interested person, the Tribunal must provide that person with a copy of the application and any accompanying documents.

(4) On receipt of an application relating to service charges, administration charges or estate charges the Tribunal must provide notice of the application to—

(a) the secretary of any recognised tenants' association within the meaning of section 29 of the Landlord and Tenant Act 1985 identified in the application; and

(b) any person whose name and address is known to the Tribunal whom the Tribunal considers is likely to be significantly affected by the application.

(5) In paragraph (4), "an application relating to service charges, administration charges or estate charges" means an application made under—

(a) section 20ZA or section 27A of or paragraph 8 of the Schedule to the Landlord and Tenant Act 1985; or

(b) section 159 of or paragraph 3 of Schedule 11 to the Commonhold and Leasehold Reform Act 2002.

(6) The Tribunal may give notice of the application to any other person it considers appropriate.

(7) Any notice given under paragraph (4) or (6)—

(a) must state that a person may apply to the Tribunal to be joined as a party to the proceedings; and

(b) may be given by publication of the notice in two newspapers (at least one of which should be a freely distributed newspaper) circulating in the locality in which the premises to which the application relates are situated.

(8) Where a rectification application under section 108(2) of the 2002 LR Act has been received by the Tribunal, the Tribunal must provide the person against whom the order is sought and any other person who the Tribunal considers should be a party to the proceedings, with—

(a) a copy of the application, and

(b) a notice specifying that if the person wishes to object, the person must send or deliver to the Tribunal an objection in response within 28 days of the date on which the person received the copy of the application provided by the Tribunal.

(9) The requirement to provide documents referred to in paragraph (1) does not apply where the Tribunal is satisfied that the circumstances to which rule 9(2)(a) (no Tribunal jurisdiction) applies exist.

(10) The requirement under paragraph (3) to provide the notice of application to an interested person does not apply in cases to which section 39, 41 or section 53 of the 1986 Act applies (succession cases); see instead rule 16(3).

30 The response

(1) In circumstances to which rule 28(1)(b) or 29(8) (certain land registration cases) apply, the respondent's response must—

(a) state the respondent's reasons for supporting or objecting to the original application or for objecting to the rectification application (as the case may be);

(b) be accompanied by copies of any documents available to the respondent which—

(i) are important to the respondent's case; or

(ii) the Tribunal or any other party to the proceedings will require in order properly to understand the respondent's case; and

(c) in circumstances to which rule 28(1)(b) applies, be the respondent's statement of case and sent or delivered to the Tribunal within such time as the Tribunal may direct.

(2) In an appeal, paragraphs (3) to (6) apply.

(3) The respondent must, unless a practice direction or direction makes different relevant provision, within 28 days after the date on which the respondent was provided with a copy of the notice of application, send or deliver to the Tribunal a response.

(4) The response must state—

(a) the name and address of the respondent;

(b) the name and address of the respondent's representative (if any);

(c) an address where documents for the respondent may be sent or delivered;

(d) where not included in the application, the name and address of every person who appears to the respondent to be an interested person, with reasons for that person's interest;

(e) whether the respondent opposes the application and, if so, any grounds for such opposition which are not contained in another document provided with the response;

(f) whether the respondent would be content for the case to be dealt with without a hearing if the Tribunal considers it appropriate; and

(g) any further information or documents required by a practice direction or direction.

(5) The respondent must provide with the response a copy of any written record of the decision appealed and any statement of reasons for that decision that the applicant did not provide and the respondent has or can reasonably obtain.

(6) The respondent must send or deliver a copy of the response and any accompanying documents to each other party at the same time as it provides the response to the Tribunal.

PART 4
HEARINGS

31 Decision with or without a hearing

(1) Subject to the remainder of this rule, the Tribunal must hold a hearing before making a decision which disposes of proceedings.

(2) The Tribunal need not hold a hearing if consent to proceeding without a hearing has been given by—

(a) each party; and

(b) each other person who has been sent a notification as being entitled, invited or permitted to attend the hearing.

(3) For the purposes of paragraph (2) a party or other person shall be taken to have consented if—

(a) the Tribunal has given that party or other person not less than 28 days' notice of its intention to dispose of the proceedings without a hearing, and

(b) no objection has been received from that party or other person within that time,

except that the Tribunal may regard such a party or other person as having consented upon shorter notice in urgent or exceptional circumstances.

(4) The Tribunal may in any event dispose of proceedings without a hearing under rule 9 (striking out a party's case) or under rule 39(4) (implementation of court order in land registration cases).

32 Notice of hearings

(1) The Tribunal must give each party reasonable notice of the time and place of the hearing (including any adjourned or postponed hearing) and any changes to the time and place of the hearing.

(2) The notice period for a hearing to consider disposal of the proceedings must be no less than 14 days, except that the Tribunal may give shorter notice—

(a) with the parties' consent; or

(b) in urgent or exceptional circumstances.

33 Public and private hearings

(1) Subject to the following paragraphs, all hearings must be held in public.

(2) The Tribunal may give a direction that a hearing, or part of it, is to be held in private.

(3) Where a hearing, or part of it, is to be held in private, the Tribunal may determine who is permitted to attend the hearing or part of it.

(4) The Tribunal may admit persons to a hearing under paragraph (3) on such terms and conditions as it considers appropriate.

(5) The Tribunal may give a direction excluding from any hearing, or part of it—

(a) any person whose conduct the Tribunal considers is disrupting or is likely to disrupt the hearing;

(b) any person whose presence the Tribunal considers is likely to prevent another person from giving evidence or making submissions freely;

(c) any person who the Tribunal considers should be excluded in order to give effect to the requirement at rule 17(8) (prevention of disclosure or publication of documents and information); or

(d) any person where the purpose of the hearing would be defeated by the attendance of that person.

(6) The Tribunal may give a direction excluding a witness from a hearing until that witness gives evidence.

34 Hearings in a party's absence

If a party fails to attend a hearing the Tribunal may proceed with the hearing if the Tribunal—

(a) is satisfied that the party has been notified of the hearing or that reasonable steps have been taken to notify the party of the hearing; and

(b) considers that it is in the interests of justice to proceed with the hearing.

35 Consent orders

(1) The Tribunal may, at the request of the parties but only if it considers it appropriate, make a consent order disposing of the proceedings and making such other appropriate provision as the parties have agreed.

(2) Notwithstanding any other provision of these Rules, the Tribunal need not hold a hearing before making an order under paragraph (1) or provide reasons for the order.

36 Decisions

(1) The Tribunal may give a decision orally at a hearing.

(2) Subject to rule 17(8) (prevention of disclosure or publication of documents and information), the Tribunal must provide to each party as soon as reasonably practicable after making a decision (other than a decision under Part 6) which finally disposes of all issues in the proceedings or of a preliminary issue dealt with following a direction under rule 6(3)(g)—

(a) a decision notice stating the Tribunal's decision;

(b) written reasons for the decision or, in cases relating to rents, notification of the right to request written reasons under paragraph (4); and

(c) notification of any right of appeal against the decision and the time within which, and manner in which, such right of appeal may be exercised.

(3) The Tribunal may provide written reasons for any decision to which paragraph (2) does not apply.

(4) Where a party is notified under paragraph (2)(b) of the right to request written reasons any such request must be made not later than 1 month from the date the Tribunal sends to the party the decision notice and notification of any right of appeal.

. . .

PART 6
CORRECTING, SETTING ASIDE, REVIEWING AND APPEALING TRIBUNAL DECISIONS

49 Interpretation

In this Part—

"appeal" means the exercise of a right of appeal from the Tribunal—

(a) on a point of law under section 11 of the 2007 Act;

(b) on a point other than a point of law where such a right of appeal is conferred—

(i) by any enactment in relation to a residential property case or a leasehold case;

(ii) by section 111(1) of the 2002 LR Act in relation to a land registration case;

"review" means the review of a decision by the Tribunal under section 9 of the 2007 Act.

50 Clerical mistakes and accidental slips or omissions

The Tribunal may at any time correct any clerical mistake or other accidental slip or omission in a decision, direction or any document produced by it, by—

(a) sending notification of the amended decision or direction, or a copy of the amended document, to each party; and

(b) making any necessary amendment to any information published in relation to the decision, direction or document.

51 Setting aside a decision which disposes of proceedings

(1) The Tribunal may set aside a decision which disposes of proceedings, or part of such a decision, and re-make the decision or the relevant part of it, if—

(a) the Tribunal considers that it is in the interests of justice to do so; and

(b) one or more of the conditions in paragraph (2) are satisfied.

(2) The conditions are—

(a) a document relating to the proceedings was not sent to, or was not received at an appropriate time by, a party or a party's representative;

(b) a document relating to the proceedings was not sent to or was not received by the Tribunal at an appropriate time;

(c) a party, or a party's representative, was not present at a hearing related to the proceedings; or

(d) there has been some other procedural irregularity in the proceedings.

(3) A party applying for a decision, or part of a decision, to be set aside under paragraph (1) must make a written application to the Tribunal so that it is received—

(a) within 28 days after the date on which the Tribunal sent notice of the decision to the party; or

(b) if later, within 28 days after the date on which the Tribunal sent notice of the reasons for the decision to the party.

52 Application for permission to appeal

(1) A person seeking permission to appeal must make a written application to the Tribunal for permission to appeal.

(2) An application under paragraph (1) must be sent or delivered to the Tribunal so that it is received within 28 days after the latest of the dates that the Tribunal sends to the person making the application—

(a) written reasons for the decision;

(b) notification of amended reasons for, or correction of, the decision following a review; or

(c) notification that an application for the decision to be set aside has been unsuccessful.

(3) The date in paragraph (2)(c) applies only if the application for the decision to be set aside was made within the time stipulated in rule 51 or any extension of that time granted by the Tribunal.

(4) If the person seeking permission to appeal sends or delivers the application to the Tribunal later than the time required by paragraph (2) or by any extension of time under rule 6(3)(a) (power to extend time)—

(a) the application must include a request for an extension of time and the reason why the application was not received in time; and

(b) unless the Tribunal extends time for the application under rule 6(3)(a) (power to extend time) the Tribunal must not admit the application.

(5) An application under paragraph (1) must—

(a) identify the decision of the Tribunal to which it relates;

(b) state the grounds of appeal; and

(c) state the result the party making the application is seeking.

53 Tribunal's consideration of application for permission to appeal

(1) On receiving an application for permission to appeal the Tribunal must first consider, taking into account the overriding objective in rule 3, whether to review the decision in accordance with rule 55 (review of a decision).

(2) If the Tribunal decides not to review the decision, or reviews the decision and decides to take no action in relation to the decision, or part of it, the Tribunal must consider whether to give permission to appeal in relation to the decision or that part of it.

(3) The Tribunal must send a record of its decision to the parties as soon as practicable.

(4) If the Tribunal refuses permission to appeal it must send with the record of its decision—

- (a) a statement of its reasons for such refusal; and
- (b) notification of the right to make an application to the Upper Tribunal for permission to appeal and the time within which, and the method by which, such application must be made.

(5) The Tribunal may give permission to appeal on limited grounds, but must comply with paragraph (4) in relation to any grounds on which it has refused permission.

54 Stay pending appeal to the Upper Tribunal

(1) A party who wishes to apply to the Tribunal to stay the implementation of the whole or part of a decision pending the outcome of the appeal must make such an application to the Tribunal at the same time as the party applies to the Tribunal for permission to appeal.

(2) The party applying for a stay under paragraph (1) must provide reasons for the application and provide notice of the application to the other parties.

(3) Before reaching a decision to stay implementation of the whole or part of a decision, the Tribunal must allow the parties the opportunity to make representations or objections.

(4) The Tribunal must notify the parties of any decision that the Tribunal makes as to granting a stay of the implementation of the whole or part of the Tribunal's decision.

(5) In a land registration case, where the Tribunal's decision to stay implementation of a decision relates to a decision disposing of the proceedings, the Tribunal must provide to the registrar a copy of the notice under paragraph (4).

(6) The notice under paragraph (4) must—

- (a) be in writing;
- (b) be dated;
- (c) specify the decision made by the Tribunal; and
- (d) include the Tribunal's reasons for the decision.

55 Review of a decision

(1) The Tribunal may only undertake a review of a decision—

- (a) pursuant to rule 53 (review on an application for permission to appeal); and
- (b) if it is satisfied that a ground of appeal is likely to be successful.

(2) The Tribunal must notify the parties in writing of the outcome of any review, and of any right of appeal in relation to the outcome.

(3) If the Tribunal takes any action in relation to a decision following a review without first giving every party an opportunity to make representations, the notice under paragraph (2) must state that any party that did not have an opportunity to make representations may apply for such action to be set aside and for the decision to be reviewed again.

56 Power to treat an application about a decision as a different type of application
The Tribunal may treat an application for a decision to be corrected or set aside or for permission to appeal against that decision, as an application for any other one of those things.

Index

References are to paragraph numbers.